WHO'S WHO IN THE DUBLIN RISING, 1916

Who's who in the Dublin Rising, 1916

Joseph E.A. Connell, Jnr

Wordwell

To Pam
M'fhíorghrá amháin

First published in 2015
Wordwell Ltd
Unit 9, 78 Furze Road, Sandyford Industrial Estate, Dublin 18
www.wordwellbooks.com

Cover image—A detail from a photograph of survivors of the GPO garrison which was taken in Croke Park on the 20th anniversary of the Easter Rising (1936). (Courtesy of Clare Cowley)

Back cover—Helena Molony (seated third from the left, second row) with other members of Inghinidhe na hÉireann/Daughters of Ireland, which was founded by Maud Gonne MacBride in 1900. (*Irish Revolutionary Women*)

ISBN 978 1 905569 94 6

British Library Cataloguing-in-Publication Data.
A catalogue record for this book is available from the British Library.

All images © National Library of Ireland except where indicated.

Typeset in Ireland by Wordwell Ltd
Copy-editor: Emer Condit
Cover design: Ger Garland
Printed by Castuera Gráficas, Pamplona

Contents

Acknowledgements

I must thank my parents for everything; without them I would have had no such love for Ireland. And, of course, my brothers and sister and their families supported me at all times.

I am most grateful to Wordwell Ltd, and it has been a pleasure to work with Nick Maxwell and Dr Una MacConville, Helen Dunne and everyone at the publisher's. Emer Condit has done an immense amount of work on the manuscript and I am most thankful. They have given polish to my efforts and all their assistance was wonderful.

Tommy Graham of *History Ireland* has been most encouraging and helpful at all times. I am indebted to him for allowing me to write a column, *Countdown to 2016*, in *History Ireland*.

Mary Mackey of the Irish National Archives has always been most helpful and has given me wonderful direction, as well as being very generous with her time.

Tom Duffy has been unstinting with his time and support, and his knowledge of Dublin, its history and its people is unequalled. Without his encouragement this book would not have been contemplated; without his advice it would not have been completed.

I am grateful to Anthony Tierney for his continuing advice and suggestions.

Dr Patrick Geoghehan and Susan Cahill have given me the privilege of a recurring spot on their NewsTalk radio show *Talking History*. It has been a joy to work with them over the years, and I am most grateful.

Mícheál Ó Doibhilín, the editor of www.kilmainhamtales.ie, has let me submit articles for his site and has published small books, *Rebels' Priests* and *Unequal Patriots,* under that imprint. I am always pleased with his editing and guidance.

Clare Cowley has been an indispensable aide for me in Ireland. Her organisation and advice are always most welcome.

Lorcan Collins kindly lets me lead his 1916 Easter Rising Tour on occasion and I particularly thank him for the opportunity.

I am extremely thankful to Lou Yovin for his kind and most patient assistance, as I am technologically challenged and completely computer-illiterate. His help was invaluable.

I have always been welcomed throughout Ireland with the greatest kindness and hospitality, and I thank everyone with whom I've spoken. I assure you that those feelings are returned with the deepest and most lasting affection.

Those individuals who have helped and encouraged me are too numerous to mention and I thank them all. Everyone I asked always gave me assistance, reassurance and direction: all heartened me when I needed that most, and from time to time most fed me when I needed that most, too. At the risk of offending someone I omit, I must especially mention Ray Bateson, Pam Boyd, Áine Broy, Dr Mary Clark, Bob Clarke, Finbar Collins, Briny M. Connell, C.B. Connell, Revd Paul Connell, Kerry Edwards, Terry Fagan, Colin and Dave Farrell, Bob Fuquea, Col. David Fuquea, Conor Goodman, James Connolly Heron, Barbara Hollandsworth, Grainne Áine Hollandsworth, Peggy Keating, Anthony Kelly, David Kilmartin, Desmond Long, Lar Joye, Sinead McCoole, Jim McIlmurray, Brenda Malone, Barbara and Dominic Montaldi, Donal Ó hUallachain, Gregory O'Connor, Maeve O'Leary, Pól Ó Murchú, Kevin O'Sullivan, Cllr Nial Ring, Detta and Seán Spellissy, Arminta Wallace, John and Judy Wohlford, and Padraig Yeates.

And, always, Pam Brewster for all things.

1. Introduction

General Headquarters April 24 1916
The four city battalions will parade for inspection and route march at 10 am today.
Commandants will arrange centres. Full arms and equipment, and one day's rations.

Thomas MacDonagh
Commandant

At noon on Easter Monday, 24 April 1916, approximately 1,000 men and women stormed buildings in central Dublin and rose against the British government. The area of Dublin between the canals was taken by an amalgamation of the Irish Volunteers, the Irish Citizen Army (ICA),[1] Cumann na mBan[2] and the Fianna. Patrick Pearse was appointed Commandant-General and James Connolly was appointed Commandant-General of the Dublin Division.[3] Connolly named the amalgam the 'Army of the Irish Republic'.

Considering the incredible confusion resulting from Eoin MacNeill's countermanding order issued on Saturday night, it is an indication of the determination of the women to take part that so many did eventually report to the fighting positions. For many, their first day was spent searching for outposts, asking to be allowed to join and sometimes being turned away.[4] Though some women carried weapons, most of the Cumann na mBan women saw their roles confined to nursing, cooking and dispatch-carrying. Not only were they the primary dispatch runners but they also passed through the British lines to get food supplies and ammunition, often hiding these in their clothes. These were all dangerous missions, and the women often held up vans, commandeering their contents at gunpoint. Most of the women who wrote accounts of their activities eliminated any trace of heroism when relating their experiences. Few of the accounts give any indication of the excitement and colour of the week. They wrote that there was little drama attached to their duties, and so they just 'got on with it'.

As far as all of the men and women listed here were concerned, they were not living history, they were living their lives. We should remember each of them who made their lives a little less ordinary by participating in the extraordinary events that took place.

There has always been disagreement about how many were 'out' during the Rising in Dublin. It is impossible to be definitive because of discrepancies in the numerous accounts of the Rising. Historical sources are complicated and they do vary. Full names are sometimes unknown, and many names occur in different versions in different accounts. Charles Dalton claimed that it was a total of 687 men, including the Citizen Army, for the duration of the Rising,[5] but it was surely more than that.

On mobilisation, total strength probably did not exceed 1,000 men and women, but this was considerably augmented as the week wore on.[6] Now it is reliably estimated that the total number of rebels in Dublin was ultimately about 2,170—1,950 Volunteers and Cumann na mBan and 220 ICA men and women.[7]

A 'Roll of Honour' that was compiled and presented to the Irish government in 1936 listed the total of all insurgent forces in Dublin as 1,358, including the names of 1,104 survivors and 254 executed, killed in action or since deceased. The Roll was divided into the following garrisons: Ashbourne, Boland's Mills, Cabra Bridge, City Hall, Four Courts, GPO, Jacob's Factory, Magazine Fort, Marrowbone Lane, Mendicity Institute, St Stephen's Green and South Dublin Union. Over the years, provisions were made to add to the Roll, and it currently lists 1,596 individuals in the Dublin garrisons and an additional 59 in counties Louth and Meath. On the 25th anniversary in 1941, however, 2,477 individuals received medals for service in the Rising. From the outset it was known that the Roll was inaccurate. 'The Roll of Honour of 1916 was presented to the government on 24 May 1936 … While accepting the rolls from [Éamon] de Valera, Liam Gogan [keeper of antiquities in the National Museum] stated that "it would be a good idea to make another attempt to correct the lists, and to include whatever names are missing, or erase names erroneously included, at the discretion of the committee", which suggests that the roll was not definitive. Over the years there have been various attempts to calculate how many people actually fought in the Rising.'[8]

There are many omissions from the Roll. Richard Mulcahy, for example, was notably absent from the Ashbourne garrison in the original Roll. Nor was James Connolly's son, Rauri (Roddy), listed, though he was in the GPO until sent to the home of William O'Brien later in the week. Further, some lists have 34 women serving in the GPO, but many more than that were 'in and out' of the GPO during the week;[9] for example, Louise Gavan-Duffy went there on Monday and stayed until she left for Jacob's on Friday.[10] Alice Mac Thomais was not listed, a girl of fifteen who reported to St Stephen's Green on Monday, then went to Jacob's Factory, then back to St Stephen's Green on Tuesday. Máire Comerford, who became one of the staunchest Republicans and was a courageous courier for Michael Collins in the War of Independence, reported to St Stephen's Green and was told to go home because she was too young; instead, she went to the GPO and spent the week on dangerous missions carrying dispatches to other garrisons—but she wasn't on the Roll. Nor was

Michael (Mick) Colgan, though he was at Jacob's and later became a senator. From the famous to the not-so-famous, those and many others were not included on the Roll of Honour, though all served in Dublin in the Rising, and all should be recognised.

Similarly, a list of those who applied for pensions for service in the Rising was released in 2014. Pension applicants had to provide very detailed accounts of their activities, and their testimony needed to be verified and clarified, sometimes through oral examinations. They were required to supply a great deal of supporting documentation. The Pension Application list, too, has noticeable omissions, however, because not all of those who served applied for a pension. The most notable of those would be Éamon de Valera.

The same uncertainty must be admitted of the numbers attached to the individual garrisons, because they, too, increased during the week. While, counting the number who passed through the GPO during the week, it can be claimed that the approximate strength of the GPO garrison was 600, it is accepted that only about 180 Volunteers and ICA members 'charged' the GPO on Easter Monday at noon, so it is unlikely that the garrison ever totalled more than 400 at any one time. The point is illustrated by the following conversation between Patrick Pearse, Desmond FitzGerald and Peggy Downie, an experienced caterer and a member of Cumann na mBan, which took place in the GPO on Tuesday 25 April:

> Pearse: 'How long will the food supply last?'
> FitzGerald: 'For how many men?'
> Pearse: 'A little over 200.'
> FitzGerald checked with Peggy Downie, who told him: 'With rigid economy, we have enough for three weeks'.
> FitzGerald to Pearse: 'With rigid economy, we have enough for three weeks.'
> Pearse: 'Then exercise rigid economy, we may be here that long.'[11]

G.A. Hayes-McCoy, however, writes that about '400 men, including those from other nearby garrisons, were driven out by the flames and that their exit onto Henry Street was hasty'.[12] To a greater degree than any other location, many Volunteers/ICA served secondarily in the GPO, having fled to it as their earlier positions were overrun, and then some were redeployed to other sites.[13] As a result, there are many more Volunteers or ICA members listed as serving in the GPO than were ever there at any one time during the Rising. Each garrison should be viewed in like manner, with many of the Irish travelling between garrisons.

As a result of this movement between garrisons and the confusion it entailed, some Volunteers, ICA and Cumann na mBan members are listed as serving at more than one garrison, particularly in the GPO, but are only counted once for the total. Unless otherwise noted, participants are counted for garrison size where they originally mustered, but one can use the List of Participants to find all the locations in which each one served.

Much of the information in these lists was taken from Bureau of Military History Witness Statements, Contemporaneous Documents and the Pension Applications, and the handwritten notes on them can be very difficult to read. In addition, many records in other collections and archives are handwritten, and often the writing is not easy to decipher. Therefore whenever a name's spelling is questionable, all forms that could be determined are listed.

Even a careful check of names can still leave room for differences. Christopher Crothers, who fought in St Stephen's Green, completed his Witness Statement [1759] using that spelling of his name, and he is so listed in the 1911 census.[14] However, in the list of Irish Citizen Army members at the Green compiled by R.M. Fox, and considered to be definitive, he is listed as Christopher 'Carruthers'.

Every event recorded comes from an individual's perspective, and that gives us an insight into what made the events important enough to be remembered. So it is with all the stories that follow. How reliable were the memories of the men and women who were in the front lines? They were under extreme stress, and many suffered wounds as well. So caveats should be made regarding oral history, as all the Witness Statements and Pension Applications were. The Applications were begun in the 1920s and continued for decades. The Statements were compiled in the 1940s and 1950s, obviously many years after the events, and individuals' memories could have changed, or been faulty from the beginning. One must be careful to recognise any bias, fabrications or misinformation when examining these kinds of primary sources. Whenever possible, the Statements and Applications were cross-checked with other sources to provide the most accurate record, and contrasts are made between contemporaneous accounts of events and those that appeared in later sources. As with all oral histories, care must be taken. A participant's memory could be right or it could be wrong. A reader must use caution in relation to the witness who may have had lapses in remembering, either intentionally or unintentionally, or through exaggeration. Anyone working with oral sources and retrospective testimony needs to familiarise himself with the methodologies of oral history and memory studies to assess and interpret them well. There are two generally agreed principles when working with oral sources: (1) they should be used in conjunction with surviving contemporary evidence; (2) recollections of events which an interviewee actually witnessed or experienced are generally more accurate than information heard at second hand. Moreover, one must consider that these Statements and Applications were recorded after the witnesses had knowledge of subsequent events, and often decades after the events occurred. Still, the Statements and Applications are a veritable gold-mine of information: they show us how vivid the memories were for all who frankly recorded them and just how proud those participants were to tell their tales.

In addition, a researcher must always question what was 'not remembered'. Take as one example the question of who raised the flags over the GPO—seemingly a simple question of fact, but the statements of Éamon Bulfin [497] and Michael Staines [294] and the joint statement of R.H. Walpole and Theobold Fitzgerald [218] clearly conflict, while Paddy Moran of Glasgow is given credit by the Ann Devlin Branch, Glasgow, 1916–1922 [UCDA, Coyle papers]. In history it is difficult to prove anything, even the simple question of who raised a flag—or who didn't raise it. Memory is a faulty instrument for recovering the past. There is always public demand for heroes and/or heroic stories, but the past is never black and white. These garrison lists attempt to give careful description, without colour or favour.

In 1916 very few participants used the Irish form of their names, although that became common shortly thereafter. For example, Michael Collins was listed as a prisoner under the name Michael Collins, but signed the Dáil Loan documents and the Treaty as Míceál Ó Coileain. These changes of name caused additional confusion when lists of participants were recorded after several years, as it was unclear whether a participant listed as 'Edward Kelly' was the same person as 'Éamonn O'Kelly' or 'Éamonn Ó Ceallaigh'. For that reason, whenever an individual used or was known by both the Irish and English versions, an attempt is made to list both names in these rosters.

Similarly, some women participants became known by the Irish version of their name, and these are listed whenever known. A maiden name and a married name are also listed if possible. In addition, many women were known by nicknames. For example, Phyllis Ryan, who served in the GPO, did change her name: Phyllis (Eilis Ni Rian) Ryan (O'Kelly) (Ui Cheallaigh). Others were known on different records by different nicknames: Mary (May, Molly) Hyland (Kelly), who served in St Stephen's Green, was one such woman, and one must try to find out whether Molly or May could be the same person as Mary or whether there were three different people. For women, the name alphabetically listed is that by which the woman was called at the time of the Rising, as far as could be determined.[15]

When only one version of a name is listed, it is because only that version was found in a list or roster, at a prison camp like Frongoch, for example. There is no official record of prisoners in the British Records Office at Kew, however, as no complete record of the number of prisoners was made.

In addition, many names are the same. Where more than one like-named participant served in a location, both names are listed.

For alphabetical purposes, the individuals are listed according to the English versions.

All of these instances are cited below, and an effort is made to point out other inconsistencies so that the reader may continue researching. Some things about the Rising are 'certain', but many are not, and the same goes for the listed participants.

While efforts have been made to verify the authenticity of every claim of a person to have been 'out' in Dublin in 1916, and to identify the location(s) at which all served, the sheer numbers of those listed here call some inclusions into question. It is perhaps inevitable that some who were not 'out' are included, but all are included for whom a reasonable claim was made. Any omissions or mistakes are mine alone.

The usual geographical areas for the residences and training of the Volunteer Battalions prior to the Rising were as follows:

> 1st Battalion: north of the Liffey and west of Sackville Street
> 2nd Battalion: north of the Liffey and east of Sackville Street
> 3rd Battalion: south of the Liffey
> 4th Battalion: south townships, Rathmines etc.
> 5th Battalion: engineers only
> 6th Battalion: south County Dublin, Kingstown

The ICA had no geographical areas, but most members resided north of the Liffey. Whenever it is possible to identify them as such, all men and women of the Irish Citizen Army are designated by 'ICA'.

Abbreviations

Ancient Order of Hibernians	AOH
Defence of the Realm Act	DORA
Dublin Metropolitan Police	DMP
Gaelic Athletic Association	GAA
General Post Office	GPO
Irish Citizen Army	ICA
Irish National Aid and Volunteers' Dependants' Fund	INAVDF
Irish Republican Army	IRA

During the Rising, James Connolly declared the amalgam of the Volunteers and Irish Citizen Army to be called the Army of the Irish Republic, and it was frequently called the Irish Republican Army thereafter. In Irish it is the *Óglaigh na hÉireann*. An individual member was usually called a 'Volunteer'.

Irish Republican Brotherhood	IRB
Irish Transport and General Workers' Union	ITGWU
Irish Women's Workers' Union	IWWU
King's Counsel	KC
Member of Parliament	MP

Queen's Counsel	QC
Reverend	Revd
Royal Irish Constabulary	RIC
Teachta Dála	TD
Trinity College Dublin	TCD
Ulster Volunteer Force	UVF
University College Dublin (formerly National University)	UCD
Voluntary Aid Detachment (of nurses)	VAD

Military/rank abbreviations

Adjutant	Adj.
Aide-de-camp	ADC
Brigadier	Brig.
Captain	Capt.
Chief of Staff	C/S
Colonel	Col.
Commandant	Cmdt
First Lieutenant	1Lt
General	Gen.
General Officer Commanding	GOC
Headquarters	HQ
His Majesty's Ship	HMS
Lieutenant	Lt
Lieutenant Colonel	Lt Col.
Lieutenant General	Lt Gen.
Major-General	Major-Gen.
Non-Commissioned Officer	NCO
Officer Commanding	O/C
Officer Training Corps	OTC
Private	Pte
Quartermaster	QM
Second Lieutenant	2Lt
Sergeant	Sgt

Street name changes/area alterations

Following the revolutionary period (1913–23), many streets, barracks, bridges and other areas were renamed, many of them in honour of those who had been leaders or served in the Rising, the War of Independence or the Civil War.

For street names containing 'Upper', 'Middle' or 'Lower', the name may be determined as follows: the 'Lower' part of a street is that part nearest to the mouth of the Liffey.

The following is a list of street/area names in italics, with their contemporary names in non-italics.

Amiens Street: Eastern end of Seán MacDermott Street.

Amiens Street Railway Station: Connolly Station.

Ancient Order of Hibernians Meeting Rooms: Kevin Barry Memorial Hall.

Broadstone Railway Station: Constitution Hill, Phibsborough, now a bus terminal.

Clarence Street (Great Clarence Street): Macken Street.

Clarence Street South: Macken Street.

Constabulary Barracks: Garda Síochána HQ in Phoenix Park.

Davy's Pub: Portobello Pub (at Portobello Bridge).

Densil or *Denzille Street*: Fenian Street.

Drogheda Street: First name of the street that became *Sackville* and then O'Connell St.

Findlater Place: Cathal Brugha Street (the first block off O'Connell Street).

Gloucester Street: Cathal Brugha Street (the continuation east from O'Connell Street).

Gloucester Street North (see *Great Martin's Lane*): Upper Seán MacDermott →Lower Seán MacDermott Street.

Great Britain Street: Parnell Street.

Great Brunswick Street: Pearse Street.

Great Clarence Street: Macken Street.

Harcourt Street Railway Station: Demolished, now housing.

Islandbridge Barracks: Partially demolished, it was renamed Peadar Clancy Barracks. Clancy Barracks was sold to developers in early 2004.

King's County: County Offaly.

Kingsbridge Railway Station: Seán Heuston Station.

Kingstown Harbour: Dún Laoghaire Harbour (seven miles south-east of Dublin).

Linenhall Barracks: Intersection of Linenhall Street and Lisburn Street.

Marlborough Barracks: McKee Barracks in Phoenix Park.

North Dublin Union: St Lawrence's Hospital.

Portobello Barracks: Cathal Brugha Barracks.

Queen's County: County Laois.

Queenstown: Cobh, Co. Cork.

Richmond Barracks: Originally on Bulfin Road, Inchicore, it became Keogh Barracks, then was taken over by the Christian Brothers and became St Michael's Primary School, then Keogh Square.

Rotunda Picture House: The Ambassador Theatre.

Royal Barracks: Collins Barracks, part of the National Museum of Ireland.

Royal University: National University.

Rutland Square: Parnell Square. The surrounding streets were once known as *Charlemont Row* (Parnell Square West), *Cavendish Row* (Parnell Square East), *Palace Row* (Parnell Square North) and *Great Britain Street* (Parnell Street).

Sackville Place (*Lane*): Ó Rahilly Parade.

Sackville Street: O'Connell Street (before *Sackville Street* it was *Drogheda Street*).

Ship Street Barracks: Government Buildings next to Dublin Castle.

South Dublin Union: St James's Hospital.

Wellington Barracks: Griffith Barracks (now a college).

Westland Row Railway Station: Pearse Station.

Fatalities by garrison

Garrison	Men	Women	Total	Executed*	Killed**
General Post Office	532	85	617	6	14
Abbey Street					
Cabra Bridge area					
Fairview area					
Headquarters (GPO)					
Henry Street					
Hopkins & Hopkins					
Imperial Hotel/Clery's					
Kelly's Fort					
Kimmage Garrison					
Metropole Hotel					
North Earl Street					
Sackville Street					
1st Battalion	407	44	451	2	11
Church Street Area					
Four Courts					
Magazine Fort					
Mendicity Institute					
North Dublin Union					
North King Street					

Garrison	Men	Women	Total	Executed*	Killed**
2nd Battalion	236	11	247	3	4
Jacob's Biscuit Factory					
Fumbally Lane					
3rd Battalion	222	0	222	0	9
Boland's Mills					
Clanwilliam Hse					
Mount Street Bridge					
Northumberland Rd					
4th Battalion	251	29	280	2	7
Jameson's Distillery					
Marrowbone Lane					
Roe's Distillery					
Sth Dublin Union					
5th Battalion	89	5	94	0	2
Ashbourne, Co. Meath					
Nth Co. Dublin					
City Hall	48	11	59	0	6
Parliament Street					
St Stephen's Green	139	30	169	1	7
College of Surgeons					
Non-assigned to a garrison[16]	0	32	32	2[17]	7[18]
Totals	**1,924**	**247**	**2,171**	**16**	**67**[19]

Names in the rosters marked by a single asterisk signify those executed; names marked by two asterisks signify those who were killed during the Rising. Officially, 64 Volunteers/ICA were killed in addition to those executed.

Executed

Thomas MacDonagh

GPO

Michael O'Hanrahan

Thomas Clarke

3rd Battalion

James Connolly

None

Seán MacDermott

4th Battalion

Patrick Pearse

Eamonn Ceannt

Willie Pearse

Con Colbert

Joseph Plunkett

5th Battalion

1st Battalion

None

Edward (Ned) Daly

City Hall

Seán Heuston

None

2nd Battalion

St Stephen's Green

John MacBride

Michael Mallin

Killed in action

GPO
Charles E. Carrigan
Edward Costello
Henry Coyle
John Keely
Gerald Keogh
Francis Macken
Michael Milvihill
*John Neale
Patrick O'Connor
The Ó Rahilly
Thomas O'Reilly
Patrick Shortis
Thomas Weafer
*Arthur Abraham Weekes

1st Battalion
Thomas Allen
Edward Costello
John Cromien
John Dwan
Patrick Farrell
Seán Howard
John Hurley
Peter Paul Manning
Patrick Joseph O'Flanagan
Philip Walsh
Peter Wilson

2nd Battalion
James Byrne
Seán Healy
Richard O'Carroll
John O'Grady

3rd Battalion
Andrew Byrne
John Costello

Patrick Doyle
Edward Ennis
Peadar Macken
Michael Malone
Richard Murphy
George Reynolds
Patrick Whelan

4th Battalion
William (Goban) Burke
Brendan Donelan
William McDowell
Richard O'Reilly
John Owens
James Quinn
John Traynor

5th Battalion
John Crenigan
Thomas Rafferty

City Hall
Louis Byrne
Seán Connolly
Charles Darcy
George Geoghegan
Seán O'Reilly
Edward Walsh

St Stephen's Green
John Adams
Philip Clarke
James Corcoran
James Fox
James McCormack
Daniel Murray
Frederick Ryan

II. General Post Office (GPO)—Headquarters Battalion

In the forenoon of Easter Monday, Patrick Pearse, James Connolly, Seán MacDermott, Thomas Clarke and Joseph Plunkett assembled about 180 Volunteers and Citizen Army men and women at Liberty Hall. Pearse and Connolly led the detachment up Abbey Street Lower to Sackville Street, where they turned north, and in his first command of the Rising Connolly ordered: 'Left wheel, GPO—charge!' Many Fianna came to the GPO, 'boys who had been sent home from some of the other positions because they were deemed to be too young to be in danger, and who had somehow or other made their way there'.[20]

The GPO was taken as the headquarters of the Rising,[21] and outposts were established at the corner of Sackville Street and Bachelor's Walk ('Kelly's Fort'), at O'Connell Bridge, at the corner of Abbey Street Lower and in the Imperial Hotel across from the GPO. Barricades were constructed in Abbey Street Lower and North Earl Street. The understanding was that once the *Proclamation* had been read and the Irish Republic established, the Irish Volunteers and the Irish Citizen Army would merge as the Army of the Irish Republic.

The 'Kimmage Garrison', comprised mostly of men who had come to Ireland from England, was the first detachment to occupy the GPO.[22] The detachment that took the GPO was not a single organised military unit, however, and had the disadvantages of a 'piecemeal organisation hurriedly put together'.[23] The men who charged the GPO were dangerously overloaded with a motley assortment of weapons. Some of them had Howth rifles, some carried the Italian Martinis that they had purchased themselves, others carried shotguns, and some were 'armed' with sledgehammers, picks and a few revolvers. Most were not in uniform, and only a few wore any military dress at all. Upon entering the building, they ordered the staff and public out; a few British soldiers were taken prisoner, and would remain so for the week. The Irish occupied every part of the building, including the roof, and immediately began to knock out windows, loopholing them with ledgers and anything else to hand.

There were no forces stationed to the east of the Sackville Street positions, and while it could be inferred that that was because there were no British barracks there, it must be noted that the pressure which ultimately crushed the GPO and brought the Rising to a halt came from exactly that quarter.

On Friday morning Pearse called the women together to praise their 'bravery, heroism, and devotion in the face of danger', and then ordered them to leave. There was an embarrassingly heated debate and the women refused. Only after Desmond FitzGerald intervened did they reluctantly agree to go with Fr Flanagan and the wounded to Jervis Street Hospital.[24] Three women remained: Winifred Carney, Julia Grenan and Elizabeth O'Farrell.

GENERAL POST OFFICE (GPO) HEADQUARTERS BATTALION: MEN

They mustered at Liberty Hall; garrison total approximately 250–300 at any one time; six executed, fourteen killed.

The Larkfield Mill in Kimmage, south County Dublin, part of a leasehold interest owned by Countess Josephine Plunkett, was the headquarters of the Volunteer 4th Battalion.[25] A small mill on the property was where Volunteers manufactured most of the pikes, buckshot and bayonets used in the Rising.[26] It also became home to about 90 Irishmen, mostly from Glasgow, Liverpool and London, who returned to Ireland to fight in the Rising, as well as a few from Ireland who were 'on the run'. They all settled in Kimmage in the months leading up to the Rising, and Larkfield became an armed camp. There were facilities for indoor and outdoor drilling, and a shooting range. After the Rising these men became known as the 'Kimmage Garrison'; along with members of the Irish Citizen Army, they comprised the core of those who first took the GPO.[27] On that Monday morning, George Plunkett waved down a tram at Harold's Cross, took out his wallet and said, 'Fifty-seven tuppenny tickets to the city centre, please'.[28]

★Thomas (Tom) Clarke (Tomás O Clerigh; executed 3 May 1916, aged 59).[29] In Kilmainham he was seen by Fr Columbus.[30]

Clarke was born on the Isle of Wight on 11 March 1857, the son of an English soldier. In 1873 he travelled to Dublin to be sworn into the IRB. After being sworn in, he returned north to Dungannon, but the police soon got on his track and he left for America in 1880. In the United States Irish separatism was inculcated in him as a member of Clan na Gael. Sent to England in 1883, he was arrested as a 'dynamiter' in an Irish separatist bombing campaign there and spent the next fifteen years as a prisoner in various English jails. Upon his release he returned to the United States, where he married Kathleen Daly from Limerick, the niece of John Daly, one of his cellmates in Pentonville Prison and the man who had sworn him into the IRB.

When Clarke returned to Ireland in 1907, he set out to bring the IRB's 'physical force' ideals to the fore in the minds of younger nationalists. The IRB was revitalised in the early twentieth century, led by this new generation of Irish patriots.[31] Clarke must be given credit for reviving the IRB, establishing its newspaper, *Irish Freedom* (a

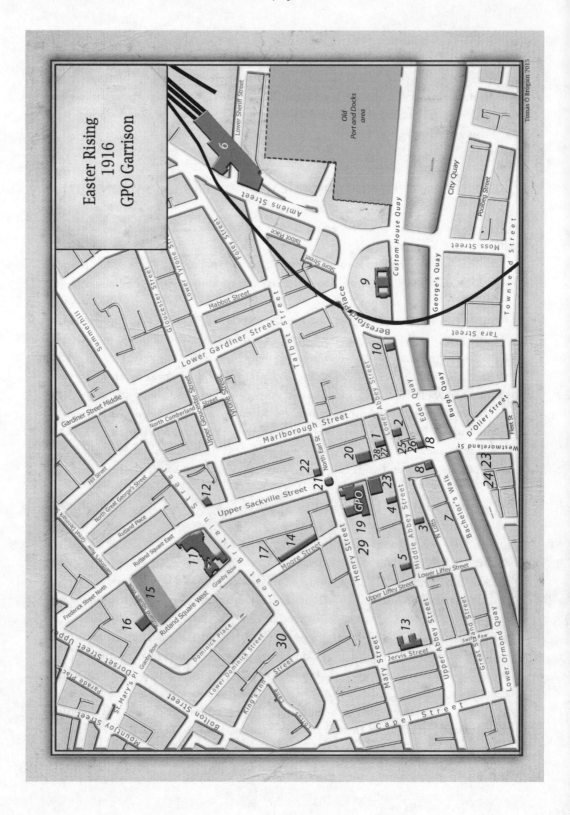

Easter Rising
1916
GPO Garrison

Tomás Ó Brógáin 2015

General Post Office (GPO)—Headquarters Battalion

No.	Address	Site	Description
1	4 Abbey St. Lower	*The Irish Times*	Very anti-ICA. Volunteers took print rolls from here, causing fires.
2	37 Abbey St. Lower	Wynn's Hotel	Meeting place for many groups.
3	55 Abbey St. Middle	*Irish Catholic*	Newspaper: very anti-ICA, anti-Volunteers.
4	84 Abbey St. Middle	*Freeman's Journal*	Newspaper: very anti-Parnell.
5	111 Abbey St. Middle	Independent House	*Independent* newspaper: anti-ICA, anti-Volunteers.
6	Amiens St.	Amiens St. Railway Station	Now Connolly Station.
7	Bachelor's Walk		Site of the Bachelor's Walk massacre, 26 July 1914.
8	56 Bachelor's Walk, at corner of Sackville St. (now O'Connell St.)	'Kelly's Fort'	The building held by the Volunteers as an outpost of the GPO.
9	Custom House Quay	Custom House	The *Helga* was moored in the Liffey here and shelled Liberty Hall.
10	18 Beresford Place	Liberty Hall	HQ of the ITGWU and the Irish Citizen Army.
11	Great Britain Street (now Parnell Street)	Rotunda Hospital	First meeting of the Volunteers was held here, 25 November 1913.
12	75A Great Britain Street (now Parnell Street)	Tom Clarke's tobacconist shop	Place for IRB and Volunteers to transfer messages.
13	Jervis Street	Jervis St. Hospital	Many casualties were treated here. Now the Jervis Shopping Centre.
14	Moore Street	The whole terrace was held by the Volunteers at the end.	No. 16 Moore St. was the last HQ of the Rising leaders.
15	Rutland Square (now Parnell Sq.)		Garden of Remembrance
16	25 Rutland Square (now Parnell Square)	Gaelic League Meeting Rooms	Many revolutionary meetings were held here.
17	Sackville Lane (now O'Rahilly Parade)		The Ó Rahilly was killed here while escaping from the GPO.
18	1 Sackville St. Lower (now O'Connell St.) and Eden Quay	Hopkins & Hopkins	A key Volunteer position right at O'Connell Bridge.
19	Sackville St. Lower (now O'Connell Street)	GPO	HQ of the Volunteers and the ICA in the Rising.
20	20 Sackville St. Lower (now O'Connell Street)	Clery's Department Store/ Imperial Hotel	Across from the GPO; the building was demolished in the fires.
21	Sackville St. Lower (now O'Connell Street)	Lord Nelson's Pillar	A great Dublin landmark, his statue was a target for many in the GPO.
22	33 Sackville St. Lower (now O'Connell Street), at the corner of North Earl Street	Pillar Café	Across from the GPO and Clery's, it was a major auxiliary position of the GPO garrison.
23	3–21 Westmoreland Street	Ballast Office	Became a British position for snipers.
24	14–18 Aston Quay	McBirney's general merchandise store	British sniper and machine-gun position.
25	10–11 Sackville St. Lower (now O'Connell Street)	Reis's Jeweller's building & the School of Wireless Telegraphy	The Volunteers tried to send messages to the world from here.
26	6–7 Sackville St. Lower	Dublin Bread Company	The Volunteers took it on Monday, but destroyed later in the week.
27	Lower Abbey Street	Hibernian Bank	Tom Weafer killed here on Wednesday.
28	17 Sackville St. Lower (now O'Connell Street)	Hoyte and Son	A druggist and oilworks; the mixture of chemicals contributed to the fires.
29		Barricade across Henry Street	A Post Office van placed here to shield the breakout to Moore Street.
30	204–206 Great Britain St. (now Parnell Stret)	Williams and Woods soap factory building	The Volunteers trapped in Moore St. contemplated fleeing to here.

militant anti-English paper), and bringing new blood into its leadership, especially mentoring his protégé Seán MacDermott.[32] Clarke became the trusted link between Clan na Gael in the US and the IRB in Ireland, and his contribution to the national revival and the events of the time was crucial:

> If any one man could be said to be responsible for the inspiration of Easter Week, or for the carrying through of the resolution to revolt—credit for that must be given to Tom Clarke. Clarke can truthfully be described as the man, above all others, who made the Easter Rising. He, it was, who inspired it originally, and he, it was, who, in broad outline, laid the plans.[33]

Though he was not a military man, Clarke took up a rifle in the GPO and sat at a window. Mary Ryan described him thus: 'I have never seen him look happier—he was like a bride at a wedding'.[34]

In Kilmainham, Fr Columbus went into Thomas Clarke's cell, where he remained for about an hour. Clarke told him that Pearse, MacDonagh and he had been court-martialled early that morning, but that sentence had not been passed on them until after 5 p.m. He also said that he had received no food since breakfast-time and that he would like something to eat. At Fr Columbus's request, one of the soldiers went to get a couple of biscuits and a tin of water. Grateful for the biscuits, Clarke gave his Volunteer badge to the priest as a souvenir. Clarke, however, later told his wife, Kathleen, that Fr Columbus told him that he would have to 'admit that he had done a great wrong' in order to get absolution. Clarke said that he threw Fr Columbus out: 'I'm not a bit sorry for what I did. I glory in it. And if that means I'm not entitled to absolution, then I'll have to go to the next world without it. To say I'm sorry would be a lie and I am not going to face my God with a lie on my tongue.'[35] He had summed up his position years before in his pamphlet *Glimpses of an Irish felon's life*: 'I was then what I had been, and what I still am, an Irish Nationalist. I asked no favours, I got none, and I am proud of it.'[36] To Kathleen, he said of Eoin MacNeill: 'I want you to see to it that our people know of his treachery to us. He must never be allowed back into the national life of the country, for sure as he is, so sure he will act treacherously in a crisis. He is a weak man, but I know every effort will be made to whitewash him.'[37]

*James Connolly (Séamus Ó Conghile; executed 12 May 1916, aged 48).[38] In Dublin Castle he recounted the story of the escape from the GPO to his daughter Nora, and said: 'We can't fail now. Such lads will never forget.'[39] Fr Aloysius attended him in Dublin Castle and at Kilmainham.[40] Connolly requested to see him, but before going Fr Aloysius was made to promise that he would act only as a priest. When he told Connolly this, Connolly said: 'It is as a priest I want to see you. I have seen and heard of the brave conduct of priests and nuns during the week and I believe that they are the best friends of the workers.' On the morning of 12 May Fr Aloysius received word to go to Dublin Castle to see Connolly. Fr Aloysius heard his confession, gave him Holy Communion, went with him in the ambulance to Kilmainham and was there when Connolly was executed.

Fr Aloysius asked Connolly to bear in mind that the men who would execute him were ordinary soldiers obeying orders, and that he should feel no anger against them but forgive them. Connolly replied, 'I do, Father. I respect every man who does his duty.'[41] Connolly was shot in a chair, as he was too badly wounded to stand.[42] The doctor who treated him in Dublin Castle was Surgeon Richard Tobin.

Dr Alfred Parsons, Alfred Fannin's brother-in-law and a doctor at the Royal City of Dublin Hospital, commonly called Baggot Street Hospital, also saw Connolly.[43] He was a leading Dublin doctor and was singled out for his great service during the Rising. He was taken to Dublin Castle to examine James Connolly, and was asked whether Connolly was 'fit to be shot'. Parsons answered, 'A man is never fit to be shot'.

George Kendall OBE was chaplain to the 59th Division of the British Army. In his 1961 memoir he described the capture and execution of Connolly. 'I saw James Connolly twice whilst he was in hospital, the second time being on the eve of his execution. Speaking to me on the first visit, he said in answer to a question of mine about his attitude—"You must know the saying." "What saying?" I asked. And he replied: "The price of liberty is eternal vigilance". This too was the saying I heard as I spoke to his men in the Dublin Castle hospital. Listening, I felt it was not my duty to condemn, or argue. Connolly was, for years, a professed agnostic, but at the hour of death, he returned to the faith of his fathers. That night a Catholic priest was admitted to the hospital and he administered Holy Communion to Connolly and gave him absolution.'[44]

After Connolly's execution, a British captain said: 'Fr Aloysius, they are the bravest and cleanest lot of men I have ever met'. Aloysius concurred that all the men were brave. 'They were clean in the eyes of the British captain and they were clean too in the eyes of God.' Aloysius always commented on the faithfulness of those executed: 'I think we owe it to the young people of this country to put the spiritual aspect of the lives of these men before them as an ideal to follow'.

*Seán MacDermott (Seán MacDiarmada; executed 12 May 1916, aged 32; crippled by polio in June 1911).[45] In Kilmainham he was visited by the Ryan sisters, Mary Josephine (Min) and Phyllis.[46]

Mary Josephine (Min) Ryan was MacDermott's fiancée; she later married Richard Mulcahy. She and her sister Phyllis were the last two to see Seán MacDermott in Kilmainham Gaol: 'He preferred to talk of casual matters, asking about different people we knew, enjoying little jokes almost as though we were in Bewley's. He had worked and planned for Irish Independence since boyhood. His last words, save for his prayers, were "God Save Ireland". At four o'clock, when the shooting was done, a gentle rain began to fall—the tears of Dark Rosaleen.'

> … If I think of any other things to say I will tell them to Miss [Mary Josephine] Ryan, she who in all probability, had I lived, would have been my wife. I will send instructions to my landlady, but she knows you all right.[47]

Fr Eugene McCarthy and Fr Augustine attended him. He was shot sitting on a soapbox, according to Fr Augustine's statement.[48]

> It was inferred that MacDiarmada did not go to Mass. If that was so he was not the first man who refused to go to Mass because of a dispute with a priest, however illogical that was. The fact was that Seán MacDiarmada was a deeply religious man, as was evidenced by his last letter to his brothers and sisters in which he wrote: 'By the time this reaches you, I will with God's mercy have joined in heaven my father and mother as well as my dear friends who have been shot during the week. I have priests with me almost constantly in the past 24 hours. One dear old friend of mine, Dr Paddy Browne of Maynooth, stayed with me up to a very late hour last night. I feel a happiness the like of which I never experienced in my life before and a feeling that I could not describe. God bless and guard you all and may the Lord have mercy on my soul'.[49]

Browne remembered that MacDermott was to be executed the day before he was actually shot. MacDermott's sentence was read to him and he was to be executed on the 11th. Browne remembered that Min Ryan had gone to see him, and when she came back to the house she told Browne that it would be a good thing if he went to see him, as he was to die the next day.[50] Browne went to Kilmainham and asked to see MacDermott, and was given permission to see him for an hour. At about 8.00 on the night of 10 May, Browne was led to MacDermott's cell. He recalled:

> I was brought up then. A soldier led me up and opened the cell door. I went in and he locked the door.
> The guard was passing up and down outside and he let me alone.
> The queer thing about my visit there was that I was to be left for an hour and a man would come and take me away at the end of that hour.
> It was when I was there that the telephone wires got busy as a result of John Dillon's speech in the House of Commons.
> It must have been—Asquith got the military authorities in Ireland to stay their hand and postpone the execution.

Browne surmised that the Gaol had been thrown into turmoil, and as a result he was left alone with MacDermott for far longer than he had permission to stay: it was 'the small hours of the morning [11 May] when I left'.

Browne said that the Gaol commander was distressed that he was still there:

> I would take it as a favour if you would say nothing about being left here so long. He brought me down, going into his office, and he told me to be on my guard during curfew while cycling home and to be sure to stop any time I was challenged by the sentries. I had a drink with him and left on my bicycle. He did not think there would be any more executions and showed great relief at that.

Browne said that he and MacDermott talked about everything, and that Kit Ryan's arrest was one of the things that was bothering him most. 'He was afraid that she would suffer in her position. He was terribly concerned about it.'

⋆Patrick Pearse (Pádraig MacPiarais; executed 3 May 1916, aged 36).[51] In Kilmainham he was attended by Fr Aloysius.[52]

On the night of 2–3 May, Fr Aloysius, walking in the corridor, saw a light shining through the spyhole in Pearse's cell: 'Pearse was there kneeling and the light showing on his face as he clasped the crucifix'. Fr Aloysius had brought this crucifix with him to the Gaol and had left it with Pearse earlier. Pearse scratched his initials, 'P.M.P.' for the Irish form of his name, on the back of the crucifix as a memento for Fr Aloysius. The crucifix was preserved in the Church Street Friary and is of wood with brass figures of Our Lord, Our Lady and the skull and crossbones.

On 3 May Fathers Aloysius and Augustine were not permitted to stay with the condemned men—Pearse, Clarke and MacDonagh—until their execution but had to leave Kilmainham Gaol between 2 and 3 a.m. Fr Aloysius protested so strongly that priests were thereafter allowed to stay with the prisoners until their executions.

⋆William (Willie) Pearse (Liam MacPiarais; executed 4 May 1916, aged 34).[53] In Kilmainham he was attended by Fr Augustine, and saw his mother and his sister, Margaret.[54] He was the only one to plead guilty to all the charges at his court martial.[55]

The younger brother of Patrick Pearse, Willie idolised his older brother and they were inseparable. When Willie was a young boy, he imagined his brother as the heroes he was learning about in his history lessons:

> He saw him [Patrick] as a bodyguard of Owen Roe and Phelim O'Neil, dreamed of him as the intimate companion of Wolfe Tone and Robert Emmet. He thought of himself beside Padraig in a national uprising, dying with him on the barricades

or on the scaffold, or if not in a tomb bearing an eloquent epitaph, he saw him buried in the quicklime pit of the felon; for him no humdrum and respectable funeral or interment in the family vault. He could not see his brother weeping after the Flight of the Earls as he shared their exile. No, on foreign soil a Fenian does not weep; he organises like Tone against the conquerors of his country, like Tone he returns to die in Ireland, or like the Fenians he returns to rouse unconquered spirits and ferments revolution against the enemies of his fatherland.

How tragically prophetic were Willie's childhood imaginings.[56]

William inherited his father's artistic abilities and became a sculptor. He was educated at the Christian Brothers School, Westland Row. He studied at the Metropolitan School of Art in Dublin under Oliver Sheppard. He also studied art in Paris. He sculpted the Fr Murphy Memorial in Wexford, and the Mater Dolorosa statue in St Andrew's Church on Westland Row.

In prison awaiting execution, he told his mother and sister that a guard had told him that he was being taken to see his brother, but as they approached the prison yard a volley of shots was heard, and another guard came and told them that they were too late. The gunfire they had heard was the firing squad that killed Patrick Pearse, Tom Clarke and Thomas MacDonagh. Another report of the incident, taken from British records, is probably more correct: that Willie Pearse was being taken to the firing squad to join his brother, but they were too late and returned him to his cell until the next day.[57]

*Joseph Mary Plunkett (Seosamh Ó Pluingcéad; executed 4 May 1916, aged 29).[58] During the storming of the GPO he carried a sword that had belonged to Robert Emmet. Fr Albert and Fr Sebastian saw him in Kilmainham.

Several years later, Plunkett's mother, Countess Josephine Mary Plunkett, recalled how she met Fr Albert:

Some friends were together in a private hospital in the Appian Way waiting for the crisis of an illness of Mrs Clarke to occur. Father Albert, O.F.M. Cap., was there in case the last absolution had to be given. The hour was late and the times not too safe to be out. Chatting to pass the time, Father Albert mentioned to me that he was with my son, Joseph, just before he was executed. Of this I was not aware until then. He told me how four priests from Church Street were sent for in the early hours of the morning of May 4th, 1916, and in twenty minutes the four had arrived at Kilmainham Gaol to find Joseph and three others [Edward Daly, Willie Pearse and Michael O'Hanrahan] were about to be executed. One priest and a prisoner were sent to a nearby cell. The prisoner had his hat on and the priest wondered to see a man going to confess and wearing his hat. A jailer put his head into the cell, and then entering, undid the handcuffs behind the man's back, and allowed him to remove his hat. It was nearly dark and there was only a candle for lighting.

The other three prisoners were together in an adjoining room, among them Joseph, by whom Father Albert was attracted. Joseph, seeing him looking at him, walked across the room to Father Albert and said: 'Father, I want you to know that I am dying for the glory of God and the honour of Ireland'. 'That's all right, my son', answered Father Albert. In a few minutes the firing squad carried out their orders.

And that was Joseph's first—and last—meeting with Father Albert here on earth. God grant they have met in heaven.[59]

Fr Eugene McCarthy, who also brought Grace back to see him, married Plunkett and Grace Gifford.[60]

Grace wrote:

I went in to see Joe in Kilmainham on the day before his execution. I have a peculiar faculty that, if somebody in Drogheda, say, was thinking about me,—some casual thought—I would instantly feel and realise it. It is a sort of telepathy.

I went out one day, and the papers had the news that MacDonagh and Pearse, and somebody else, had been executed. The next morning, although we had been up all night, I woke up as if I were being pulled out of bed by an unseen force, and dead beat after being awakened. I dressed, and went to the priest; and I told him Joe was going to be executed. I had no notion what I was doing, except I was being pulled on. I got a paper from the priest. I went down to a man named Stoker to get the wedding ring. He lived opposite the Gaiety. I went to Kilmainham then, to see Joe. His thoughts were so powerful that I was simply pulled out of the bed. I was let in to see him; and the prison chaplain must have been there; and he married us. I don't remember how it came about that they got the chaplain. Next morning, Joe was executed.

When I saw him, on the day before his execution, I found him in exactly the same state of mind. He was so unselfish, he never thought of himself. He was not frightened—not at all, not the slightest. I am sure he must have been worn out after the week's experiences, but he did not show any signs of it—not in the least. He was quite calm.

I was never left alone with him, even after the marriage ceremony. I was brought in and was put in front of the altar; and he was brought down the steps; and the cuffs were taken off him; and the chaplain went on with the ceremony; then the cuffs were put on him again. I was not alone with him—not for a minute. I had no private conversation with him at all. I just came away then.

I saw Joe twice that day before his execution—when we were married, and again that night. I saw him again that night, to say good-bye.

I saw Pearse's letter to his mother lying on the British Governor's desk. I very nearly stole the letter; but they gave it to her alright. I did not see Pearse himself. I was allowed to stay only a short time with Joe, yet I believe that Min Ryan and Father Browne were allowed to stay a long time with Seán MacDermott. Min Ryan was there with Seán MacDermott for ages and ages. In fact, she said her conversation ran out altogether. She did not know what to say to him. There would be a guard there, and you could not talk. I can't understand how she managed to stay quite a while. I was just a few moments there to get married, and then again a few minutes to say good-bye that night; and a man stood there, with his watch in his hand, and said: 'Ten minutes'.

After my second visit to Joe, I could not get home. The priest brought me to a convent. They would not let me in. Then they brought me to the house of a bell-founder, called Byrne, and I had something to eat there. For the second visit, a policeman, in a car, brought me a note from the Governor. I did not see any of the other prisoners. They were all locked up in their own cells.

Arthur P. Agnew; a member of the Kimmage Garrison from Manchester, he was born in Liverpool and joined the IRB in 1910. He recalled that as they left Kimmage 'we knew there was to be a fight, but we did not know when or what it was to be like'.[61] On arriving at the GPO, he was posted to guard O'Connell Bridge at the north end from Hopkins Corner to Kelly's Corner, with orders to stop any British troops crossing the bridge. On Wednesday, owing to heavy fire, they were ordered to retreat to the GPO. After an unsuccessful attempt to reoccupy Kelly's on Thursday, he spent Thursday and Friday in the Metropole Hotel. On Friday he received instructions to evacuate the hotel and return to the GPO. On returning to the GPO, he joined the general evacuation to Moore Street, where he remained until the surrender. After grounding arms on the western side of Sackville Street, he spent the night on the open ground at the Rotunda, and on Sunday morning marched to Richmond Barracks for interrogation. From Richmond Barracks he was taken to the North Wall and put on a cattle-boat for Holyhead and then to Stafford Jail. In July he was transferred to Frongoch and was released at Christmas 1916.[62]

David Timothy Begley; a member of the Kimmage Garrison from Manchester.[63]

James Behan; he was a Volunteer in the 2nd Battalion. He was imprisoned for eight days and released because of his youth.

Michael Behan; an ICA member, he lived on Richmond Road.

Andrew J. Bermingham; he was mobilised on Easter Monday for Blackhall Place but could not reach his company, joining the forces at the GPO instead. After the surrender, he was arrested and deported to Knutsford Prison on 1 May 1916, and then to Frongoch.

John Joseph Bermingham; ICA. He was in Knutsford and Frongoch until July 1916.

Joseph Patrick Billings; ICA. He was imprisoned at Frongoch.

Patrick Bird; ICA. He was in the Hibernian Bank and was imprisoned at Frongoch.

Thomas Blanchfield; he came with the men who had reported to Cabra Bridge.[64] (He went to the 5th Battalion and is counted in that garrison.)

Edmund (Ned) Boland, Harry's brother; ICA. He was in the Imperial Hotel and escaped to Cathedral Street.

Harry Boland; he came in from Fairview with the group led by Capt. Frank Henderson.[65] On Monday his company held a post at Goulding's Manure Works at Fairview Bridge, and later in the day transferred to Gilbey's Wine Merchants on the corner of Richmond Avenue, where he remained until Tuesday. On Tuesday, along with his brother Ned and William Whelan, he took three prisoners, British Army instructors from the Bull Wall, to the GPO, returning to Gilbey's on Tuesday evening. One of these prisoners later identified him at his trial. By Wednesday the British were encircling Gilbey's, so the men there decided to evacuate to the GPO. He and Diarmuid Lynch were underground making the ammunition safe, unknown to Pearse and the others, so Boland was the penultimate person to leave the GPO.[66] He was imprisoned in Mountjoy, then Dartmoor, then Lewes in Sussex, and finally in Maidstone Prison. He was killed in the Civil War.[67]

Lt Michael Boland; ICA. He was leading his men across Sackville Street from Abbey Street when the Lancers trotted down Sackville Street. He formed his men into two ranks and they fired on the Lancers, but too soon. Later he was in command on the roof; he was imprisoned at Frongoch. He had fought in the Boer War and thought it 'madness' to take and hold buildings. 'Shut in here with our leaders, and the flags over our heads to tell the enemy just where to find us when they want us. We should have taken to the hills like the Boers.'[68]

James Bolger; a member of the Kimmage Garrison from Liverpool.[69]

John Bolger; a member of the Kimmage Garrison from Liverpool.[70]

David J. Bourke (Dáithí de Burca); he was in Reis's Jewellers Building and the Hibernian Bank. Along with Fergus O'Kelly and Con Keating, Bourke had been assigned by Plunkett to set up a 'pirate' transmitting and receiving station in Kimmage. They found it impossible to build a transmitter, but thought they had constructed a receiver using a gramophone speaker. When this, too, refused to operate, Keating and Bourke were sent to Kerry to seize the government's apparatus on Valencia Island, but Keating lost his life in an accident and Bourke returned to Dublin.[71]

John Boylan; he was at Annesley Bridge in Fairview. He was sent to the City Hall.

Joseph Bracken; he was a member of the Volunteers from the beginning, and was imprisoned until August.

Capt. Peadar Bracken (Peadar Ó Briacain); a member of the Kimmage Garrison from Tullamore.[72] He joined the Gaelic League, but felt that it was just a cover for the IRB. He was the O/C of the Athlone area. After a fight between the RIC and Volunteers in Tullamore on 20 March, he fled to the Kimmage camp. While at Kimmage, he honed his marksmanship skills and was a very accomplished marksman. He came to Dublin because 'they needed experienced fighting men there'; he was appointed captain by Pearse, then sent to O'Connell Bridge by Connolly. He had been in charge of three others at O'Connell Bridge at the outset of the Rising and then led the men in 'Kelly's Fort', ultimately having about 35 in his command.[73] He sent Séamus Robinson to take over Hopkins & Hopkins on the north side of the Bridge.[74]

Michael Brady; ICA. He was interned until June 1917.

_____ **(1) Breaslin**; a member of the Kimmage Garrison from Glasgow.[75]

_____ **(2) Breaslin**; a member of the Kimmage Garrison from Glasgow.[76]

Capt. Liam Breen; ICA. He was detailed to the Reis's Jewellers Building and imprisoned at Frongoch.

James Michael (Séamus) Brennan; a member of the Kimmage Garrison from Tullamore,[77] he was in the tram commandeered by George Plunkett, who demanded 'fifty-seven tuppenny tickets'. Brennan prodded the driver in the back with a shotgun and told him to keep going without stopping until they reached Nelson's Pillar. He was posted at the Tower Bar directly across Henry Street from the GPO.

Maurice Brennan; he came with the men who had reported to Cabra Bridge, and was interned until June 1917.

Cmdt W.J. Brennan-Whitmore; aide to Joseph Plunkett. He helped Michael Collins get Plunkett to the GPO,[78] and led some Volunteers in the Imperial Hotel and North Earl Street.[79]

Brennan-Whitmore was one of the few to argue for a guerrilla-type campaign, and held that 'the one really big flaw in our effort was the decision to stand and fight in Dublin'. He regarded the defensive plan adopted by the Military Council as a wasted opportunity. The Volunteers might have 'put up a prolonged resistance that would appeal to the fighting instincts of our race and rouse our people out of the apathy they had sunk into', but the defensive strategy consigned them to 'another chapter of failure'. He argued so often and so forcefully that the Military Council told him to put his ideas into a book and submit it to them, but his advice was ignored.[80]

He was charged with taking the Imperial Hotel and the North Earl Street area and building barricades. He tried fruitlessly to stop the looting, until he shot into the air.

When Brennan-Whitmore entered the Pillar Café as his HQ, he was told of a publican who had a very important message for him. Brennan-Whitmore descended the stairs to find an elderly man who said that in the 'Fenian days' the area had been scouted for the best firing positions. He showed them to Brennan-Whitmore, who took the man's advice and deployed his men accordingly.

It was his command that set up the 'string and can' communication system from the Imperial Hotel across Sackville Street to the GPO. When Brennan-Whitmore was captured he met the Australian sniper, stationed in Trinity, who hit one of his cans and tried to hit the string.[81] The sniper, 'snap-shooting' from a corner of Trinity College, hit the can several times but was disappointed to have missed the string—from over half a mile away.

Brennan-Whitmore was wounded while escaping from the hotel. When he was captured he gave his name as 'William Whitmore', and it was under that name that he was always listed.[82] He wrote *Dublin burning* and *With the Irish in Frongoch*.[83]

Joseph A. Briggs; he is listed on the Roll of Honour.

#[84] Daniel (Dan) Brophy: he was interned until July 1916.

Thomas Brophy; he came in from Fairview and was in the Imperial Hotel.

Donal Buckley (Domhnall Ó Buachalla); he joined the Maynooth Company of the Volunteers,[85] and they mobilised and proceeded to Dublin to join the Rising. He was sent to City Hall on Tuesday and returned to the GPO.[86] He fought at the Exchange Hotel in Parliament Street, sniped from the glass turret/dome of Arnott's on Henry Street, sniped on Trinity College from the Dublin Bread Company and was involved in the retreat from the GPO. He did not go to Moore Street with the rest of the Volunteers, and after wandering around Dublin for some time he was arrested at Broadstone Station on Saturday morning. He was taken to Richmond Barracks and then to Knutsford Jail in England, then was transferred to Frongoch. He was elected a TD for Kildare North in the First Dáil.

Edward (Éamon) Bulfin; a member of the Rathfarnham Company, he lived at St Enda's while studying for a degree in science, and the students there made munitions under the direction of Peadar Slattery.[87] On Easter Monday morning he received orders signed by Pearse that instructed him to mobilise the Rathfarnham Company and proceed to Liberty Hall. The company assembled outside Rathfarnham Church; about twenty out of a total strength of 35 mustered. From Liberty Hall they proceeded to the GPO, gaining entry through a window on Prince's Street. On the roof, Bulfin was given the job of hoisting one of two flags. He was given a green flag with a golden harp and the words 'Irish Republic'. 'The thing I remember most about hoisting it is that I had some kind of hazy idea that the flag should be rolled up in some kind of a ball, so that when it was hauled up, it would break out.' Looking down from the parapet, he saw that people had begun to loot the shops on the street below. (See statement of Robert Walpole, below.)

Bulfin was sentenced to death by British military court martial after the surrender,[88] but the fact that he was an Argentine citizen, born in Buenos Aires, saved his life. The Argentine ambassador intervened and, eventually, on 21 March 1917, Bulfin was deported under Britain's Aliens Restriction Act of 1914. The Argentine government did not want to anger the British Empire, with which they were already having problems, and arrested Bulfin when he arrived in Buenos Aires, sentencing him to jail for leaving Argentina for the purpose of 'deserting from military service'. Bulfin was released in 1919 and was later appointed ambassador to Argentina by Éamon de Valera.

Bartholomew (Bart) Burke; a member of the 4th Battalion, he was interned until December.

David Burke; a Marconi radio operator, he operated the radio in the Wireless School until the Wednesday afternoon of the Rising, when the position had to be abandoned owing to heavy shelling from the HMY *Helga*.

Fergus (Frank, Fergus de Burca) Burke; a teacher at St Enda's. He said that he saw 'bullets like hailstones, hopping off the street'. He was imprisoned at Frongoch.[89] He became a second lieutenant in E Company during the War of Independence.

Nicholas Burke; a member of the Hibernian Rifles, he was sent to the *Dublin Evening Mail* newspaper office, Parliament Street, and to Smith & Weldon's Ironmongers.

Christopher Columba Byrne; he became a captain in the War of Independence.[90]

Edward Byrne; aged fifteen, he joined the Volunteers on Easter Monday at Fr Mathew Park, and became a member of Michael Collins's 'Squad'.

James Byrne; he was in the Metropole Hotel and was imprisoned at Frongoch.

Joe Byrne; an IRB member. He was *not* a Volunteer or an ICA member, but reported to the GPO on Tuesday.

Louis Byrne (15); an ICA member listed as a 'boy'.[91] He ran messages from Liberty Hall and City Hall to the GPO. He went on to fight in the Civil War on the anti-treaty side, and was interned in Ballykinlar Barracks, Co. Down. He was the son of Louis Byrne (below), who was also sent to City Hall and was killed there.

Louis Byrne (46); ICA. He was sent to the City Hall, where he was killed. (Counted in the City Hall garrison.)

Patrick Joseph Byrne; ICA. He was one of those who came in from Cabra Bridge and Annesley Bridge.

Peter Sylvester Byrne; a Fianna member, he took part in the Howth gunrunning. He was imprisoned for two weeks after the Rising.

Thomas (Tom) Francis Byrne (O'Byrne); a member of the Kildare Volunteers, he travelled from Kildare, joined with the Maynooth Volunteers and came to the GPO.[92] He fought in the Boer War with John McBride and was thereafter known as 'the Boer'.[93] He was sent to City Hall and occupied the roof of Shortall's, next to the Exchange Hotel. He took Ned Walsh with him but not Ned's teenage son, who never saw his father alive again because Ned was killed in Shortall's. O'Byrne married Lucy Smyth, who was in the GPO.

 # Patrick Caddell; he fought in the retreat from Kelly's Corner, Rathmines, into

Dublin city centre by way of O'Connell Bridge, to the GPO, before finally retreating to Moore Street. Imprisoned at Frongoch.

John Caffrey; his death in 1933 was deemed to be attributable to the wound he received on Wednesday 26 April 1916.

Matthew Caffrey; he was in the Dublin Bread Company and in Westmoreland Street. He was interned until December.

Patrick Caldwell; a member of the Kimmage Garrison from Liverpool,[94] he was part of a small group that occupied the Ship Hotel after they failed to force entry into Mooney's public house in Abbey Street. After some time in the Ship Hotel, the group were ordered to the GPO and given various positions to defend in the building.[95]

Joseph Callen; ICA. He was in Lambe's public house, then came to the GPO. He was posted in the Coliseum Theatre and Arnott's.

Daniel Canny; ICA. He came from Annesley Bridge in Fairview.

Joseph Canny; he came in from the Cabra Bridge.

Alex Carmichael; a member of the Kimmage Garrison from Glasgow. He was involved in a large raid on Uddington Colliery, Scotland, for explosives that were smuggled to Ireland.[96]

Bernard Carmichael; is listed on the Roll of Honour as a carpenter from Kimmage.

Peter Carpenter, brother of Walter (below); he was at Annesley Bridge in Fairview, then went to the Metropole Hotel.

Walter Patrick Carpenter, brother of Peter (above); ICA.[97] He was O/C of the ICA Boys' Corps.[98] 'I was one of the members of the committee of the Citizen Army (Old Comrades) Organisation who supplied information to Mr R.M. Fox for inclusion in his *History of the Irish Citizen Army,* which was subsequently published in 1943.'

**Charles E. Carrigan (Caragan, Kerrigan) (34 on the day he was killed).[99] Born in Glasgow, he was a Gaelic Leaguer and a member of the IRB, becoming the Scottish representative on the Supreme Council. He was part of The Ó Rahilly's group that charged up Moore Street, and was killed on Friday evening in Sackville Place. He is buried in Glasnevin Cemetery.

James Carrigan; ICA. He became a member of Michael Collins's 'Squad'.[100]

> I was not mobilised for any parade on Easter Monday morning. I strolled down O'Connell Street and mingled with the crowd and to my great surprise I saw a crowd of Volunteers marching into the General Post Office. This conveyed to me that some event of importance was about to take place. ... We went along there and we were marched off again into the city to occupy the GPO and Hibernian Bank. My party was about 25–30 strong. We were divided and the group that I was with broke into the Hibernian Bank with Captain Tom Weafer in charge. This building would have been occupied between 5 and 6 p.m. Orders were immediately issued to have the windows barricaded and vessels filled with fresh water. For barricading the windows we used the caretaker's bedding and other articles of furniture that were lying around. We were only in possession of the building about an hour when we saw women going down O'Connell Street with goods looted from shops in the surrounding streets there. We were ordered by Tom Weafer to shout at these women from our windows and order them to drop their loot. The majority of them obeyed our instructions and piled up the loot in the middle of O'Connell Street or Sackville Street as it was then known and Abbey Street Junction.

John Carroll; a member of the Kimmage Garrison from Liverpool.[101]

Patrick Carroll; a member of the Fianna, he later joined the ICA and is listed as a 'boy'.[102] After reporting to the GPO he was sent to St Stephen's Green. He was a member of the Volunteers in both the War of Independence and the Civil War.

Peter Carroll (Peadar Ó Cearbhail); he is listed on the Roll of Honour and was imprisoned at Frongoch.

James Cassels; he originally reported to Jacob's but came to the GPO later in the week. (Counted in the Jacob's garrison.)

James Philip Cassidy; he was imprisoned until December 1916.

 # John Clarke.

Lt Liam Clarke; one of the first casualties, he was badly wounded when a homemade bomb exploded prematurely.[103] When he got to hospital, one Volunteer remarked: 'So much for those bloody canisters. If it didn't blow Liam's head off, the divil use it is to us.' He went to work for Kathleen Clarke and the Irish National Aid and Volunteers' Dependants' Fund, but he never fully recovered from his injuries.[104] He received the maximum pension of £350 per year.

Peter Clifford; a member of the Louth Battalion.

Patrick J. Clinch; a member of the Kimmage Garrison from Liverpool.[105] Imprisoned at Frongoch.

John (Seán) Coate; he is listed on the Roll of Honour.

Joseph Coghlan; a member of the Kimmage Garrison from Manchester.[106]

Seán Cole; ICA. He lived on Buckingham Street.

 # Capt. Richard (Dick) Coleman; mobilised with the Fingal Brigade at Saucerstown, went to the GPO, and was then sent to the Mendicity Institute. (See 5th Battalion, Ashbourne, and 1st Battalion, Mendicity Institute.)

Patrick Colgan (Padraic Colgain); a member of the Maynooth Company.[107] He married Delia Larkin, sister of 'Big Jim' Larkin.

Harry Colley; on Sunday he had taken his three rifles to Fr Mathew Park, expecting the Rising to start then. An ICA member, he was imprisoned at Frongoch. He became a TD, as did his son George, born in 1922.[108]

Capt. Michael Collins (Míceál Ó Coileain); aide-de-camp to Joseph Plunkett. He was not listed as a member of the Kimmage Garrison but went to Kimmage almost daily to attend to Plunkett. It seems the Volunteer Military Staff had given him specific responsibility for the garrison.[109] Joe Good said that he was 'impressed with the hurry and earnestness in Collins, but had little sympathy for his drastic methods … since he was abusive to us. He was not well liked.'[110] Collins led the main body of the garrison out of the GPO into Moore Street.

Patrick (Paddy) Connaughton; originally from Longford, he was imprisoned at Richmond Barracks and sent to Stafford, then Frongoch.

Joseph Connolly; ICA. Brother of Capt. Seán Connolly, who was killed at City Hall. He was sent to St Stephen's Green.

Rory (Rauri, Roddy) Connolly; James's son, he was sent to William O'Brien's home later during the week.

James Patrick Conroy; he was in the Dublin Bread Company and the Hibernian Bank.

Herbert 'Andy' Conroy; an ICA sharpshooter, he was sent to Hopkins and Hopkins, where his sharpshooting from the roof slowed the fire from TCD. Later he was wounded there.[111] He became a member of Michael Collins's 'Squad'.

Seán Conway; ICA. He was at Annesley Bridge in Fairview, then went to Church Street and then to the GPO.

John Dutton Cooper; ICA. He was in the Dublin Bread Company.

Laurence Corbally; ICA. Son of Richard (below), he was listed as a 'boy'.[112] They escaped into Moore Street.

Richard Corbally; ICA. Imprisoned at Frongoch.

Thomas Corbally; imprisoned at Frongoch.

Patrick John Christopher Corless; he came in from Cabra Road and was sent to Harcourt Street. Interned until December.

★★Edward Cosgrave (43);[113] some sources have him as a member of the ICA, but he is not mentioned in the list of ICA casualties.[114] He is listed as being killed in the GPO on Tuesday, and buried in Glasnevin Cemetery.[115] He is not on the list issued by the Irish National Aid and Volunteers' Dependants' Fund as 'men who were killed whilst fighting for Ireland during Easter Week, 1916'.

Daniel Courtney; ICA. He was known as the 'Grandfather of the Citizen Army'. He was at Annesley Bridge in Fairview, came to the GPO and escaped to Moore Street. His brother, Bernard, was at St Stephen's Green and both were imprisoned at Frongoch.

Michael Patrick Cowley (M.L.?) (Mícheál Padraig Mac Amhalghaidh); IRB Dublin centre. He became the manager of National City Bank.[116]

★★Henry (Harry) Coyle (28);[117] an accomplished hurler, he was a strict teetotaller and an ICA member. One report said that he was killed in the escape down Henry Place on Friday night, when he shot himself while trying to break open a door with a rifle.[118] Another report, however, said that he was killed at the same place by a sniper.[119] He is buried in Glasnevin Cemetery.

Thomas Craven (Tomás MacCraibhain); a member of the Kimmage Garrison from Liverpool.[120]

Michael Cremin; he marched in from Rathfarnham.[121] 'One individual at this post did not appear to me to have had any military training, so I asked him if he was a member of the Volunteers or Citizen Army, and he replied in the negative. I then asked him how he got in there, and he said he was in O'Connell Street when James Connolly appealed for volunteers and he considered it his duty to come along.' He received the maximum pension of £350 per year.

 # James Crenigan; a member of the Fingal Brigade, he became battalion adjutant.[122]

Joseph Cripps; a druggist, he made many forays to find medical supplies and was on Red Cross duty. He was a photographer and went to the GPO to take photographs as soon as he heard of the Rising, then stayed in the GPO.[123]

Lt Gerald Crofts; a famous singer, he was second in command and was with the men in the Imperial Hotel who 'escaped' towards Marlborough Street but were captured.[124] The O/C, Cmdt William Brennan-Whitmore, 'provisionally' promoted him to lieutenant.[125]

Michael Croke; ICA. He was first stationed in Lower Abbey Street.

Thomas Croke (Tomás Crok, Crooke?); he was in the Irish School of Telegraphy in the Reis's Jewellers Building.

William F. (Liam) Cullen; he became one of Michael Collins's most trusted lieutenants. An ICA man, he was imprisoned at Frongoch.

Mark Joseph Cummins; he was interned until August.

Tom Cummins; he was wounded in Moore Street during the attempted escape with The Ó Rahilly.

John Cusack; he came in from Cabra Road.

Patrick Dalton; he was in Cole's Lane, then went through Henry Street to Moore Street.

Denis (Dinny) Daly; a member of the Kimmage Garrison from London.[126] He worked for the Post Office in London, joined the IRB there and was great friends with Michael Collins.[127] Daly was the leader of the party sent to Cahirsiveen to commandeer a wireless system and transmitter.[128] Four other Volunteers made up the raiding party: Dan (Donal) Sheehan, Charles Monahan, Colm Ó Lochlainn[129] and Con Keating. They went by train to Limerick, where they met Tommy McInerney, who obtained the two cars that were to be used in the venture. Keating, Sheehan and Monahan travelled on with McInerney and were to go to Tralee with the equipment after it had been taken; Daly and Ó Lochlainn were to travel in the second car with the tools. The cars were to stay together but somehow became separated. When Daly and Ó Lochlainn got to Cahirsiveen, the other car never showed up; as neither of them knew anything about wireless, they decided to return to Dublin. On the train back, they heard that McInerney had driven off the Ballykissane Pier; Sheehan, Monahan and Keating drowned.[130]

Patrick (Paddy) J. Daly (O'Daly); he was imprisoned in Frongoch, and went on hunger strike as a result of being punished for a minor infraction of the camp rules. The strike was successful and he was released to the general prisoner population.[131] He became the leader of Michael Collins's 'Squad'. Later he became a major-general in the Irish Army.[132]

Séamus Daly; he was in the Metropole Hotel.[133] An IRB member, he became a commandant.[134]

> On Thursday, I called over to No. 2 Dawson St. and I saw Michael O'Hanrahan, and I asked him how were things. He asked me how were things in the Workshop. I said that everything was practically cleared out now, that we delivered all the stuff [bombs], and was there any use in carrying on with any more work, and he said 'I don't think there will be any time to'; and then he said 'as a matter of fact, we may be in the field—any time now. Expect anything that happens'. And then he said 'Keep in touch with your Company, and wait for any orders'.

William Daniel (Liam) Daly; a member of the Kimmage Garrison from London.[135] A telephone operator, he installed a telephone on the roof of the GPO, and was wounded in the arm when escaping with the leaders. Imprisoned at Frongoch.[136]

William Darcy (Darcey, D'Arcy); he was an IRB organiser and allegedly died from the effects of captivity.

William Darker; he reported to the GPO, then moved to outside locations, latterly a series of barricades in the north city area, until taking ill, allegedly from lying on cold cobblestones, and collapsing on Thursday.

Daniel Davitt; he was in Cole's Lane, then went to the Pillar House in Henry Street.

James Dempsey; he came with the men who had reported to Cabra Bridge. He became a member of Michael Collins's 'Squad'.

Patrick Dennany; ICA. He was interned until December 1916.

Joseph Derham; ICA. He was at Ballybrough and Summerhill and was imprisoned at Frongoch.

Patrick Devereux; ICA. He was in the Imperial Hotel and Delahunt's public house.

Francis Devine; he was one of the men sent to Parliament Street.

Thomas William Devine; he was an early Volunteer.[137] When he reported on Monday he came directly from work and had no weapon. Capt. Liam Tannam pointed him to a pile of weapons and bandoliers and told him to take his pick.

> Towards [Friday] afternoon the order was issued for all present to assemble in the large room just inside the entrance to the building, and I remember Pearse standing up on a table and seeing his fine head in relief against a sunlit window. It was my last sight of him and the picture is still very clear in my memory.
>
> In his address he paid tribute to the spirit and exertions of his followers. I don't remember all he said on that historic occasion, but I do remember the (prophetic) words: 'Win it we will although we may win it in death', and the cheer that went up from the garrison. He then outlined his immediate plans. Evacuation had been decided on. The wounded would first be removed to the Coliseum Theatre in Henry Street. Next an advance party with bayonets would leave with The Ó Rahilly, attack the enemy barricade in Moore Street, and if successful in breaking through, take possession of Williams and Woods Jam Factory nearby …
>
> The removal of the wounded out of doors began at once, conspicuous amongst them a stretcher case covered in white linen which I was told was James Connolly. I remember thinking, he was dead …
>
> Volunteers for the advance party were now called for and out of a large number who put up their hands, about thirty—though I can't be sure of the number—were chosen, myself among them.
>
> We lined up in Henry Street just outside windows, when The Ó Rahilly briefly inspected our ranks, noting, I daresay, that more than one rifle lacked a bayonet. The inspection finished, we formed fours …
>
> The Ó Rahilly drew his sword and took his place in front. Then at the words

of command 'Quick March—at the double', we moved off along Henry Street and at a brisk trot rounded Moore Street corner. We were met with bursts of machine-gun fire from the barricade and I heard groans and thuds as several of my comrades fell. One of them was my friend Patrick Shortice. R.I.P. I forget the exact number of casualties we suffered but they were comparatively heavy. The wonder is our small force wasn't wiped out there and then. … [T]he fleet-footed Ó Rahilly—he could run like a deer—kept nearer the right-hand pavement and led the nearest of us by six or seven yards. The charge carried us and him within 25 or 30 yards of the barricade, when perceiving, or sensing, that the bulk of his party had failed to keep up with him, The Ó Rahilly swerved into a doorway (the private door of Leahy's licensed premises) … At this time I don't suppose a cat could have crossed Moore Street unscathed … For about half a minute Ó Rahilly stood tensely in the doorway, then taking advantage of a momentary lull in the firing, he nodded swiftly in our direction and blew two blasts on his whistle. A few seconds he waited, then dashed out into mid street in the direction of Henry Street … He had covered only a few yards when he was hit from the barricade and he fell face forward, his sword clattering in front of him. He lay motionless for a few seconds and we thought him dead.

Then with a great effort he raised himself a little on his left arm and with his right made the sign of the Cross. Again he lay down and again such was the greyness of his face we thought him dead; then minutes, seconds—I cannot tell—later he stirred and, by supreme efforts, slowly and painfully dragged himself inch by inch into Sackville Lane a few yards away where he lay down for the last time. The present memorial plaque overlooks the spot where he died. R.I.P.

James (Séamus) (Peter, Peadar?) Devoy; one of the ICA who carried Connolly's stretcher out of the GPO into the Moore Street buildings. Nephew of Clan na Gael founder John Devoy.

William Dickinson; he was from Liverpool.

Charles Donnelly; a member of the Rathfarnham Volunteers.[138]

While presenting printed copies of the Proclamation of 1916 to three members of the Dublin Typographical Society who set up the Proclamation of 1916 in Liberty Hill, Mr [Oscar] Traynor, Minister for Defence, stated he was aware that 2500 copies were printed and that probably they were intended for distribution throughout the country. He was in the GPO for the best part of the week and did not see the Proclamation. He did not see a copy afterwards except the one the President of Ireland had framed at present, and the time had come when someone more closely connected with this aspect of the Rising would have to fill the void.

On Easter Monday evening 1916, while on a window barricade at the GPO, Commandant-General P.H. Pearse instructed me to hand bundles of the Proclamation to the newsboy for distribution through the city. I called a newsboy of about eighteen years of age whom I asked to have the Proclamation distributed. He took a large bundle of same and, in less than an hour, he came back holding his cap by the peak and the back, full of silver coins, mostly 2/- and 2/6d pieces. I refused the money, telling him he was told to give them out free. He said he thought we wanted the money to buy food for the garrison. I asked him who he had at home and he informed me he had a widowed mother and small brothers and sisters, so I told him to go and give the money, which he had got for the Proclamation, to his mother. (This I believe he did.) He came back again and collected the balance of the Proclamations, stating he would give them out without charge (which I believe he did).

Patrick (Paddy) Donnelly; the greenkeeper at the Grange Golf Club. He became the QM of E Company, 4th Battalion, in the War of Independence—the 'Rathfarnham Company'.

Éamonn T. Dore; Seán MacDermott's 'bodyguard'. He was from Limerick and married Nora Daly, Kathleen Clarke's sister, in May 1918.[139]

Michael Dowling; the big toe of his left foot was amputated as a result of a gunshot wound received while retreating from the GPO, and he was interned until September 1916 at Frongoch.

Edward Doyle; ICA. He was in Hopkins & Hopkins and the Dublin Bread Company.[140]

John Doyle; ICA. Imprisoned at Frongoch.

John Doyle; he was on the Ballybrough Road then went to the Coliseum Theatre.

John Joseph (J.J.) Doyle; he came in from Fairview.

Peter Doyle; ICA. He was one of the men sent to the City Hall and was imprisoned at Frongoch.

Capt. Seán (John J.) Doyle; he acted as medical officer until Jim Ryan arrived.

Connolly had him lead twelve women, 23 men and 30 wounded through the holes in the walls to the Coliseum Theatre, and then to Jervis Street Hospital. When they got to the British lines, an officer let the women and wounded through and sent the rest back to the GPO. Imprisoned at Frongoch.[141]

Thomas Doyle; he came in from Kimmage and was sent to the Four Courts.[142]

 # William Doyle; he was interned at Knutsford and Frongoch until September.

Capt. Frank Drennan; he led a party of men who tunnelled through the walls of the Imperial Hotel to Allen's stores on North Earl Street.[143]

Patrick Joseph Drury; he was in Fleet Street, Westmoreland Street and the Imperial Hotel.

Edward Duffy; imprisoned at Frongoch.

Joseph Duffy; a member of the Kimmage Garrison from Liverpool.[144] Along with John McGallogly, he was ordered to barricade the houses at the top of Lower Abbey Street.[145]

Francis (Frank) Dunne; ICA. Imprisoned at Frongoch.

John Dunne; imprisoned at Frongoch. He became a member of Michael Collins's 'Squad'.

Joseph Dunne; ICA. Imprisoned at Frongoch.

Patrick Dunne; he came with the men who had reported to Cabra Bridge. Imprisoned at Frongoch.

Thomas Dunne; ICA. Imprisoned at Frongoch.

Michael Dwyer; an ICA member, he also fought at St Stephen's Green and was imprisoned at Frongoch. (Counted in the GPO garrison.)

Albert Dyas; he went to William's in Henry Street, then into Moore Street.

John Early; ICA. He was in Mary's Lane, then went to the Coliseum Theatre.

Joseph Egan; a member of the Kimmage Garrison from Liverpool.[146]

Patrick English; he was a 4th Battalion Volunteer and was interned until December.

Patrick Francis (Frank) English (Frainnc Inglis); he was in the Imperial Hotel.

Thomas (Tom) Ennis; ICA. On Wednesday afternoon he entered Henry Street with a party led by James Connolly and went down to Liffey Street, returning by way of Abbey Street the next morning. He was part of the company that went to the Hibernian Bank. He was imprisoned at Frongoch. He led the Custom House attack in 1921. He became a member of Michael Collins's 'Squad' and later a major-general in the Free State Army.

Robert Eustace; he came in from Clontarf.

Denis Farrell; ICA. He came to the GPO on Monday evening.

John Faulkiner; he came with the men who had reported to Cabra Bridge.

Christopher Feekery; he carried dispatches to Jacob's, the Four Courts and Boland's Mills.

Michael Finegan; ICA. He was in Bowe's public house in Fleet Street and the Imperial Hotel.

Thomas Desmond FitzGerald; quartermaster in the GPO.[147] He led the party of Cumann na mBan and wounded to Jervis Street Hospital. He became editor of *The Irish Bulletin* and subsequently Irish Free State Minister for Foreign Affairs and then Minister for Defence. He wrote *Desmond's Rising*.[148]

John J. Fitzharris; ICA. He was sent to St Stephen's Green, then came back to Henry Street.

Andrew Joseph (Andy) Fitzpatrick; on Good Friday, he led Martin King on a tour of the principal telephone trunk line centres with a view to disrupting communications on Sunday. He and Arthur King were to cut the cables at Talbot Street, and did so on Monday morning.[149] He was at Hopkins & Hopkins.[150]

Francis Flanagan (brother of Michael); a member of the Kimmage Garrison from Dublin.[151] Both brothers worked as poulterers in Moore Street, but had been ordered to be arrested by the RIC and so went 'on the run'. They moved to Glasgow, but returned to Kimmage with other Glasgow Volunteers.

James Michael Flanagan; he was interned until December.

Fr John (O'?) Flanagan; a priest who came to the GPO from the Pro-Cathedral.[152] A secluded corner was set aside for him to hear confessions and he gave conditional absolution to the Volunteers. The priests of the Pro-Cathedral told some of the garrison that if they wanted to leave their guns in the vaults they could do so; some did and escaped capture. (See statement of Leslie Price, below.)[153]

Matthew Flanagan; ICA. He was employed at Jacob's.

Maurice Daniel Flanagan; he was interned until December.

Michael (Mick) Flanagan (brother of Francis); a member of the Kimmage Garrison from Dublin.[154] He became a member of Michael Collins's 'Squad'.

James Fleming; he evaded capture and prison.

Ignatius George Flynn; he was in the Hibernian Bank.

Patrick Flynn; he was in North Earl Street.

Thomas Fogarty; he was in the Hibernian Bank and Reis's Jewellers Building and was imprisoned at Frongoch.

Michael Fox; a Volunteer, he was interned until August 1916.

Bernard (Barney) Friel (Frick?); a member of the Kimmage Garrison from Glasgow.[155] He collected swords, and was often seen marching with two or three at his belt. Imprisoned at Frongoch and Perth.

Andrew Furlong; a member of the Kimmage Garrison from London, he was wounded in the leg and tried to go to Jervis Street Hospital.[156] When the men carrying him couldn't get there, they returned to the GPO but it had already been evacuated. They ended up at a British barricade on Henry Street. As the men were crowding together to leave the GPO, a bullet hit Furlong's ammunition pouch, and one of the exploding bullets hit John Neale, killing him.[157]

Matthew Furlong; a member of the Kimmage Garrison from Manchester.

Joseph Gahan; a member of the Kimmage Garrison from Dublin. He was in the Ship Inn in Abbey Street.

Patrick Gallagher; one of the men who came in from Fairview.

Peter Paul Galligan; he came from Wexford, where he was in charge of a training camp. A member of the IRB, he reported to the GPO, then cycled from Dublin to Wexford carrying James Connolly's orders that the Enniscorthy Volunteers were to rise.[158] After the surrender he cycled to Cavan, but was arrested at the family home and was imprisoned in Dartmoor. He received the maximum pension of £350 per year.

Henry Gannon; a member of the 4th Battalion, he was interned until December 1916.

Patrick Garland; he was one of the men who went to the *Irish Independent* offices.

John James Gavan (Gavin); an ICA man, he was in Lambe's pub in Fairview. He went to the Coliseum Theatre and was imprisoned at Frongoch.

John Joseph Geoghegan; he came in from Annesley Bridge and was in the Metropole Hotel.

Richard Gibson; an ICA man, he came from Annesley Bridge in Fairview and was imprisoned at Frongoch.

Michael Giffney; a member of F Co., 2nd Battalion. He was at Mason's corner shop on the Clonliffe Road, and later in a house next to the 'Old Maids' home on Portland Row. He was wounded in Henry Place and was treated in Dublin Castle. He was imprisoned at Stafford, then at Frongoch.

Joseph Gleeson; a member of the Kimmage Garrison from Liverpool.[159] He was an active member of the GAA and said he encountered the IRB through the GAA. By 1913 he was IRB representative for the north of England.[160] He always used 'Richmond' as an alias.

Martin Gleeson; a member of the Kimmage Garrison from Liverpool.[161] Imprisoned at Frongoch.

Thomas Gleeson; he reported to the GPO, but was sent to St Stephen's Green and is counted in that garrison.[162]

William Gleeson (brother of Thomas); he reported to the GPO, but was sent to St Stephen's Green and is counted in that garrison.

Richard P. (Dick) Gogan; he was one of James Connolly's stretcher-bearers on the escape. He became a TD.

David Thomas Golden; he was in the Dublin Bread Company and the Hibernian Bank.

Alfred Joseph (Joe) Good (21); a member of the Kimmage Garrison from London, he encountered the Volunteers mostly through his participation in the Gaelic League.[163] He was assigned to O'Connell Bridge at the outset of the Rising, then he was in Kelly's Fort. He was imprisoned at Frongoch. He wrote *Enchanted by dreams: the journal of a revolutionary*.[164]

John (Jack) Graves; he was a member of the Maynooth Company and was sent to the Royal Exchange Hotel in Parliament Street.[165]

John Halpin; he was at Liffey Junction and Broome Bridge.

Patrick Halpin; ICA. He lived at Summerhill.

William Halpin; ICA. He was one of the men sent to the City Hall garrison.

Arthur Hannon; he was at the Dublin and Wicklow Manure Works in Fairview and came to the GPO; later he was sent to the Four Courts.

John Harling; a member of the Kimmage Garrison from London.[166]

Thomas (Tom) Harris; a member of the Kildare Volunteers, he travelled from Kildare, joined the Maynooth Volunteers and came to the GPO.[167] He was slightly wounded in the foot and was imprisoned in Frongoch.[168]

James Joseph (J.J., Séamus) Hayes; ICA. He was at Annesley Bridge in Fairview. Imprisoned at Frongoch.

Seán Hayes; he was imprisoned at Frongoch.

Richard (Dick) Healy; a member of the IRB and the ICA. Healy joined the Volunteers and bought his Martini-Henry rifle by paying at the weekly meetings. A member of the 2nd Battalion, he reported to St Stephen's Green but was sent to the GPO. Healy was in the Reis's Jewellers Building, the Hibernian Bank (where he saw Tom Weafer killed) and the Dublin Bread Company. He was imprisoned in Knutsford Jail and then transferred to Frongoch. Commenting on the Rising, he said: 'We were only semi-organised and we knew it wasn't going to be a success. Our hope was to kindle a flame and start the ball rolling. Up until then, there was no national movement worth speaking of except the Irish Republican Brotherhood, which was a small secret society.'[169]

James Michael Heery; he was interned until July.

Michael Heffernan; he was an employee of the Dublin Bread Company, and was interned until August 1916.

Seán Hegarty; a member of the Kimmage Garrison from Glasgow.[170] He helped raise the *Irish Republic* flag on the Prince's Street corner with Gearóid O'Sullivan.[171] (See Robert Henry Walpole note below.)

Capt. Frank Henderson (Prionsios MacFounraic); ICA. After the countermanding order was issued by Eoin MacNeill on Easter Sunday, Henderson's company was ordered to parade in St Stephen's Green at 10 a.m. on Easter Monday. After some confusion and disagreement among the officers and a short demobilisation, the company remobilised with a strength of between 80 and 100 Volunteers and they marched off from Fr Mathew Park at about 3 p.m. They occupied their positions until late Tuesday, when they were ordered by James Connolly to try and make it to the GPO. When they eventually made it to the front entrance of the GPO, they were fired on by Volunteers in the Imperial Hotel who thought that they were enemy forces because they had some prisoners in British Army uniform with them. Once inside the GPO, Henderson was ordered along with 21 other Volunteers to occupy McDowell's jewellery shop and Bewley's provision store in Henry Street. The group secured as much food as they could from the shops in Henry Street, sending a large proportion of this back to the GPO. As they erected barricades across Henry Street using goods from the shops, a large mob removed the items from the barricade as quickly as the Volunteers put them there. The Volunteers first fired a volley of shots over the heads of the mob but this had no effect, so they were forced to fix bayonets; the bayonet charge had the desired effect and the mob fled. Sometime on Thursday everyone was withdrawn to the GPO, as an attack was felt to be imminent; they remained in the GPO until the evacuation. Henderson was imprisoned at Frongoch.[172]

Capt. Leo James Henderson; ICA. He was imprisoned at Frongoch and became O/C in charge of the 1st Dormitory. He organised the 'Belfast Boycott', and was arrested in a raid on Ferguson's Garage at the start of the Civil War.

Richard Hickey; he was at the Portobello Bridge, then went to Prince's Street and Henry Street.

Frederick Paul Higgins; he was wounded on a mission to the *Freeman's Journal* in Abbey Street and was taken to Jervis Street Hospital.

Peter Higgins; ICA. He went into Moore Street, but evaded capture.

Hugh Holohan (a brother of Paddy in the 1st and 5th Battalions, and the cousin of Garry and Patrick, who were in the 1st Battalion); ICA. A friend of the Lemass brothers, he told them to come into the GPO on Tuesday, even though their unit, the 3rd Battalion, was at the Four Courts. He was imprisoned at Knutsford and Frongoch.

John Joseph Horan; a member of the Kimmage Garrison.[173]

Martin Hore; he was a 2nd Battalion Volunteer and he evaded capture.

George Howard; he was sent to the South Dublin Union.

Patrick Hughes; an ICA man, he was imprisoned at Frongoch. He received the maximum pension of £350 per year.

Thomas Hughes; he came in from Fairview Park.

Richard (Dick) Humphreys (Risteard MacAmblaoibh); The Ó Rahilly's nephew.[174]

James Hunter; ICA. He was a friend of the Ring brothers and, like them, a carpenter. He was imprisoned at Frongoch.

Joseph Hutchison; ICA. He came in from Fairview and went to the Imperial Hotel.

 # John F. (Jack) Hynes; he went to Kelly's gun store, where he was wounded, and was taken to Jervis Street Hospital.

Peter Jackson; he was imprisoned at Frongoch.

Thomas Jones; he is listed on the Roll of Honour.

Brian Joyce (Seoighe); he was elected hurling captain while he was a student at St Enda's. He was imprisoned at Frongoch.

Séamus Kavanagh; he was lame in one leg, and was given clerical duties as a result. Imprisoned at Frongoch.[175]

Thomas Kearney; ICA. He was at Annesley Bridge in Fairview.

Hubert (Hugh) Kearns; he was sent home by Seán MacDermott because he was ill and avoided capture.

Cornelius (Con) Keating; he was in Liffey Street and was imprisoned until August.

Christopher Keeling; he is listed on the Roll of Honour.

**John Keely (Kealy, Kiely);[176] a Gaelic Leaguer, he was particularly good at Irish and helped Francis Macken teach his Irish class at St Enda's. He mobilised with the Rathfarnham Volunteers and they made their way to Liberty Hall and then to the GPO. They arrived just as the Lancers came down Sackville Street, and Keely was killed in the cross-firing.[177]

Edward J. Kelly (Éamonn Ó Ceallaigh); a member of the Hibernian Rifles.[178] He was sent to the *Dublin Evening Mail* office in Parliament Street.

Fergus Kelly; he seized the Wireless School with Johnny (Blimey) O'Connor.

Francis Matthew (Matt) Kelly; ICA. In the War of Independence he worked in an office for Michael Collins.

Frank Kelly; a member of the Kimmage Garrison from Manchester.[179]

 # John J. (Jack) Kelly; he was imprisoned at Frongoch.

Joseph Kelly (16); his brother, Thomas, was in Boland's Mills. He was deemed too young to be imprisoned, but his boots were taken from him and he was released. He was caught making bombs in the War of Independence, was imprisoned for eighteen months in Dartmoor Prison and was released at the Truce. He fought on the anti-treaty side in the Civil War.

 # Richard (Dick) Kelly; he was sent to Boland's Mills, then to the Mendicity Institute.

Austin (Gilbert?) Kennan; a member of the Kimmage Garrison from London.[180]

Luke Kennedy; after the Rising he was imprisoned in Knutsford Prison in Cheshire, then in Frongoch, and during the War of Independence was Volunteer O/C at the Ballykinlar internment camp in County Down. He was an IRB centre in Dublin[181] (in the IRB, small groups were set up and called 'circles' and the 'leader' was called the 'centre'). He received the maximum pension of £350 per year.

Henry Vincent Kenny; ICA. He was an engineer and was sent to bore through buildings on Moore Street.

James Kenny; shot but survived. He was recruited to fight the English on the day of the Rising and was not a Volunteer or a member of the ICA. He was shot in the foot by either the Swede or the Finn who reported to the GPO to fight 'for small nations' but who had no experience with weapons.

Joe Kenny; he was seriously wounded in his leg and never properly recovered.

John Kenny; he came in from Fairview and was sent into Henry Street.

Michael Kenny; he was held for two weeks after the Rising, but then released because of his age.

Bernard Patrick Keogh; he was in the Hibernian Bank and was imprisoned at Frongoch.

**Gerald Anthony Keogh (20);[182] he was a Fianna member and was killed in front of Trinity College early on Tuesday morning.[183] He had been sent to summon Volunteers from Larkfield and was returning when he was killed. His body lay in a room in Trinity for three days, and was then buried in Trinity until after the Rising. He was reinterred in Glasnevin Cemetery.[184]

Joseph James Keogh; he came in from Fairview and was in the Imperial Hotel.

Michael Keogh; he lived at 18 Synge Street and is listed on the Roll of Honour.

John (Seán) Kerr; a member of the Kimmage Garrison from Liverpool.[185] On

Wednesday afternoon he went into Henry Street with a party led by Connolly, down to Liffey Street, and they returned by way of Abbey Street the next morning.

Thomas Kerr; a member of the Kimmage Garrison from Liverpool.[186]

Thomas Kilcoyne; he came in from Fairview and went to the Imperial Hotel.

John A. Kilgallon; an American citizen studying at St Enda's, he was interned until December and was then deported to the USA in 1917.

Thomas (Tom) Kilgallon; he went into the waxworks next door and returned with an officer's uniform including a coat with a high fur collar and an Australian hat—even Connolly had to laugh at him.[187]

Robert Killeen; ICA. He was in the Magazine Fort, then reported to the GPO. He was imprisoned at Frongoch.

Patrick (Paddy) Kilmartin; prior to the Rising, he was very adept at acquiring weapons from British soldiers, and many of these were stored at his home. He collected explosives from Michael Staines at the GPO on Tuesday, and then returned to his company at Broadstone Station late that evening. When their position was overrun on Wednesday, Capt. O'Sullivan ordered the men to surrender. Upon capture, Paddy was sent to Richmond Prison, then to Kilmainham Gaol and Arbour Hill Prison, and then finally to Wakefield Prison in Yorkshire.

King brothers (George, John and Patrick); they were from Liverpool and joined the Volunteers in 1914.[188] George managed to open a manhole cover at the corner of Lombard Street East and Great Brunswick Street and cut Dublin Castle's vital cable to London. Pat was the adjutant at Kimmage. John was wounded in the retreat to Moore Street. They were taken from Frongoch and handed over to the English military for desertion, and eventually discharged as 'persons not likely to give loyal and faithful service to His Majesty'.[189]

Sam King; he was in the Imperial Hotel and Gardiner Street.

Patrick Kirwan; he was a member of the Maynooth Company.[190] He was sent to the City Hall and was in the *Dublin Evening Mail* office.

Michael Knightly; a journalist and ICA man, he was imprisoned at Frongoch. He became Press Intelligence Officer for the Volunteer HQ.[191]

John Lafferty; he was interned until December.

Thomas Lambert; ICA. He was sent to the City Hall on Monday evening and is counted in that garrison.

Séamus Landy (Lundy); a member of the Kimmage Garrison from Liverpool,[192] he was in the Hopkins & Hopkins detachment.[193]

Michael Largan; he was in the Imperial Hotel and Marlborough Street.

Patrick Lawler; he was in Clery's and Marlborough Street.

 # Edward Lawless; he was imprisoned at Frongoch.

Thomas Leahy; a shipyard worker, he moved to England, then moved back to Dublin in 1914 after war was declared. He was involved in the attack on the Magazine Fort, and then served in Fairview, Ballybrough and the O'Connell Street area. (Counted in the 1st Battalion.) An ICA man, he was imprisoned at Frongoch.[194]

Joseph Ledwith (Ledwidge); he was a member of the Maynooth Company and was in the Royal Exchange Hotel and the Coliseum Theatre.[195]

Hugh Lee; he was wounded in the escape to Moore Street.

Joseph Lee; he was imprisoned at Frongoch.

Noel Lemass (19); he was with Brennan-Whitmore in the Imperial Hotel and was wounded while escaping. He was imprisoned at Frongoch.

Seán Lemass (17); he took up a position on the roof on Tuesday. The Lemass brothers were members of the 3rd Battalion. In the confusion they reported to the Four Courts; then, when they passed the GPO, Hugh Holohan called them in and they were absorbed into that garrison.[196] Lemass noted: 'Many people have claimed to have helped in carrying the wounded Connolly from the GPO. In fact, the process was so slow and frequently interrupted that almost everyone in the GPO helped … at some stage'. He became a member of Michael Collins's 'Squad', and served as taoiseach from 1959 to 1966. On 29 January 1916 Herbert Phelan Lemass, the youngest brother, was shot by mistake by Seán. The coroner's verdict held it was an accident, but said 'it was a result of young men playing with guns'.

Capt. Dermot (Diarmuid) Lynch; he was a member of the Supreme Council of the IRB. He and Harry Boland were underground making the ammunition safe, unknown to Pearse and the others, so Lynch was the very last person to leave the GPO.[197] During the War of Independence he organised Sinn Féin's blockade of food exports in 1918 and was deported to the US for doing so. (He was a US citizen.) While deported, he was elected TD for Cork South East.[198] He received the maximum pension of £350 per year.

Gilbert Lynch; he was a member of the Kimmage Garrison from Manchester.[199]

John Lynch; an ICA man, he was imprisoned at Frongoch.

Martin Lynch; an ICA man, he was imprisoned at Frongoch.

Patrick Leo Lynch; on Wednesday afternoon he went into Henry Street with a party led by Connolly, down to Liffey Street, and they returned by way of Abbey Street the next morning.

John McArdle; he came with the men who had reported to Cabra Bridge.

Garrett (Gearóid) McAuliffe (MacAuliffe); a member of the Kimmage Garrison from Manchester.[200]

Kevin J. McCabe; an ICA man, he was imprisoned at Frongoch. When he was captured he was told that the men would be shot. McCabe shouted back, 'Might as well shoot us now, then'. One of the British officers heard him and sent medics over to care for the men.

Jack McCabe; he was in the Metropole Hotel.[201]

William (Billy) McCleane; he became a member of Michael Collins's 'Squad'.

Bernard McCormack; he was sent to College Green.

Miceal MacCraich; he is listed on the Roll of Honour.

Pat McCrea; he accompanied M.W. O'Reilly to an arms depot in Rutland [Parnell] Square to get more weapons.[202] 'On Tuesday in the Post Office our first job was to commandeer the National Volunteer rifles and the Hibernian Rifles weapons out of Parnell Square, and the man in charge of that was M.W. O'Reilly. We succeeded in this mission. When we loaded them in the car we walked back to the Post Office again, and on the way there was a skirmish in Jervis St. where I got slightly wounded in the hand.' He became a member of Michael Collins's 'Squad', and was often used as a getaway driver.

Patrick McDermott; a member of the Kimmage Garrison from Liverpool.[203]

Rory MacDermott (Ruaidhri MacDiarmada); he was in Reis's Jewellers Building.

Joseph McDonagh; an ICA man, he was imprisoned at Frongoch.[204]

John McDonald; ICA. He lived on St Brigid's Avenue, North Strand.

John Quinlan MacDonnell (McDonnell?); ICA. He was at Annesley Bridge and Gilbey's in Fairview, then went to the Imperial Hotel.

James John (J.J.) McElligott; he led some men to the GPO from the Imperial Hotel when it was on fire.

John McEntagart; he was wounded in the escape and received a wound pension.

Seán MacEntee; he was sent to Ardee to rouse his unit and he returned to the GPO on Wednesday. He was a Belfast engineer and led a Volunteer unit at Castlebellingham in County Louth, where he lined up Constable McGee and an English Grenadier officer named Dunville against some railings with other prisoners and shot them (McGee died and Dunville survived). Only a year previously he had been an enthusiastic Redmond supporter and tried to get a commission in the British army. He became tánaiste of the Republic.[205] He received the maximum pension of £350 per year.

Dominick McEvoy; he is listed on the Roll of Honour.

James McEvoy; he was in the Reis's Jewellers Building.

Thomas Richard McEvoy (MacEvoy) (17); ICA. He carried dispatches to St Stephen's Green and North King Street.

James (Séamus) McGallogly; a member of the Kimmage Garrison from Glasgow.[206] He worked in a colliery in Uddington, Scotland, and planned a large raid for explosives that were to be smuggled to Ireland; he was detained, however, and so his brother took his place on the raid.[207]

John (Seán) McGallogly (younger brother of James); a member of the Kimmage Garrison from Glasgow.[208] He was involved in many raids for explosives that were then smuggled to Ireland.

Milo McGarry; a member of the Kimmage Garrison from Glasgow.[209] His mother was recruited by Marie Perolz on Easter night, and then went to the Dalys in Limerick with the news that the Rising would go ahead on Easter Monday.[210]

Seán McGarry; ICA. A great friend and confidant of Tom Clarke. Of Clarke he wrote:

> To him the Irish nation was very real. He spoke of fighting for Ireland as casually as he did about any item of the day's news. To fight England was to him the most natural thing in the world for an Irishman … He was slow to condemn, always ready to hear the other side, and was perhaps over-tolerant to his friends … He was always content to do the work and get it done; the credit could go anywhere … It is not for us who were the contemporaries of these seven gallant men who signed the Proclamation of 1916 to apportion greatness nor indeed to say if any of the seven signatories were great. But, if one may hazard a guess, it is that history will write Tom Clarke as a great Irishman—great in his love for Ireland, great in his faith in her destiny, great in his purpose, great in his achievement, and great in his death.[211]

Michael McGarvey; a member of the Kimmage Garrison from Liverpool.[212]

C. McGinley (Coniobhar Mac Fionnlaic); he is listed on the Roll of Honour.

Patrick McGinley; ICA. He came in from Fairview and went to the Imperial Hotel.

William (Liam) McGinley; a member of the Kimmage Garrison from Glasgow.[213]

Michael Conway McGinn; ICA, brother of Tom (below). He was the caretaker of the Clontarf Town Hall, where the Volunteer Military Council frequently met prior to the Rising. McGinn was a friend of Patrick Pearse and was an old IRB man himself. He came in from Fairview and went to the Imperial Hotel.

Tom McGinn; ICA. He was from Clontarf, and came in to the GPO with his brother.

Séamus McGowan; an ICA member, he supervised the removal of the war stores from Liberty Hall on Monday afternoon.[214] He was a sergeant and the assistant QMG.

Christopher McGrane; a member of the Fianna, he was at the Howth gunrunning.

Michael McGrath (Micéal MacGrait); a member of the Kimmage Garrison from London.[215]

Patrick Joseph McGrath Jnr; ICA. He and his father were in the Hibernian Bank and Reis's Jewellers Building.

Patrick Joseph McGrath Snr; ICA.

Thomas (Tom) McGrath; he was a 2nd Battalion Volunteer and was imprisoned at Frongoch.

Leo MacKey; he lived at 23 North William Street and is listed on the Roll of Honour.

Michael MacKey; he was on the Ballybrough Road, then came to the Imperial Hotel. He was imprisoned at Frongoch.

Dan McLaughlin; he attended medical school for several years and assisted Jim Ryan in treating the wounded.

Dr Daniel Aloysius MacLaughlin; he was not a Volunteer but offered medical services.

John (Seán) McLoughlin (MacLoughlin) (16); he was a messenger, often shuttling between the Mendicity Institute and the GPO. (Counted in the 1st Battalion garrison.) He was appointed a commandant by Connolly and was in command of a group of 30 assigned to take the *Irish Independent* offices on Thursday afternoon.[216] Connolly led them to the *Independent*, and it was on this foray that Connolly was wounded in the ankle. (Some report that McLoughlin was later promoted to 'Commandant-General by Connolly, and thus it was he, not de Valera, who was the highest-ranking survivor of 1916'.[217]) McLoughlin asked Connolly what would happen to the men, and Connolly replied: 'Oh, I think those of us, including myself, who have signed the Proclamation, will be shot. Some good, however, might come from what we have done.' Connolly told him not to reveal his rank: 'You're a young man; you'll be able to pick up the thread; men such as you will be needed'.[218]

Charles MacMahon (12); at twelve, he was one of the two youngest to fight in Dublin (Thomas Keenan, in St Stephen's Green, was the other).

Donal (Dan) McMahon;[219] ICA. He was imprisoned at Frongoch.

Patrick MacMahon; he was sent to North King Street.

Patrick McMahon; a member of the Kimmage Garrison from Liverpool.[220]

Seán McMahon; he was imprisoned at Frongoch and later died of TB, which was related to his imprisonment.

Patrick McManus; an ICA man, he was imprisoned at Frongoch.

Bernard McMullan; he was interned until August 1916.

John McNally; he was imprisoned at Frongoch.

William (Liam) MacNeive (MacNiamh); he was an IRB member and one of the Kimmage Garrison from Liverpool.[221] Imprisoned at Frongoch.

Frank McPartland; he is listed on the Roll of Honour.

Peter Celestine McPartlin; he was a member of the Hibernian Rifles and was at Hopkins and Hopkins.[222] Imprisoned at Frongoch.

**Francis (Frank) Macken (29);[223] taught Irish at St Enda's. He mustered with the Rathfarnham Company on Monday morning, and then reported to the GPO. His body was found next to that of The Ó Rahilly in Sackville Place.[224]

Laurence Mackey; ICA. He was in the Imperial Hotel. Imprisoned at Frongoch.

Michael Mackey; he was on the Ballybrough Road, then went to the Imperial Hotel.

John (Seán) Madden; ICA. He went to a position on Liffey Street, and he was imprisoned at Frongoch.

John (Jack) Maguire; he was a member of the Maynooth Company and was sent to City Hall and Parliament Street, then returned to the Coliseum Theatre.[225]

Matthew Maguire; a Volunteer from Maynooth.[226]

Patrick J. Maguire; a member of the Kimmage Garrison from Glasgow.[227]

Patrick Mahon; ICA. He was interned until August 1916.

Patrick (Paddy) Joseph Mahon Jnr; ICA. He was at Gilbey's and Annesley Bridge, then went to the Imperial Hotel. He was imprisoned at Frongoch.

Thomas Christopher Mahon; ICA. A cousin of Paddy, he only joined the Volunteers on Tuesday. He was released after the Rising because of his age.

Louis Maire; he was at the Magazine Fort and is counted in the Four Courts garrison.

Antle (Tony) Makapaltis (Makanaltis); on Monday afternoon Makapaltis, a sailor from Finland, and a Swedish sailor turned up at the GPO and offered to fight for the Irish.[228] Capt. Liam Tannam talked to the two men. The Swede could speak no English. Makapaltis told Tannam that they wanted to fight for Ireland because, like Ireland, Finland and Sweden were small countries threatened by a much larger country (Russia). Tannam admitted the two men; the Swede was given a rifle and the Finn a shotgun and they were posted to the front right section of the GPO. Both men remained in the GPO until the surrender and were captured by the British. The Swede was released almost immediately when the Swedish consul intervened on his behalf. Makapaltis was detained in Kilmainham Gaol and later transferred to Knutsford.[229]

Jerome Joseph Malone; he came in from Kimmage and was sent to Price's Stores on Henry Street, then to the Ship Hotel in Abbey Street.[230]

Thomas Mangan (Ó Mangain); a member of the Maynooth Company, he was sent to the *Dublin Evening Mail* office in Parliament Street.[231]

Henry (Harry) Manning; he was in North Earl Street and was shot through the foot while attempting to retreat in the early hours of Friday morning, part of a group of Volunteers attempting to break out of the British cordon.[232] These men had been in various positions, including the Imperial Hotel and surrounding buildings. Frank Thornton had taken the first group and Séamus Daly was to lead the second group ten minutes later. When they reached the intersection between Railway Street and Gardiner Street they came under heavy fire. Some of the first group did not make it through the cordon and were forced to retreat into the Pro-Cathedral. Manning was severely wounded and had to be supported by two Volunteers.

Thomas Markham; he came in from Annesley Bridge and was interned until September.

 # James Marks; he was sent to the Mendicity Institute.

Thomas Mason; ICA. He was imprisoned at Frongoch.

Patrick Meagher; ICA. He was in Blackhall Place, then came to the GPO. He was interned until July 1916.

 # William Meehan; he was sent to the Mendicity Institute.

Seán Milroy; a Sinn Féin journalist and an ICA member. He was TD for County Cavan from 1921 to 1924.

James Minahan; he came in from Cabra Bridge and was interned until December.

James Mooney; ICA. He had been at the Fairyhouse Races, where he won on the favourite in the first race. When he reported to the GPO he was sent to St Stephen's Green, then back to the GPO. Imprisoned at Frongoch.

John Francis Mooney; he was at the Magazine Fort, then Church Street. (He reported to the GPO but is counted in the 1st Battalion garrison.)

Patrick Mooney; he was sent to McDowell's Jewellers in Henry Street, then to the Coliseum Theatre. He was imprisoned at Frongoch.

Edward John Moore; he reported to Columcille Hall in Blackhall Place, then went to the Coliseum Theatre.

John Moore; ICA. He was in the Imperial Hotel.

Patrick Thomas Moore (Padraig Ó Mordha); he was sent to the Coliseum Theatre and was imprisoned at Frongoch.

Patrick J. (Paddy) Morrin (Moran?); a member of the Kimmage Garrison from Glasgow.[233] Very handy with any kind of tool, he was designated the 'Foreman of Works' at Kimmage. He had been assigned to O'Connell Bridge at the outset of the Rising. According to the account of the Scottish Brigade, he was a steeplejack and Pearse asked him to hoist the *Irish Republic* flag.[234] (See statement of Robert Walpole, below.) Imprisoned at Frongoch. Helena Molony and Winifred Carney were part of a small core group of women at Liberty Hall who produced the flags. Molony recalled: 'We made the flags—three, measuring six feet by four and a half feet. There was a very nice sailor from Glasgow called Morrin, who looked at the flagstaff in the G.P.O. and said: "We could get a flag on that. I will do it, and they won't get it off in a hurry".'

Henry Moughan; he went to McDowell's Jewellers in Henry Street.

Andrew J. Mulhall; assigned to the 1st Battalion, he was a scout and reported to the GPO. He was arrested on Tuesday and released. (Counted in the 1st Battalion garrison.)

Andrew Mulligan; ICA.

Dominick Mulvey; he was in the Dublin Bread Company.

Stephen Mulvey; a Volunteer from Bray, he was in the Dublin Bread Company and the Hibernian Bank. Imprisoned at Frongoch.

William Robert Mulvey; he carried a dispatch from Eoin MacNeill to Éamon de Valera on Sunday.

**Michael Mulvihill (Moynihan?) (36);[235] a member of the Kimmage Garrison from London.[236] He went to Dublin at Easter on holiday and immediately volunteered. His body was found in Moore Lane near Henry Place.[237] He is buried in Glasnevin Cemetery. Not on the list issued by the Irish National Aid and Volunteers' Dependants' Fund as 'men who were killed whilst fighting for Ireland during Easter Week, 1916'.

Charles Murphy; he lived at 7 Albert Place and is listed on the Roll of Honour.

Fintan Patrick Murphy; he was QM of the Dublin Brigade after 1917.[238] He received the maximum pension of £350 per year.

Martin Murphy; he was in the Metropole Hotel.

Michael Murphy (Mícheál Ó Murchu); he married Martha Kelly, who was in the Imperial Hotel. An ICA man, he was imprisoned at Frongoch.

Peter Murphy (Peadar Ó Muirchadha); he was interned until December.

Robert Joseph Murphy; he was in the Metropole Hotel.

Capt. Séamus Murphy; he was a captain in the Dublin Brigade since 1914.[239]

Stephen Murphy; ICA.[240] He was sent to Jacob's Biscuit Factory.

Thomas Murphy (Ó Murchadha); a member of the Kimmage Garrison from Liverpool.[241]

William Murphy; he was in the Coliseum Theatre.

Joseph Murray; on his pension application he indicated that he was 'Deputy Chief of Staff to James Connolly'.[242] He was imprisoned in Frongoch.

Patrick Joseph (Paddy) Murray; he was from Galway and was imprisoned in Frongoch.

Thomas Murray; a Volunteer in the 2nd Battalion, E Company. The rest of his company were in the Jacob's Garrison, but as he arrived late in Fairview on Easter Monday he ended up in the GPO. He was sent to the Metropole Hotel and Manfield's. He was imprisoned in Frongoch and was released at Christmas 1916.

Francis Dominic (Frank) Murtagh; an ICA man, he was imprisoned at Frongoch.

Joseph (Moggy) Murtagh; a member of the Fianna and the ICA, he was a small lad from Clontarf. When they left the GPO, he carried a cross on his shoulder across Henry Street and was unscathed. Later he was in Hanlon's Fish Shop in Moore Street, when he got up and said he'd 'take a stroll over to the GPO'.[243]

**John Neale (Neal, Neill);[244] a cockney member of the ICA, he often used the term 'comrade' and claimed to be a socialist from London. He took 'potshots' at Nelson's nose on the Pillar until Connolly ordered him to desist.[245] He ruined his stockings and shoes on Monday and replaced them with a guest's pair from the Metropole Hotel.[246] He was supposed to have been in the party that blew up the Great Northern railway line across the viaduct on Monday. Joe Good described him as being a socialist speaker in London and as dying in the GPO, but Good noted that 'I never found out his name'.[247] When the garrison was leaving the GPO, the men were crowding together and a bullet hit Andrew Furlong's ammunition pouch. As the pouch exploded, bullets went in every direction and one hit Neale, causing him to fall against Charles Saurin: 'Can't you stand away and let a fellow lie down?' Neale asked gently. He was laid on a pile of mail-bags; when Oscar Traynor asked him whether he was badly hurt, Neale responded, 'I'm dying, comrade'.[248] Very little is known about him, and some question whether he is the same man as Arthur Abraham Weekes (see below). Not on the list issued by the Irish National Aid and Volunteers' Dependants'

Fund as 'men who were killed whilst fighting for Ireland during Easter Week, 1916'.

John Patrick Newman; an ICA man, he was in the Hibernian Bank and was imprisoned at Frongoch.

Shaun (John Michael) Nolan; ICA. He was sent to City Hall.

Lt Alfred George Norgrove; ICA. He was sent to City Hall and was captured on Monday.

Frederick Norgrove; ICA. He was sent home by James Connolly on Wednesday on account of his age, and Fox lists him as a 'boy'.[249]

James Norton; an ICA man, he was imprisoned at Frongoch.

 # Joe Norton; he came in from Ashbourne.

Michael Nugent; he was in the Imperial Hotel and was imprisoned at Frongoch.

Patrick Nugent; an ICA man, he was imprisoned at Frongoch.

Ernest Nunan (Ernan Ó Nunain),[250] brother of Seán (below); both were members of the Kimmage Garrison and had been sent from London by their father to join the Rising.[251] They were taken from Frongoch and handed over to the English military for desertion, and were eventually discharged as 'persons not likely to give loyal and faithful service to His Majesty'.[252]

Seán Nunan (Seán Ó Nunain), brother of Ernest (above); Seán later accompanied Michael Collins when Ned Broy let them in to see the G-Division files.[253] Seán became the secretary to President de Valera in the USA in 1919, and was a registrar of the Dáil bonds in 1919–21.

Tomás Ó Briain; he is listed on the Roll of Honour.

Eugene (Eoghan) O'Brien (Ó Briain); a 4th Battalion Volunteer.

John O'Brien; he came from Lambe's public house in Fairview, and was imprisoned at Frongoch.

Matthew (Matt) O'Brien; he was imprisoned at Frongoch.

Michael O'Brien; he came in from Kimmage, and was imprisoned in Frongoch.[254]

William Joseph O'Brien; he went to the Coliseum Theatre.

James O'Byrne; an ICA man, he came in from Fairview and went to the Metropole Hotel. He was imprisoned at Frongoch.

James O'Byrne; ICA. Imprisoned at Frongoch.

John O'Callahan; he was at the Magazine Fort, then was sent to Liffey Street.

Padraig Ó Caoimh; he is listed on the Roll of Honour.

Kevin O'Carroll (Caoinghalla Ua Cearbhaill) (that is the 'first' name as signed on the Roll of Honour); he was next to The Ó Rahilly when he was killed, and was himself badly wounded in the stomach. He was taken to the Thomas McKane home at 10 Henry Place, at the corner of Moore Street (behind Cogan's greengrocer's shop). The family had remained indoors for the previous two days, having seen a looter shot and unceremoniously thrown upon a barricade by British troops. Mr McKane, on hearing an attempt to enter the cottage, made for the rear door. At that moment, a Volunteer broke the glass panel with his rifle, which accidentally discharged. A bullet passed through Mr McKane, killing his teenage daughter behind him. Bridget McKane (16) was the first civilian casualty of the retreat from the GPO.[255] Fr McInerny anointed her. Her mother signed her death certificate with an 'X'. The Volunteers were very traumatised by her death.[256] O'Carroll was imprisoned at Frongoch.

Richard Joseph O'Connell; he was in the Imperial Hotel.

James O'Connor; he came from the North Circular Road Bridge, and was imprisoned at Frongoch.

John Thomas O'Connor; a Fianna member, he was in the Reis's Jewellers Building and was imprisoned in Frongoch until December.

Lt Johnny 'Blimey' O'Connor; a member of the Kimmage Garrison from London.[257] It was at one of the campfire concerts at Kimmage that he received the nickname 'Blimey' and it stuck for the rest of his life.[258] Like most of the men from Kimmage, he was armed with a shotgun, and that had very limited range. He had joined the Gaelic League and the Volunteers while he lived in London, and came to Ireland in

January 1916. An electrician, he installed communications throughout the GPO; he and others had attempted to restore wireless equipment from the Telephone Company School opposite the GPO in the Reis's Building at the corner of Sackville Street and Abbey Street. '[Blimey] was climbing up the wireless mast to fix some wires and he was being sniped at the whole time. How he had the pluck to carry on and how he was not riddled is beyond me.'[259] They broadcast 'Ireland Proclaims Republic today. Irish troops have captured the city and are in full possession. Enemy cannot move in city.' He was able to set up the transmitter but their attempts to set up the receiving apparatus failed, so there was no way of knowing whether the transmissions had been heard. They broadcast from Monday night until they were driven out by fire later in the week. He was imprisoned at Frongoch and fought on the Republican side during the Civil War, serving mostly in County Cork.[260]

**Patrick O'Connor;[261] a native of County Kerry, he was active in the GAA. He was killed on a reconnaissance mission in Thomas Lane on Friday morning.[262] Not on the list issued by the Irish National Aid and Volunteers' Dependants' Fund of 'men who were killed whilst fighting for Ireland during Easter Week, 1916'.

Patrick O'Connor; he was imprisoned at Frongoch.

Peter O'Connor; originally sent home because he was only sixteen, his mother told him to return to 'fight for his country'.

Rory O'Connor; an assistant to Joe Plunkett before the Rising, he would be the information officer for the anti-Treaty IRA. He was executed in 1922 in reprisal for Seán Hales's assassination.

Séamus Ó Donnagain; a member of the Kimmage Garrison from Manchester.[263]

Patrick (Paddy) O'Donoghue; he was in the Hibernian Bank. He was taken from Frongoch and handed over to the British military for desertion, and was eventually discharged as 'a person not likely to give loyal and faithful service to His Majesty'.[264]

Séamus O'Donoghue (Ó Donnchadha); a member of the Kimmage Garrison from Manchester.[265]

William O'Donoghue; a member of the Kimmage Garrison from Liverpool.[266]

Liam O'Gorman; ICA. He lived in Drumcondra Place.

Brian O'Higgins (Brian Ó hUiginn); one of the party who moved the explosives into the GPO basement. He was unwell for several months prior to the Rising, and he and several others like him were 'relegated in this way to the Reserve very much against their will; but they were in touch with things all the same, helped in propaganda work and in whatever way they could, and were ready to do our best when the call came. We called ourselves the "Lame Ducks" and joked and laughed over our extreme military knowledge, but were very proud that we had not been passed over and we were to have our own special place in the great mobilisation that was at hand.'[267] He wrote *The soldier's story of Easter Week*. He was imprisoned in Frongoch, became a TD and fought on the Republican side in the Civil War.

James O'Higgins; he came with the men who had reported to Cabra Bridge.

Padraig (Patrick, Paudeen) O'Keefe; he led some men to the GPO from the Imperial Hotel.[268] While he was on guard at the GPO, he lowered a ladder so that the men from Hopkins and Hopkins could retreat back into the GPO.[269] He was imprisoned at Frongoch. From 1918 he was assistant secretary of Sinn Féin. He served as a TD for County Cork, North-East. He supported the Treaty and was the deputy governor of Mountjoy Prison during the Civil War executions.

Fergus Francis O'Kelly; along with David Bourke and Con Keating, O'Kelly had been assigned by Joseph Plunkett to set up a 'pirate' transmitting and receiving station in Kimmage.[270] They found it impossible to build a transmitter but thought they had constructed a receiver using a gramophone speaker. When this, too, refused to operate, Keating and Bourke were sent to Kerry to seize the government's apparatus on Valencia Island, but Keating lost his life in an accident and Bourke returned to Dublin.[271] O'Kelly led six other Volunteers (including Seán O'Connor, who was an electrician, Arthur Shields, the well-known Abbey actor, and Bourke, who was to be the radio operator) to the Wireless School, which was occupied along with Reis's Jewellery Shop. The tower of the Dublin Bread Company restaurant, at 6–7 Lower Sackville Street, dominated the roof of the Wireless School. O'Kelly sent word to James Connolly that the DBC would have to be occupied in order to ensure safe operation of the radio. Connolly sent a company of Volunteers under the command of Capt. Tom Weafer, who was killed while taking these buildings. It was not possible to set up a receiving radio but a transmitting radio was successfully put into operation. O'Kelly stated that, as far as he could remember, the first message broadcast was to announce the proclamation of the Irish Republic and the taking over of Dublin by the Republican Army. The radio was kept in operation until Wednesday afternoon, when shelling from the HMY *Helga* became so intense that the position of the radio was no longer viable. Attempts were made to bring the radio apparatus to the GPO, but owing to the weight of some of the equipment this proved impossible.[272]

Joseph O'Kelly; he lived at 11 Upper Dominick Street.

Joseph O'Kelly; he lived at 93 Lower Dorset Street.

Seán T. O'Kelly (Seán T. Ó Cellaigh) (president of Ireland from 1945 to 1959); ICA. He was Pearse's adjutant during the Rising and was sent to release Bulmer Hobson on Monday evening from Martin Conlon's home in Cabra Park.[273]

Lt Ted O'Kelly; a member of the Kildare Volunteers, he travelled from Kildare, joined the Maynooth Volunteers and came to the GPO, where he was slightly wounded.[274]

_____ O'Laughlin; he was wounded in the breakout and taken to the McKane house in Moore Street.

David O'Leary; a member of the Kimmage Garrison from London.[275]

Diarmuid O'Leary (Ó Laoghaire); a member of the Kimmage Garrison from London.[276]

Edward Joseph (Éamon) O'Mahoney; ICA. He was imprisoned until 12 May. During the War of Independence he was a training officer for the Volunteers.

Matthew O'Mahoney; he was in Gilbey's in Fairview Strand, then went to the Imperial Hotel.

Seán O'Mahoney; ICA. He lived in Gardiner Place.

Sgt George Oman; an ICA member, he was in the Imperial Hotel. He was the older brother of William, who was the ICA bugler and who was in City Hall and St Stephen's Green. George managed to escape when the Rising ended and was not imprisoned. Later he would join the same IRA company as William, and from pension records seems to have dealt with supplies, particularly ammunition, during 1919–21. Their uncle, Robert, was in the Four Courts.

Donagh O'Moore; ICA. He was detained until May—released because of his youth.

Patrick Michael O'Moore (Padraig Ó Mordha); he was sent to Capel Street. After the Rising, he joined the British Army.

Colm Ó Muirchadha; he was interned until December.

James (Jim) (Séamus) O'Neill; an ICA officer who acted as QM during the Rising. He waited at Liberty Hall to load all the weapons, ammunition and bombs, before shuttling it all to the GPO. He was primarily responsible for the issuance of 'bombs'. He was appointed the ICA QM on Easter Sunday.[277] Following the Rising, he became the O/C of the Citizen Army.

John O'Neill; he was imprisoned at Frongoch.

John O'Neill; ICA. His widow filed a claim for a pension, which was unsuccessful because, according to medical opinion, his death was attributed to natural causes rather than to shock and heart trouble arising from military service in the Rising.

Patrick Joseph O'Neill; his pension application noted that he was in the GPO for two days and was sent home. Fox lists him as a 'boy'.[278]

William O'Neill; he was in Tyler's shoe shop and Noblett's confectionery. Interned until December 1916.

**The Ó Rahilly (Michael Joseph O'Reilly, aged 41);[279] brigade munitions officer. He said to Countess Markievicz at Liberty Hall just before marching off: 'It is madness, but it is glorious madness'.

He left the GPO at about 8.00 p.m. on Friday night to find a way to Williams and Woods: 'It will either be a glorious victory or a glorious death'. (Some commentators have his party as comprising twelve men, some about 30 and others 40 men.[280]) He carried a Mauser pistol in one hand and a sword in the other. He was hit first crossing Moore Street, then ran further up the street and fell into Sackville Lane (now Ó Rahilly Parade).[281] The Ó Rahilly crawled up this lane after being wounded, and died there.

Another Volunteer in the GPO, Thomas Devine, reported:

> Volunteers for the advance party were now called for and out of a large number who put up their hands, about thirty—though I can't be sure of the number— were chosen, myself among them.
>
> We lined up in Henry Street just outside windows, when The Ó Rahilly briefly inspected our ranks, noting, I daresay, that more than one rifle lacked a bayonet. The inspection finished, we formed fours . . .
>
> The Ó Rahilly drew his sword and took his place in front. Then at the words of command 'Quick March—at the double', we moved off along Henry Street and at a brisk trot rounded Moore Street corner. We were met with bursts of

machine gun fire from the barricade and I heard groans and thuds as several of my comrades fell. One of them was my friend Patrick Shortice. R.I.P. I forget the exact number of casualties we suffered but they were comparatively heavy. The wonder is our small force wasn't wiped out there and then . . . the fleet-footed Ó Rahilly—he could run like a deer—kept nearer the right-hand pavement and led the nearest of us by six or seven yards. The charge carried us and him within 25 or 30 yards of the barricade, when perceiving, or sensing, that the bulk of his party had failed to keep up with him, The Ó Rahilly swerved into a doorway (the private door of Leahy's licensed premises) . . . At this time I don't suppose a cat could have crossed Moore Street unscathed . . . For about half a minute Ó Rahilly stood tensely in the doorway, then taking advantage of a momentary lull in the firing, he nodded swiftly in our direction and blew two blasts on his whistle. A few seconds he waited, then dashed out into mid street in the direction of Henry Street . . . He had covered only a few yards when he was hit from the barricade and he fell face forward, his sword clattering in front of him. He lay motionless for a few seconds and we thought him dead.

Then with a great effort he raised himself a little on his left arm and with his right made the sign of the Cross. Again he lay down and again such was the greyness of his face we thought him dead; then minutes, seconds—I cannot tell—later he stirred and, by supreme efforts, slowly and painfully dragged himself inch by inch into Sackville Lane a few yards away, where he lay down for the last time. The present memorial plaque overlooks the spot where he died. R.I.P.[282]

The Ó Rahilly died slowly: at least four hours after he was shot he was heard calling for water. It is noted that at the moment of surrender, nineteen hours later, a British ambulance came across him, barely alive, but that is probably incorrect. The ambulance driver, Albert Mitchell, made a statement that The Ó Rahilly was alive the next day and that a British officer then remarked, 'The more of them that die naturally, the fewer we'll have to shoot',[283] but that seems quite unrealistic.

On Saturday morning Seán McLoughlin led a group of twenty Volunteers from the headquarters of the Volunteers at No. 16 Moore Street towards the Parnell Street end of the terrace to reconnoitre the area in preparation for an attack towards the Four Courts. They emerged into the rear yard of the last house, Kelly's, at No. 25, halting to await further orders. McLoughlin opened the rear gate and stepped into Sackville Lane at the side of the house. He wrote that he was shocked to see the body of The Ó Rahilly lying along the roadway in a pool of blood, with Paddy Shortis lying dead beside him. At this very moment Seán Mac Diarmada arrived and on seeing The Ó Rahilly became deeply upset. They placed covers on both bodies and then, on receiving an order delivered by a messenger, returned to No. 16 to be informed that all preparations for an attack were to be cancelled for one hour.[284]

Elizabeth O'Farrell saw The Ó Rahilly's body when she returned from her first meeting with Brig. Gen. W.H.M. Lowe in Tom Clarke's shop. Her recollection, and that of McLoughlin, is more likely than that of Mr Mitchell. Miss O'Farrell related that it was 2.30 p.m. on Saturday when she reached Moore Street, and as she passed Sackville Lane again 'she saw Ó Rahilly's corpse lying a few yards up the laneway, his feet against a stone stairway in front of a house, his head towards the street'.[285]

The Ó Rahilly wrote this note to his wife:

Written after I was shot—Darling Nancy, I was shot leading a rush up Moore Street, took refuge in a doorway. While I was there I heard the men pointing out where I was + I made a bolt for the lane I am in now. I got more [than] one bullet I think. Tons + tons of love dearie to you + to the boys + to Nell + Anna. It was a good fight anyhow. Please deliver this to Nannie O'Rahilly, 40 Herbert Park, Dublin. Goodbye darling.

He wrote this note on a letter he'd received from his son, Aodghan; it had a bullet hole through it. A plaque replicating his note was carved by Shane Cullen and placed in Ó Rahilly Parade in 2005.

Liam O'Regan; a member of the Maynooth Company, he was sent to the Royal Exchange Hotel in Parliament Street.[286]

Desmond O'Reilly; ICA, brother of Kevin (below). Their brothers Sam and Thomas were in the 1st Battalion. He was at the North Circular Road Bridge and was interned until August.

John O'Reilly; he was imprisoned until August.

John K. O'Reilly; ICA. He lived on North Circular Road.

Joseph O'Reilly; ICA. He was in Price's hardware shop in Moore Street, and was imprisoned until December.

Joseph (Joe) O'Reilly; a member of the Kimmage Garrison from London,[287] he became Michael Collins's 'assistant' after Frongoch.

Kevin O'Reilly, brother of Desmond (above); their brothers Sam and Thomas were in the 1st Battalion. He was one of the men who came in from Cabra Bridge.

Capt. Martin O'Reilly; he led the party of wounded and women to Jervis Street Hospital. The party consisted of Fr Flanagan, British Army Lt George O'Mahoney (captured on Monday), thirty wounded men and twelve women.

Capt. Michael William (M.W.) O'Reilly (M.L. Ó Raghallaigh); he was QM on the brigade staff and became O/C at Frongoch.[288] 'On Tuesday in the Post Office our first job was to commandeer the National Volunteer rifles and the Hibernian Rifles weapons out of Parnell Square, and the man in charge of that was M.W. O'Reilly. We succeeded in this mission. When we loaded them in the car we walked back to the Post Office again.'[289] At the surrender, he carried a white flag out the door of 17 Moore Street. A British officer approached him and told him that there were still some snipers in Cole's Lane, and O'Reilly took care of that. Subsequently, he was director of training for the IRA. He received the maximum pension of £350 per year.

★★Thomas O'Reilly (21);[290] a member of the ICA, he was killed on Thursday. One brother, Patrick, was in St Stephen's Green, and another, John, was in City Hall. It is not clear where Thomas was killed; one report has him killed in the Railway Fitting Shop in the 3rd Battalion area,[291] but his brother John said that he was sent to the GPO and was there all week until he was killed.[292]

William Joseph O'Reilly; imprisoned until December.

Joseph Francis O'Rorke; he came in from Gilbey's in Fairview Strand and went to the Coliseum Theatre.

Michael O'Shea; a member of the Kimmage Garrison from Liverpool.[293]

Gearóid O'Sullivan (Gearóid Ó Suilleaváin); a cousin of Michael Collins. A few months younger than Collins, he moved to Dublin in 1909 to attend St Patrick's Training College on his way to becoming a teacher, then attended the Royal University. He was the youngest officer in the GPO. He raised the Irish tricolour on the Henry Street corner between 1 and 2 p.m. on 24 April with Seán Hegarty.[294] Later, he ran with a mattress wrapped around himself from Clery's to the GPO, fell, got up and made it across unscathed. He was sent to Frongoch and was released in the general amnesty on 21 December 1916. On 19 October 1922 he married Maud Kiernan, Kitty's sister, in what was to be a double wedding with Kitty and Michael Collins. Kitty was a bridesmaid, but dressed all in black. He became adjutant-general of the Free State army. He died on Good Friday 1948 and was buried in Glasnevin Cemetery on Easter Monday.[295]

James O'Sullivan; a printing compositor, employed by the Gaelic Press, who assisted in printing the *Irish War News* during the Rising. The *Irish War News* was printed at the premises of James O'Keeffe's Printing Plant in Halston Street.

William O'Toole; an ICA member, he was imprisoned until December.

Matthew Parnell; ICA. He was in the Imperial Hotel.

Liam Parr; a member of the Kimmage Garrison from Manchester.[296]

Liam Pedlar; he was in Reis's Jewellers Building.

 # Thomas Peppard; he was the intelligence officer for the Fingal Brigade.[297] He was sent to the Mendicity Institute.

Capt. George Plunkett; brother of Joseph and Jack. He was the O/C of the Kimmage Garrison.[298] On Monday morning Capt. Plunkett waved down a tram at Harold's Cross, took out his wallet and said, 'Fifty-seven tuppenny tickets to the city centre, please'.[299] He became chief of staff of the IRA during the 1940s.

John (Jack) Plunkett; brother of Joseph and George.[300]

John Poole; he was sent to City Hall and is counted in that garrison.

Capt. Vincent Poole; ICA. He was at Annesley Bridge in Fairview. When he came to the GPO, he was assigned to Mansfield's boot shop, where they fired at close range on some British soldiers crossing the road. The British were decimated. Connolly promoted Oscar Traynor over his head, much to Poole's chagrin. When the fires started, the Poole brothers offered to explore the sewers to see whether an exit could be found, but were driven back by the filth.[301]

Seán Price; he was a member of the IRB and the Volunteers, and later fought in the War of Independence.

> Early on Friday morning British military opened fire. After some time the roof was ablaze. One could see the liquid from the shells running down the wall, ablaze, so we were brought to the ground floor where we were lined up for evacuation. Connolly was lying on a stretcher on the floor. Dr Jim Ryan asked for Volunteers to take the stretcher. R. Gogan of the 1st, Paddy Ryan of the 2nd, and myself took the stretcher across Henry Street into Henry Place. There was

heavy machine gun fire into Henry Place from Moore Lane, where the British were established behind barricades. When we reached the Mineral Water factory [4–8 Henry Place: Michael O'Brien and Co., mineral water company], we were stopped by Seán MacDermott, as the barricade which the Volunteers were putting across the end of Moore Lane, to afford some protection to the Volunteers passing towards Moore St., was not completed. We lowered Connolly to the ground, who turned on the stretcher and told the men to keep to the wall and burst open the factory gate on the left [*sic*]. Just then a Volunteer in uniform was shot in the breast and fell over the handles of the stretcher. Connolly, seeing the uniform, and thinking it was Plunkett, got very excited. He tried hard to get off the stretcher, shouting to get Plunkett into the factory at once. Just then, Plunkett came strolling up from the G.P.O. and pacified Connolly. Liam Cullen then came back with word from MacDermott to bring Connolly forward to the foot of the barricade. MacDermott told us to rush across at the first lull in the firing. We darted forward towards Moore Street, turned into the hallway of a grocer's shop at the corner of Henry Place and Moore St. The first man Connolly saw was a D.M.P. man sheltering. Connolly let a roar to throw him out to hell. We put Connolly in a bed in a small room. Later, we took him to a bedroom over a chandler's shop in Moore St.[302]

Charles Purcell; an ICA man, he was imprisoned at Frongoch.

James Quinn; he was a Volunteer, then joined the Hibernian Rifles. He evaded capture.

Patrick Rankin; he became O/C of an IRA unit in the War of Independence.

Thomas Rath (Roth?); he was at Annesley Bridge and then went to the Hibernian Bank.

Seámus Reader (18); a Scottish piper and a member of the Glasgow Volunteers. He was involved in a large raid on Uddington Colliery, Scotland, for explosives, and left Glasgow on 15 January carrying explosives to Ireland.[303] Following the Rising, he was interned in Reading jail.

Andrew (Andy) Redmond; he came in from Annesley Bridge in Fairview and went to the Metropole Hotel, then to the Imperial Hotel.

John Redmond; ICA. He was in the Imperial Hotel.

John Reid; he was one of the party who moved the explosives into the GPO basement. An ICA man, he was imprisoned at Frongoch.

Matthew Reilly; he was in Findlater's Place.

Sam Reilly; he was a sniper on the roof with Joseph Sweeney. He became a caretaker at Columbia University in New York.

John Richard Reynolds; after the Rising he opened an office on College Green, which was also the first office used by Kathleen Clarke for the Irish Volunteers' Dependants' Fund, prior to its amalgamation with the Irish National Aid Association. Reynolds was ordered by the English military officials to deport himself to Coventry, England, and remained there until 1917.[304] His daughter, Molly, was also in the GPO and was arrested.

Peter Joseph Reynolds; he carried dispatches throughout Dublin, and evaded capture after the Rising.

Henry (Harry) Ridgeway; ICA. He wore a Red Cross armlet, which was ripped off by British soldiers.[305]

Ring: five brothers—**Christopher, Joseph, T.W. (Leo), Liam and Patrick**. Four of them were carpenters and they were put to good use in 'burrowing' passages through buildings, especially in the Moore Street area under the command of Frank Henderson. All were ICA members. Liam, who began using the Irish form of his name, Liam Ó Rinn, became the chief translator to the Oireachtas and translated *A Soldier's Song* into Irish in 1926.

James (Séamus) Robinson; a member of the Kimmage Garrison from Glasgow,[306] he led the men in Hopkins and Hopkins.[307] He was born in Belfast, then moved to Scotland.[308] He was instrumental in acquiring explosives from munitions factories and mines and smuggling munitions from Scotland to Ireland. He received the maximum pension of £350 per year.

Thomas J. Roche; he was imprisoned at Frongoch.

William (Liam) Roche; a member of the Kimmage Garrison from Liverpool.[309]

Michael Rogers (Mícheál Mac Ruaidhri); at St Enda's he was the school gardener and taught practical horticulture.

Fenton Christopher Ronan; he was in Hopkins and Hopkins.[310]

William Ross; he was one of the men who came in from Cabra Bridge.

Charles Rossiter; an ICA man, he came in from Fairview and was imprisoned at Frongoch.

Seán Russell; ICA. At first he was in Lambe's pub, on the north-east side of Tolka Bridge. In Fairview he and his men set up a 'fort' to hold off the British coming in from the north and the Bull Wall. It was said that in a few hours Russell had built his fort with enough supplies to last a month, but later the fort was reluctantly abandoned[311] and his men went to the GPO with the rest of Henderson's men.[312] Then he was in the Metropole Hotel.

Desmond Ryan; he lived at St Enda's and was a prolific writer about Pearse and St Enda's.[313]

James (Jim) Ryan (Séamus Ó Riain); a medical student at UCD nearing his final exam, he bandaged Connolly's arm after Connolly was first wounded on Wednesday. Later he helped care for Connolly's leg after Connolly was severely wounded on Thursday.[314] He was a friend of Connolly's but had been sent to Cork to relay Eoin MacNeill's cancellation order to the Cork Brigade. Imprisoned at Frongoch, he was TD for Wexford from 1918 and later became a senator. He served in de Valera cabinets after 1932.[315]

Laurence (Larry) Ryan; a member of the Kimmage Garrison from Manchester.[316]

Oliver Ryan; a member of the Maynooth Company, he was sent to the Royal Exchange Hotel in Parliament Street.[317]

Thomas Ryan; a printing compositor, employed by the Gaelic Press, who assisted in printing the *Irish War News* during the Rising. The *Irish War News* was printed at James O'Keeffe's premises in Halston Street.

Major Charles (Charlie) Saurin; as part of a small party under the command of Lt Joe Tallon of C Company, he was stationed in McCabe's public house and remained at this position until Tuesday night/Wednesday morning, when the whole column occupying the area were ordered to evacuate to the GPO and Saurin led a party of 66 men in from Fairview. On arriving at the GPO he received serious cuts to his right hand when attempting to gain entry and was also hit by a bullet in the right hand. He was sent to the Metropole Hotel, then returned to the GPO.[318] Imprisoned at Frongoch.[319]

Martin Savage; he was killed during the failed Ashtown ambush of Lord French in 1919.

John Joseph Scollan; he was appointed National Director of the Hibernian Rifles. The Hibernian Rifles paraded as usual on Easter Sunday in North Frederick Street, and although Scollan saw the countermanding order from Eoin MacNeill he ordered his men to parade again on Easter Monday. Scollan, with about 60 men, paraded at the hall in Frederick Street, and sometime soon after noon they received word that the Volunteers had taken the GPO. On arriving at the GPO, the Hibernian Rifle men were ordered to barricade the upper windows. At about 6 a.m. on Tuesday Scollan received orders to go to the Royal Exchange Hotel, along with eighteen of his own men and nine Maynooth men. Arriving at the hotel, they occupied the roof and fired on the British troops who had taken over the City Hall[320] and who had the Volunteers pinned down in the offices of the *Dublin Evening Mail*. The Volunteers and ICA came under heavy and sustained attack from units of the Irish Fusiliers and Enniskilling Fusiliers; these attacks were repelled, and the British troops suffered heavy casualties. On Thursday morning Scollan received orders from Connolly to go to Broadstone Railway Station to find out what conditions were like there. As he was going up the steps of the station he was challenged and taken prisoner by a British soldier. He was held overnight at Broadstone Station and the next day taken to Ship Street Barracks, and then detained in Wandsworth Prison. In July 1916 he was moved to Frongoch, where he was held until October, when he was transferred to Reading Jail.[321]

Francis (Frank) Scullen (Scullion); a member of the Kimmage Garrison from Glasgow.[322] He was involved in a large raid on Uddington Colliery, Scotland, for explosives that were smuggled to Ireland.[323]

Patrick Scullen (Scullion); a member of the Kimmage Garrison from Glasgow,[324] he was imprisoned at Frongoch.

Patrick Joseph Seely; he came in from Kimmage.[325]

James Seville; he was in the Dublin and Wicklow Manure Works in Fairview and evaded capture after the Rising.

James Sexton; an ICA man, he was imprisoned at Frongoch.

Michael Sexton; ICA. He was sent to the City Hall on Monday evening and is counted in that garrison.

Fr Eugene Sheehy; he was an uncle of Hanna Sheehy-Skeffington, and she met him when she brought food to the GPO. 'My God, Hanna, what are you doing here?' She asked him the same question. He explained that he was there to offer spiritual consolation, and she told him that she had something more substantial to offer.[326]

Frank Sheridan; he was detained at Richmond Barracks and is listed on the Roll of Honour.

James Sheridan; he came in from Kimmage and was interned until June.[327]

Arthur Shields; he went to the wireless school in the Reis's Jewellers Building with Fergus O'Kelly. An ICA member and a Protestant, he was imprisoned in Frongoch. Both he and his brother, William Joseph Shields (who changed his name to Barry Fitzgerald), were actors at the Abbey Theatre, and both made many films in Hollywood.

**Lt Patrick (Paddy) Shortis (23);[328] originally from Ballybunion, he attended All Hallows College for a short time but decided that he did not have a vocation to the priesthood. He attended the wireless college in Cahirsiveen, then moved to England and was a member of the Kimmage Garrison from London.[329] On Wednesday afternoon he went into Henry Street with a party led by Connolly, down to Liffey Street, returning by way of Abbey Street the next morning. He was shot dead in Moore Street with The Ó Rahilly on their attempted escape. He died just beyond Henry Place.[330]

> We moved off along Henry Street and at a brisk trot rounded Moore Street corner. We were met with bursts of machine gun fire from the barricade and I heard groans and thuds as several of my comrades fell. One of them was my friend Patrick Shortice. R.I.P.[331]

Not on the list issued by the Irish National Aid and Volunteers' Dependants' Fund as 'men who were killed whilst fighting for Ireland during Easter Week, 1916'.

Peadar Slattery (O'Slattery, Ó Slatara); a teacher at St Enda's, he taught the students there to make munitions later used by the Volunteers.[332] They continued making the munitions right up to Easter Week, when Dr Kathleen Lynn transported them to Liberty Hall in her car; on Easter Monday she retransported some to City Hall.[333] Slattery was Director of Munitions in the GPO.[334]

Charles (Charlie) Smith; ICA. He was in Westmoreland Street and then the Imperial Hotel.

John Stafford; he was in the Hibernian Bank. A sniper in the window, he fired several shots until his rifle stock was hit and he was severely wounded.

Matthew Stafford; at 63 he was the oldest man to fight in the Rising. He was a sniper, and on his pension application Oscar Traynor said that as a teenager Stafford had been involved in the escape of IRB founder James Stephens from Dublin to Paris in March 1866.

Michael Staines (Miceal Ó Stainear, de Stainer, de Stainar?); QM of the Volunteers. He took the telegraphy room upstairs in the GPO. He was one of James Connolly's stretcher-bearers during the escape.

> I went on to the roof where I hoisted a flag on the corner near to Henry St. on the front. It was a tricolour, probably about 6ft. by 3ft. green next the flag post. I can't say definitely what other flags were there. I also hung a green flag with harp from the ceiling in front of a low window in the ground floor. When on the roof I had a look round generally and I saw Pearse reading the proclamation. We stood on the edge of the footpaths at a point in front of the window where there is now a door, on the Prince's St. side of the portico. There was a large number of people around when this was happening, but there was no demonstration.[335]

(See statement of Robert Walpole, below.)

He became QM of the Dublin Brigade after returning from Frongoch, and was a TD in the first three Dáils. He was the first commissioner of the Garda Síochána, then retired from politics. Subsequently he became director of the New Ireland Insurance Company, with offices on Bachelor's Walk formerly occupied by the Kapp and Peterson and 'Kelly's Fort' premises.

Joseph Michael (Joe) Stanley; an IRB member, he was imprisoned at Frongoch. He was the one who printed the *Irish War News* from the GPO at the direction of Pearse and Connolly. Later he was the owner of the Drogheda *Argus* and other regional newspapers.[336]

Charles Steinmayer; he was in the breakout party with The Ó Rahilly.[337] He was imprisoned for eighteen months.

Patrick J. (Paddy Joe) Stephenson; he and Seán MacLoughlin were the dispatch carriers, especially to and from the Mendicity Institute.[338] (Counted in the 1st Battalion garrison.) An ICA member, he was imprisoned at Frongoch.

James (Jim) Strich; ICA. He was imprisoned at Frongoch.

Capt. James J. Sullivan (O'Sullivan); he came from the North Circular Road in Cabra. (He is counted in the 1st Battalion garrison.)

Padraig Supple (Stupple?); a member of the Kimmage Garrison from Liverpool,[339] he was imprisoned at Frongoch.

Anthony (Tony) Swann (14); ICA. He was with The Ó Rahilly when the latter was shot. He was to be deported but was deemed to be too young. His brother was at King Street.

Paddy Swanzy; he was in North Earl Street and was imprisoned at Frongoch.[340]

James Sweeney; he was imprisoned at Frongoch.

Joseph Aloysius Sweeney (Sweeny); he lived at St Enda's and was a student at Trinity. He was a sniper on the roof of the GPO. When one of the improvised armoured cars came in front of the Gresham, Good shot the driver through the windscreen slit; the truck remained in front of the Gresham for several hours—filled with sweltering British soldiers. He was imprisoned at Frongoch and later fought for the Free State in the Civil War. He served as a TD for County Donegal in the first three Dáils, and retired as a major-general in the Irish army.[341]

Lt Patrick E. Sweeney; his pension application claimed that his health was affected by an explosion in close proximity to him during the fighting in 1916 and the beatings he received from British personnel following his capture/surrender after the Rising.

Charles Tallon; brother of Christopher, James and Joseph. He was imprisoned at Frongoch.

Christopher Tallon (Cristoir Ó Tallainain), brother of Charles, James and Joseph; ICA. The brothers were at Lambe's public house in Fairview and all were imprisoned at Frongoch.

James Tallon (Séamus Ó Tallainain), brother of Charles, Christopher and Joseph; imprisoned at Frongoch.

Joseph (Joe) Tallon, brother of Charles, Christopher and James; he was known as 'the chef' because he cooked in the Metropole Hotel.[342] An ICA man, he was imprisoned at Frongoch.

William (Liam) Tannam; when the Lancers charged down Sackville Street, he was the one who gave the order to fire.[343] When Tom Weafer was wounded in the Dublin Bread Company, Tannam rushed to be his replacement. When Weafer recovered, Tannam turned command back over to him. Weafer was killed later. During the fires on Friday night, but before the garrison left the GPO, he and Madge Fagan (MacSherry) were afraid that some panic might set in, so they led them all in a rousing version of *A Soldier's Song*. He was one of James Connolly's stretcher-bearers during the escape. Imprisoned at Frongoch.

Capt. Francis Joseph (Frank) Thornton; he brought the armoury from Liberty Hall, then led the garrison in the Imperial Hotel and Clery's. He was the leader of the Liverpool Volunteers before the Rising.[344] When he was captured, he was queried about a 'contribution card' that he had in his possession, and he explained to the British officer that it was to keep track of the contributions the Volunteers made to purchase their own weapons. The British officer was incredulous: 'Well, I never could understand this damned country anyway!'[345]

Hugh Thornton; a member of the Kimmage Garrison from Liverpool.[346]

Patrick Thornton; a member of the Kimmage Garrison from London.[347]

William Toole (O'Toole); ICA. He was in the Metropole Hotel and was imprisoned in Frongoch.

Joseph (Joe) Toomey, brother of John Charles, who was in the 1st Battalion; their sister, Statia, was also in the GPO. An ICA member, he was imprisoned at Frongoch. Their brother Eddie was sent home from the GPO because he was only sixteen.

Lt Oscar Traynor (30); after Fairview Strand fell, he led the Fairview Volunteers and ICA members to the GPO, then was sent to the Metropole Hotel; after its fall, he returned to the GPO. He led his men to bore through the walls of the hotel to the corner of Messrs Manfield's premises on the corner of Abbey Street Middle.[348]

> Some time on Thursday a barricade which stretched from the Royal Hibernian Academy to a cycle shop—I think the name of it was Keating's—on the opposite side of the street, took fire as a result of a direct shell hit. It was the firing of this

barricade that caused the fire which wiped out the east side of O'Connell St. I saw that happen myself. I saw the barricade being hit, I saw the fire consuming it and I saw Keating's going up. Then Hoyt's [*sic*] caught fire, and when Hoyt's caught fire the whole block up to Earl St. became involved. Hoyt's had a lot of turpentine and other inflammable stuff, and I saw the fire spread from there to Clery's. Clery's and the Imperial Hotel were one and the same building, and this building was ignited from the fire which consumed Hoyt's. I had the extraordinary experience of seeing the huge plate-glass windows of Clery's stores run molten into the channel from the terrific heat.

He was imprisoned at Frongoch. He fought for the Republicans/IRA in the Civil War, and became the chief of staff. Still later he became a minister in the Dáil.[349] He received the maximum pension of £350 per year.

Joseph George Trimble; ICA. He was interned until December.

George Tully; ICA.[350] He reported here and was sent to St Stephen's Green, then to Jacob's Biscuit Factory, and finally came back to the Imperial Hotel.

Dr J.J. Tuohy; he is listed on the Roll of Honour.

Patrick Coleman Tuohy; he was in the Imperial Hotel and was imprisoned at Frongoch.

Cormac Turner; a member of the Kimmage Garrison from Glasgow.[351] He was involved in a large raid on Uddington Colliery, Scotland, for explosives that were smuggled to Ireland.[352] He took the explosives to Liberty Hall and was to go on with them to Larkfield, but this was during the period of discord between the ICA and the Volunteers; finally a deal was made between Connolly and Thomas MacDonagh, and Turner went on to Kimmage.[353] He was one of the Hopkins and Hopkins garrison.[354]

Francis (Frank) Turner; brother of Harry and Joseph.

Henry (Harry) Turner, brother of Francis and Joseph; ICA. He was in the Coliseum Theatre.

Joseph Turner, brother of Francis and Harry; ICA. He was in the Coliseum Theatre and the Metropole Hotel.

John Joseph Twamley; a lineman in the engineering office of the Post Office. Prior to the Rising, he was detailed to determine how to cut all lines of communication with England. He was to cut the telephone cables at Bray and Shankill. On Sunday he was sent to Bray, then returned to Dublin via Lamb Doyle's, where he stopped in for a pint![355]

Timothy Tyrrell; he was a member of the Maynooth Company and was sent to the *Dublin Evening Mail* office in Parliament Street.[356]

Patrick Villiams; ICA.

Joseph Vize; a member of the Kimmage Garrison from Liverpool,[357] he was sent to Jacob's.

Michael Wade; ICA. He was interned until August.

Charles Walker; he helped print the *Irish War News* from the GPO.[358]

Robert Henry (Harry) Walpole; Connolly's 'bodyguard' since he was 'kidnapped' in January 1916.[359] Walpole indicated that, soon after the takeover, Connolly handed him a flag and told him to raise it over the GPO. He went to the roof, where he met Seán Hegarty, who offered to help; Hegarty raised it halfway and Walpole the rest of the way.[360] This was the *Irish Republic* flag on the Prince's Street corner. The flag was of green poplin, with *Irish Republic* in white and orange letters, and had a gold border. It was made in Fry's Poplin Factory, Cork Street, Dublin, and the words *Irish Republic* were painted on it by Theobald Fitzgerald in the home of Countess Markievicz, Surrey House, Leinster Road, Rathmines. The flag was captured by the Royal Irish Regiment and hung upside down in their mess hall for many years. It was returned to Ireland in 1966 and is now in the National Museum.[361] Walpole was imprisoned at Frongoch.

Christopher Walsh; a member of the Hibernian Rifles, he was sent to City Hall.

Edward (Ned) Walsh (43);[362] he was the only member of the Hibernian Rifles to be killed in the Rising. He was sent from the GPO to the Dolphin Hotel and then to the Exchange Hotel in Parliament Street, where he was killed. (Counted in the City Hall garrison.)

James Joseph (J.J.) Walsh; originally from Cork, he marched in from Fairview with a section of 30 Hibernian Rifles. He knew Morse Code and sent out queries from the GPO, hoping for replies. He would be Ireland's first Minister for Posts and Telegraphs after the Treaty.

Mark William Walsh; he was in the Dublin and Wicklow Manure Company in Fairview and then came to the GPO.

Martin Walsh; a member of the Kimmage Garrison from Liverpool.[363]

Thomas (Tom) Walsh; ICA. He was sent to the City Hall on Monday evening and is counted in that garrison.

Gilbert Ward; a member of the Kimmage Garrison from Liverpool.[364]

James Wardock; he is listed on the Roll of Honour.

Patrick Weafer; an ICA member from Maynooth, he was in Lambe's public house in Fairview, then came to the GPO.[365]

★★Capt. Thomas Joseph (Tom) Weafer (Wafer) (26);[366] ICA. He and Capt. Frank Henderson were at Fr Mathew Park in Fairview at the outset. On Monday afternoon, Weafer led his company at Clark's Bridge over the Royal Canal and blocked British troops from coming down the railway lines to Amiens Street Station. Weafer and his men were taken by surprise but acquitted themselves well and stopped the British advance. He split his forces between the Ballybrough Bridge and the Annesley Bridge, and then after the British had pulled back he led his men to the GPO.[367] Weafer was killed in the Hibernian Bank on Lower Abbey Street on Wednesday. The strategic importance of the building is clear. It allowed Weafer and his men to control access to the street from Amiens Street Station, for example, and members of the GPO garrison were occupying a number of buildings on each side of Sackville Street. The building was completely destroyed and his body was totally consumed in the fire.[368] Some reports, however, note that he was killed on Monday in the Reis's Jewellers Building, where he was sent to erect a wireless.[369]

★★Arthur Abraham Weekes (Weakes, Wicks)[370] (see John Neal, Neale, Neill, *supra*); he was from Norwich, England, and died in Moore Lane. Very little is known about him, and some claim that he is the same man as John Neal. It is said that Weekes joined the GPO garrison on Tuesday. He is listed among the ICA casualties[371] but is not on the list issued by the Irish National Aid and Volunteers' Dependants' Fund of 'men who were killed whilst fighting for Ireland during Easter Week, 1916'.

Thomas Wheatley; ICA. He was at Annesley Bridge in Fairview, then came to the GPO.

Joseph Whelan; ICA. He was at the Dublin and Wicklow Manure Company and Annesley Bridge in Fairview, then went to the Metropole Hotel.

Laurence Whelan; he was in Reis's Jewellers Building and the Dublin Bread Company, then went to Westmoreland Street.

William Whelan; he was in Fairview, then went to Clery's. After escaping from Clery's, he was captured near Great Britain Street. His long blonde hair led some of the British to think that he was German, and he was severely beaten.

Christopher John Whelehan (Whelan?); a member of the Kimmage Garrison from Liverpool,[372] he was sent to Jacob's.

Capt. John J. (Jack) White DSO; an ICA officer and trainer, he left the ICA in 1914.[373]

Michael White; he was sent to the South Dublin Union and is counted in that garrison.

Michael (Mick) White; he was in William's Stores and in Marlborough Street.

Henry Joseph Williams; he was in Reis's Jewellers Building and the Hibernian Bank.

Henry Christopher Willis; he was at Annesley Bridge in Fairview, then came to the GPO.

 # James Wilson; he was sent to the Mendicity Institute.

 # Peter Wilson; he was sent to the Mendicity Institute.

 # William (Beck) Wilson; he was sent to the Mendicity Institute.

 # William (Cody) Wilson.

James Wren; he was not a member of the Volunteers or ICA, but came to the GPO with his cousins Tommy and Paddy Mahon. He came in on Monday, but owing to ill health he only served for one day.

GPO HEADQUARTERS BATTALION: WOMEN

There were about 84 women from the ICA and Cumann na mBan in the GPO, but only a fraction of that number at any one time.[374] Only three of them—Winifred Carney, Julia Grenan and Elizabeth More O'Farrell—remained after the other women and the wounded were evacuated early on Friday.

Mary (Molly, Mollie) Adrien (Adrian);[375] she was sent from Dublin with Pearse's message, 'Strike at one o'clock today', and cycled between Ashbourne and Dublin several times during the week.[376]

Elizabeth (Lillie) Burke (née McGinty); she was involved in attending the wounded in the GPO and she remembers leaving the GPO on Friday and going to the Coliseum Theatre, escaping through a hole in the wall. She was in Jervis Street on Saturday at the surrender.

Ellen Sarah Bushel; an usher at the Abbey Theatre, she carried many messages to and from the GPO. She was imprisoned after the Rising.

Alice Byrne; sister of Catherine (below).

Catherine Byrne (Rooney); when she joined the Central Branch of Cumann na mBan early in 1915, she was twenty years old. She was the first Cumann na mBan woman to enter the GPO on Monday. Her sister Alice and their older brother, Patrick Byrne (Paddy), also took part in the Rising. Catherine served in the GPO throughout the week. On Monday night she was sent to the Hibernian Bank to prepare food for the garrison there; she returned early on Tuesday morning, bringing dispatches with her. Later on Tuesday Pearse sent her to the Four Courts with dispatches that she concealed in her hair under her bonnet. She was sent to Clarke's Dairy with bandoliers of ammunition, and while looking out a window was nearly shot—her beret had two bullet holes in it![377] Unable to return to the GPO, she spent the night in an armchair in a tenement; early next morning she went to King Street, where she spent the rest of the week until the surrender.

Elizabeth (Lillie) Byrne; she was a courier, particularly to the 1st and 2nd Battalions.

(Maria) Winifred Carney (McBride); an ICA member, she was James Connolly's secretary.[378] She changed her opinion of Joseph Plunkett when at his capture she was given his ring to pass on to Grace Gifford. In Moore Street she knelt at Connolly's side and asked of the surrender: 'Was there no other way?' Connolly replied that he would not see his brave boys burned to death and there was no other way.[379] (On some lists she is identified as Winifred Conway.[380])

Catherine Gertrude (Gertie) Colley (Murphy); she was detained for a short time at Broadstone Railway Station.

Máire Comerford; she reported to St Stephen's Green, but was turned away because she was deemed too young and spent the week carrying dispatches from here.[381]

Brigid (Bridie, Brid) Connolly (Brigid Ni Conghaile); she was sent to Cmdt Ned Daly on Monday, along with Sarah (Sorcha) MacMahon (Rogers) and Leslie Price (Barry). She carried dispatches between James Connolly in the GPO and Cmdt Daly in Church Street. She left the GPO on Friday, and was arrested as she was on her way towards Jervis Street Hospital with May Gibney (O'Neill).

Mary (May) Cullen; she was sent with Brigid Grace to the 25 Northumberland Road garrison to warn it of the arriving troops, and then to Mount Street Bridge to warn the Volunteers there.

Laura Daly (O'Sullivan); she came from Limerick with her sister Nora and finally reached the GPO about midnight on Tuesday. Later, the two left Dublin to return to Limerick to try to get the Volunteers there to rise.[382]

Nora Daly (Dore); sister of Laura (above).[383]

> The order was given to lodge us in Kilmainham Jail and hither we were finally marched, arriving after dusk and being received by the light of candles, which only served to intensify the gloom. Finally our quarters were allotted, one cell to each four prisoners, and one blanket and one 'biscuit' doled out to us. Our cell doors were banged shut and we were left to make the best we could of the means at our disposal.

Éamon Dore accompanied Nora and Laura back to Limerick, and Nora later married him.[384]

Evelyn Mary (Aoife) de Burca (Eva Burke).[385]

> At 6-30, or thereabouts, Commandant Joseph Plunkett gave the Captain over our division orders to get the wounded men and nurses ready to evacuate Headquarters immediately; we all got ourselves in readiness as quickly as possible.

We had only three stretcher cases, which was well, as our means of egress was difficult. About eight men or more were told off, by Commandant Pearse, to act as our escort, we had nine wounded, and two doctors, one being the R.A.M.C. Lieutenant [George O'Mahoney]. Commandant J. Plunkett kindly asked our Captain if we would wish to take this prisoner with us, and, as he had done such good work for the wounded, our Captain decided that we would. We had only a dozen Red Cross workers at this time, as some had been sent on early in the afternoon to Jervis Street Hospital. I expect it was now about 7 p.m. when all were ready and the order given to march; so, off we started, accompanied by Fr —— who carried the Red Cross Flag.

Eileen Dempsey; employed at McCrad Collar Manufacturers, she lost her job after the Rising.

Brid Dixon; a great friend of Leslie Price, she and Price spent much of the week under fire as couriers.[386]

Frances Downie, sister of Peggy (below); they arrived on Holy Thursday specifically with a view to attending a training camp.[387]

Margaret (Peggy) Downie (Viant); from Liverpool, she was the chief cook and helped take the wounded to Jervis Street Hospital.[388]

Louise Gavan-Duffy (Luise Ghabhanach Ni Dhubhthaigh); she travelled through Dublin on Easter Monday, arriving finally at the GPO, where she was made the chief assistant to QM FitzGerald.[389] She asked to see Pearse: 'I said to him that I wanted to be in the field but that I felt that the Rebellion was a frightful mistake, that it could not possibly succeed, and that it was, therefore, wrong'. Pearse suggested that she help out in the kitchens, and she agreed to this, since it was not active service. She stayed there until the GPO was evacuated on Friday, and next morning went to Jacob's Biscuit Factory 'to see what they were going to do there'.[390]

Máire English; she was in the Hibernian Bank and Reis's Jewellers Building.

Margaret Mary (Madge) Fagan (MacSherry); during the fires on Friday night, but before the garrison left the GPO, she and Liam Tannam were afraid that some panic might set in, so they led them all in a rousing version of *A Soldier's Song.* [391]

Brighid Foley (Brid Ni Foghludha, Breeid) (Martin); one of a group of Cumann na mBan women sent to save a batch of guns shortly before the Rising. The Volunteers asked Foley, Effie Taaffe and Kitty O'Doherty to find and protect the guns, which had come into the country in boxes marked as 'cutlery'. The women successfully transported these two boxes across town, past a couple of policemen, and hid them under the stairs in O'Doherty's house.[392] In the weeks immediately preceding the Rising, Foley travelled to Birmingham, England, to assist Liam Mellows. He had been deported to England and she helped him return to Ireland before the Rising. In the week before the Rising she travelled to Cork with dispatches from Seán MacDiarmada and Éamonn Ceannt for Terence MacSwiney and Tomas MacCurtain, finally travelling there on Sunday 23 April, before returning to Dublin on Monday and reporting to St Stephen's Green.[393] She was imprisoned and interned until July 1916.

Mary (May) Gahan (O'Carroll); from Dublin, she remembered people pelting her with bottles as she walked to imprisonment in Kilmainham Gaol.[394] During the War of Independence she and her husband opened a pub, and she often bought weapons from British soldiers. She even bought a machine-gun and had it lowered out of Ship Street Barracks.

Lucie Gethings; she is listed on the Roll of Honour.

Maura (May) Gibney (O'Neill);[395] she was in the GPO all week and left on Friday. She was arrested as she was on her way towards Jervis Street Hospital with Bridie Connolly. May wrote of her involvement: 'On Easter Monday 1916 I volunteered for service at the GPO. I was not a member of a Republican organisation at the time but as a reference I mentioned the name of a Volunteer whom I knew was on duty at one of the points. I asked to be allowed to remain at the GPO and was lucky enough to be accepted as a member of the garrison.'

Brigid Grace; she was sent with Mary Cullen to the 25 Northumberland Road garrison to warn Brigid's brother of the arriving troops.

Julia Grenan (sometimes named as 'Sheila Grennan'); *Who's Who* claims that 'Sheila' was the one who conveyed the instructions for the surrender with Elizabeth More O'Farrell, but most commentators agree that the woman's name was Julia Grenan, although Brian O'Higgins has it spelled 'Grennan'.[396] For example, *Last Words* by Piaras Mac Lochlainn names her as Julia Grenan.[397] See also her own articles published shortly after the Rising.[398] It should be noted, however, that she is buried in Glasnevin Cemetery in the same grave as her great friend Elizabeth O'Farrell, and the gravestone reads: 'And her faithful comrade and lifelong friend—Sheila Grenan'.[399]

She was a member of the Irish Citizen Army. She was recruited by Marie Perolz on Easter night, and went to Carrickmacross with the news that the Rising would go ahead on Easter Monday.[400] After leaving the GPO, she was arrested and taken with the men to the gardens at the Rotunda. The following day they were marched to Richmond Barracks and then moved to Kilmainham Gaol, where she was held until early May 1916. While being held in the Gaol, the women realised that the leaders were being executed: 'At first the wardress said it was distant fighting, but we knew the truth'.

Grenan worked at the Irish Hospital Sweepstakes office in Ballsbridge, and also worked as a furrier. She maintained her strong republican beliefs for the rest of her life, and shared a house with her old friend Elizabeth O'Farrell on Mount Street.

Mary Hanley (Máire Ni Ainle); she is listed on the Roll of Honour.

Annie (O'?) Higgins; a talented musician and teacher, she invented a new method for teaching harmony that was widely adapted. On Thursday she was sent north with dispatches; she cycled to Kingscourt and then was taken by car to Cavan. When she returned, she was arrested.[401]

Patricia Hoey; she is listed on the Roll of Honour.

Ellen (Nell) Humphreys; she was a sister of The Ó Rahilly. Although she was in and out of the GPO several times during the week, she was not involved in the fighting. She was captured in the vicinity of her home at 54 Northumberland Road and was imprisoned.[402]

Maeve (Maud) Kavanagh (Cavanagh) (McDowell); she was sent from the GPO by James Connolly and Thomas Clarke to Waterford to deliver messages and orders to Seán Matthews.[403] Connolly called her the 'Poetess of the Revolution'.[404] Maeve was the sister of Ernest (usually spelt Kavanagh), the cartoonist with Connolly's paper. He was shot on the steps of Liberty Hall.

Linda Kearns (McWhinney); during Easter Week, she transported ammunition and guns from Hardwicke Street and North Great George's Street to the GPO. She also set up a first aid station in North Great George's Street and worked as a courier for the Volunteers, but evaded capture after the Rising.[405]

Kathleen J. Kelly (Barber); she is listed on the Roll of Honour.

Martha Kelly (Murphy); she married Michael Murphy, who was also in the GPO. She was in the Imperial Hotel and was imprisoned in Kilmainham.

Mary (May) Kelly (Chadwick); she was mobilised for Easter Sunday. She spent Monday night in the GPO and was in Jacob's Factory from Tuesday until the surrender.

Bridget Lambert (Doran); sister of Ellen (below).

Ellen (Nellie) Lambert (Stynes); on Monday she followed a group of ICA members to the GPO and she was there until Friday. She carried dispatches for Pearse between the GPO and the College of Surgeons. She was also involved in cooking and attended the wounded. On Friday she was arrested, taken into Broadstone Station and interrogated. She was released and given a pass; she spent the night with other women in the Refuge on Henrietta Street.

Mary Lawless; she is listed on the Roll of Honour.

Mabel McConnell (Fitzgerald); she is listed on the Roll of Honour.

Mairead McElroy; she is listed on the Roll of Honour.

Mary McLoughlin; a member of the Hibernian Rifles, she was Seán's schoolgirl sister and a Cumann na mBan member from the start.[406]

Sarah (Sorcha) MacMahon (Sorcha Bhean Mhic Ruaidhri) (Rogers); with Kathleen Clarke, she was primarily responsible for establishing and operating the Irish National Aid and Volunteers' Dependants' Fund. She was back and forth between the GPO and the Four Courts.[407]

Máire Mapother; she was in Reis's Jewellers Building and the Hibernian Bank.

Kathleen Murphy (Patton); she arrived in Holy Week from Liverpool with a view to attending a training camp.[408] She carried many supplies to the Hopkins and Hopkins corner.[409] She was imprisoned.

Eileen Murphy (née Walsh); a Cumann na mBan officer, she was in the Hibernian Bank.[410]

Rose Ann Murphy (née Byrne); she was from Liverpool, and on Monday she was sent to Dundalk with dispatches to ask the Volunteers there to join the Rising.[411]

Eileen Murray; ICA. She was in the Hibernian Bank.

Mary (May) Murray; she was an organiser and mobilised the Walsh sisters. They carried dispatches all week until Thursday, when the fires were too great for them to get out of and back to the GPO.[412]

Ellen Noone; she helped with the cooking and serving on a voluntary basis from Tuesday until Friday morning, when she was advised to leave. While leaving the GPO on Friday, she was arrested with others on Dorset Street and was taken to Broadstone Station. She was released later in the day and went to the 'Sisters' in Henrietta Street.

Elizabeth (Eilis) O'Brien; she went to Reis's Jewellers Building on Abbey Street, opposite the Hibernian Bank. She helped with dispatches for Capt. Tom Weafer there, and attended the wounded in Fr Mathew Hall while still carrying dispatches to the Four Courts and to the Linenhall area.

Mary O'Connell; she is listed on the Roll of Honour.

Aileen Mary O'Connor (O'Reilly); she was in the Munster and Leinster Bank.

Elizabeth More O'Farrell; she was recruited by Marie Perolz on Easter night, and went to Athenry and Galway with the news that the Rising would go ahead on Easter Monday.[413]

Elizabeth O'Farrell saw The Ó Rahilly's body when she returned from her first meeting with Brig. Gen. W.H.M. Lowe in Tom Clarke's shop. She related that it was 2.30 p.m. on Saturday when she reached Moore Street, and as she passed Sackville Lane again 'she saw Ó Rahilly's corpse lying a few yards up the laneway, his feet against a stone stairway in front of a house, his head towards the street'.[414]

She went out the door of 15 Moore Street at about 12.45 p.m. on Saturday in order to find the British commander, Brig. Gen. Lowe, to convey the leaders' wish to surrender. Subsequently, Lowe asked her to go to the other garrison commanders and convey the terms. She later became a nurse and midwife at Holles Street Hospital.[415]

Mary O'Hanrahan; ICA. She was arrested and held for questioning at Broadstone Railway Station following the surrender but was released after a few hours.

Máire O'Neill; she is listed on the Roll of Honour.

Cathleen O'Reilly; she is listed on the Roll of Honour.

Mary Teresa (Molly, Mollie) O'Reilly (Corcoran); she carried messages back and forth from the City Hall. (See City Hall garrison).

Nora O'Reilly (Sister Lourdes); she was in the Hibernian Bank. She became a nun with the Society of Missionary Catechists in the US.

Leslie Price (Barry, Leslie de Barra); she married Tom Barry.[416] She cooked meals and while assisting the men in the Hibernian Bank she witnessed the death of Capt. Thomas Weafer. As she stood beside Weafer, a bullet whizzed past her and hit Weafer in the stomach. As she was about to help Weafer, another bullet hit another Volunteer who had already gone to Weafer's aid. She had just enough time to whisper a prayer in Weafer's ear before he died.

Tom Clarke sent her to the Pro-Cathedral to fetch a priest on Thursday; she brought Fr Flanagan back. When she called at the presbytery, Flanagan's first reaction was to refuse. He indicated that two priests had already been sent to Jervis Street Hospital especially to tend to the spiritual needs of the Volunteers, but Price convinced him to come back with her by a circuitous route. Flanagan said that he was aware that it was essential not to compromise the Catholic Church by appearing to aid or comfort the rebels, but in the end he decided that his priestly duty overrode every other consideration.[417]

> I got safely to the door of the [Pro-Cathedral] Presbytery ... I kicked and kicked, and pressed all the bells ... The door was opened a little bit and I was let in by a priest, Father O'Flanagan. I said to him, 'I have been sent over by Tom Clarke for the priest'. He said, 'You are not going to the Post Office. Let these people be burned to death. They are murderers.' Mrs Wyse Power was the only one to whom I ever told this. I knew then, by some other remark Father O'Flanagan made, that it was the linking up with the Citizen Army he did not like. It took a certain amount of courage to fight a priest. I said, 'If no priest is going to the Post Office, I am going back alone. I feel sure that every man in the Post Office is prepared to die, to meet his God, but it is a great consolation to a dying man to have a priest near him.' Whatever effect I had on him, he said, 'Very well. I will go.' ...
>
> We passed a man in Moore Street who had been shot and was dying on the road, but he had drink taken. The priest did not stop for him. I was horrified. Further down Moore Street on the left we came to Henry Place, I think. At that place, a white-haired man was shot but not dead. He was lying, bleeding, on the kerb ... I remember the priest knelt down to give him absolution. You see the difference. Here he knew a man who was respectable ...
>
> We got to the Post Office and I brought Father O'Flanagan to Tom Clarke. I remember Tom Clarke took Mick Staines aside, and he said on no account was he [the priest] to be let out of the Post Office.[418]

Margaret Quinn; she was in the Hibernian Bank.

Annie Redmond; she is listed on the Roll of Honour.

Mary Catherine (Molly, Mollie) Reynolds; she helped store some of the Howth rifles under the floor of her father's office in No. 1 College Street. Her father was John R. Reynolds, who also took part in the Rising. On Easter Monday morning she helped issue the mobilisation order for her father's company, notifying the members in Clontarf; when she returned to her home, her own mobilisation orders were waiting for her and with another member of her branch she arrived at St Stephen's Green. Unable to locate other members of Cumann na mBan, she waited around until the arrival of Margaret Skinnider, who informed both women that women volunteers were needed in the GPO. On arriving at the GPO she met The Ó Rahilly, whom she knew well, as he had been a frequent visitor to her father. The Ó Rahilly helped the two women to select the best place for the first aid station at the back of the main hall of the GPO. She helped treat James Connolly when he received a bullet wound to the left shin; his leg was set in splints and a waste-paper basket was cut in two to make a cage for it. On Friday evening, with the Red Cross men and women and the wounded, the prisoners and Fr Flanagan, she was evacuated from the GPO. They went towards Arnott's through holes in the walls that had been made by the Volunteers during the week in an attempt to get the wounded to Jervis Street Hospital. They made it to Liffey Street; when they halted, Fr Flanagan and the prisoners, one a British Medical Officer (Lt George O'Mahoney), went off to make arrangements for the wounded to be admitted to the hospital. Fr Flanagan returned with an officer and a number of soldiers and escorted the party to the hospital. On arrival at the hospital the Red Cross men were arrested, as were those with minor wounds. The women were allowed to wait in the dispensary waiting room, where they stayed for the remainder of Friday night and most of Saturday. On Saturday evening Fr Flanagan arrived and told them that the Volunteers had surrendered and that they should go home.[419] Later she was very active in the anti-conscription campaign.[420]

Bridie Richards; she mobilised on Monday and was instructed to go to the Priory in Dominick Street. On Tuesday she was sent to the Hibernian Bank before being sent to the GPO, where she was mainly involved in cooking and in attending the wounded.

Ann Noreen Ryan (Ni Riain); she was in Reis's Jewellers Building and the Hibernian Bank.

Phyllis (Eilis Ni Rian) Ryan (O'Kelly) (Ui Cheallaigh); a sister of Jim Ryan, she later became Mrs Seán T. O'Kelly. (O'Kelly had first married her sister, Mary Kate

[Kit], and married Phyllis after Kit passed away.) She and other members of her Cumann na mBan branch reported for duty in full kit to Palmerston Place at noon on Monday, and at 6.00 p.m. a dispatch rider told them to go home. She decided, however, to go by the GPO, where she was ordered to go to the Imperial Hotel, and then on Tuesday she and other women were sent to the Four Courts.[421]

Mary Josephine (Min) Ryan (Mulcahy); sister of Jim. She was Seán MacDermott's fiancée, and later married Richard Mulcahy. She and her sister Phyllis were the last two to see Seán MacDermott in Kilmainham Gaol: 'He preferred to talk of casual matters, asking about different people we knew, enjoying little jokes almost as though we were in Bewley's. He had worked and planned for Irish independence since boyhood. His last words, save for his prayers, were "God Save Ireland". At four o'clock, when the shooting was done, a gentle rain began to fall—the tears of Dark Rosaleen.'[422]

Veronica (Bheronica) (Ni Rian) Ryan (Gleason) (Ui Glasam); she was in the Hibernian Bank, and evaded capture.

Hanna Sheehy-Skeffington; she met her uncle, Fr Eugene Sheehy, when she brought food to the GPO. 'My God, Hanna, what are you doing here?' She asked him the same question. He explained that he was there to offer spiritual consolation, and she told him that she had something more substantial to offer.[423]

Matilda (Tillie) Simpson; ICA. She helped with first aid, and made several trips to Jervis Street Hospital.

Lucy Agnes Smyth (Byrne); she was sent to 27 Hardwicke Street to get some rifles, then reported to the GPO and was sent to the Hibernian Bank, where she remained until going to Jervis Street Hospital with the other women. She was romantically involved with Con Colbert. Elizabeth Colbert wrote of her:

> I went to a céilidhe with Con shortly before the Rising. There were a lot of prominent people in the movement at it and many of them have since become well known. In the course of the evening he said to me "I'll show you the nicest girl in Dublin". He introduced me to Lucy Smith [sic]. I think he was in love with her and would probably have married her if he had lived. She was a nice, gentle, refined girl, a member of Cumann na mBan and a great worker in the movement. She afterwards married Tom Byrne of Boer War fame who was also keen on her at the same time. He was Con's rival.[424]

Brigid Lyons Thornton, 1st Battalion, and **W.T. Cosgrave**, South Dublin Union. Brigid Lyons (left) was studying to be a doctor when she reported to the 1st Battalion. Later she became the first female medical officer in the Free State Army. W.T. Cosgrave (middle) was a Sinn Féin councillor in Dublin, and succeeded Arthur Griffith and Michael Collins as the head of the Free State government. (Women's Museum of Ireland)

Con Colbert (in kilt on right), 4th Battalion. He was in command at Watkins's Brewery/Ardee Street Brewery, Jameson's Distillery and the entire Marrowbone Lane post. Executed 8 May 1916. (Courtesy of the Trustees of the National Library of Ireland)

Countess Markievicz, St Stephen's Green. Originally she was to liaise between the GPO and St Stephen's Green, but Michael Mallin told her that he needed her as second in command. Markievicz only arrived at the Green sometime late on Monday afternoon. (Courtesy of the Trustees of the National Library of Ireland)

Denis O'Callaghan, 1st Battalion. O'Callahan led the assault on the Linenhall Barracks and ordered the British occupying it to surrender. Thirty-two clerks and a policeman surrendered, and the barracks was set on fire. The fires were difficult to control, and they burned until after the Rising was over. (O'Callaghan family)

Edward Lyons, 1st Battalion. A member of the 1st Battalion, he was one of the men who took the Four Courts on Monday and held them until the surrender on Saturday. (Lyons family)

Elizabeth O'Farrell, GPO. Nurse O'Farrell left 16 Moore Street to tell the British that the GPO garrison would surrender. Following Pearse's surrender, she took the surrender orders to the other garrisons. She became a midwife at Holles Street Hospital. (Donna Cooney)

Fr Albert Bibby, 1st Battalion. Fr Albert Bibby, OFM Cap., was one of several Capuchin friars from the Church Street Priory who ministered to the rebel garrisons. In the aftermath of the Rising, Fr Albert ministered to a number of rebel prisoners in Kilmainham Gaol and in other locations. (Irish Capuchin Provincial Archives)

Fr Augustine Hayden, 1st Battalion. Fr Augustine Hayden, OFM Cap., helped the Cumann na mBan women in the hospital in Fr Mathew Hall, and then on Thursday he went to the Volunteer position in the Four Courts. Fr Augustine dismissed his bravery by saying, 'Well, I felt that I might be badly wounded, but I would not be killed outright'. (Irish Capuchin Provincial Archives)

Cathal Brugha, 4th Battalion. Vice-Commandant of the 4th Battalion, he suffered 25 wounds in the South Dublin Union: five were considered 'very dangerous', nine were 'very serious' and eleven were 'superficial'. The British deemed that he would not survive and released him to his family. His wounds bothered him greatly for the rest of his life, and he was never able to walk well again. He was the first Ceann Comhairle of Dáil Éireann and was killed in 1922, fighting on the anti-Treaty side during the Civil War. (Courtesy of the Trustees of the National Library of Ireland)

W.T. Cosgrave, 4th Battalion. W.T. Cosgrave addressing a crowd. He succeeded Michael Collins as the chairman of the Provisional Government of the Free State. He served as the first president of the Executive Council of the Free State from 1922 to 1932. (Courtesy of the Trustees of the National Library of Ireland)

Harry Boland (centre), GPO. On Monday his Company held a post at Goulding's Manure Works at Fairview Bridge, and later in the day transferred to Gilbey's Wine Merchants on the corner of Richmond Avenue, where he remained until Tuesday. On Tuesday, along with his brother Ned, he took three prisoners, British Army instructors from the Bull Wall, to the GPO. (Courtesy of the Trustees of the National Library of Ireland)

Hanna Sheehy-Skeffington (left), GPO, and **Margaret Pearse.** A pacifist, Hanna brought food and medical supplies to the GPO, where she met her uncle, Fr Eugene Sheehy. 'My God, Hanna, what are you doing here?' She asked him the same question. He explained that he was there to offer spiritual consolation, and she told him that she had something more substantial to offer. (Courtesy of the Trustees of the National Library of Ireland)

David Sears, 4th Battalion. He was the youngest in the garrison. He and his father were journalists, and his father became a TD in the first four Dáils. (Courtesy of the Trustees of the National Library of Ireland)

Dr Kathleen Lynn, City Hall. An ICA captain, Kathleen Lynn delivered arms to City Hall. After both Seán Connolly and Seán O'Reilly were killed, as the Medical Officer and the highest-ranking officer she surrendered the garrison, causing a minor flurry among the British, as they did not know whether they could accept a surrender from a woman. Subsequently founded St Ultan's Hospital for Infants.

Thomas Ashe, 5th Battalion—Ashbourne. Ashe was known as an inspirational but somewhat impractical leader. In 1917 he was imprisoned and led a hunger strike in Mountjoy Prison. His lung was pierced during force-feeding on 23 September and he was taken to the Mater Hospital, where he died on 25 September. (Courtesy of the Trustees of the National Library of Ireland)

Eamonn Duggan, 1st Battalion. He was the Battalion Adjutant and was in Church Street and North Brunswick Street. He became a plenipotentiary in the Treaty negotiations of December 1921. He received the maximum pension of £350 per year. (Courtesy of the Trustees of the National Library of Ireland)

In April 1919 she married Thomas Byrne, known as 'the Boer', who was also in the GPO.

Christina Stafford (Brooks); she was in Reis's Jewellers Building and the Hibernian Bank. She was imprisoned in the North Dublin Union and Kilmainham Gaol during the Civil War and was given a medical release.

M.J. Stapleton (née Slevin): she is listed on the Roll of Honour. She married William (Bill) Stapleton, a member of Collins's 'Squad'.

Annie Tobin (Soalfield); she is listed on the Roll of Honour.

Aoife (Effie) Taaffe; she is listed on the Roll of Honour. Shortly before the Rising the Volunteers sent a group of Cumann na mBan women to save a batch of guns; they asked Brighid Foley, Effie Taaffe and Kitty O'Doherty to find and protect the guns, which had come into the country in boxes marked as 'cutlery'. The women successfully transported these two boxes across town, past a couple of policemen, and hid them under the stairs in O'Doherty's house.[425]

Anastasia (Statia) Toomey (Byrne); her brother Joe was also in the GPO, and her brother John was in Jacob's and at St Stephen's Green. After her activities during Easter Week (mostly first aid and making cartridges) she was appointed secretary of the Fairview Branch of Cumann na mBan and was also active on the staff of the Irish National Aid and Volunteers' Dependants' Fund.

Cesca Chevenix Trench (Sadhbh Trinseach); a Cumann na mBan member who was born in County Wicklow. She delivered her homemade medical supplies to the GPO on Tuesday, and then, as she was opposed to the Rising, she asked to see Pearse and told him that she was going to see Eoin MacNeill.

Unaware of the coup, Cesca was incredulous when she heard that the 'Sinn Féiners had risen and had got all the principal bridges'. But she was in no doubt that she was called out. 'I took all the ammunition for a rifle in my bag and also some bandages and compressed food,' she wrote in her diary that evening. 'There's war in the City', an idle tram man told them at the terminus. She reflected that she must 'get to some people to see what was doing', as she hurried on, finding it 'hard to believe that Eoin sanctioned this apparent madness'. 'Dublin is ours and the Castle after 700 years', a nice brown-faced man with his bandolier, belt and rifle told Cesca when she checked that there were first-aiders in the makeshift garrison being created that afternoon at St Stephen's Green. She was determined at least to deliver her first aid things and she did this at the GPO, where the tricolour was now flying and Pearse had just read the Proclamation of the Republic.

> I decided to go to Eoin MacNeill's headquarters and ask him whether I'd be more use inside than out. I went in first and left the first aid appliances ... They had volunteers with arms at every window of which the glass was all broken and thrown about in the street and a little inside ... They were protected behind boards and bags, letter bags a good many I expect ... I went off by Camden Street. There we passed Jacob's Factory, in the hands of the Volunteers, who were sitting quietly at each window, while some women were yelling at them below. There were bullet holes in the windows and in some of the shops opposite, hence a lot of broken glass ...
>
> I asked Mr Pearse had he any message he wanted sent to Eoin MacNeill. He said 'Have you seen him? ... What does he think?' I intimated what I believed he thought. 'You don't seriously think you'll succeed, do you?' said I. 'We would have,' said he, 'if it'd been on Sunday. Eoin MacNeill spoiled it.' 'It seems to me mad', said I, as I took the little note he gave me for his mother or sister as I was going out that way, 'and I thought your idea was to be on the defensive.' 'Our idea was to win Irish freedom', said he with a glow in his voice. ...
>
> I am aware that I ought to have spoken with more vigour, but while I'd been walking up and down waiting for his note to be written I saw things I shall never forget, a row of young fellows kneeling saying their prayers and two priests came in while I was there, and began to hear confessions kneeling by the side of them; at a little distance a Proclamation to the people of Ireland—of the Irish Republic ... I read it, it included the phrase 'our countrymen in America' as far as I remember, and 'our gallant allies', either 'in Europe' or 'on the Continent'. Of course that will damn them. If they don't win, and it is impossible that they should, they'll all be shot.[426]

Cathleen (Catherine?) Treston; she was imprisoned.

Brigid Bean Ua Faoithe (White, Whyte); she is listed on the Roll of Honour.

Bridie Walsh (Slater); sister of Margaret and Mary Josephine.

Helena Walsh; she worked in the kitchen with Peggy Downie.

Margaret Walsh (Jenkinson); sister of Bridie and Mary Josephine.

Mary Josephine (Mary Jo) Walsh (Rafferty); sister of Margaret and Bridie. They all helped with the nursing in the GPO.

Esther Wisley (O'Moore); she worked in the kitchens with Louise Gavan-Duffy.

Dr Nancy Wyse-Power (de Poer); she joined Cumann na mBan in 1915. She undertook her first mission to Cork on Ash Wednesday and had a brush with the authorities as she was delivering the message. Upon her arrival, she discovered that a priest had taken the bag, mistaking it for his own. This led to much trouble on her part, as she and the MacSwiney family, to whom she was delivering the message, spent all the next day trying to retrieve it. Her only consolation was that a priest was less likely to go to the police, and in fact he returned the bag without even mentioning its contents.[427] On Easter Monday she carried a dispatch from Pearse to Dr Dundon, Borris, Co. Carlow, and on Tuesday delivered dispatches to Kilkenny before returning to the GPO. In a later mission during Easter Week, Nancy sewed a message that she was given into the hem of her skirt.

Prisoners in the GPO

Upon the seizing of the GPO, a total of thirteen British soldiers and DMP men were taken prisoner. As conditions in the GPO worsened, The Ó Rahilly addressed the men guarding the prisoners in the courtyard. 'Let every man remember this—as custodians of the prisoners every man must keep in mind the honour of his country. Whatever happens to the rest of us—they must be our first concern.'[428]

Lt A.D. Chalmers; a British officer from the 14th Royal Fusiliers who was using the postal facilities in the GPO at the time the Rising began. He was 'trussed up' with telephone cord by Michael Collins and remained captive all week. The Ó Rahilly 'appointed' him to keep a watch to note that nothing had been 'stolen' by the Volunteers. 'I want this officer to watch the safe to see that nothing is touched. You will see that no harm comes to him.' The British shot him in the thigh when the prisoners were released in advance of The Ó Rahilly's escape bid.

Pte James Doyle, Royal Irish Regiment; escaped and hid in the Coliseum Theatre, and was discovered only on 3 May.

DMP Constable Edward Dunphy; he was on guard when the GPO was taken over and remained in custody until the retreat. He was wounded in the hand as he ran down Moore Lane in the retreat.

Sgt Henry, School of Musketry; escaped and hid in the Coliseum Theatre, and was discovered only on 3 May.

2Lt King, Royal Irish Fusiliers; he was taken prisoner outside the GPO, having been caught spying.[429]

Lt George O'Mahoney (Mahony); a doctor in the English Indian Army Medical Corps, he was originally from Cork and was on convalescent leave after injuring his leg in a fall in the Himalayas. He was returning to Dublin on Tuesday morning, and when he stepped off the train at Harcourt Street Station in his uniform he was told that the rebellion was on and that he should get off the streets. He was taken to the north of Dublin by Canon Hemphill, but was taken prisoner and brought to the offices of the Dublin and Wicklow Manure Company. Later he was taken to the GPO. He described Chalmers as 'in a bit of a funk', expecting to be shot at any moment. As a prisoner O'Mahoney helped to take care of the wounded, and he treated Connolly's leg wound. Connolly told him: 'You are the most valuable thing we've captured!' O'Mahoney treated the rebels with compassion, and was helped by Dan McLaughlin, who had attended medical school for several years. In contrast, Jim Ryan, another medical student, also treated the wounded but was 'punctilious about Mahony's [sic] position and took care to have as little truck with him as possible'.[430]

Pte Peter Richardson, Connaught Rangers. 'We were placed near the door where we could run for our liberty. Then, shaking hands with each of us in turn, The Ó Rahilly said "Good-bye … I may never see you again. Good-bye and good luck to you". Then the door was pulled open.'[431]

III. 1st Battalion

Commandant Edward (Ned) Daly first set up his headquarters in North Brunswick Street (North Dublin Union) and later in Church Street, and established his defences for the 1st Battalion in the Four Courts area around buildings that allowed his limited forces as much movement between positions as possible.[432] Because of Eoin MacNeill's cancellation order, Daly's command was greatly reduced in size.[433] Daly's troops engaged the British in a haphazard and widespread battle, and the area they were to hold presented many tactical problems to them as defenders, as well as to the attacking British.[434] Daly knew that his troops needed to take their positions rapidly, as these were the Irish most exposed to the quick British response. He had reconnoitred his command area exhaustively and established his posts in positions allowing crossing fields of fire, cover and concealment.[435] The 1st Battalion was to occupy and hold the Four Courts area and to form a line from there to Cabra, where it was to link up with the 5th Battalion. Daly's command area extended from the Cabra and North Circular roads to the north, east towards the Bolton Street approach to North King Street, and west to North Brunswick Street as far as Red Cow Lane.[436] This area controlled the main approach routes from the west of Dublin to the centre of the city.[437] As regards his preparations, strategy and the actual tactics used during the week, the British noted that 'in this North King Street they [the Irish] had situated themselves as to be able to inflict maximum casualties on the English troops with minimum loss to themselves', and they gave Daly much credit.[438] Daly placed his forces in areas that allowed them to intercept British troops coming from Marlborough Barracks and Royal Barracks toward the GPO.

Mendicity Institute

Capt. Seán Heuston led twelve Fianna members to take and hold the Mendicity Institute, which lay to the west of Daly's other positions and was located on Usher's Island on the south side of the Liffey (opposite side to the Four Courts). Heuston was originally charged to hold the Institute for the afternoon, but he asked for and received a small number of reinforcements from the GPO, bringing his garrison to about 35 men. He was ordered to control the route between Royal Barracks and the Four Courts, and to prevent the British from crossing Church Street Bridge. A tall wall with wooden gates

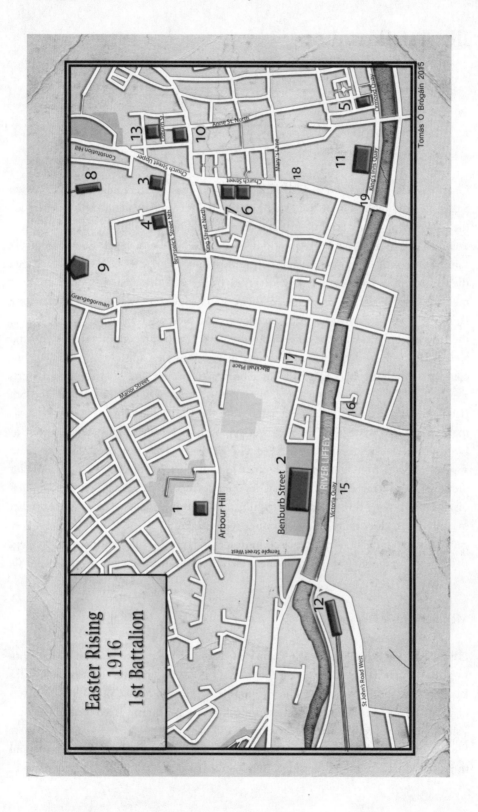

Easter Rising
1916
1st Battalion

Tomás Ó Brógáin 2015

No.	Address	Site	Description
1	Arbour Hill	Arbour Hill Detention Centre	The Rising's executed leaders are buried here.
2	Benburb Street	Royal Barracks	British Lancers and troops were based here. Now Collins Barracks, part of the National Museum of Ireland.
3	4 Brunswick Street North	North Dublin Union	Briefly occupied by the Volunteers at the beginning of the Rising.
4	5–9 Brunswick Street and Red Cow Lane	Richmond Hospital	Many casualties of the Rising were treated here.
5	Charles Street West	Medical Mission and Collier's dispensary	Lancers retreated here after they were fired upon from the Four Courts.
6	139–142 Church Street	Capuchin Franciscan Friary	Home of the friars who ministered to the Rising's garrisons and to the leaders when they were in prison.
7	131–137 Church Street	Fr Mathew Hall	Used as a hospital during the Rising.
8	Constitution Hill, Phibsborough	Broadstone Railway Station	Volunteers tried to take it early in the Rising. Now a bus station.
9	Grangegorman Road	Richmond Penitentiary	Used as an insane asylum, some British troops were billeted here.
10	King Street North		British atrocities were committed here by the South Staffordshire Regiment.
11	King's Inn Quay	Four Courts	Major position of the 1st Battalion.
12		Kingsbridge Railway Station	Never taken by the Volunteers, it was a major conduit for the British reinforcements from the west. Now Heuston Station.
13	6–8 Lisburn Street	Linenhall Barracks	Captured by the Volunteers and set on fire.
14	Cabra	Marlborough Barracks	Lancers were billeted here. Now McKee Barracks.
15		Guinness Buildings	
16	Usher's Island	Mendicity Institute	A Fianna/Volunteer position under Seán Heuston from Monday afternoon until Wednesday.
17	Blackhall Place	Columcille Hall	The 1st Battalion mustered here.
18	Chancery Street	Bridewell	The Volunteers captured DMP constables and two Lancers here.
19		Church Street Bridge	

surrounded the large building, and Heuston's men immediately barricaded themselves into the rooms of the Institute. Windows were knocked out and loopholed with furniture and sandbags, and the Fianna, expecting the British to use incendiaries, strategically placed buckets of water throughout. The Fianna were well-trained marksmen and disciplined troops, and were told to remain stealthily at their posts until Heuston gave the signal to fire on any British attempting to advance on the interior positions of the Four Courts garrison. When the 10th Royal Dublin Fusiliers left Royal Barracks, they marched up the north quays with no advance scouts and did not reconnoitre the area. As they came abreast of the Institute, Heuston's men fired in unison on the column, taking it completely by surprise. Here the Volunteers and Fianna were much better prepared than the professional British soldiers. It could always be argued that an 'ambush' will favour an amateur, but in this case the British simply marched down the road without taking any fundamental precautions, and suffered heavy casualties for their arrogance. Ultimately, Heuston estimated that his small garrison faced an assault by about 300–400 British troops and the Institute was finally surrounded on Wednesday, necessitating Heuston's surrender. He had been asked to hold for three hours, but he had held for three days.

1ST BATTALION: MEN

A, B and C Companies mustered at Columcille Hall in Blackhall Place under Cmdt Edward (Ned) Daly and proceeded to Brunswick Street. D Company mustered in Temple Street under Capt. Seán Heuston and proceeded to Liberty Hall, and then to the Mendicity Institute. Garrison total about 400 men and women; two executed, eleven killed.

Locations: North Brunswick Street, Church Street, Constitution Hill, Four Courts, Fr Mathew Hall, North King Street ('Reilly's Fort'), Magazine Fort, Mendicity Institute, North Dublin Union.

Magazine Fort: a contingent of Fianna was deployed to the Fort in Phoenix Park, intending to blow up the munitions there. They had a mock football game just outside the gate, and when the ball was kicked over the fence they asked the sentry to throw it back. When he turned his back, they rushed him and took over the Fort. The explosion was to 'signal' the start of the Rising, but the key to the main arms room had been taken by the O/C when he went to the Fairyhouse Races, so they were able to explode only a small portion of the munitions.[439]

Mendicity Institute: garrison about 35. This was on the south side of the Liffey at Usher's Quay, about half a mile to the west of the Four Courts. It controlled the route between Royal Barracks and the Four Courts. Most of the Volunteers were Fianna, and most were between twelve and 25 years of age (Heuston was only 25 years old). He was instructed to hold this position for three hours to delay English deployment; they held for three days. They were reinforced with thirteen men from north County Dublin, and there were 24 survivors and two killed. The Fianna only surrendered when they ran out of ammunition on Wednesday, infuriating the British that so few youngsters had held them off for so long. Heuston was the youngest executed.

*Cmdt Edward (Ned) Daly (Éamonn Ó Dalaigh; executed 4 May 1916, aged 25);[440] prior to the Rising he told Phyllis Morkan that 'if there was going to be fighting, [we] will need all the women [we] can get!'[441]

Daly's 1st Battalion occupied the Four Courts and the adjacent streets on the north bank of the River Liffey, almost a mile to the west of the GPO.[442] Daly first set up his headquarters in North Brunswick Street, then later in Church Street, and established his defences for the 1st Battalion in the Four Courts area around buildings that allowed his limited forces as much movement between positions as possible.[443] Because of Eoin MacNeill's cancellation order, Daly's command was greatly reduced in size.[444] His troops engaged the British in a haphazard and widespread battle, and the area they were to hold presented many tactical problems to them as defenders, as well as to the attacking British.[445] Daly knew that his troops needed to take their positions rapidly, as these were the Irish most exposed to the quick British response. He reconnoitred his command area exhaustively and established his posts in positions allowing crossing fields of fire, cover and concealment.[446] The 1st Battalion was to occupy and hold the Four Courts area and to form a line from there to Cabra, where it was to link up with the 5th Battalion. Daly's command area extended from the Cabra and North Circular roads to the north, east towards the Bolton Street approach to North King Street, and west to North Brunswick Street as far as Red Cow Lane.[447] This area controlled the main approach routes from the west of Dublin to the centre of the city. As regards Daly's preparations, strategy and the actual tactics used during the week, the British noted that 'in this North King Street they had situated themselves as to be able to inflict maximum casualties on the English troops with minimum loss to themselves', and they gave Daly much credit.[448] Daly placed his forces in areas that allowed them to intercept British troops coming from Marlborough Barracks and Royal Barracks towards the GPO.

Daly moved his HQ to Fr Mathew Hall, as it was more central to his command area, and then finally moved to the Four Courts.

One of his command summed up Daly's call to arms on Easter Monday:

On my arrival in 5 Blackhall Street I found about 250 men gathered in the hall and rooms on the ground floor, while upstairs a Battalion Council Meeting was being held … I saw the Comdt. come out to the back room and he called all the men to take their places in their Cos. When all had got into the ranks he called the men to attention, and spoke to them about the training they had gone through for the past 16 months, and that he was glad to see such a muster of the Batt. While he was speaking he was handed a written message. When he read it he looked earnestly at the men, and then told them that 'The Irish Republic' had been proclaimed at 12 noon by Comdt. Gen. Patrick Pearse who had, with some of the Kimmage Garrison and Head Quarters staff, and Comdt. James Connolly with the Irish Citizen Army, taken over the G.P.O. and were preparing to defend the Republic with their lives. The Comdt. then said that if any man present did not agree with the opinions of the Supreme Council of the Irish Republic he was at liberty to return home, but if anyone did so, he would ask him to leave his arms, ammo., and equipment behind as some of the men present were not fully armed. No man left the ranks, and the Comdt. said he was glad he had the men 100 per cent behind him and the officers of the Supreme Command.[449]

At the surrender, when a British officer called out 'Who is in charge of these men?', Daly stepped forward and answered 'I am the commander. At all events I was in charge.' In Kilmainham he was in cell no. 66 and was attended by Fr Columbus, who knew him from the Four Courts. When he entered Daly's cell, Fr Columbus saw a look of relief and gladness appear on Daly's face. When it was realised that Holy Communion had not been brought to Plunkett, who was in a different wing, Fr Columbus went there and literally gave him the Sacrament as he was being led from his cell. Anxious to see Daly for the last time, Fr Columbus rushed back, only to discover that he had already been led out to be executed. As Fr Columbus proceeded to follow him, the shots rang out.[450]

Daly was also seen by his sisters Madge, Laurie (his favourite) and Kathleen (Kattie) Clarke. Madge felt Laurie falter and told her: 'Remember, you're a Daly'.[451] He was the second youngest to be executed.

*Seán ('Jack', J.J.) Heuston (Seán MacAodha; executed 8 May 1916, aged 25);[452] he commanded D Company at the Mendicity Institute, held by Fianna and Volunteers, most aged between twelve and 25. This was the first garrison to capitulate, and did so on Wednesday. In Kilmainham he was in cell no. 19, where he was visited by Fr Albert,[453] by his brother Michael, who was studying to be a Dominican priest, and by Fr Patrick (Paddy) Browne,[454] the Dominican novice master. In addition, his mother, sister, aunt and a first cousin saw him.[455]

In *The Capuchin Annual* of 1942, Fr Albert gave a remarkable account of his time with Heuston. According to that account, Heuston was 'kneeling beside a small table with his Rosary beads in his hand and on the table was a little piece of candle and some letters which he had just written to some relatives and friends. He wore his overcoat as the morning was extremely cold and none of these men received those little comforts that are provided for even the greatest criminals while awaiting sentence of death.'

Fr Albert said that Heuston had been to confession and Mass that morning and was not afraid to die. According to Fr Albert's account, Heuston 'awaited the end not only with the calmness and fortitude which peace of mind brings to noble souls, but during the last quarter of an hour he spoke of soon meeting again Padraig MacPhiarais and the other leaders who had already gone before him'.

Heuston wrote to his sister, a Dominican nun: 'Let there be no talk of "foolish enterprises". I have no vain regrets. If you really love me, teach the children the history of their own land and teach them that the cause of Caitlin ni h-Uallachain never dies. Ireland shall be free from the centre to the sea as soon as the people of Ireland believe in the necessity for Ireland's freedom and are prepared to make the necessary sacrifices to obtain it.'[456]

Fr Albert walked to the Stonebreaker's Yard with Heuston, and they saw Fr Augustine and Michael Mallin as they passed in the hallway. When they reached the Yard, the blindfolded Heuston bent and kissed a cross that Fr Albert held in his hand. In the Yard, Fr Albert wrote, 'there was a box (seemingly a soap box) and Seán was told to sit down on it. He was perfectly calm and said with me for the last time "My Jesus, mercy". I scarcely had moved away a few yards when a volley went off, and this noble soldier of Irish freedom fell dead. I rushed over to anoint him. His whole face seemed transformed, and lit up with a grandeur and brightness that I had never before noticed.'

Fr Albert said that Heuston's last message to him was 'Remember me to the boys of the Fianna. Remember me to Miceal Staines and to his brothers and to all the boys at Blackhall Street.'

Of Heuston's death, Fr Albert wrote:

Later on his remains and those of the others were conveyed to Arbour Hill military detention barracks, where they were buried in the outer yard, in a trench which holds the mortal remains of Ireland's noblest and bravest sons. Never before did I realise that man could fight so bravely, and die so beautifully and so fearlessly as did the heroes of Easter Week. On the morning of Seán Heuston's death, I would have given the world to have been in his place, he died in such a noble and sacred cause and went forth to meet ....

Lt Thomas Allen (30);[457] he ordered a policeman to turn over the keys to the Chancery Place entrance to the Four Courts, and the Volunteers entered at that point. He was only promoted to Lt on Monday morning. There are conflicting accounts of the date of his death: some note that he was killed on Monday in a barricaded window of the Four Courts by a British sniper whose bullet ricocheted off Seán O'Carroll and hit Allen in the chest,[458] while others record his death later in the week in one of the windows of the Records Office.[459]

Liam Aloysius Archer; he was in the Bow Lane Distillery. Later he became chief of staff of the Free State army.[460]

William Francis Ashton; he was in Church Street and the Four Courts.

Capt. Richard (Dick) C. Balfe; Mendicity Institute. He was badly wounded when Liam Staines picked up a grenade and tried to throw it back, but the grenade exploded near Balfe. He was imprisoned at Frongoch and became O/C of E Co. of the North Camp.

> When we reached the Mendicity Institute we broke one small door and entered ... On the stroke of twelve o'clock a small party of sappers came along unarmed. We allowed these to pass knowing what was coming along. In a few minutes the main body of troops in column of route came into view. We had sixteen men altogether including officers. All had Lee-Enfield rifles. Every man had at least 100 rounds of ammunition. Myself and some others had 500 rounds each. Two shots were fired rapidly and the commanding officer dropped. I heard afterwards that he was shot between the eyes and in the heart. The column halted right opposite to us after the two shots and it was a case of fire and one could not miss. The column were [sic] four deep. There were from 200 to 250 at least in the column. At the time we had been putting out a tricolour flag and we saw the officer in front drawing his sword and pointing towards it. This was the officer who was immediately shot dead. The firing became continuous and rapid and it eased off. Some of the British soldiers tried to protect themselves against the quay wall and eventually ran up side streets and in through houses. The casualties were numerous and the ambulance was a considerable time removing the wounded. At four o'clock p.m., they came down eight deep. They must not have known where the first attack had come from, as the officer who first saw us was immediately shot dead. We altered our tactics then and we concentrated firing on the rear of the column. As they were nearly at Queen Street Bridge [now Liam Mellows Bridge, connecting Queen Street and Arran Quay] we suddenly concentrated the firing on the head of the column. The column stopped. It was just a matter of firing as rapidly as possible into a solid body.[461]

Tom Bannon; he came up from Longford to Dublin with Brighid Lyons (Thornton) and Frank McGuinness.[462]

Benedict Barrett; he was in the Four Courts.

Piaras Béaslaí, Vice-Commandant; became editor of *An tÓglach* (*The Soldier*). Born and educated in Liverpool, he moved to Dublin at the age of 23. He was stationed in 'Reilly's Fort'.[463] Along with Éamon Morkan, he moved the ammunition and bombs to the Four Courts. He was TD for Kerry East in the first three Dáils and published one of the first biographies of Michael Collins.

Robert Beggs; he was in North King Street and the Four Courts.

Daniel Joseph Begley; he was in the Magazine Fort, then went to the Four Courts. Imprisoned at Frongoch.

John Bent; he came from Cabra to the Four Courts. Imprisoned at Frongoch.

Charles Stewart Bevan (brother of James and Thomas); Four Courts. He led the men in barricading the windows of the chancellor's office.

James (Séamus) Bevan (brother of Charles and Thomas); a Fianna member, he was in the Four Courts.[464]

> In those days I had a keen interest in the Flags of Nations and their significance. And hence, when on the Wednesday of Easter Week I arrived within sight of the G.P.O. with a dispatch from Commandant Daly of the Four Courts area, I was immediately struck by the appearance of the flag which flew from the Henry St. corner of the G.P.O. I have a vivid recollection of that flag [the Irish tricolour]. It was very large, much larger than any flag I had ever seen. It blew in a stiff breeze almost half-way across Henry St. and the bottom edge of this flag almost touched the top of the balustrade.

Joseph Bevan; Four Courts.

Thomas Joseph Bevan (brother of Charles and James); was in the Four Courts library.

Fr Albert Bibby, OFM; he was one of several Capuchin friars from the Church Street priory who ministered to the rebel garrisons. In the aftermath of the Rising, Fr Albert ministered to a number of rebel prisoners in Kilmainham Gaol and in other locations.[465]

James Bird; ICA. He was at the Church Street Bridge, then at the Four Courts. Imprisoned at Frongoch.

Peter (Peadar) Blanchfield; he was at Cabra Bridge and escaped from Phibsborough. Imprisoned at Frongoch. (He went to the 5th Battalion and is counted in that garrison.)

Patrick (Paddy) Boland; a Fianna member, he was at the Magazine Fort and then went to Church Street. Imprisoned at Frongoch.

Joseph Brabazon; Four Courts. He was wounded at the Church Street Bridge barricade.

Edward Brennan (Éamonn Ó Braoináin); Four Courts. Imprisoned at Frongoch.

James Joseph (Séamus) Brennan; Mendicity Institute.

> Our tiny garrison of twenty-six had battled all morning against three or four hundred British troops. Machine-gun and rifle fire kept up a constant battering of our position. Seán [Heuston] visited each post in turn, encouraging us. But now we were faced with a new form of attack. The enemy, closing in, began to hurl grenades into the building. Our only answer was to try and catch these and throw them back before they exploded. Two of our men, Liam Staines and Dick Balfe, both close friends of Seán's were badly wounded doing this. We had almost run out of ammunition. Dog-tired, without food, trapped, hopelessly outnumbered, we had reached the limit of our endurance. After consultation with the rest of us, Seán decided that the only hope for the wounded and indeed, for the safety of all of us, was to surrender. Not everyone approved but the order was obeyed and we destroyed as much equipment as we could before giving ourselves up …[466]

James Breslin; he was in North King Street, Monks' Bakery and then the Four Courts.

Peadar Breslin; Four Courts. He was sent with the party to take Broadstone Station.[467] While he was in Moore's Coach Factory, the British attacked it and he shot the first British soldier who broke cover.[468]

Thomas Breslin; he was in North King Street, Red Cow Lane and Monks' Bakery.

Edward Bridgeman (Bridgemor?); he was in the Four Courts. Imprisoned at Frongoch until September 1916.

Frederick John Brooks; he was one of the Fianna garrison at the Mendicity Institute who surrendered on Wednesday.

James Burns; he was in North Brunswick Street and then the Four Courts.

George Butler; Four Courts. He was one of the party sent to reconnoitre Broadstone Station; in order to provide cover for the Volunteers retreating from the station, several times he dropped to his knees and fired at the British while he was in clear view of their lines.

Ambrose Byrne; he was at the Church Street Bridge and then the Four Courts. Imprisoned at Frongoch.

Bernard Christopher Byrne; he was in North King Street and Carter's Lane.

Charles Bernard Byrne; he was in the Four Courts. He became a member of Michael Collins's 'Squad'. He was called 'the Count' because of his cheerful mien in all situations.

James Byrne; Four Courts. He was guarding the front gate with his Howth rifle, and fired on the Lancers who had been ambushed on Church Street and were fleeing toward Chancery Place.[469]

John Joseph Byrne; he was one of the Fianna garrison at the Mendicity Institute who surrendered on Wednesday. Imprisoned at Frongoch.

Laurence Byrne; he was in North Brunswick Street and Monks' Bakery.

Patrick Byrne; he was in Watkins's Brewery, then Jameson's Distillery and then the Four Courts. Imprisoned at Frongoch.

Seán Byrne; Four Courts. He was a member of F Company.[470]

> On Wednesday of Holy Week I attended a meeting in Keating Branch Gaelic League Hall, North Frederick Street, presided over by Dermot Lynch. Others attending were Andy Fitzpatrick, J. Tyrrell, J. Twamley, Martin and George King, all employees of the Engineering Branch Post Office. We were told that a special squad was being formed to deal with communications and that specific tasks would be allotted to those present. Plans were to be prepared immediately for cutting communications so as to isolate the city. We were not told at this meeting

that action had been decided upon but that we were to have plans prepared immediately. After some discussion the meeting adjourned until the following evening. On Thursday evening at the same place, the meeting reassembled and was attended by Thomas McDonagh [sic], who informed us that we were going into action on the following Sunday at 6 p.m. and that we were to submit our plans for the isolation of the city. A plan was then hurriedly prepared and the following decided on: Andy Fitzpatrick to cut cross-channel cable from G.P.O. at a point in Talbot Street; J. Tyrrell to cut cables at Dunlaoghaire and Blackrock; J. Twamley to cut cables and wires at Bray and Shankhill. Martin and George King to cut cables in Westland Row area. We were informed that the Telephone Exchange, Crown Alley, was being attended to by G.H.Q. staff. I was detailed to cut the trunk telephone and telegraph lines at 7th Lock Bridge between Inchicore and Clondalkin. On Good Friday I surveyed the position at 7th Lock and made notes of equipment required for the job. We met at Liberty Hall that night and submitted our reports to James Connolly; we were supplied with such tools as pliers, hacksaws, axes, sledges and ropes which we brought to our homes to be kept in readiness. We made a further survey on Saturday and noted all police private wires which were to be cut to isolate all barracks. F. Byrne was to do this job. We met again on Saturday night in Liberty Hall and completed arrangements. On Sunday morning, on seeing the parade cancellation notice in the paper, I proceeded to Liberty Hall and there met members of the Executive Council. I waited until the Executive Council meeting was over. I was then informed by Seán McDermott [sic] that the Rising had been postponed and that I was to cancel all 'action orders' until further notice. I proceeded to Blackrock, Dunlaoghaire and Bray and contacted M. Tobin, J. Tyrrell, M. Higgins (Loughlin's town) and J. Kenny (Bray) and gave instructions not to proceed with demolition work. I returned to Dunlaoghaire at about midnight. On Monday morning I received an order from Dermot Hegarty to mobilise company at Blackhall Place. I went to Summerhill and left instructions for J. Costelloe, company mobiliser, to carry out the mobilization. I then went to Liberty Hall and met James Connolly, who told me to join my battalion at Blackhall Place, and that the battalion officers there would decide on whatever demolition was to be carried out in the area. I was instructed by Comdt. E. Daly to select a Point near Liffey Junction for the cutting the western trunks (Athlone, Sligo, Galway).

I proceeded to Broome Bridge via Royal Canal and, with the help of a bridge demolition party in the area, cut down the pole and wires.

Séamus Byrne; he was in the Four Courts and was interned in Stafford Jail.

William Byrne; he was in the Four Courts.

James Cahill; he was in North Brunswick Street and was imprisoned at Frongoch.

Ignatius Callendar; when he went off to fight, his mother pinned a badge of St Thérèse of Lisieux, the 'Little Flower of Jesus', on his chest with the remark, 'You're all right now—the Little Flower will protect you'.[471] A courier, he made ten trips between the GPO and the Four Courts garrison.[472] His mother owned the Lucan Restaurant, 2 Sarsfield Quay, from which the last meals for Pearse were prepared on 1 and 2 May. The restaurant closed in June 1916 when the personnel from Royal Barracks learned of Mrs Callender's sympathy for the executed rebel leaders and stopped eating there. The restaurant was declared out of bounds for Royal Barracks, and as a result of the drop in business it was forced to close.

Michael John Campbell; he was in North Brunswick Street.

Peter Carroll (Peadar Ó Cearbhaill); Four Courts.

Hugh Casey; he was at North Brunswick Street, then Church Street and then in Moore's Coach Builders, North Brunswick Street.

Thomas Cassidy; he was in Church Street.

John Patrick Catlin; he was in Church Street and then the Four Courts.

Lt Peadar (Peter) Clancy; Four Courts. He was in command of a section at a barricade at the junction of Church Street and the quays. A detachment of Lancers had been detailed to escort munitions lorries from the North Wall to the magazine in Phoenix Park; when they reached Clancy's barricade, his men opened fire, killing one Lancer and wounding others.[473] The Lancers fell back under fire from many locations and finally took cover in Collier's Dispensary and the nearby Medical Mission in Charles Street, where they defended their position throughout the Rising. Later Clancy led a detachment to build a barricade at 5 Church Street. After coming under fire for hours, Clancy and Thomas Smart climbed the barricade with cans of petrol, ran across Church Street and poured the petrol through the ground-floor windows of the house facing them. No. 1 Usher's Quay was consumed in the flames and the British position was broken. As a leader of the Dublin Brigade in the War of Independence, he was murdered in Dublin Castle on Bloody Sunday, 21 November 1920.[474]

James Clarke; he lived at 31 Bachelor's Walk.

#[475] **John Clarke**; he came from the 5th Battalion via the GPO. (Counted in the 5th Battalion.) He was in the Mendicity Institute.

Seán (John) Cody; Mendicity Institute. Imprisoned at Frongoch.[476]

> On our way … We also met a British recruiting sergeant who gave a very sharp look at my rifle, but I believe now he understood why I had my hand in my uniform pocket in which I had my revolver. It was a strict order to all Volunteers never to part with their weapons without defending them, and I took the precaution of having my hand on the revolver in case I should have to use it.

Cody was with a group of Volunteers in Moore's coach works but was separated from his unit when they made a withdrawal under fire.

Joseph Coffey; he was in North King Street and Church Street.

Francis Xavier Coghlan;[477] he was in North King Street, Church Street and St Mary's Lane.

Patrick Cole; he was in North King Street and Church Street.

Thomas Cole; he was in Keegan's Gunshop in Chancery Street.

Capt. Richard (Dick) Coleman; he mobilised with the Fingal Brigade at Saucerstown, went to the GPO and then was sent to the Mendicity Institute (see GPO and 5th Battalion). He was one of the garrison at the Mendicity Institute who surrendered on Wednesday.

Lt Maurice John Collins; he took up his post in Lambe's public house after he was released from guarding Bulmer Hobson on Monday evening, then went to the Four Courts. (See Martin Conlon.) He took command of the small garrison holding 'Reilly's Fort'. He was imprisoned in Wandsworth. After his release he opened a tobacconist and confectioner's shop, with a billiard room.[478]

Éamon Comber; he was in North King Street.

Luke Condron; Four Courts. Imprisoned at Frongoch.

Martin Conlon; he was in charge at Fr Mathew Hall after guarding Bulmer Hobson until Monday evening, when Seán T. O'Kelly was sent from the GPO to have him released. Hobson was held at Conlon's home in Cabra Park from just before the Rising by Conlon, Michael Lynch, Con O'Donovan,[479] Maurice Collins and Seán Tobin.[480] Conlon was a member of the IRB Supreme Council.[481]

James Conroy Snr; he was in Church Street and Mary's Lane, and then the Four Courts.

Patrick Vincent Coogan; he was in Blackhall Place and the North Dublin Union.

Joseph Cooling; he was in the Four Courts and was deported until September.

Lt Michael Cosgrave; he was in Church Street and the Four Courts and was interned until September.

★★Lt Edward J. Costello (24);[482] a native of County Kildare, he was killed by a shot to the head while he was in Church Street. He was carried to Jervis Street Hospital, where he died, and is buried in Glasnevin Cemetery. Not on the list issued by the Irish National Aid and Volunteers' Dependants' Fund as 'men who were killed whilst fighting for Ireland during Easter Week, 1916'.

Redmond Cox; he was in North King Street, then the North Dublin Union and then the Four Courts.

William Coyle; he was in North King Street and the Bridewell in Chancery Street, and then in the Four Courts. Imprisoned at Frongoch.

 # James Crenigan (Corrigan?); he came from the 5th Battalion via the GPO. (Counted in the 5th Battalion.) He was in the Mendicity Institute.

★★John Cromien (23);[483] there is no definitive account of his death, but it seems that he was killed in a running battle along the railway line between Broadstone Station and the Cabra Bridge. The Volunteers were attempting to destroy the bridge but were unsuccessful. His date of death is uncertain, and it is unclear whether he was killed in Prussia Street.

John Francis (Frank) Cullen; he was one of the Fianna garrison at the Mendicity Institute who surrendered on Wednesday. Imprisoned at Frongoch.

Joseph Cullen; he was in North Brunswick Street and the Four Courts.

Thomas Cullen; he came in from Cabra and was in the Four Courts. Imprisoned at Frongoch.

 # Francis (Frank) Daly; he was in Church Street. (He came in from the 5th Battalion and is counted in that garrison.)

Patrick Daly; he was in North King Street and Church Street.

Patrick (Paddy) Daly (O'Daly) (Pádraig Ua Dalaigh); a Fianna member. Some months before the Rising he got a job with a building firm making repairs at the Magazine Fort and he knew its layout. He was the leader of the attack on the Fort that was supposed to provide the signal to start the Rising. He was the engineer for the whole brigade. He was wounded in his right arm in an attack on the Lancers in the Medical Mission,[484] and was imprisoned at Frongoch.

Michael Darker; he was in the Four Courts.

Luke Darling; he was in North King Street.

Henry Delaney; he was a member of the Royal Dublin Fusiliers on leave from the Curragh. He took off his uniform and joined the 1st Battalion in the Four Courts.

Edward Delemere; Four Courts. He volunteered to run from Reilly's Fort to Fr Mathew Hall for ammunition and he made it back, but his fellow Volunteer Patrick O'Flanagan was killed on the return journey.[485] Imprisoned at Frongoch.

James Dempsey; he was in the Magazine Fort and then North King Street.

Michael Derham; he was at the Church Street Bridge and Cleary's public house and was imprisoned at Frongoch. His sister, Margaret, was also in the Four Courts.

John (Seán) Derrington; he was one of the Fianna garrison at the Mendicity Institute who surrendered on Wednesday.

William Patrick (Liam) Derrington; he was one of the Fianna garrison at the Mendicity Institute who surrendered on Wednesday.

Paul Dervin; he was in Brunswick Street and Church Street.

Christopher Doggett; he was in Church Street and then in Moore's Coach Builders.

John (Seán) Domican; he was in the North Circular Road Bridge garrison and North King Street. Imprisoned at Frongoch.

Robert Donohoe; he was in Chancery Street and North Greek Street.

Sylvester Donohoe; he was in Blackhall Street and North Brunswick Street.

Andrew Dowling; Four Courts.

James Thomas Dowling; he was in Mary's Lane, Church Street and Bow Lane.

John Dowling; Four Courts.

Thomas Dowling; Four Courts. He was part of a detail that constructed a barricade across Bow Lane with materials taken from Jameson's Distillery.[486]

John Doyle; Four Courts.

William Drennan; he was in North King Street.

Christopher Duffy; he was in Fr Mathew Hall and was imprisoned at Frongoch.

Éamonn J. Duggan; the battalion adjutant, he was in Church Street and North Brunswick Street. He became a plenipotentiary in the Treaty negotiations of December 1921. He received the maximum pension of £350 per year.

Thomas Dunne; he was in Antwerp Street and Moore's Coach Builders. Imprisoned at Frongoch.

Thomas John Dunne; he was in North King Street and North Brunswick Street.

**John Dwan (25);[487] along with Volunteers William Murphy, William Hogan, John Williamson and Thomas Sherrin, he watched a makeshift British armoured vehicle (actually a Guinness boiler mounted on a lorry body) come up North King Street and fire a broadside at the Volunteers. This began the battle on the street, which was the most sustained fighting of the week. The British use of the armoured 'car' kept their casualties down, and the Volunteers used the opportunity to bore through building walls to keep under cover.[488] Dwan was one of a small detachment of Volunteers in Lagan's public house, and was killed on Friday in North King Street[489] while manning a barricade on North King Street and Church Street.[490] When Dwan was shot in the head, Hogan carried the body of his friend back to Coleraine Street, where it lay until the stretcher-bearers could take him to hospital. He lived in Lower Gardiner Street and was employed at the railway works in Inchicore.

Michael Edwards; he was in North King Street and Moore's Coach Builders. Imprisoned at Frongoch.

John (Seán) Ellis; Four Courts. Imprisoned at Frongoch.

John Fagan; he was in Church Street and North King Street.

Michael Fagan; he was in Fr Mathew Hall.

Patrick Fagan; he was in Monks' Bakery and Bull Lane.

Capt. Frank Fahy, O/C of C Company; his men stormed the Chancery Street entrance and occupied the Four Courts. On the retreat from Church Street and North King Street he was found lying in the street; he was thought to have been wounded, but in fact had suffered a heart attack. He became Ceann Comhairle (Speaker of the Dáil).[491]

John Farrell; he was in Bridge Street.

John Farrell; he was in Church Street and North King Street.

**Patrick Farrell (19);[492] he was shot on Friday on the top floor of Moore's Coach Builders on Church Street.[493]

Thomas Farrell; he was in the Four Courts.

Christopher Farrelly Jnr; he was in the Four Courts.

Seán Farrelly; he was in the Four Courts.

Stephen Farren; he was in North Brunswick Street and Clarke's Dairy. Imprisoned at Frongoch.

Peter Fearon; he was in North Brunswick Street and Broadstone Railway Station.

Gerald Feeny; he was in Church Street and the Four Courts.

John Fisher; he was in the Church Street Bridge area and the Bridewell in Chancery Street.

Denis Fitzpatrick; he was in Moore's Lane and Greek Street, and the Bridewell in Chancery Street.

Maurice Fitzsimons; he was sent over to the GPO and was imprisoned at Frongoch.

Michael Flanagan; he was ordered to take his detachment to reinforce Reilly's Fort. He led very effective fire against the South Staffordshire troops. Imprisoned at Frongoch.

Seán Flood; Four Courts. 'We had plenty of food in the Four Courts. A man used to go out early every morning, bring in bread, meat and other food for the day. We knew him as "Looter" Flood.'[494] Imprisoned at Frongoch.

John Fogarty; he and his brother, Patrick (below), came from Cabra and went to the Four Courts. He was imprisoned until July 1917.

Patrick Fogarty, brother of John (above); he was in the Four Courts. Imprisoned until July 1917.

Michael Patrick Foley (Mícheál Ó Foghludha); Four Courts.

Seán Forde; he was in the Magazine Fort, then North Brunswick Street and North King Street.

Frederick Foy; he came from Kimmage,[495] went to the GPO and was sent to the Four Courts. Imprisoned at Frongoch.

Denis Frawley; he was in North King Street.

Matthew Gahan; he was in Moore's Coach Builders, the Linenhall Barracks and Clarke's Dairy.

Patrick Gartlan; he was in North King Street and Broadstone Railway Station.

Frank Gaskin; he was in the Magazine Fort.[496]

I did not parade on Easter Sunday as I got word that the Rising was off, I paraded on Easter Monday with my Company at Emerald Square. Garry Holohan came along and asked for four volunteers. I volunteered along with Paddy McGrath and two others. We went to Rutland Street, off Summerhill, from there to the Magazine Fort with Paddy Daly in charge. Paddy Boland and I went and disarmed the sentry and held up the guard. We disarmed the guard. The remainder of our party tried to get into the explosives store but did not succeed. They set fire to some of the building. After about twenty minutes we left and I went to Marrowbone Lane.

Arthur Gaynor; he was in the North Dublin Union and Church Street. Imprisoned at Frongoch.

Christopher (Christy) Geraghty; he was in the North Dublin Union, then in Church Street and then went to the Four Courts

John (Seán) Geraghty; he was in the Four Courts. Imprisoned at Frongoch.

Robert (Bob) Gilligan; a member of the Fianna, he was in the Magazine Fort.

Patrick Gilsenan; he was in Moore's Coach Builders and the Bridewell in Chancery Street.

Vincent Joseph Gogan; he was in Cabra, at the Midland Railway Bridge and in Drumcondra.

Gerry Golden (Jeremiah Golden, James Barry); a member of the 1st Battalion, he escaped capture in Phibsborough, fleeing to the 5th Battalion. (Counted in the 5th Battalion.)

On my arrival in 5 Blackhall Street I found about 250 men gathered in the hall and rooms on the ground floor while upstairs a Battalion Council Meeting was being held … When the B.C. Meeting was over I saw Comdt. [Daly] and other officers come down, and on my speaking to the Comdt. I asked him if I would be sent down the country. He replied 'No', as the Countermanding Order of Sunday had upset all the plans. He then enquired about my mother and I informed him that she had left for Longford on the 9 a.m. train. He said he was glad she had got out of town in time and then asked me what arms I had brought with me. I replied, 'Everything I had in the house'. I also told him I was keeping the Service Rifle, but that all the others could be given to anyone who had no arms or ammunition only small arms. He then told me to take my place with 'B'

Co. men, as he was about to make a very important announcement. On my taking my place in the ranks of 'B' Co. in the Hall, I saw the Comdt. come out to the back room and he called all the men to take their places in their Cos. When all had got into the ranks he called the men to attention, and spoke to them about the training they had gone through for the past 16 months, and that he was glad to see such a muster of the Batt. While he was speaking he was handed a written message. When he read it he looked earnestly at the men, and then told them that 'The Irish Republic' had been proclaimed at 12 noon by Comdt. Gen. Patrick Pearse who had, with some of the Kimmage Garrison and Head Quarters staff, and Comdt. James Connolly with the Irish Citizen Army, taken over the G.P.O. and were preparing to defend the Republic with their lives. The Comdt. then said that if any man present did not agree with the opinions of the Supreme Council of the Irish Republic he was at liberty to return home, but if anyone did so, he would ask him to leave his arms, ammo., and equipment behind as some of the men present were not fully armed. No man left the ranks, and the Comdt. said he was glad he had the men 100 per cent behind him and the officers of the Supreme Command.[497]

James Graham; Four Courts. Imprisoned at Frongoch.

Patrick Green; he was in the Four Courts.

William Greene; he was in Monks' Bakery in Church Street and Fr Mathew Hall.

Gerald Griffin; he was in North King Street.

William Griffith; he was in North King Street.

Michael Grimley; he was at the Church Street Bridge.

John Halpin; he was in the Four Courts.

Peter (Peadar) Halpin; he was in the Four Courts. Imprisoned at Frongoch.

Thomas Hamill; he was in North King Street. Imprisoned at Frongoch.

Stephen Hanlon; he was in North King Street.

Thomas Hannigan; he was in Cabra and at the railway bridge on the North Circular Road.

Frank Harding; he was in the Four Courts.

Seán Harling (14); he was in the North Dublin Union. At the very beginning of the Rising he was selling race cards for the Fairyhouse Race Meeting outside the Broadstone Station.[498] He became aide to de Valera, witnessed the dictation of the letters appointing the plenipotentiaries to the Treaty negotiations, and delivered the letters to them. He fought for the Republicans/IRA in the Civil War.[499]

James Harmon; imprisoned at Frongoch.

Alfred (Alf) Harnett; he was at the Church Street Bridge. Imprisoned at Frongoch.

John Harpur; he was imprisoned at Frongoch.

Seán Harrington; he was sent to the Mendicity Institute.

Christopher Haughton; he was in Church Street.

Fr Augustine Hayden, OFM; during Easter Week, Fr Augustine helped the Cumann na mBan women in the hospital in Fr Mathew Hall, and then on Thursday he went to the Volunteer position in the Four Courts.[500] Fr Augustine wrote a detailed account of his activities under fire in the Four Courts area on Thursday and Friday, dismissing his bravery by saying, 'Well, I felt that I might be badly wounded, but I would not be killed outright'.[501]

Diarmuid Healy; he was imprisoned at Frongoch.

Peadar Healy; a ticket-collector at the Broadstone Railway Station, he was taken by surprise that the Rising was on and reported to his battalion position late.[502]

John Hegarty; he was imprisoned at Frongoch.

Thomas Henderson; he was in North Brunswick Street, Red Cow Lane and Monks' Bakery. Imprisoned at Frongoch.

Edward Hendrick; he was at the Church Street Bridge. Imprisoned at Frongoch.

James Joseph Hendrick; he came in from Cabra Road and was in Church Street.

James Higgins; he was imprisoned at Frongoch.

Patrick Joseph Hogan; he was in Blackhall Street and Church Street.

William Conor Hogan; he was in North King Street. Along with Volunteers William Murphy, John Dwan, John Williamson and Thomas Sherrin, he watched a makeshift British armoured vehicle (actually a Guinness boiler mounted on a lorry body) come up North King Street and fire a broadside at the Volunteers. This began the battle on the street, which was the most sustained fighting of the week. The British use of the armoured 'car' kept their casualties down, and the Volunteers used the opportunity to bore through building walls to keep under cover.[503]

Denis Holmes; he was in the Four Courts.

Gerard (Garry) Holohan (Gearóid Ó hUallachain) (brother of Patrick Hugh; their cousin, Hugh, was in the GPO, and his brother, Paddy, was sent to the 5th Battalion). He was a Fianna member; they met at the house at 8 Rutland Cottages. It was his assignment to buy a football for the game at Phoenix Park in the area known as the Fifteen Acres, and he was in the Magazine Fort. With Denis O'Callahan, he set Linenhall Barracks alight.

> When [I] reached Rutland cottages the house was packed with men and they were still arriving on foot and on bicycles. We distributed automatic pistols to the men who had no small arms and made everyone leave his rifle in the house and remove his equipment. Then we sent them to the Phoenix Park in batches, some on bicycles and some on the Ballybough tram. Paddy Daly and I went on bicycles and called at Whelan's on Ormond Quay, where we bought a football. After a few minutes' chat together, as if we were a football team with followers, we moved around to the front of the [Magazine] Fort in a casual way, some of the lads kicking the ball from one to the other. When we got near the gate they rushed the sentry who was standing outside, and then another party rushed in and took the guardroom completely by surprise. I was detailed off with Barney Mellows to take the sentry on the parapet. I rushed straight through the Fort, which is a rather large place, and I had some difficulty in locating him. I eventually saw him looking at me over a roof. I rushed towards him, calling on him to surrender. He came towards me with his bayonet pointed towards me. I fired a shot and he fell, and at that moment Barney came along the parapet. The poor sentry was crying, 'Oh, sir, sir, don't shoot me. I'm an Irishman and the father of seven children.' ... When I met Paddy Daly he told me he could not find the key of the high-explosives store and he had set the charges in the small-arms ammunition store. Éamon and I lit the charges and my brother Pat gave us a hand. While we were placing the charges, most of the attacking party were clearing away. We informed

the prisoners that one of their men was injured and told them to give him attention. We also ordered them not to go down the Park in the direction of the city. We took the guards' rifles and went to the waiting hackney car ... I followed behind the car on my bicycle. As the car turned towards the gate leading to the Chapelizod Road we noticed a youth of about 17 years of age running towards the gate. He stopped and spoke to the policeman who was in the middle of the road directing the traffic, and then ran away in the middle of the road towards Islandbridge. I left the hack and followed him, and when he got to the corner of Islandbridge Road he ran towards one of the big houses, evidently with the intention of giving the alarm. I jumped off my bicycle, and just as the door opened I shot him from the gate. At that moment the car arrived at the junction of the road and two large explosions took place in the Fort. The lads on the car started to cheer, and then they thought it wiser to put the rifles that were in their hands into the well of the car.[504]

Paddy Holohan (brother of Hugh in the GPO, and the cousin of Garry and Patrick, who were in the 1st Battalion); a member of the 1st Battalion, he escaped capture in Phibsborough, fleeing to the 5th Battalion and then back to North King Street. He was in charge of the top floor of Clarke's dairy, and commanded his men to bore through the walls towards Reilly's Fort. Imprisoned at Frongoch. (Counted in the 1st Battalion garrison.)

Patrick Hugh (Paddy) Holohan (brother of Garry); a Fianna member, he was in the Magazine Fort. He was attached to the Church Street/North Brunswick Street unit and became O/C in the North Dublin Union after Capt. Nicholas Laffan was injured on Saturday.[505] After Elizabeth O'Farrell and Fr Columbus carried the order to surrender to Daly, Holohan still prepared an assault on the British in North King Street, saying that his Volunteers had decided to fight to the finish. He was finally convinced to surrender by Fr Augustine and Fr Aloysius.[506] His detachment consisted of 58 Volunteers; they were marched to Dublin Castle, searched and then sent to Richmond Prison, then to Knutsford, and finally were imprisoned at Frongoch.

Con Howard; Four Courts.

**Seán Bernard Howard (17);[507] Four Courts. A friend of Seán Harling and a member of the Fianna Pipers Band, he and a few members of the Fianna blew up a railroad bridge to block the British. He was wounded on Saturday during a charge down Church Street and was taken to Fr Mathew Hall, where he died.[508]

Michael Howlett; he was in Mary's Lane and the Four Courts.

**John (Jack, Seán) Hurley (29);[509] wounded in the head during a charge down Church Street,[510] he was taken to Fr Mathew Hall and then to Richmond Hospital, where he died.[511] He was a great friend of Michael Collins from west Cork, and his sister, Catherine, married Collins's brother.

Christopher Hyland; he was in the Monks' Bakery and Fr Mathew Hall.

Thomas Hyland; he was in North King Street and North Brunswick Street, and was imprisoned at Frongoch.

Seán Hynes; he was in Columcille Hall in Blackhall Place.

Nicholas Jackman; he was in Church Street.

Thomas Kane (Tomas Ó Canain); Four Courts.

Denis Kavanagh; he was in Brunswick Street and Manor Street.

James Joseph (Séamus) Kavanagh; he was in North King Street. Imprisoned at Frongoch.

Patrick Kearns; he was in the Four Courts. Imprisoned at Frongoch.

Joseph Kelly; he was at Church Street Bridge. Imprisoned at Frongoch.

Michael J. Kelly; he was at Moore's Coach Builders. Imprisoned at Frongoch.

Patrick Kelly; Four Courts. He opened fire on the Lancers as they escaped to the Medical Mission. After the Linenhall Barracks was set alight, the fires engulfed several other buildings; he was detailed to try to control the blaze, but the Volunteers were unsuccessful as firemen.[512] Imprisoned at Frongoch.

 # Patrick Kelly (Padraig Ó Ceallaigh); he came from the 5th Battalion via the GPO. (Counted in the 5th Battalion.) He was a member of the Lusk Company and was sent to the Mendicity Institute. He was court-martialled on 4 May along with Seán Heuston, Willie O'Dea and James Crennigan. Heuston, Kelly and O'Dea received the death sentence. On 8 May Heuston's death sentence was confirmed and Kelly's was reduced to three years and confirmed.

 # Richard Kelly; he came from the 5th Battalion via the GPO and was in the

Mendicity Institute. (Counted in the 5th Battalion.)

 # Tom Kelly; he came from the 5th Battalion via the GPO. (Counted in the 5th Battalion.)

James J. Kennedy; he was in North Brunswick Street and the Linenhall Barracks.

John Kennedy; he was in King Street and Greek Lane.

Joseph Kennedy; he was in the Magazine Fort and Columcille Hall in Blackhall Place.

Seán Kennedy; he was at Church Street Bridge.

John Kenny; he was in Columcille Hall in Blackhall Place and the Monks' Bakery. Then he went to the Four Courts.

Patrick Killion; he was in North King Street and St John's Convent in Church Street at North Brunswick Street.

Capt. Nicholas Laffan; O/C of G Company. His force set up barricades across North Brunswick Street and occupied buildings on North King Street and Brunswick Street. He set a barricade from Moore's coach factory to North Brunswick Street. Seriously wounded when shot in the head in Moore's and evacuated to Fr Mathew Hall.[513]

John Larkin; he was imprisoned at Frongoch.

Francis J. (Frank) Lawlor (brother of Laurence, below); he was in North Brunswick Street and the North Dublin Union and was imprisoned at Frongoch.

John (Seán) Lawlor; he was in the Four Courts and was imprisoned until August.

Laurence James (Larry) Lawlor (brother of Francis, above); he was in the Linenhall Barracks and the Broadstone Railway Station and was imprisoned at Frongoch.

Thomas Leahy; a shipyard worker, he moved to England but moved back to Dublin in 1914 after war was declared. An ICA man, he was involved in the attack on the Magazine Fort, then served in Fairview, Ballybough and the O'Connell Street area. Imprisoned at Frongoch.[514]

Peter Ledwith; he was at Church Street Bridge.

Robert Leggett; he was at Church Street Bridge. Imprisoned at Frongoch.

Michael Lennon; Four Courts. His house at 5 Church Street Upper was taken over by Volunteers led by Peadar Clancy. Lennon was wounded but survived, after having his wound dressed by Brigid Lyons (Thornton) in his own home. Imprisoned at Frongoch.[515]

Nicholas Lennon; he was at Church Street Bridge.

George Levins; he was one of the Fianna garrison at the Mendicity Institute who surrendered on Wednesday.

Arnold Lowe; he was in the Four Courts and was imprisoned until August.

Charles Lynch; he was in the Four Courts.

Capt. Fionan Lynch (Fionan Ó Loinsigh, Ó Loingaigh); Four Courts. He was in command of F Company, and set up the first barricade on Upper Church Street.

He was a prisoner in Mountjoy in 1917 when Tom Ashe was carried away to be force-fed. Lynch cried out, 'Stick it, Tom'. Ashe replied, 'I'll stick it, Fin'.[516] A TD for Kerry South from 1918, he was the Minister for Education in the first Irish Free State government, and then Minister for Fisheries. In early 1919, Lynch was in Strangeways Prison in Manchester with Piaras Béaslaí and Austin Stack, among others. After Lynch got out, he wrote a coded message to Béaslaí and Stack, telling them how to escape. He wrote that he had 'studied the syllabus' and he was satisfied that 'the examination could be passed quite easily'. He had laid the plan for escape before Michael Collins, who took it up. It was decided to send Rory O'Connor to Manchester. To advise Béaslaí and Stack of developments, a letter was received by them from 'Cousin Maud', marked as from a convent school in Lancashire, informing them that 'We are all busy preparing for the examination. Professor Rory has arrived. He is a very nice man.'[517] They successfully escaped in October 1919.

Gilbert Lynch; he was in North King Street.

Michael Lynch (Miceal Ó Loinsigh); he was in the Four Courts. He was interned until August.

Charles (Charlie) Lyons; he was in the Four Courts. Imprisoned at Frongoch.

Edward Lyons; he was in the Four Courts. Imprisoned at Frongoch.

John E. Lyons; he was in the Four Courts. Imprisoned at Frongoch.

Joseph Lyons; he was in Fr Mathew Hall.

Joseph MacDonagh; he was at Columcille Hall in Blackhall Street and Church Street Bridge. He was building a barricade in Hammond Lane when he was approached by Fr O'Callahan from the nearby St Paul's Church on Arran Quay. Fr O'Callahan could see nothing but evil in the Rising and told the barricade-builders, 'You are all going to hell for this'.

M. McAntee (MacMeachtaigh?); he was in the Four Courts.

Patrick McArdle; he was at Church Street Bridge and the Bridewell in Chancery Street.

Frank McCabe; he was in North King Street.

Michael McCabe; Four Courts. He was captured but was released because of his age (he was sixteen). He subsequently joined the British Army and fought in France.

Thomas Joseph McCann; he was in Church Street.

Daniel McCarthy; he was in the Four Courts.

Christopher J. McCormack; he was in Moore's Coach Builders.

John McCormack; Four Courts. He was one of a small detachment sent towards the North Dublin Union; they were pinned down for several hours by heavy British fire.

Andy MacDonald; he was a member of the Fianna.

Thomas McDonnell; he was in Church Street.

Louis McEvatt; Four Courts. He was one of a small detachment sent towards the North Dublin Union; they were pinned down for several hours by heavy British fire.

Christopher McEvoy; he came in from north Dublin and was in the Four Courts.

Joseph McGill; he was at Church Street Bridge.

Edward (Eunan) MacGinley; a member of the Fianna, he was imprisoned at Frongoch.

Frank McGuinness (brother of Joseph, below); Four Courts. He was an uncle of Brigid Lyons (Thornton) and was wounded in Gardiner Place.

Lt Joseph McGuinness (brother of Frank, above); an uncle of Brigid Lyons (Thornton). He was in command of the first twenty Volunteers sent to take the Four Courts; they stormed the Chancery Street entrance. He won the South Longford election on 9 May 1917 while imprisoned in Lewes Gaol: 'Put him *in* to get him *out*' was the election slogan.

Michael McHugh; he was in Church Street.

William McKeon; he was at Church Street Bridge and North King Street.

Owen McKeown; he was in Moore's Coach Builders in North Brunswick Street. Imprisoned at Frongoch.

Peter McLaughlin; Four Courts.

John (Seán) McLoughlin (MacLoughlin) (16); he was a messenger, often shuttling between the Mendicity Institute and the GPO. (Counted in the 1st Battalion garrison.) He was appointed a commandant by Connolly and was in command of a group of 30 assigned to take the *Irish Independent* offices on Thursday afternoon.[518] Connolly led them to the *Independent* and was wounded in the ankle. Imprisoned at Frongoch.[519] (Some report that MacLoughlin was later promoted to 'Commandant-General by Connolly, and thus it was he, not de Valera, who was the highest-ranking survivor of 1916'.[520]) His father, Patrick 'Ruggie' McLoughlin, was a leader in the Lockout of 1913 and helped organise the union. In 1921 Seán helped Roddy Connolly to found the Communist Party of Ireland. He fought on the anti-Treaty side during the Civil War and was imprisoned in Mountjoy Prison.

Peter McMahon; Four Courts.

Maighnas MacMearigh (McMerry); he was in the Four Courts.

Francis Joseph McMenamy; he was in Blackhall Street, Dorset Street and North Brunswick Street.

Manus McMenamy; he was in Blackhall Street, North Brunswick Street and Fr Mathew Hall.

Joseph McMenarigh; Four Courts.

Francis (Frank) McNally; he was in the Four Courts. Imprisoned at Frongoch.

Peter McNally; he was one of those guarding Bulmer Hobson on Sunday 23 and Monday 24 April following Hobson's kidnapping by the Volunteers. (See Martin Conlon, above.) Following Hobson's release, McNally reported that he tried to rejoin the garrison but was arrested by British military at Binn's Bridge and subsequently interned until December.

James McNamara (MacNamara); he was in North Church Street. On Bloody Sunday, 21 November 1920, he was arrested and charged with the murder of 'Captain Bagly', i.e. Captain G.T. Bagallay, who was killed during that day's attacks on suspected British intelligence operatives in Dublin. Although acquitted, McNamara was interned until December 1921.

Patrick J. McNamara (MacNamara); he was in North King Street and Church Street, and was interned until December.

Patrick McNestry; he was in Church Street.

Michael McNulty; he was in North Brunswick Street and Blackhall Street. Imprisoned at Frongoch.

Peadar Joseph McNulty; he was in North King Street and North Brunswick Street.

Thomas McQuaid; he was in Church Street and King Street.

Patrick Macken; he was at Church Street Bridge.

Michael Magee; he was in North King Street.

Thomas (Tomás) Maguire; he was at the Broadstone Railway Station. Imprisoned at Frongoch.

Louis Maire; he was at the Magazine Fort and is counted in the Four Courts garrison, though he also spent time at the GPO. (R.M. Fox lists him at St Stephen's Green.[521])

**Peter (Peadar) Paul Manning (25);[522] he was shot on Saturday on the top floor of Moore's Coach Factory.[523]

 # James Marks; he came from the 5th Battalion via the GPO and was in the Mendicity Institute. (Counted in the 5th Battalion.)

Christopher Martin; a Fianna member, he was in the Magazine Fort.

Éamon (Edward) Martin; a Fianna member, he lived on Shelbourne Road near Beggar's Bush Barracks. He was in the Magazine Fort.[524] Later he was shot through the lung while reconnoitring Broadstone Station.[525] He received the maximum pension of £350 per year.

Frank Mason; he was at Church Street Bridge.

George Mason; he was in the Four Courts.

Henry Meade; he was in King Street and Church Street.

Walter Meade; he was in North Brunswick Street and the North Dublin Union, and was imprisoned at Frongoch.

William Christopher Meade; he was in Red Cow Lane and the North Dublin Union. Imprisoned at Frongoch.

 # William Meehan; came from the 5th Battalion via the GPO and was in the Mendicity Institute. (Counted in the 5th Battalion.)

Herbert Charles (Barney) Mellows; a Fianna member. In the taking of the Magazine Fort, he went with Garry Holohan to take care of the sentry on the parapet. He went in the group to 5 Church Street. Imprisoned at Frongoch.

Michael Merrigan; he was in the Four Courts.

Thomas Merrigan; he was in May Lane and King Street.

Michael Mervyn; he was tried on 3 May and was sentenced to death, but that was commuted to ten years' penal servitude. He lived at 54 Bayview Avenue, North Strand, or 590 North Circular Road.

Philip Monaghan; imprisoned at Frongoch.

Thomas Joseph Monroe; he was in Blackhall Place and then the Four Courts.

John Francis Mooney; he was at the Magazine Fort and then Church Street. (He had gone to the GPO but is counted in the 1st Battalion garrison.)

Patrick Mooney; Four Courts. Imprisoned at Frongoch.

John W. Moore; he was at Cabra Bridge. His death was attributed to ill-treatment by the British Army while a prisoner.

John Morgan; he was in Blackhall Place and North King Street.

Éamonn (Ned) Morkan; Battalion Quartermaster, Four Courts. Along with Piaras Béaslaí, he hauled boxes of ammunition from Fr Mathew Hall to the Four Courts when Daly moved his HQ there. Imprisoned at Frongoch.

Andrew J. Mulhall; assigned to the 1st Battalion, he was a scout and reported to the GPO. He was arrested on Tuesday but released. (Counted in the 1st Battalion garrison.)

Andrew Mulligan; ICA. He was interned until December.

James Joseph Mulkearns; he was in North King Street and Cuckoo Lane. He was imprisoned at Frongoch, where he was known as 'the Rajah of Frongoch', after the drama company in the prison camp, in which he played a leading role.

Michael Mullen; he was imprisoned at Frongoch.

Peter Mullen; he was in North King Street and Church Street.

Thomas J. Munroe; he lived at 7 Little Denmark Street.

William (Liam) Murnane; Mendicity Institute. He was one of the first into the building and helped barricade the windows. Imprisoned at Frongoch.

Bernard (Barney) Murphy; he was in Church Street and the Four Courts.

Colm Murphy; he was imprisoned at Frongoch.

Edward Murphy; he was in Fr Mathew Hall.

Frederick Charles Murphy; he was in North King Street and Hammond Lane. Imprisoned at Frongoch.

Gregory Murphy; he was a Dublin IRB centre. In the weeks preceding the Rising, he assisted in the distribution of arms throughout the Dublin area and in general preparations for the Rising. He avoided arrest and assisted in the removal of war material, wounded and hospital staff from Fr Mathew Hall following the surrender.[526] He received the maximum pension of £350 per year.

Hubert Joseph Murphy; he was in Upper Church Street and North King Street. Imprisoned at Frongoch.

John (Seán) Murphy; a member of the Fianna, he was in the Magazine Fort. Imprisoned at Frongoch.[527]

Martin Murphy; he was at Church Street Bridge and Camden Row. Imprisoned at Frongoch.

Michael Murphy (Mícheál Ó Murchadha); he was in Columcille Hall and North King Street.

Michael Murphy; he was in Church Street and North Brunswick Street.

William Murphy; he was one of a small detachment of Volunteers in Lagan's public house and was in North King Street. Along with Volunteers William Hogan, John Dwan, John Williamson and Thomas Sherrin, he watched a makeshift British armoured vehicle (actually a Guinness boiler mounted on a lorry body) come up North King Street and fire a broadside at the Volunteers. This began the battle on the street, which was the most sustained fighting of the week. The British use of the armoured 'car' kept their casualties down, and the Volunteers used the opportunity to bore through building walls to keep under cover.[528]

Joseph Michael Murray; he was in the Four Courts.[529] He was a courier back and forth from the GPO. 'Each day I marked on a map for Joe Plunkett the overnight positions of the British Forces.'

Laurence Joseph Murtagh; he was at Church Street Bridge. Imprisoned at Frongoch.

Patrick Murtagh; he was at Jameson's Distillery and King Street.

Denis Joseph Musgrave; Four Courts. He was interned until July.

Denis Neary; he was in the Four Courts.

Joseph Neary; he was imprisoned at Frongoch.

Arthur James Neilan; Four Courts. In one of the cruel ironies of the Rising, his older brother, Lt Gerald Neilan of the Royal Dublin Fusiliers, was one of the first casualties when the British attacked the Mendicity Institute.

Patrick Nevin; he was in Church Street. Imprisoned at Frongoch.

Thomas Francis Nolan (Tomas Ó Nuallain); he was in North Brunswick Street and the Monks' Bakery.

Christopher Noonan; he was in Church Street and North Brunswick Street.

 # Joseph Norton; came from the 5th Battalion via the GPO and was in the Mendicity Institute. (Counted in the 5th Battalion.)

John O'Brian (Seán Ó Briain); a member of the Fianna, he was in the Magazine Fort and then the Four Courts.

John O'Brien (Seán Ó Briain); he was at Church Street Bridge.

Joseph O'Brien (Seosamh Ó Broin); he was in the Mendicity Institute.

Michael O'Brien; at King Street and Church Street and went to St Stephen's Green.

Patrick J. O'Brien; he was in Blackhall Place and North Brunswick Street.

Thomas O'Brien; he was a scout throughout the area.

Thomas O'Brien; he was in North Brunswick Street and Church Street.

Thomas O'Brien (Tomas Ó Briain); he was in the Four Courts. Imprisoned in Frongoch.

Charles (Cathal) O'Byrne; he was imprisoned at Frongoch.

William O'Byrne; he was imprisoned at Frongoch.

Capt. Denis (Dinny, Duncan?) O'Callahan (Donnchadh Ó Ceallachain); an early Fianna member, he joined the IRB in 1901 and became a centre in 1908. He recruited for the IRB from then until the Rising. He established a drill centre at the offices of the *Irish Freedom*, 5 Findlater Place, and drilled Volunteers there after 1913. In 1914 he took his motor boat north from Dublin with orders to tow in Erskine Childers's yacht *Asgard* if it could not make it into Howth Harbour.

A deputy to Daly, he commanded A Company.[530] On Tuesday a small group of about twelve men, under the command of O'Callahan, were ordered by Daly to occupy Broadstone Railway Station, at the top of Constitution Hill. Included in this group were two senior Fianna officers, Dublin Fianna Commandant Éamon Martin and Capt. Garry Holohan. The Volunteers in the party included, amongst others, Peadar Breslin, Seán Cody and Nicholas Laffan. The original plan was to take this position at the beginning of hostilities but it was postponed until Tuesday, by which time a small detachment of British forces had occupied the station. Before the men set out on their mission they were blessed by Fr Albert in front of St John's Convent, and the Sisters of St Vincent de Paul prayed for their safe return.

Leading the mission were Martin and Holohan. They advanced up the road with fixed bayonets. As they approached the station, Holohan noticed a dark figure running behind the entrance of the building. It was getting dark and it was hard to make out whether it was an enemy soldier or a fellow Volunteer. Holohan shouted back to the others that there was somebody ahead. Martin moved to Holohan's right side and tried to look inside the building. As he moved further along for a closer look, a sniper fired upon their position. Martin was hit by a rifle shot, which went through his chest, and almost instantly he began bleeding heavily; nevertheless, he managed to run back a short distance to a relatively safer position, where he collapsed on the ground. His comrades lifted him up and retreated back down the hill, but they were subjected to enemy fire as they made their way back. Two Volunteers, Nicholas Laffan and George Butler, covered their retreat and they managed to get back safely. Martin was brought to Richmond Hospital, where his wounds were treated.[531]

Later O'Callahan led the assault on the Linenhall Barracks and demanded the surrender of the British occupying it.[532] When they refused, the Volunteers set bombs at the gate; finally the British did surrender, and the barracks was set on fire. Thirty-two clerks and a policeman surrendered and were taken to Fr Mathew Hall as prisoners. The fires were difficult to control, and although the Volunteers tried to extinguish them they burned until after the Rising was over.[533] He was imprisoned in Portland Prison until Christmas 1916, then sent to Lewes Prison and finally back to Portland, from where he was released in June 1917.

John Stephen O'Carroll; he was in Church Street and May Lane.

Michael O'Carroll (brother of Peter and William, below); he was in Blackhall Street, North Brunswick Street and North King Street.

Peter (Peadar) James O'Carroll (brother of Michael and William); he was in Blackhall Street and North King Street.

Robert J. O'Carroll; he was at Church Street Bridge and then the Four Courts. Imprisoned at Frongoch.

Seán O'Carroll; he was in Church Street and then the Four Courts. Imprisoned at Frongoch.

Lt William (Liam) O'Carroll (Liam Ó Cearbhaill) (brother of Michael and Peter, above); Four Courts. He used his revolver to blow the lock off the gate at Cullen's Builders' Yard, and his men hauled lorries and building material to erect a barricade across Red Cow Lane.[534] He observed a group of civilians trying to force their way into the Monks' Bakery, and detailed Volunteers to guard the bakery and its workers. Imprisoned at Frongoch.

M. Ó Conallan; Four Courts.

Mortimer O'Connell (Mort Ó Conaill); he was on sentry duty near Smithfield, and was often a courier back to Daly's HQ with news of the British troops massing in that area. Later he was in a unit trying to reinforce the Volunteers in Clarke's and Moore's Coach Factory, and finally had to turn back to the Four Courts.[535] He became chief clerk of Dáil Éireann.

Patrick John (Seán) O'Connell; he was in the Four Courts and was engaged in intelligence-gathering.

Fergus O'Connor; he was in Church Street and was imprisoned until July 1917.

James S. O'Connor (brother of Patrick and Thomas); he was in the Four Courts. Imprisoned at Frongoch.

John Stephen O'Connor; he was in May Lane and Church Street. Imprisoned at Frongoch.

Patrick J. O'Connor (brother of Thomas, below); he was at Church Street Bridge and then the Four Courts. Imprisoned at Frongoch.

Thomas (Tommy) O'Connor (brother of Patrick, above); he was in North King Street and Church Street. Imprisoned at Frongoch.

Michael O'Dea; Four Courts. He was severely wounded by a sniper firing from the Bermingham Tower in Dublin Castle.[536]

William O'Dea; he was one of the Fianna garrison at the Mendicity Institute who surrendered on Wednesday.

Fionan O'Doherty; Four Courts.

Florence J. O'Doherty; in the days immediately preceding the Rising, O'Doherty was entrusted by Thomas Clarke with the task of securing IRB funds, as well as serving as one of the Irish Volunteers holding Bulmer Hobson prisoner. (See Martin Conlon, above.) He evaded arrest/capture following the Rising.

Liam O'Doherty; he was in North King Street.

Cornelius (Con) O'Donovan (Ó Donnaghain, Ó Donnobhain); he was in Blackhall Street and North King Street. On Holy Saturday he had been one of those detailed to guard Bulmer Hobson. (See Martin Conlon, above.) While he was at his position in the Four Courts, an artillery shell hit the roof, which collapsed on him. Those who were buried in the rubble were finally pulled out.

Lt Seán Martin O'Duffy; Four Courts. When he mustered at Columcille Hall, he heard Cmdt Daly tell the Volunteers that an Irish Republic was to be declared that day and that the men would be required to defend it with their lives—but that if any man couldn't do so, he could withdraw and nothing would be said.[537] He was in Moore's Coach Factory when it was attacked by a wave of British troops, and was imprisoned at Frongoch. He became the registrar of the Republican Courts.

Francis (Frank) O'Flanagan; he was at Church Street Bridge. Imprisoned at Frongoch.

George O'Flanagan; he was in Blackhall Place and was imprisoned at Frongoch. 'Ned Daly addressed us from a platform at one end of the hall and said "Now, boys, the time has come which you are all wishing for when you have the chance of striking a blow for Irish Freedom".'[538]

Maurice O'Flanagan; Four Courts.

Michael O'Flanagan (brother of Patrick, below); Four Courts. He was a section commander who led his men on a search of the Bridewell. They found two Lancers in one of the cells and took them to the Four Courts as prisoners. They also found 23 members of the DMP in the basement; they were taken to the Four Courts and interrogated, then released. O'Flanagan's men also released two prisoners—a man and a woman—who were being held on charges of being drunk and disorderly.[539]

Patrick Joseph O'Flanagan (25);[540] he volunteered to run from Reilly's Fort to Fr Mathew Hall for ammunition but was killed on the return journey.[541] He was sent out in a desperate attempt, as the men were determined to keep fighting to the very end of their ammunition.[542]

Liam O'Gorman; he was in the Four Courts.

Bernard O'Hanlon; he was in Church Street.

Patrick O'Hanlon; he was in Church Street, the Bow Street Distillery and Blackhall Street. Imprisoned at Frongoch.

Jeremiah O'Healy; he was in the Linenhall Barracks and Broadstone Railway Station.

Lt Diarmuid O'Hegarty (Hegarty) (Ó hEigeartaigh); Four Courts. A Cork man, he became a director of organisation for the IRA. He became a member of Michael Collins's 'Squad'.

Michael O'Kelly; he was in the Four Courts. Imprisoned at Frongoch.

Thomas O'Kelly; he was in the Mendicity Institute, and was imprisoned until June 1917.

Patrick Joseph O'Leary; he was in North Brunswick Street and Cuckoo Lane. Imprisoned at Frongoch.

Miceal Ó Lorgas; he is listed on the Roll of Honour.

Seán O'Mahoney; he was imprisoned at Frongoch.

Robert (Bob) Oman; he was at the Linenhall Barracks. The uncle of William (City Hall) and George (GPO), he was imprisoned in Staffordshire Prison after the Rising. Bob was a lieutenant and later captain of G Company, 1st Battalion, Dublin Brigade, until his imprisonment during the Civil War. His health suffered terribly at that time and he was confined to a convalescent home for the remainder of his life.

Seán O'Moore; he was in North Brunswick Street, North King Street, Broadstone Railway Station and the Linenhall Barracks. In 1948 he unsuccessfully ran for the Dáil as a National Labour Party candidate from this very district.

Charles O'Neill; he was in North King Street.

Joseph O'Neill; he was in North King Street, North Brunswick Street and Red Cow Lane. Imprisoned at Frongoch.

Michael Edward O'Neill; he was in North Brunswick Street and North King Street. Imprisoned at Frongoch.

Patrick O'Neill; he was at Church Street Bridge.

Patrick Francis O'Neill; he was in Church Street. Imprisoned at Frongoch.

William O'Neill; he was in the Four Courts. Imprisoned at Frongoch.

Michael O'Reardon; he was in North King Street.

Luke O'Reilly; he was at Church Street Bridge.

Peter O'Reilly; he was in North Brunswick Street and Red Cow Lane.

Samuel Patrick (Sam) O'Reilly; brother of Kevin (GPO), Desmond (GPO) and Thomas. On Monday night he was put in charge of a detail to blow up the Midland Railway lines near Broadstone Station; they cut telegraph lines and destroyed the signal system but not the railroad. The official report described their work:

> During Monday night troops had been ordered over the line and the rebels, having become aware of this, prepared to wreck expected troop trains. An abortive effort to destroy a culvert near the Liffey Junction was made, and during the early hours of the morning, the cattle special, proceeding in advance of the troop train, was derailed and wrecked. On the same morning an engine in steam at the Broadstone was seized by the rebels and placed on the up-line, and started, those in charge jumping off as soon as the engine began to gather speed. This would have resulted in disaster if the locomotive had met a troop train coming from the opposite direction but it was thrown off the line at the Liffey Junction points. In consequence of this derailment, the troop trains could not come into the city. All telegraph wires were cut and service from Dublin was completely suspended.[543]

He went to the GPO on Tuesday. Imprisoned at Frongoch.

Thomas O'Reilly (brother of Samuel, above); he was in Blackhall Place. Imprisoned at Frongoch.

Thomas O'Reilly; he was in North Brunswick Street and Broadstone Railway Station.

—— **Ó Snodaigh**; he is listed on the Roll of Honour.

Miceal Ó Srollaigh; he is listed on the Roll of Honour.

Capt. James (Séamus) O'Sullivan; Battalion Adjutant. He occupied positions on the Cabra Road and South Circular Road, then went to the GPO. (Counted here in the Four Courts garrison.)[544]

John O'Sullivan; he was in Blackhall Place and North Brunswick Street.

Bernard Parker; a member of the Fianna, he was in the Magazine Fort and North Brunswick Street.

 # Thomas Peppard; he came from the 5th Battalion via the GPO. (Counted in the 5th Battalion.) He spent Easter Monday night guarding the road near Blanchardstown; although the railway was damaged nearby, he did not take part in any action. On Tuesday morning he was detailed to proceed into Dublin city in order to reinforce Volunteer units there. After reporting to the GPO, he was posted to the Mendicity Institute. He remained in the Mendicity Institute until Wednesday, when it had to be evacuated after coming under heavy attack by the British and the Volunteers were forced to surrender. He was detained in Kilmainham Gaol, was sentenced to death— commuted to three years' penal servitude—and was transported to Portland Prison, UK. After a spell in Portland he was transferred to Lewes Jail.

James P. Plunkett; he was in Blackhall Place, in North King Street and at Church Street Bridge.

Frank Dominic Pollard; he was in Church Street and then the Four Courts. Imprisoned at Frongoch.

Stephen Patrick Pollard; Four Courts.

Seán Prendergast; he was in the Four Courts and was interned until August.

Albert Sylvester Rawley; he was at the Cabra Road Bridge and went to Columcille Hall in Blackhall Place.

(Timothy) John Redmond; he was at Moore's Coach Builders and was imprisoned at Frongoch.

Laurence Regan; he was an engineer and was in the Four Courts.

John James (Seán) Reid; he was in the Four Courts and was interned until June.

Joseph Francis Reynolds; a Fianna member, he was often sent as a messenger to the GPO. Late in the week he was sent to reconnoitre the Capel Street area and found that it was held by the British; he was sent to the GPO with this information and then made his way back to Daly's HQ.[545]

John Richmond; he was in Columcille Hall in Blackhall Place and Cleary's pub in Church Street. Imprisoned at Frongoch.

Edward Joseph (Eddie) Roach (de Roiste); Mendicity Institute. He took his position at the windows to fire onto the quays.

Joseph Roche (Roach); he was in the Mendicity Institute and Blackhall Place.

Liam Roche (de Roiste); he was one of the Fianna garrison at the Mendicity Institute who surrendered on Wednesday.[546]

Michael Joseph Roche; he was in Jameson's Distillery in Bow Street. Imprisoned at Frongoch.

Timothy (Tim) Roche; he commandeered the jaunting car for the Fianna escape from the Magazine Fort. He was to have commandeered a car, and did, but did not know how to drive it; after driving it into a lamppost, he went to get the hackney. Paddy Daly, Éamonn Martin, Barney Mellows, Seán Ó Briain, Paddy Holohan and Jack Murphy all climbed aboard the cab, while the others took off on foot or on their bicycles.

William Ryan (Liam S. Ó Riain); he was in Blackhall Place.

William Ryan; he was in Fr Mathew Hall and at Capel Street Bridge.

Michael Saunders; he was in North Brunswick Street and Blackhall Place.

Leo Patrick Scullen; he was at Cabra Bridge, then came to Blackhall Place.

Michael Scully (Mícheál Ó Scollaighe); he was in the Mendicity Institute and Blackhall Place.

William Scully; he was in North King Street and Church Street.

Thomas P. Sheerin; he was one of a small detachment of Volunteers in Lagan's public house and was in North King Street. Along with Volunteers William Murphy, William Hogan, John Williamson and John Dwan, he watched a makeshift British armoured vehicle (actually a Guinness boiler mounted on a lorry body) come up North King Street and fire a broadside at the Volunteers. This began the battle on the street, which was the most sustained fighting of the week. The British use of the armoured 'car' kept their casualties down, and the Volunteers used the opportunity to bore through building walls to keep under cover.[547]

Charles Shelly; he was in North King Street and Broadstone Railway Station.

James Sheridan; Four Courts. Imprisoned at Frongoch.

John Sheridan; he came from the GPO and was in the Four Courts.

Henry (Harry) Shiels; he was at North King Street, then Church Street, and then at the Linenhall Barracks in Lisburn Street.

Seán Shortall; he was a coachbuilder and escaped capture after the Rising.

William Shortall; he was in North King Street.

Frank Shouldice; in Fr Mathew Hall: 'It was a terrible slaughter'. Younger brother of Jack (below), his men occupied the Jameson's Malt House, from which he was a very effective sniper, firing from a perch on the Jameson's Tower.[548] Imprisoned at Frongoch.

Lt John Francis (Jack) Shouldice; commanded the Volunteers who occupied the very strategic position at Reilly's public house ('Reilly's Fort') at the intersection of North King Street and Church Street.[549]

Liam Siuptal; he was in the Four Courts.

Lawrence Slevin; he was a Land Leaguer and member of the IRB from Offaly. He was wounded in the leg while escaping from the Four Courts and running across Fr Mathew Bridge, and he limped for the rest of his life. He was taken to Richmond Hospital, and the staff there helped him to escape capture.

Thomas Smart; Four Courts. He and Peadar Clancy took cans of petrol across Church Street Bridge and burned out buildings on the south side of the bridge, forcing the British to evacuate. He was later sent to the Bridewell as one of the reinforcements on the roof, where they had a fine view of the South Staffordshire troops advancing, and many were shot to pieces in their advance.

Henry Vincent Staines; he was in North King Street.

James Staines; he was in Church Street.

William F. (Liam) Staines; Mendicity Institute. On Wednesday the Institute was heavily attacked by British forces, who were able to get close enough to throw hand-grenades. One grenade entered a room occupied by several Volunteers; Staines attempted to throw the grenade out the window but it exploded before he was able to get rid of it and he was badly wounded.

Patrick Joseph (Paddy Joe) Stephenson; Mendicity Institute. Taking his position at the windows, he was challenged by a DMP man who told the Volunteers to 'quit going so far with this playing of soldiers'. After the policeman was told to 'get the hell off' and didn't move, Stephenson fired a shot in his general direction and the policeman 'shot off down the quays so quickly that his helmet fell off his head'.[550] Stephenson and Heuston were at the window, trying to light the fuses on their canister bombs, but the bombs refused to light. His father, Patrick Stephenson Snr, a civilian, was killed on 24 April 1916 and is buried in Glasnevin Cemetery. His brother, Edward, was serving with the British army in France; he returned to Dublin on compassionate leave shortly thereafter but never returned to duty in the British army.[551] Paddy was imprisoned in Knutsford Jail and Frongoch, and became chief librarian of Dublin City. He was greatly involved in the restoration of Kilmainham Gaol.

Capt. James J. Sullivan (Séamus O'Sullivan); O/C of B Company and Battalion Adjutant. He erected barricades on North Circular Road and on Cabra Road. His men tried to destroy the Cabra Bridge but were unsuccessful. The men withdrew to Glasnevin, and some later managed to link up with the 5th Battalion in north

Dublin.[552] Sullivan went to the GPO. (Counted in the Four Courts garrison.)[553]

Patrick Joseph (Paddy) Swan; deported after the Rising. His brother was in the GPO.

James Joseph Sweeney; he was in the Four Courts.

Éamonn Tierney; from London. On the escape from North King Street he 'fetched the flag' that was still flying on the lance that had been planted in the street on Monday and was unscathed.

Michael Tierney; he is listed on the Roll of Honour.

Liam Tobin; Four Courts. 'Commandant Ned Daly was in the hall in Blackhall Place and, just before we left, he addressed us and told us we were going out to fight. As well as I can remember he said that if there was anybody who did not feel like going out to fight they could leave, but I think they all stood firm. I have an idea that perhaps one or two did back out, but in the main, all stood firm.'[554] He became one of Michael Collins's most trusted lieutenants and a member of his 'Squad'.

Michael Tobin; he was in the Four Courts.

Fr Aloysius Travers, OFM; the Fr Mathew Feis was scheduled during Easter Week, and a small boy was shot on Monday afternoon in the Hall. The children were quickly rounded up and placed under the stage for safety, and from that time on Fr Aloysius helped in the Fr Mathew Hall, which was quickly turned into a hospital by the Volunteers and Cumann na mBan.[555]

Edward Travers; he was in North King Street.

Daniel Tynan; he was in the Magazine Fort and Columcille Hall.

James Walsh; he was in North King Street and Broadstone Railway Station. Imprisoned at Frongoch.

**Philip Walsh (Walshe) (27);[556] he was in the Four Courts. He was a section commander and was killed on Saturday at the head of a unit reconnoitring Church Street.[557] They were to occupy Broadstone Station but did not have enough men, so they took up positions in the area. On Saturday his small group of men was trapped in Clarke's Dairy on North King Street, and he was killed on a reconnaissance mission to Reilly's Fort after Pearse's surrender to Gen. Lowe.

Thomas Walsh; he was in Cleary's public house in Church Street.

George Ward; he was in the Bow Street Distillery.

Seán Ward; he was in Moore's Coach Builders in North Brunswick Street.

James Weldon; he was imprisoned at Frongoch.

George Whelan; he was in Blackhall Place. Imprisoned at Frongoch.

William Whelan; a member of D Company, he was imprisoned at Frongoch.[558]

John Joseph Williams; he was in North King Street.

John Williamson; he was one of a small detachment of Volunteers in Lagan's public house and was in North King Street. Along with Volunteers William Murphy, William Hogan, Thomas Sherrin and John Dwan, he watched a makeshift British armoured vehicle (actually a Guinness boiler mounted on a lorry body) come up North King Street and fire a broadside at the Volunteers. This began the battle on the street that was the most sustained fighting of the week. The British use of the armoured 'car' kept their casualties down, and the Volunteers used the opportunity to bore through building walls to keep under cover.[559]

 # James Wilson; came from the 5th Battalion via the GPO. (Counted in the 5th Battalion.) He was in the Mendicity Institute.

Mark Wilson; he was in the Four Courts. Imprisoned at Frongoch.

#**Peter Wilson (40);[560] a Swords Volunteer, he was sent first to the GPO and then to the Mendicity Institute. A British sniper killed him when the Volunteers were being formed up to leave the Mendicity Institute after surrender.[561] (Counted in the 5th Battalion.) Wilson was unmarried and lived with his widowed mother, two brothers, William and John, and a sister, Molly. He worked for the County Council as a road worker, earning £2 a week, and was the principal earner in the household. His brother William was incapacitated by a spinal disorder and John's work was infrequent. The family had to rely on the Irish National Aid and Volunteers' Dependants' Fund until the 1930s, when William was granted a pension by the state on the basis that he had been a dependant of the deceased. His mother had died by the time the pension was awarded.

Wilson is interred in the grounds of Dr Steevens's Hospital along with another Volunteer, Seán Owens, who was killed while fighting at the South Dublin Union.

 # William Wilson; came from the 5th Battalion via the GPO. (Counted in the 5th Battalion.) He was in the Mendicity Institute.

Thomas Yourell; he was in Queen Street, Church Street and the Hay Market.

1ST BATTALION: WOMEN

Margaret Byrne (Copeland); she was in the Four Courts.

Mary Byrne; during the Rising she was in the Michael Dwyer Club, Skippers Alley, opposite the Four Courts. She was involved in carrying ammunition daily from her own home and from Mícheál Staines's home (Murtagh Road) to the barricades, and was also involved in cooking for the Volunteers (principally at Glynn's Builders Yard).

Máire (May, Meg) Carron (Máire McCarron); she was arrested after the Rising and was sent to Kilmainham Gaol and Richmond Barracks.

Mrs (Martin) Peig Conlon (Peig Bean Uí Channallan [Callanan]); she was in the Four Courts. She carried Eoin MacNeill's cancellation order to Galway, and then the message that the Rising was to go ahead.[562]

Katie Daly (Beatty); she is listed on the Roll of Honour.

Margaret (Maggie, Kate?) Derham (Durham?) (Mulligan); she and Brigid Lyons went from the Four Courts to set up a canteen and first-aid station at 5 Church Street Upper. She had met Áine Ní Riain on Tuesday and they had gone to the GPO, but then Maggie volunteered to go to the Four Courts because her brother, Michael, was in that area.[563]

Eilís Elliott (Ní Briain); she was in the Four Courts and Fr Mathew Hall. After the surrender she slept in the Hall, and then left on Sunday morning with the other churchgoers.[564]

Emily Elliott (Ledwith); she was in the Four Courts and Fr Mathew Hall. After the surrender she slept in the Hall, and then left on Sunday morning with the other churchgoers.

Ellen (Nellie) Ennis (Costigan); she was in the Four Courts and was imprisoned.

Anna (Mrs Frank) Fahy; she was in the Four Courts. She had been sent to Athenry with Pearse's message: 'Collect the premiums, 7 pm, Sunday'.[565] Her husband was mobilised and she went to Blackhall Place on Monday and to the GPO the following day. She was sent to the Four Courts. She joined others on Church Street in Fr Mathew Hall. She stayed in the Four Courts until the surrender.

Mary Christina Hayes (O'Gorman); she was in the Four Courts and was put in charge of the first-aid station at Fr Mathew Hall, on Church Street.

Cathleen Healy; Four Courts. A member of the Hibernian Rifles, she was mobilised on Sunday at the Hibernian Hall and the following day at St Stephen's Green. She was sent by Tim O'Neill to collect things at St Mary's Road and to Gardiner Street (to Tom Clifford's place). She collected more goods to bring them to Cabra. She carried dispatches and also helped with the cooking and first-aid work at Fr Mathew Hall. Her brother, Seán Healy, was killed during the Rising.[566] On Tuesday he had reported to Jacob's. He was given an urgent dispatch to carry to Phibsborough Bridge, but was shot on the way.[567] The youngest Fianna/Volunteer to be killed, he died at the Mater Hospital on 27 April. Cathleen was dismissed from her employment on 3 May.

Teresa Healy (Byrne); she started out in Croyden Park, then came to the Four Courts.

Áine Heron; a captain in Cumann na mBan, she was married in 1912 and had two children and another on the way when the Rising started. She set up a first-aid station in a small shop on Church Street on the Monday of the Rising; on Tuesday she spent some time in the Hibernian Bank on the corner of Abbey Street and then volunteered to set up a first-aid station in the Four Courts. She left the Four Courts on Wednesday morning to deliver dispatches and was unable to re-enter the Four Courts. After the Rising she worked with the Volunteers' Dependants' Fund and the campaign for the election of Desmond FitzGerald in the 1918 election. She was active in assisting the IRA throughout the War of Independence.[568] Later she became a judge of the Dáil/Republican Courts.

Mary (May) Kavanagh (Duggan); she was in the Four Courts. She spent most of the week nursing in Fr Mathew Hall.

Kathleen Kenny (Hensey?) (Blackburn); she was in the Four Courts and Fr Mathew Hall. After the surrender, she slept in the Hall and then left on Sunday morning with the other churchgoers.

Mary (Mamie) Kilmartin (Stephenson); Four Courts.[569] She married Patrick Joseph (Paddy) Stephenson, who was in the GPO and the Mendicity Institute.

Brighid Lyons (Thornton); she went with Katie Derham from the Four Courts to set up a canteen and first-aid station at 5 Church Street Upper. Imprisoned in Kilmainham Gaol.[570] She became the first female officer in the Medical Corps after the Free State was established in 1922.[571]

Lt Catherine (Katy) McGuinness; she was in the Four Courts. She was the wife of Joe McGuinness and the aunt of Brighid Lyons.

Rose McGuinness; a cousin of Brighid Lyons, she was wounded by flying glass.

Rose McManners; vice-commandant of the Inghinidhe branch of Cumann na mBan and chief cook of the garrison.

Brid S. Martin; she was in the Four Courts.[572]

Kathleen (Kate) Martin; she is listed on the Roll of Honour.

Margaret Martin (Murnane); she was in the Four Courts. She helped with first aid in Fr Mathew Hall.

Florence (Flossie) Meade (Griffin); she was in the Four Courts.

Caroline (Carrie) Mitchell (McLoughlin); as a messenger, she went back and forth between the 1st Battalion and the GPO.

May Moloney (McQuaile); she was in the Four Courts.[573]

Mary Pauline Morkan (Keating); she was in the Four Courts and was imprisoned. 'We had plenty of food in the Four Courts. A man used to go out early every morning, bring in bread, meat and other food for the day. We knew him as "Looter" Flood. We spent all our time in the kitchen, except that we once visited the living quarters where we saw clothes &c. I don't know whose quarters they were. There was no first aid to be done; the hospitals were too near. I am not aware that anyone was wounded in the Four Courts.'[574]

Philomena Morkan (née Lucas); she was a first-aid matron in Fr Mathew Hall.

Phyllis Morkan; a long-time member of Cumann na mBan, she was in the Four Courts.[575]

Elizabeth (Lily) Murnane (Coleton); she was in the Four Courts. She was also in the Michael Dwyer Club off Merchant's Quay, and helped with nursing the wounded.

Eileen (Mrs Séamus) Murphy; her house was used as a storehouse for supplies on Easter Sunday. Some supplies were to be distributed among the 3rd Battalion positioned on Camden Row.

Brigid Murnane (McKeon); she was in the Four Courts. She helped with the cooking in Fr Mathew Hall.

Mary Murray (Allen); she was in the Four Courts.

Josephine Neary (Flood); she reported on Tuesday and stayed until the surrender.

Mary (Dolly) O'Carroll (Lawlor); she was in the Four Courts. She was in the Michael Dwyer Club, Skippers Alley, off Merchant's Quay. She assisted in the carrying of arms, first-aid supplies and dispatches, as well as supplying information regarding the movements of British forces. She was not arrested or interned following the surrender.

Ellen O'Flanagan (Parker); she was in the Four Courts. She was in the hospital in Fr Mathew Hall.

Annie O'Keefe (O'Carroll); she was in the Michael Dwyer Club and the Four Courts. She was Mary (Dolly) O'Carroll (Lawlor)'s sister-in-law, and became Peter O'Carroll's (1st Battalion) wife. She also was in Cumann na mBan with Dolly.

Emily O'Keefe (Hendley); she was in Jameson's Distillery, Marrowbone Lane.

Maura O'Neill (Mackay); she is listed on the Roll of Honour.

Eilís Ní Riain (Bean Uí Chonaill); she was in the Four Courts and Fr Mathew Hall. After the surrender she slept in the Hall, then left on Sunday morning with the other churchgoers.[576]

Louisa (Dolly) O'Sullivan (Pollard); she was in the Four Courts. She started at Cabra Bridge before reporting here. She was imprisoned at Kilmainham.

Mary (Mollie) O'Sullivan (O'Carroll); she was one of the first-aid detachment in the Four Courts.

Eileen Walsh (Murphy); she was in the Four Courts.

IV. 2nd Battalion

On the south side of the River Liffey, Jacob's Biscuit Factory was then located in the buildings that are now occupied by the Dublin Institute of Technology and the National Archives. (The other Dublin battalions had been assigned posts in the areas in which their Volunteer members lived, but the 2nd Battalion was the Dublin north-east battalion. As a result, many of the men who occupied Jacob's were not particularly familiar with their area. Because the 2nd Battalion did not report to a building in its 'area', many men normally assigned to it reported to the GPO.) The Jacob's building was on the route that British troops would take from Portobello Barracks to support Dublin Castle, and the main action for the Jacob's garrison was sniping at Portobello Barracks and other military positions that were overlooked by the two towers in the main factory building. Its outposts on Malpas Street, Fumbally Lane and Camden Street would hinder any city-bound movement from Wellington Barracks on the South Circular Road.

The factory was a massive triangular structure filling most of the area between Peter Street and Bishop Street. It was difficult for the British to assault, as a labyrinth of streets surrounded it and myriad small houses hindered the use of artillery.[577] It had two tall towers, which provided a view over much of the city. MacDonagh posted men in buildings in Camden Street, Wexford Street, Aungier Street and other streets in the area, making Jacob's an even more difficult target for the British military. As 150 men and women invaded the building, they informed the caretaker, Thomas Orr, and the watchman on duty, Henry Fitzgerald, what they were doing, and Orr called George Jacob and the manager, Mr Dawson. Both Jacob and Dawson came to the building, where the Volunteers had assembled all the workers and placed them under guard. After a short time all the workers were released, but Orr remained in his apartment in the building for the duration of the Rising, and Fitzgerald stayed with him.[578]

Within hours of the garrison's take-over, Volunteers on Wexford Street and Camden Street put to flight a company of British soldiers travelling from Portobello Barracks to Dublin Castle.

In addition to Jacob's factory, MacDonagh's men occupied Barmack's Malthouse in Fumbally Lane, as well as positions in Camden Street, Malpas Street and Kevin Street. After the fighting started, however, the outposts were quickly withdrawn to the main Jacob's building.[579] While MacDonagh sent out patrols throughout his area, most

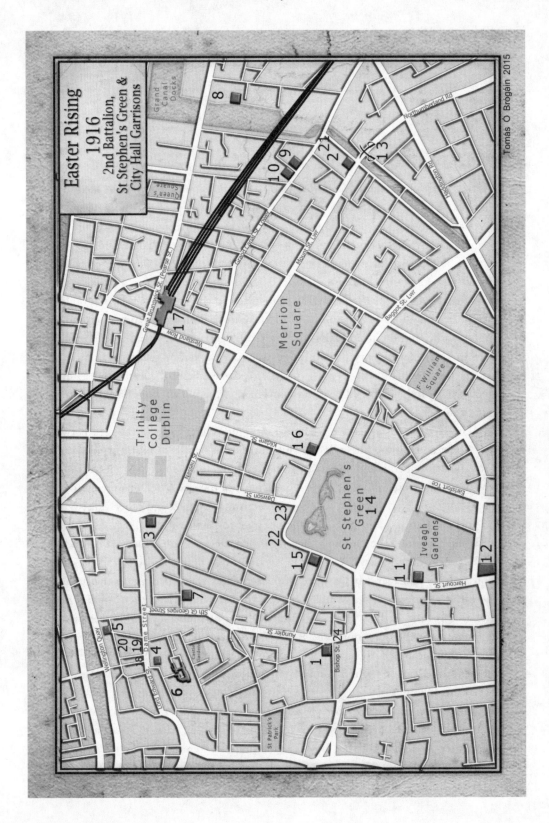

Easter Rising
1916
2nd Battalion,
St Stephen's Green &
City Hall Garrisons

Tomás Ó Brógáin 2015

No.	Address	Site	Description
1	26–50 Bishop St. at corner of Peter Row and Aungier St.	W. & R. Jacob Biscuit Factory	HQ of the Volunteer 2nd Battalion (part of the building is now in Dublin 8).
2	1–2 Clanwilliam Place	Clanwilliam House	Central position of the Volunteers at Mount St. Bridge.
3	College Green	Trinity College Dublin	Field HQ of the British Army.
4	Castle Hill	Dublin City Hall	One of the first positions taken by the Volunteers.
5	6 Crown Alley	Telephone Exchange	Had the Volunteers disabled this at the outset, it would have severely affected British communications.
6	Cork St./Lord Edward St.	Dublin Castle	Administrative centre of British government.
7	10 Exchequer St.	Irish National Aid and Volunteers' Dependants' Fund	After the Rising, it provided funds to survivors and their families.
8	Grand Canal Docks at Ringsend Road	Boland's Mills	Main position of the 3rd Battalion.
9	Grand Canal St.	Boland's Bakery	Main position of the 3rd Battalion.
10	Grand Canal St. and Great Clarence St. (now Macken St.)	Dispensary	HQ of the 3rd Battalion.
11	Harcourt St.	Russell Hotel	Held by the British during the Rising.
12	Harcourt St.	Harcourt St. Railway Station	Volunteers attempted to take it but did not hold it.
13	Mount St. Bridge over the Grand Canal	Mount St. Bridge	Scene of the largest single battle of the Rising.
14	St Stephen's Green	Taken by the ICA at the start of the Rising.	HQ of the ICA in the area.
15	St Stephen's Green and York St.	Royal College of Surgeons	Volunteers and ICA retreated from the Green to the College on Tuesday.
16	St Stephen's Green North	Shelbourne Hotel	Taken by the British, it overlooked the Green.
17	48–52 Westland Row	Westland Row Railway Station	Taken and held by the Volunteers. Now Pearse Station.
18	Cork Hill and 3–4 Parliament St.	*Mail and Express* office	A Citizen Army outpost of the City Hall garrison.
19	Cork Hill and 1–3 Parliament St.	Henry & James outfitters	A Citizen Army outpost of the City Hall garrison.
20	5–7 Parliament St.	Royal Exchange Hotel	A Citizen Army/Volunteer outpost of the City Hall garrison.
21	Grand Canal St. and Clanwilliam Place	Robert's Builders' Yard	A Volunteer position of the Mount St. Bridge area.
22	St Stephen's Green West	Turkish Baths	The Citizen Army held this position at the north-west end of the Green.
23	St Stephen's Green North	United Services Club	Held by the British.
24	Overview of Redmond Hill and Wexford St.	Kelly's pub	A Volunteer outpost of the Jacob's garrison.

of his men remained in Jacob's for the entire week, or were sent to augment the St Stephen's Green garrison.

MacDonagh surrendered the garrison on Sunday at about 2.30 p.m. after reading the unconditional surrender to the men. Because they had seen so little action during the week, and had been kept in the dark as to the progress of the Rising, the surrender came as a surprise to many of the men and women of the garrison.

2ND BATTALION: MEN

Most mustered at St Stephen's Green and primarily occupied Jacob's Biscuit Factory on Peter Street and Bishop Street, as well as the surrounding streets. About half of the battalion went to the GPO after mustering at Fr Mathew Park in Fairview.

Jacob's Biscuit Factory Building: garrison total about 180 men and women, with another 50 sent on to other garrisons; three executed, four killed.

Barmack's Malthouse in Fumbally Lane, as well as positions in Camden Street, Malpas Street and Kevin Street.

Many men and women reported to Jacob's Factory and were then redeployed to St Stephen's Green.[580]

*Major John MacBride (Seán MacBhríde; executed 5 May 1916, aged 48).[581] 'Liberty is a priceless thing and anyone of you that sees a chance, take it. I'd do so myself but my liberty days are over. Good luck, boys. Many of you may live to fight another day. Take my advice, never allow yourselves to be cooped inside the walls of a building again.'[582] MacBride constantly checked the men's positions and it was said that he had the consummate skills of an officer, able to calm men just by his presence. In Kilmainham he was attended by Fr Augustine, who recorded him as saying: 'I have looked down the muzzles of too many British guns in the South African war to fear death, and now please carry out your sentence'.[583] 'Mind the Flag' were reportedly his last words before the firing squad.

MacBride was a native of Westport, Co. Mayo, and was a draper's assistant there in his early life. He emigrated to South Africa, and during the Boer War took a leading part as one of the leaders of the Irish Brigade fighting the British. The government of South Africa conferred the rank of major on him. Upon his return he married Maud Gonne and they had one son, Seán. In the years leading up to the Rising he was a water bailiff for Dublin Corporation. He had been the witness at the New York wedding of Tom and Kathleen Clarke. Éamonn Ceannt, charged with being a member of the Jacob's garrison, called him as a witness at his court martial.[584] He testified that Ceannt was *not* a member of that garrison.

*Cmdt Thomas MacDonagh (Tomás MacDonnchada; executed 3 May 1916, aged 38).[585] He was the last man to be invited onto the Military Council of the IRB, and was by all accounts a warm-hearted, humorous and talkative individual. Originally from Cloughjordan, Co. Tipperary, he had been brought up in a house full of music, story and prayer. His parents were teachers and his mother, a convert to Catholicism, inculcated in her children a belief in acts of individual charity and morality that would considerably influence his character. During his life he was a schoolmaster, a poet, a theatre manager, an astute literary critic, a supporter of women's rights and the Gaelic League, and a friend to some of the best-known and most influential artistic and political figures in literary Dublin. He sought fairer pay and better working conditions for secondary school teachers through the foundation of the ASTI, while his involvement with the Dublin Industrial Peace Committee in 1913 was underlined by a recognisable desire to seek a fair resolution to the Lockout. MacDonagh was sympathetic to the ambitions of the ITGWU; while not a member of the union, and far removed from the realities of its socialist policies, he greatly favoured the workers rather than the employers owing to his sense of justice, fairness and a natural support for the underdog. Finally, he joined the Irish Volunteers out of a sense that nationalist Ireland needed to defend Home Rule.[586]

In Kilmainham he was seen by Fr Aloysius and Fr Columbus.[587] The governor told Fr Columbus that Tom Clarke's wife and Willie Pearse were on their way, but that the visit of MacDonagh's sister, a nun, was out of the question because of practical difficulties. When MacDonagh was told this he was so disappointed and upset that Fr Columbus promised that he himself would bring her to the prison if at all possible.[588] Later Fr Columbus was given a car to fetch her and he was able to bring her to the prison, along with the Mistress of Novices. He conducted Sister Francesca to her brother's cell with only the flickering of a candle to light the way, then left to get the holy oils for anointing the men. When he returned he found that the governor was anxious to get the nuns to leave, as the time was almost up. Sister Francesca was numbed and dazed with grief. To gain more time, she asked for a lock of her brother's hair as a keepsake, but there were no scissors. The governor then produced a penknife with a small scissors attached. It was given to Sister Francesca but she could not use it, as her shaking fingers refused to work. A soldier took it from her and, cutting a lock of her brother's hair, handed it to her. Finally, after she had hung her mother's rosary beads around her brother's neck, Fr Columbus led her away and supported her down the stairs to the military car outside. Sister Francesca wrote that she received the rosary back the next day from Fr Aloysius, though six beads had been shot off.[589]

When Fr Columbus re-entered the prison, the governor informed him that both priests would have to leave immediately, as it was now 3.20 a.m. 'We have not finished giving the rites of the church to the men', said Fr Columbus, and he explained that the anointings could only be given after the shootings. 'Well, in that case,' said the governor, 'it cannot be done at all, as it is written in the regulations that all except officials have to leave the prison.' The priests were surprised and indignant but were unable to change the governor's mind. Having administered the Sacraments of Confession and Holy Communion, the priests accepted the ruling but lodged a formal complaint. Then they said a last farewell to the three prisoners, without telling them that they would not be present at the shootings.

*Vice-Cmdt Michael O'Hanrahan (Mícheál Ó hAnnrachain, executed 4 May 1916, aged 39).[590] In Kilmainham he was in cell No. 67; he was seen by his sisters and was attended by Fr Albert.[591]

His sister Eily wrote:

At last we arrived at Kilmainham. This was the first time we knew where we were. We were shown into a little white-washed room off the hall, with two candles. We were sitting there for a while. I went to the door once or twice and asked the soldiers in the hall why we were not being brought to my brother. I heard a woman's voice in the hall. 'That seems to be Mrs Clarke', I said to Cis. I went to her and she said, 'What brings you here, Eily?' 'I don't know, except that we were told Mícheál was being deported.' I said to Mrs Clarke: 'Is there anything you want to tell us?' as she seemed to hesitate. 'They are executing the men', she said. I said, 'Could it be possible that Mícheál would be executed?' She then told us that she had been there the night before to see her husband before his execution, and she had been called this night to see her brother, Ned Daly.

After a short time some soldiers came and brought us up the dark iron stairs and along the iron corridor to Mícheál's cell. There was nothing in it, no light even, but an old bag, thrown in the corner, and a bucket, no bed, no chair, no table, a place in which you would not put a dog. Mícheál was standing in the cell. When we rushed forward he caught us in his arms …

He asked us did we know the circumstances that brought us, and where was Mother. We told him why we had not brought her and we said we knew now why we had been sent for. He said he would have loved to see Mother and Máire, but that it was better after all Mother had not come. He was not in any way agitated. The only thing that worried him was what was to become of my Mother and us. He said he did not know where Harry was. They were devoted to each other and did everything together. He told us not to fret, and we tried to reassure him that we would be all right and that the women of '98 had to endure that too …

There were six soldiers and two officers, and any time we said anything referring to the Volunteers and the Movement, one of the officers came forward and said we must speak of nothing but personal matters. I mentioned that Tom

Clarke and Pearse were gone and one of the officers interrupted me. Again in the course of conversation I mentioned that MacDonagh was gone and again I was stopped. We told him that Ned Daly and two others were going with himself. We rushed in all this information in a hurry and with the greatest need we should do so without delay. We were left there only a short time, although we had been told that the interview would be for 20 minutes. We asked to be permitted to stay to the end, but the officers said that would be out of the question. I asked Mícheál if he had anything to eat. He said some bully-beef had been left in to him in a billycan, but he had not eaten it. I asked had he not had a bed. He said no. Then one of the officers said to Mícheál if he had any affairs to settle he should do so without delay. I said, how can anyone situated as he is without a table or chair even settle anything. A table and chair and a candle in an old candlestick were brought. It was then we saw how bad the cell really was. Mícheál wrote his will on paper headed with the Kilmainham stamp. He left all he had—which was only his books—to Mother and to his sisters after her death. Only for that will we would not have afterwards got his medals, as a brother of ours who had married early and had no sympathy with Ireland applied for them, and the affair went on for months. The record of this is in the Department of Defence.

When he had finished the will he said he would be seeing Father in a few hours. We asked him had he seen a priest.

An officer said his clergy had been sent for and would be here presently. Mícheál said he had asked for Father Augustine and Father Albert. These priests were marvellous. They saved the reason of many people whose sons and brothers were executed. Father Aloysius and Father Sebastian were very good too. The two former used to come and see us regularly, sometimes they came twice a day in a cab.

The two officers witnessed the will.

Although these men did their duty they were not aggressive …

We said goodbye to Mícheál. He did not weep, but kept up his courage. We did not give way either then. He kissed us several times and told us to give his love to Mother and Máire and to Harry when we found out where he was. I think he was afraid Harry would be executed too.

We came downstairs and I got weak, and when I got to the ground floor I fainted. A stretcher was brought and I was laid on it. One of the soldiers, an Irishman, made himself very objectionable and seemed to gloat over the executions. When I became conscious again I was brought back to the same room we had been in before. One soldier—an Englishman—was very kind, he brought water and tried to console us. He said, 'After all, ladies, your brother is getting the death he would have wished for'.

As we were passing into the room Cis asked me, 'Who is that girl sitting in the hall?' I said, 'That is Grace Gifford', and while we were in the room we heard an officer ask her who she was. She answered, 'I am Mrs Plunkett'. We did not know she had been married.

James Barrett; he was in Malpas Place.

William Barrett; he was in the Jacob's building.

Joseph Patrick Begley; ICA. He was sent to St Stephen's Green.

John Bermingham; he was at Barmack's in Fumbally Lane and was imprisoned at Frongoch.

William Berry (Barry, Derry?); ICA. He was in the Jacob's building.

William J. Blake; he is listed on the Roll of Honour.

Gerald Boland (Gearóid Ó Beolain); Harry's brother. He led the men tunnelling through the walls from Jacob's into Kelly's pub, which had a commanding view over Redmond Hill and Wexford Street. He was imprisoned in Frongoch with Michael Collins, where his dislike of Collins increased.[592]

John Boyne; he was in the Jacob's building.

Luke Bradley; he was sent to St Stephen's Green.

Francis Brady; he was in Delahunt's public house in Camden Street.

James Joseph Brady; he was sent to Merrion Square.

Patrick Brady; he was sent to St Stephen's Green. Imprisoned at Frongoch.

James Brennan; he was sent to St Stephen's Green.

Laurence Brennan; he was in Barmack's in Fumbally Lane.

Patrick Breslin; ICA. He was imprisoned at Frongoch.

John Brien; he was in Delahunt's public house in Camden Street.

James Brougham; he was sent to the Turkish Baths in St Stephen's Green.

Joseph Brown (Browne) (Seosamh de Brúin); he went from Jacob's to Boland's Bakery/Mills.

William Joseph Buckley; ICA. He was in the Jacob's building.

Thomas Burke; he was sent to St Stephen's Green. Imprisoned at Frongoch, he became a vice-president of the General Council.

Denis Byrne; he was sent to St Stephen's Green, and was in Little's public house.

**James Byrne (46);[593] originally assigned to Camden Row, he was based in Jacob's. He was shot while visiting his mother at her home in 31 Lower Stephen Street, and died in Mercer's Hospital.[594]

Joseph John Byrne (Seosamh de Bruin, de Brun; Seorais De Bruin?);[595] he was setting off to spend the day at the seaside when he met some Volunteers who told him that the Rising was on, so he reported to St Stephen's Green.

> The people of the neighbourhood gathered with lively curiosity. They seemed at a loss to know whether we were in action or merely on manoeuvres: as the day wore on they too began to realise the seriousness of their position, especially when a tall Volunteer not quite seasoned to arms during a false alarm that the British were approaching let his Howth gun fall to the ground, a charge was released with a report that made his comrades as well as a number of the people jump with the shock. It was the first shot, though an accidental one, fired by our lot. One chap declared it nearly took the tip of his ear off. After this the people kept a respectful distance, though numbers considered at the time to be British soldiers' dependants or sympathisers were definitely hostile. Several times they essayed to tear down the barricades, our men displayed great good temper.[596]

Patrick Byrne (Pádraig Ó Broin); he was in the Jacob's building.

Vincent (Vinnie) Byrne (14); he was coming up Grafton Street with his .22 rifle when he met Lt Sheils, who told him to go home. Later he met Mick Colgan and they reported to St Stephen's Green.

> Between 5 and 6 o'clock on Sunday evening, we were all called to the basement floor where we were informed by Commandant McDonagh [*sic*] that a surrender

had been called by the Commander-in-Chief, Patrick Pearse. There was a Franciscan Father in the building at the time, and he was pleading with the men to lay down their arms quietly. I remarked to the reverend father: 'Is there no chance of getting out to the hills and fighting it out?' He said: 'No, my son, and come along with me'. James Carbury and myself were brought along by the reverend father to a low window in Bishop Street and just dropped out into the street and told to go home. At this time, our clothes were all white from flour bags which were being used as sandbags at the windows. There was a lot of people outside, women especially, who tried to manhandle us down the street. One woman took us into her house and brushed off the flour from our coats. She let us out and we proceeded on our way home.[597]

He became a member of Michael Collins's 'Squad'.

Lt William Byrne; he was in the Jacob's building, and led a twelve-man squad to occupy the tenement houses on Malpas Street.

Patrick Cahalan; he was in Barmack's in Fumbally Lane.

Arthur John Cahill (Ó Cahill); he was in the Jacob's building and was appointed garrison medical officer.

James Carberry (Carbury); he was in the Jacob's building.

Francis Joseph Carney; he was sent to St Stephen's Green.

James Joseph Casey (Séamus Ó Casaigh, Ó Caghahaigh); he was in the Jacob's building and was imprisoned at Frongoch.

James Cassels; he was sent to the GPO. Imprisoned at Frongoch.

Daniel Francis Chambers; he was sent to St Stephen's Green.

Peter Christie; he was in Fumbally Lane, then was sent to St Stephen's Green. Imprisoned at Frongoch.

Robert John Clarke; he was in the Jacob's building.

Seán Colbert; he was in the Jacob's building.

Michael John (Mick) Colgan; a participant in the landing of the guns at Howth in July 1914, he was a section commander in E Company. He founded the Irish Bookbinders and Allied Trades Union, was president of the Dublin Trades Union Council in 1937 and president of the Irish Trade Union Congress in 1941–2. He was elected to the Seanad in 1943, 1948 and 1951.

Charles Tottenham Collins; he was sent to Jacob's from Boland's Mills.

Andrew Comerford; he was in the Jacob's building and was imprisoned at Frongoch.

Jimmy Conroy Jnr; he bought the paraffin to burn the Custom House in 1921. He became a member of Michael Collins's 'Squad'.

James Cooney; he received a disability pension.

Joseph Alphonsus Francis Cotter; brother to Richard and Thomas (below), he was sent to the Turkish Baths in St Stephen's Green.

Richard (Dick) Cotter; he lived at 32 St Anne's Road, Drumcondra.

Thomas Cotter; he lived at 32 St Anne's Road, Drumcondra.

Peter Cullen; he was in the Jacob's building.

James Cunningham; he was in the Jacob's building. Imprisoned at Frongoch.

Michael Curtain (Curtin) (Mícheál Ó Cortain; Míceál Ó Corgain?); he is listed on the Roll of Honour.

William Joseph Daly (Liam Ua Dáilaigh); he was in the Jacob's building. Imprisoned at Frongoch.

James Darcy; he was in Meredith's Pawn Office in Bishop Street.

Patrick Leo Darcy; he was imprisoned at Frongoch.

Richard Patrick Davys (Riseard MacDaibhis); called as a witness by Éamonn Ceannt at Ceannt's court martial, he testified that Ceannt had *not* been a member of the Jacob's garrison.

Seán Deegan; he is listed on the Roll of Honour.

Frederick Victor Devine; he was in the Jacob's building.

Peter Dolan; he was sent to St Stephen's Green.

John Donnelly; he was in Camden Street.

John Doogan; he was in the Jacob's building.

Patrick Doyle; he lived at 96 South Circular Road and is listed on the Roll of Honour.

Thomas Doyle; he was sent to St Stephen's Green. Imprisoned at Frongoch.

James Drannon (?); he is listed on the Roll of Honour.

Thomas Drumm; he was in Fumbally Lane and was sent to St Stephen's Green.

Francis Duggan; he was in the Jacob's building.

Samuel Ellis; he was sent to St Stephen's Green. Imprisoned at Frongoch.

Christopher Ennis; he was in the Jacob's building. Imprisoned at Frongoch.

Michael Ennis; he was in Malpas Street. Imprisoned at Frongoch.

James Fairhill (Séamus Ó Maoilfinn, Ua Maoilfinn); he was in the Jacob's building.

James Farrell; he was sent to St Stephen's Green.

Christopher Farrelly; he was in the Jacob's building.

Gerald Fitzmaurice; he was sent to the Turkish Baths in St Stephen's Green.

Michael Fitzpatrick; he is listed on the Roll of Honour.

Matthew Flanagan; employed at Jacob's and imprisoned at Frongoch. His supervisor at Jacob's, Mr Nesbitt, was asked after the Rising whether Flanagan's job would be held for him, and replied that his job would be there for him whenever he wished to return.

Michael Fleming; he was imprisoned at Frongoch. In 1920, during the War of Independence, he hid Seán Treacy following Treacy's escape from Professor Carolan's house in Drumcondra after it was raided by the RIC; Treacy was killed the following day.

Joseph Fogarty; he was in Barmack's in Fumbally Lane.

John (Jack) Furlong; he married Kathleen Kearney, with whom he had two sons, Seán and Rory. He died of influenza in 1918. She subsequently married Stephen Behan and became the mother of Brendan.

Joseph Furlong; an IRB member from Wexford. Prior to the Rising he was engaged in undercover work for the IRB. When he arrived he did not have a weapon, so MacDonagh handed him his Mauser C96 pistol.

Matthew Furlong; he lived at 70 Seville Place.

Tadhg Gahan; he was sent to St Stephen's Green.

Daniel Patrick (Doctor P.) Gleeson; he was in the Jacob's building.

Charles Goulding; he was imprisoned at Frongoch. His son, Cathal, born in 1922, became chief of staff of the IRA from 1962 until the split between the Official and Provisional IRA in December 1969, when he became a founder member of Official Sinn Féin.

James Goulding; he was imprisoned at Frongoch.

Richard Grattan; he was in the Jacob's building.

John Gregory; he was sent to St Stephen's Green and was imprisoned at Frongoch.

James Joseph Hannon; he was in Malpas Place.

James Hayes (Séamus Ó hAodha); he was imprisoned at Frongoch.

Michael Hayes (Ó hAodha); a founding member of the Volunteers in 1913, he managed to avoid arrest after the Rising. He sheltered Sinn Féin colleagues during the War of Independence in Ballykinlar camp. While in prison, he was elected as a Sinn Féin TD for the National University of Ireland in the 1921 general election. He was released after the July 1921 truce, supported the Treaty and served as Minister for Education from January to September 1922. He was Ceann Comhairle (Speaker of the Dáil) from 1923 to 1932, and later a senator. Of the Rising he said, 'This was the only course, but the venture was a hopeless one'.[598]

Seán Healy (15);[599] a Fianna member, he was apprenticed to his father as a plumber. He never received any mobilisation orders, so on Tuesday he reported to Jacob's. He was given an urgent dispatch to carry to Phibsborough Bridge, but was shot at Byrne's corner on the way.[600] The youngest Fianna/Volunteer to be killed, he died at the Mater Hospital on 27 April. His sister, Cathleen, was in the Four Courts.

George Heuston; he was in Delahunt's public house on Camden Street.

James J. Hughes; he was in the Jacob's building.

Robert Humphreys; he was imprisoned at Frongoch. He was the first to sing *A Soldier's Song* in public at a Volunteers' concert, and became an announcer for RTÉ.

Capt. Thomas (Tom) Hunter; Battalion Vice-Commandant. He was an IRB centre ('centre' was the name given to a leader of an IRB 'circle') of the Henry Joy McCracken Circle in Dublin. Hunter and a small detachment were ordered to take and hold an outpost position at New Street and Fumbally Lane. After a few hours, they were ordered back to Jacob's. Hunter was the one who tearfully told the rank and file about their surrender. He broke his sword in two on the stairway before he informed his men. He was de Valera's ADC in Lewes Prison and was TD for Cork North East in the first two Dáils.

Thomas Michael Jennings; he was sent to St Stephen's Green.

John Joyce; he was in Barmack's in Fumbally Lane. Imprisoned at Frongoch.

Joseph James Joyce; he was sent to St Stephen's Green.

Daniel Kavanagh; he is listed on the Roll of Honour.

John Kavanagh; he was sent to St Stephen's Green.

Patrick Kavanagh; he was sent to St Stephen's Green.

Séamus Kavanagh; he was sent to St Stephen's Green.

Peadar Kearney (Peadar Ó Cearnaigh); he was one of a group that seized Barmack's Malthouse in Fumbally Lane. Upon being informed of the surrender, he was one of those who argued for a mass breakout to the hills. He escaped from Jacob's and avoided capture. He wrote *A Soldier's Song/Amhrán na bhFiann*. He took part in the War of Independence, serving time in Collinstown camp, Co. Dublin, and Ballykinlar camp, Co. Down. He took the pro-Treaty side in the Civil War but lost faith after the death of Michael Collins. He returned to his original trade of house-painter, taking no further active part in politics.

Frank Kearns (brother of Hubert, John, Joseph and Thomas, below); he was imprisoned at Frongoch.

Hubert Kearns (brother of Frank, John, Joseph and Thomas); he was imprisoned at Frongoch.

John Kearns (brother of Frank, Hubert, Joseph and Thomas); with his brothers, he was in Barmack's in Fumbally Lane and was imprisoned at Frongoch.

Joseph John Kearns (brother of Frank, Hubert, John and Thomas); he was imprisoned at Frongoch.

Thomas Kearns (brother of Frank, Hubert, John and Joseph); he was imprisoned at Frongoch.

Thomas Kehoe; a Wicklow man, he became a member of Michael Collins's 'Squad'. He was killed in the Civil War.

Francis Kelly; he was sent to St Stephen's Green.

Hugh Kelly; he was sent to St Stephen's Green.

John Emmanuel Kelly; he was in the Jacob's building and was interned until September.

Patrick Kelly (Padraig Ó Ceallaigh); he went to the Fairyhouse Races on Easter Monday, and while there heard about the Rising. He arrived at the GPO that night and was told to go to Jacob's.[601] Imprisoned at Frongoch.

James Joseph Kenny; he was in Fumbally Lane. Imprisoned at Frongoch.

Daniel King; he was sent to City Hall.

Seán Joseph Francis King; he was sent to St Stephen's Green.

John Watson Lake; he is listed on the Roll of Honour.

Edward (Ned) Lane; he came from Fr Mathew Park.

Patrick Lanigan; he was in Barmack's in Fumbally Lane and was imprisoned at Frongoch.

James Joseph Lawless; he was in the Jacob's building.

Michael J. Lawless; he was sent to St Stephen's Green, and is counted in that garrison.[602]

Joseph (Joe) Leonard; he was imprisoned at Frongoch. He became a member of Michael Collins's 'Squad'.[603]

Patrick Long; he is listed on the Roll of Honour.

Thomas Losty (Loohy?); he was in New Street and was imprisoned at Frongoch.

Michael Love; he was in the Jacob's building.

Seán Lynch; he was in Malpas Street.

William Lynch; he was imprisoned at Frongoch.

Edward (Ned) Lyons; a member of B Company. Ned joined the Volunteers in 1914 and as an engineer was involved in the repair, maintenance and manufacturing of arms in the run-up to the Rising, including the manufacture of trench mortars to be used against barracks. He was part of an armed guard in Fr Mathew Park on Easter Sunday, and was a sniper in Barmack's in Fumbally Lane. He was imprisoned in Knutsford, transferred to Frongoch and released in December 1916.

Richard McDavitt (Risteard MacDaibhis); he is listed on the Roll of Honour.

Owen McDermott; he was in Fumbally Lane and was sent to St Stephen's Green.

John MacDonagh (McDonagh); brother of Thomas. He was sent to St Stephen's Green and was imprisoned at Frongoch. He was a theatre manager and directed Michael Collins's film promoting the Dáil Loan.[604]

John Bernard McDonald; he went to St Stephen's Green. Imprisoned at Frongoch.

Matthew McDonnell; he was sent to St Stephen's Green. Imprisoned at Frongoch.

Lt Michael (Mick) McDonnell; imprisoned at Knutsford and Frongoch, he became a member of Michael Collins's 'Squad'.[605]

Patrick McDonnell; he was in Fumbally Lane and was sent to St Stephen's Green. Imprisoned in Frongoch.

William McDonnell; he was in Fumbally Lane and was sent to the Turkish Baths in St Stephen's Green.

Patrick McEvoy; he was in the Jacob's building.

John McGlure; he was in the Jacob's building.

Claude McGowan; his brother Charles was in the 3rd Battalion, and his sister Josephine (Josie) was in Marrowbone Lane in the 4th Battalion.

Thomas McGrane; he was sent to St Stephen's Green.

Daniel McGrath; he was in the Jacob's building.

Richard (Dick) McKee; he was born in 1893 in Finglas, and after the Rising he was imprisoned at Frongoch. He became O/C of the Dublin Brigade and was murdered on Bloody Sunday.[606]

Bernard J. MacMahon; he was in Barmack's in Fumbally Lane.

Peter (Peadar) MacMathghamhna; he was sent to St Stephen's Green.

James McParland; he was in the Jacob's building.

William Joseph Maher; he was in the Jacob's building.

Patrick Manning; he is listed on the Roll of Honour.

Peter Martin; he was imprisoned at Frongoch.

Michael Meade; he is listed on the Roll of Honour.

Owen Meade; he was in Barmack's in Fumbally Lane.

John Meldon; he was in the Jacob's building.

Thomas J. Meldon; he was in the Jacob's building.

James (Séamus) Melvinn; he was in the Jacob's building.

Michael J. Molloy; one of the printers of the *Proclamation*, he was chosen by James Connolly to oversee the printing, as he was an experienced compositor.[607] He was detailed to Fumbally Lane at the start of the Rising, and later did duty on one of the Jacob's towers, where his keen eyes helped him as a sniper. Later he was sent to St Stephen's Green. He carried with him the piece of paper signed by the signatories to the *Proclamation* until he found himself in Richmond Barracks after the surrender, when he chewed it up and spat it out to prevent its discovery. He was sent to Knutsford Prison and thence to Frongoch.[608] He was released in August 1916.

Richard Molloy; he was in the Jacob's building and was imprisoned at Frongoch.

Andrew Monks; he was in Fumbally Lane and was sent to St Stephen's Green.

James Moran (Séamus Ó Murain).

Patrick (Paddy) Moran; imprisoned at Frongoch. He was hanged at Mountjoy Prison on 14 March 1921 for his 'participation' in the Bloody Sunday killings at 38 Upper Mount Street, even though he was not there. The Volunteers at the Gresham Hotel on Bloody Sunday were, however, actually under his command.[609]

Seán Morgan; he is listed on the Roll of Honour.

Martin Mullen; he was at Portobello Barracks and in New Street and was imprisoned at Frongoch.

Frederick Murphy; he was sent to St Stephen's Green.

John J. (Seán) Murphy; imprisoned at Frongoch.

> Later that evening I sent one of the men to report to Captain Hunter that [British] reinforcements were going from Back Lane into Ship Street Barracks in very large numbers and what was I to do about it, was I to open fire, we had not enough men to tackle a large body like that. By the time he returned the military had all passed into the Barracks. That night MacDonagh instructed Captain Hunter to evacuate our positions and fall back into Jacob's Factory. We did so, and I was given a position on the top of the building on the Peter Street side. A series of windows overlooked the Adelaide Hospital and were in view of the Tower in the Castle from where we were under fire on the Wednesday night by machine guns. No casualties occurred among the men under my charge.[610]

James Joseph Murran; he was sent to St Stephen's Green.

Bernard Murtagh; he was sent to St Stephen's Green.

Joseph Neary; he was in the Jacob's building.

Patrick Nolan; he was imprisoned at Frongoch.

Patrick O'Byrne; imprisoned at Frongoch.

John O'Callahan (Seán O'Callaghan, Seán Ó Ceallacháin); he was in the Jacob's building and in Camden Street.

James (Jim) O'Carroll; he was the brother of Frank, Larry and Peter, who were in the 1st Battalion.

James Joseph O'Carroll; he was sent to St Stephen's Green.

**Richard O'Carroll (40);[611] he was promoted to Lt and assigned to Delahunt's public house in Camden St, which had been seized on Monday night by a party of Volunteers led by Lt James Shiels. After the Volunteers had vacated the building, he was murdered there by Capt. J.C. Bowen-Colthurst. O'Carroll was travelling along Camden St when he was pulled from his motor-cycle combination by Bowen-Colthurst and shot; he died nine days later in Portobello Hospital.[612] He was a Labour Party member of Dublin Corporation, representing the Mansion House Ward from 1908, and was the general secretary of the Incorporated Brick and Stone Layers' Union. He left a widow and seven children, aged from thirteen years to a few weeks. He is buried in Glasnevin.

Patrick O'Connell; he was in the Jacob's building.

Christopher O'Donnell; he was in Barmack's in Fumbally Lane.

James O'Donnell; he was in Barmack's in Fumbally Lane.

William O'Donnell; he was in the Jacob's building and in Kelly's public house in Aungier Street.

★★John O'Grady (27);[613] he joined the Volunteers just four months before the Rising and was one of fifteen cyclists who set off to relieve some of de Valera's men in Boland's. They were unable to force their way in, and he was killed on the return journey: 'I fear they got me'.[614] He had been married for only eight months.

Hugh O'Hagan; he is listed on the Roll of Honour.

Edward O'Hanrahan; he was in the Jacob's building and was imprisoned at Frongoch.

Henry (Harry) O'Hanrahan; he was a brother of Michael, 2nd Battalion O/C.[615]

Joseph John O'Hanrahan; he was in Fumbally Lane and was sent to St Stephen's Green.

Patrick O'Kelly (Padraig Ó Ceallaigh); 'The rank-and-file of all the volunteers in Jacob's were practically all of the middle and working class ... the great common people of Ireland. In Jacob's, I met many GAA players I knew. The GAA played a big part in the Rising and the subsequent Black and Tan War.'[616]

Christopher Robert O'Malley; he was in the Jacob's building.

Francis Thomas O'Reilly; he was in Barmack's in Fumbally Lane and was imprisoned at Frongoch.

Patrick O'Reilly; he was imprisoned at Frongoch.

Thomas O'Reilly; he was in Delahunt's public house.

Lt Danny O'Riordan (Donal O'Reardon, Domhnall Ó Riordain); he is listed on the Roll of Honour. He was put in charge of twenty cyclists sent to relieve Westland Row Station. When they passed Merrion Square they came under fire and dismounted to return fire. Realising that they would be overrun, O'Riordan ordered a withdrawal, in the course of which John O'Grady was wounded; he later died of his wounds.

Frederick O'Rorke (O'Rourke); he was in Barmack's in Fumbally Lane and was sent to the St Stephen's Green garrison.

John O'Rorke (O'Rourke) (Seán T. Ó Ruairc); he was sent with a party to Jacob's for food and brought back supplies to the College of Surgeons. 'Then some of the E Coy men who had been in the Surgeons during the week, rejoined, by permission of Commandant Mallin, our Company which was in Jacob's.'[617] (Counted in the Jacob's garrison.)

John Joseph O'Rourke; he was in Malpas Street.

Michael O'Rourke; he was imprisoned at Frongoch.

Thomas O'Rourke (Tomas Ó Ruairc); he is listed on the Roll of Honour.

Dermot O'Shea; he was from Cork and was interned until September.

James O'Shea; he was in the Jacob's building and was sent to St Stephen's Green. Imprisoned at Frongoch.

Michael Phelan; he was in New Street and was imprisoned at Frongoch.

James S. (Séamus) Pounch; a member of the so-called 'Surrey House Clique', a group of Fianna boys who used to meet regularly at Countess Markievicz's house in Leinster Road, Rathmines.[618] He met Garry Holohan, who was headed to the Magazine Fort, but Holohan told him that he would be of no use in that job, since Pounch was in uniform. He was the Assistant QM of the Fianna and in Jacob's he was responsible for provisions; he raided the surrounding shops for bread, potatoes and other food. He was given an order by MacDonagh stating that he was an officer of the Irish Republican Army authorised to commandeer food, for which compensation would be paid after the Rising. He also described a 'miniature céilí' in the factory and the assembly of an improvised Tricolour. At the surrender, he put a greatcoat over his uniform and escaped.

Éamon (Bob) Price; Capt. of C Company. Imprisoned at Frongoch, he became O/C of J Company of the North Camp.[619] He became director of organisation of the IRA in 1920, and a major-general in the Irish Army. He married Máire Nic Shiubhlaigh, whom he met in Jacob's during the Rising.

Thomas Pugh; a member of the Socialist Party of Ireland. Richard Mulcahy persuaded him to join the Volunteers rather than the Citizen Army. When the order for the Rising was countermanded, he went to an exhibition of paintings in the Royal Hibernian Academy, and mobilised the next day. He later met his wife in Knutsford Prison, where he was sent after the surrender.[620]

John Purfield; ICA. He lived on Fitzgibbon Street.

Daniel Reardon; he was sent to St Stephen's Green.

Laurence Reardon; he was in the Jacob's building.

Patrick Redmond; he was in Fumbally Lane and was imprisoned at Frongoch.

William J. Redmond; he was sent to Merrion Square.

James J. Renny; he is listed on the Roll of Honour.

John Arnold de Vere Reynolds; he was in Barmack's and was sent to St Stephen's Green.

Seán Augustine Roche; he was in the Jacob's building and evaded capture.

Richard Roe; he was in Camden Street.

Patrick Rooney; he is listed on the Roll of Honour.

Albert Rutherford; he was in Fumbally Lane and was sent to St Stephen's Green.

John Ryder; he was in Barmack's in Fumbally Lane.

William Ryder; he was in the Jacob's building.

Frederick Schweppe; he was in Barmack's in Fumbally Lane and was imprisoned at Frongoch.

Philip Shanahan; imprisoned at Frongoch. He was originally from Tipperary and his pub on Foley Street was 'home' to Volunteers from 'the country'.

Lt James Sheils; on Monday night Sheils led the raiding party when the Volunteers seized Byrne's store and Delahunt's public house at the junction of Lower and Upper Camden Street. When the British troops attacked the position, the Volunteers retreated. Richard O'Carroll was fatally wounded there on Wednesday by British Capt. J.C. Bowen-Colthurst.[621] Sheils was imprisoned at Frongoch.

Denis Shelly; he was in Fumbally Lane and was sent to St Stephen's Green.

Thomas Shelly; he was in Fumbally Lane and was imprisoned at Frongoch.

Michael I. Sheppard; he was imprisoned at Frongoch.

Terence Simpson; he was sent to St Stephen's Green and was imprisoned at Frongoch.

Michael Slater; he was in Barmack's in Fumbally Lane.

Thomas Slater (brother of William, below); a member of the IRB since 1905. 'He [MacDonagh] told us one of the places which we were to occupy was Trinity College, and an officer named Paddy Walsh of "D" Company was detailed for this job. As, however, the numbers which could be spared from the main body at Stephen's Green were so small, Tom MacDonagh decided to call off the taking of Trinity College as it would have meant a heavy loss of life with no hope of getting in. All that we could have spared for this job would be about twenty men.'[622]

William Slater (brother of Thomas, above); he was in the Jacob's building. He had returned from England on Good Friday and was mobilised by his brother.

James Joseph Slattery (14); imprisoned at Frongoch. He became a member of Michael Collins's 'Squad' and lost an arm in the Custom House attack/fire in 1921.[623]

Michael Smyth; he was in Fumbally Lane and was imprisoned at Frongoch.

Daniel Charles Somers; he came from the GPO and was in the Jacob's building.

William J. (Bill) Stapleton; he was the guard commander over the main gate. Imprisoned at Frongoch. He became a member of Michael Collins's 'Squad'.[624]

Richard (Dick) Stokes; he was sent to St Stephen's Green.

Patrick Emmet (Dermot?) Sweeney; called as a witness by Éamonn Ceannt, he testified that Ceannt was *not* a member of the Jacob's garrison.

John Charles Toomey; an ICA man, he was sent to St Stephen's Green and was imprisoned at Frongoch.

Joseph Tormey (Seosamh Ó Torma).

John Turner; he was sent to St Stephen's Green.

Andrew Tyrrell; he is listed on the Roll of Honour.

Joseph Edward Vize; he was sent to St Stephen's Green.

John Walker; he was sent to St Stephen's Green. He and his brother Michael (below) were Olympic cyclists.

Michael Walker (brother of John, above); he was sent to St Stephen's Green. In the 1912 Olympic Games, Michael cycled for Ireland but under the banner of Great Britain. He finished 67th in the individual road race.

John Peter Walsh; he was in the Jacob's building.

Patrick (Paddy) Walsh; 'He [MacDonagh] told us one of the places which we were to occupy was Trinity College, and an officer named Paddy Walsh of "D" Company was detailed for this job. As, however, the numbers which could be spared from the main body at Stephen's Green were so small, Tom MacDonagh decided to call off the taking of Trinity College as it would have meant a heavy loss of life with no hope of getting in. All that we could have spared for this job would be about twenty men.'[625] He was imprisoned at Frongoch.

Martin Walton (15); a Feis Ceoil prizewinner on the violin, he was just fifteen when he took part in the Rising, although he was already 6ft tall. His parents did not want him to fight, so they took the valves from his bicycle tyres and he was unable to get to Jacob's until Tuesday morning. He arrived at the garrison with a 'murderous-looking shotgun'. He worked as a courier between Jacob's and the GPO during the Rising. Afterwards he was interned in Ballykinlar Camp, Co. Down, where he taught music.

> After the Rising we started to reorganize immediately—to look for guns, try and buck up the language, the Gaelic League and any other organization that wasn't banned and that we could get into. It was a terrible time. There were still thousands of Irishmen fighting in France and if you said you had been out in Easter Week one of their family was liable to shoot you. With the surrender in 1916 and the

immediate raids by the military and the round-up, the country was disarmed. Here and there we managed to hold onto a few guns, but very few, so looking for arms was a very high priority. I remember getting the key of an old Sinn Féin Hall from an old Fenian, and we started there, about eight, 10 or 12 of us, drilling and organising. I always thought that was the great test of a man—if he was able to keep coming to meetings, without any arms and with nothing happening, just drilling and going through the long haul until he could see combat. It was in that hall that one of the most famous of the guerrilla fighters, Ernie O'Malley, was brought into the movement. That little hall dissolved then and we took up headquarters in the painters' union—the Tara Hall, Gloucester Street, which is now Seán MacDermott Street. We met and drilled there. We were under cover of the painters' union, you see, so we got away with it. We more or less just kept in touch until the prisoners were released from Frongoch, because they were the ones who would be able to lay the foundations for the fight to come.

He fought for the Free State in the Civil War. A great friend of Michael Collins,[626] he founded the Walton Publishing and Music Stores in Dublin.

George Ward; imprisoned at Frongoch.

Nicholas Ward; he was sent to St Stephen's Green.

Christopher John Whelehan; one of the Kimmage men,[627] he came from the GPO (counted in the GPO garrison).

Peter Williams; he was sent to St Stephen's Green and was imprisoned at Frongoch.

2ND BATTALION: WOMEN

Cecilia Conroy (Courcy?) (O'Neill); a member of the Hibernian Rifles, she went back and forth to St Stephen's Green and the GPO.

Máire Deegan; she is listed on the Roll of Honour.

Saoirse Hayes (MacAodha); she is listed on the Roll of Honour.

Sara Kealy (17); she was the one who suggested that all the men write letters to their families and the women would deliver them, and she stayed to collect them all.[628]

Kathleen Lane (McCarthy); on her way to Jacob's she came into contact with a crowd of 'separation allowance women', who berated the Volunteers.[629]

Teresa Magee (McGee); she often carried dispatches to St Stephen's Green.

Annie O'Hagan (McQuade); she reported to the Sinn Féin office at 6 Harcourt Street and was ordered to Jacob's.[630]

Eileen (Eily) (Lily) O'Hanrahan (O'Reilly);[631] on the Wednesday before the Rising she undertook to go to Enniscorthy, Co. Wexford, to deliver a dispatch (sewn into the lining of her red fox fur) to the leader of the Volunteers there, Séamus Doyle. She assumed this dispatch to be an order to rise. On her way back she met Min Ryan, whom, she later concluded, had delivered MacNeill's countermanding order. This was confirmed years later by Doyle, who was the recipient of both dispatches. She immediately returned to Dublin. She was the sister of Mícheál O'Hanrahan and saw him in Kilmainham Gaol.

Josephine (Josie) Pollard (Daly); she was a member of the Liberty Players at Liberty Hall.

Kathleen Pollard (McDonald); sister of Josie (above).

Máire Nic Shiubhlaigh (née Molly Walker) (Mrs Éamonn Price); she was in command of the women, and was a famous actress in the early days of the Abbey. She recounts in her autobiography how she spent much of early 1916 making first-aid kits. On Monday morning she was at Mass when a telegram came from Lily O'Brennan (sister of Áine Ceannt); Máire went home, changed, went to St Stephen's Green, and then cycled to the Ceannts' house in Dolphin's Barn because she was to report to his battalion (they had already left). Then she went to Jacob's.[632] She wrote that MacDonagh told her: 'We are going to surrender. I want you to thank all the girls for what they have done. Tell them I am issuing an order that they are to go home.' She added: 'I started to protest, but he turned away. One could never imagine him looking so sad.'

Her remarkably honest recollections convey an impression of loneliness and fear:

> Though calls could be heard from the upstairs rooms, the sound of footsteps, an occasional clatter as a rifle fell, there was an eeriness about the place; a feeling of being cut off from the outside world ... Our isolation and occasional periods of inactivity were not pleasant. We heard many of the rumours that travelled around the building as the days passed and we had no means of telling if they were true or not.[633]

V. 3rd Battalion

The 3rd Battalion was positioned around Boland's Mills and Boland's Bakery in the Grand Canal Street area, an important strategic stronghold because it covered the railway line out of the Westland Row terminus. Commandant Éamon de Valera's Rising HQ was actually in a small dispensary next door, at the corner of Grand Canal Street and Great Clarence Street (now Macken Street). De Valera's positioning of garrisons on approaches to the city centre slowed the British advance and funnelled them into areas where the rebels were well situated with interlocking fields of fire and under effective cover. For example, the British troops marching in from Kingstown were led into a trap on Northumberland Road, where they suffered their greatest losses. De Valera knew every inch of the territory and he did not reduce his area of responsibility, though Eoin MacNeill's order cancelling the Rising greatly reduced the number of men who mustered. James Grace, who survived the battle at 25 Northumberland Road, reported to his position on Easter Monday, but only about 34 members of his company's roster of over 100 showed up. De Valera has been depicted as one who scorned danger almost to recklessness. All his men believed that, as a leader, he was capable of the unexpected stroke that would extricate them from danger. 'De Valera certainly knew every inch of the area under his command … It was characteristic of de Valera to attempt the impossible and he made no reduction in the scale of his operations notwithstanding the fact that less than one fifth of the men allotted to his command had responded to the mobilization order. He might have sat down in Boland's and waited to be dug out of it, but that was not his way.'[634] In contrast, others regarded de Valera's leadership at Boland's Mills as questionable.[635] His failure to relieve the hard-pressed garrison at Mount Street Bridge remains one of the most extraordinary aspects of the battle. Seventeen men kept a whole regiment of English soldiers at bay for almost five hours, yet de Valera made no attempt to reinforce or relieve them, though he was only 600 yards away.[636]

The inexperience of the British troops was most notably demonstrated when one of the first British soldiers fired a volley and then fell to the ground crying out, 'I've been shot'. His company commander, Capt. Frank Pragnell, examined the boy and exclaimed angrily, 'Good God, man! You're not hit—it's only the recoil'.[637] It should be emphasised that the British commander at the site requested permission to deviate from the planned route upon seeing the rebel positions but was ordered to proceed 'directly to Beggar's Bush Barracks', a fatal command decision which led to the greatest British casualties of

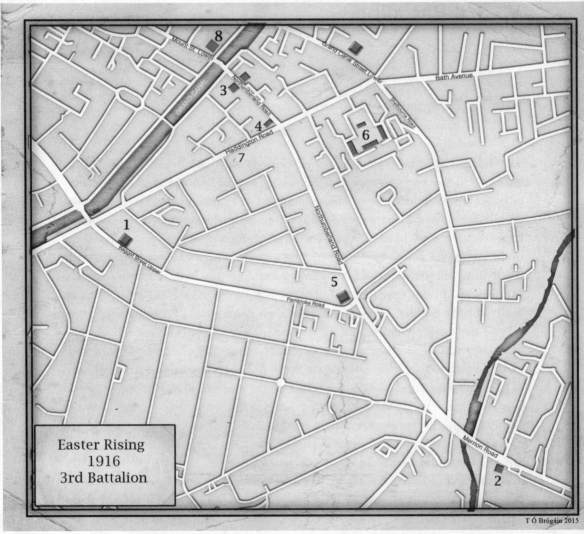

Easter Rising
1916
3rd Battalion

T Ó Brógáin 2015

No.	Address	Site	Description
1	16–18 Baggot Street Upper	Royal City of Dublin Hospital	Commonly called Baggot Street Hospital. Used to treat British and Irish casualties of the Rising.
2	Merrion Road, Ballsbridge	Pembroke/Ballsbridge Town Hall	Éamon de Valera was held here after the Rising.
3	1–5 Northumberland Road	St Stephen's Schoolhouse and Parochial Hall	Held by the Volunteers, right at Mount Street Bridge.
4	25 Northumberland Road, at corner of Haddington Road	Single family home	Held by two Volunteers, whose fire inflicted great damage on the British advancing on Mount Street Bridge.
5	122–124 Pembroke Road, at Northumberland Road	Carrisbrook House	Taken early by the Volunteers, it was quickly abandoned.
6	Shelbourne Road	Beggar's Bush Barracks	Main training depot for the British Army, it was very lightly garrisoned.
7	Haddington Road S	t Mary's Church	The British had snipers in the bell-tower here.
8	1–2 Clanwilliam Place	Clanwilliam House	Seven Volunteers held this key post. Three were killed and four survived.

the fighting. The British employed tactics used in the trenches of the Western Front to try and get through, and the casualties were terrible.

The British failure to reconnoitre properly, and to adapt their plans to a changed situation, contributed greatly to the number of casualties they suffered in attacking Mount Street Bridge. They stubbornly attacked the house at 25 Northumberland Road, then continued towards town on Northumberland Road, coming under murderous fire from Clanwilliam House and the Parochial Hall right at Mount Street Bridge. They could have outflanked all the Volunteer positions by withdrawing and using other bridges to cross the Grand Canal, but they did not send out scouting parties and just threw their men into the Volunteers' fire. Reminiscent of the carnage in France, this was a clear example of a commander remaining committed to a plan that had already proven disastrous. All commanders are expected to show initiative in the midst of a battle, but the British officers showed no such initiative on Northumberland Road or at Mount Street Bridge. After eight hours of charges the British had lost 240 killed and wounded. Most of the seventeen Irish rebels assigned to those positions escaped with their lives.

As another note on preparation, the men in the Mount Street Bridge garrisons expected the British to use incendiary weapons, and so they took the precaution of having several buckets of water available, and even placed siphons filled with water throughout their positions. Fire ultimately sealed their fate, however, as Clanwilliam House burned to the ground, killing three of its seven defenders.

3RD BATTALION

Boland's Bakery/Mills; A, B and D Companies mustered in Great Brunswick Street; C Company mustered in Earlsfort Terrace; garrison totals about 200; none executed, nine killed.

Boland's Bakery/Mills, Clanwilliam House, Grand Canal Street, Northumberland Road, Westland Row Station, St Stephen's Schoolhouse and Parochial Hall, the Dublin and South Eastern Railway Offices, Works and Line, and the Mount Street Bridge area.

Cmdt Éamon de Valera; in Kilmainham he was in cell no. 59. (While in penal servitude at Princetown in Dartmoor, Devonshire, however, his number was Convict 95, and there was a song written with that number in the title:

"Twas in Kilmainham prison yard our fifteen martyrs died
And cold and still in Arbour Hill they are lying side by side,
But we will yet pay back the debt for the spirit is still alive
In men who stood through fire and blood with Prisoner 95'.)[638]

De Valera was the only battalion commandant who did not allow women in the garrison.[639] In the 1937 Dáil Éireann debates on the Constitution, de Valera admitted that he had turned some Cumann na mBan members away from the Boland's garrison 'due to their lack of soldierly training'.[640] According to George Lyons, who fought in Westland Row Station, de Valera 'decided they [the women] would probably be an encumbrance where an extremely mobile force was necessary, and that anyhow women should be spared, as far as possible, from witnessing the horrors of war, especially the class of war we expected to develop'.[641] Nevertheless, de Valera did call for women to carry dispatches, though one reported that she was not allowed to actually enter Boland's Mill.[642] Eventually the women who were to have joined the 3rd Battalion made their way back to Harcourt Street, and when they received no further orders from de Valera they made their way to any garrison where their help would be accepted.[643]

Boland's Mills and Boland's Bakery were important strategic strongholds because they covered the railway line out of the Westland Row terminus. De Valera's Rising HQ was actually in a small dispensary next door, at the corner of Grand Canal Street and Great Clarence Street (now Macken Street).[644]

Joseph Allwell; he was in B Company and is listed on the Roll of Honour.

Thomas R. Atkins; he was in Camden Street and Harcourt Street. He was accidentally wounded by fellow Volunteer Joseph Clarke on Monday.

Henry Banks; imprisoned at Frongoch. 'While I was in the 1st Battalion, I bought my rifle, and paid £4.5.0 or £4.10.0 for it, not in a lump sum but on the easy payment system. I owed £1.0.0 on the rifle when I transferred to the 3rd Battalion, and the 1st Battalion tried to claim it, but they did not get it. I paid the £1.0.0 for it. These rifles, I think, were got through the I.R.B., and it was I.R.B. men got preference when they were given out. They were long Lee Enfields.'[645]

Seán Banks; he is listed on the Roll of Honour.

P. Begley; Battalion Adjutant and Vice-Commandant at Boland's, he was O/C of D Company. He left his post on Thursday.

John Bermingham; he lived on St Ignatius Road and is listed on the Roll of Honour.

Stephen Boylan; he was at 144 Great Brunswick Street and Boland's Bakery/Mills.

John Bracken; he was at Boland's Mills and Westland Row Railway Station. Imprisoned at Frongoch.

John Bracken Jnr; he was in A Company and was imprisoned at Frongoch.

John (Seán) Breen; he was in Boland's Mills and Grand Canal Street and was imprisoned at Frongoch.

Patrick Brennan; he lived in Milltown Park, was a member of E Company and is listed on the Roll of Honour.

Patrick Brennan; he was in D Company and is listed on the Roll of Honour.

Tobias (Toby) Breslin; he was in both Boland's Bakery and Boland's Mills, then Grand Canal Street, and was sent to the offices of the Dublin and South Eastern Railway, overlooking Grand Canal Street and Beggar's Bush Barracks.

James Browne; he was in Boland's Bakery and Grand Canal Street.

William Browne; he was in Boland's Bakery and the offices of the Dublin and South Eastern Railway. Imprisoned at Frongoch.

William Bruen; he was in Boland's Bakery and the sugar distillery in Great Brunswick Street.

Frederick Burton; he was in B Company and is listed on the Roll of Honour.

**Andrew Joseph Byrne (33);[646] a labourer originally from Wicklow, he was stationed as a sniper on the roof of the railway workshops of the Dublin and South Eastern Railway.[647] He was killed late in the week; he died in Sir Patrick Dun's Hospital and is buried in Deansgrange Cemetery.

Christopher Byrne; brother of Thomas (below). He was in Boland's Mills and Grand Canal Street. Then they went to the railroad crossing at Lansdowne Road, where they smashed the lines and dug a trench.

Daniel Byrne; he was dispatched to Boland's with a request for supplies and reinforcements for the men at 25 Northumberland Road. He returned with pieces of fruit cake, and George Reynolds sent him back to the bakery to get more men and food more substantial than cake.[648]

Denis Byrne; he was in Boland's Bakery and then went to Jameson's Distillery in Marrowbone Lane.

Dermot Byrne; he is listed on the Roll of Honour.

Henry Byrne; he was in A Company and was imprisoned at Frongoch.

James Byrne; he was in A company and is listed on the Roll of Honour.

John (Seán) Byrne; he was a member of C Company and was in charge of first aid for the battalion.

> Some time after I had joined the Volunteers as an ordinary Volunteer there was a call for men for the first aid classes. Most of the Volunteers did not seem to like the idea of going to these classes, they seemed to think that they would not be good soldiers if they attended them. It was pointed out from time to time that a medical man was just as important as anybody else. Following these appeals I decided I would give in my name to the Captain to go to the first aid classes. I attended some lectures given to our own Company.[649]

He was imprisoned at Frongoch.

Michael Byrne; he was in Boland's Bakery and Grand Canal Street. Imprisoned at Frongoch.

Michael Byrne; a member of the Fianna and under sixteen years of age, he was in No. 25 Northumberland Road up to 2.30 a.m. on Wednesday. Lt Malone gave orders that he and another Fianna member, Paddy Rowe, deliver dispatches. The boys guessed that this was a ruse to get them away from the battle and strenuously objected, but Malone, knowing the hopelessness of the situation, ordered them to go and not return.

Michael Byrne; he was in Boland's Mills.

Patrick Byrne; he was in Boland's Bakery and Grand Canal Street. Imprisoned at Frongoch.

Patrick (Paddy) Byrne; he was in the 25 Northumberland Road detachment and at Clanwilliam House, and was sent home because of his youth.

Peter Byrne; he was in Boland's Bakery and Grand Canal Street. He was imprisoned at Wakefield Prison, then at Frongoch.

Thomas Byrne; brother of Christopher (above). He was in Boland's Bakery and then went to Jameson's Distillery, Marrowbone Lane. He took shots at Beggar's Bush Barracks and was sent to the dock area to determine whether the HMY *Helga* could be attacked. He was imprisoned in Frongoch.

William Byrne; he was in Boland's Mills and Grand Canal Street.

John Campbell; he was in the Harcourt Street Railway Station.

Christopher (Christy) Carberry (Carbury) (Christoir Ó Cuirbre); he was in Boland's Bakery and Grand Canal Street. He was tortured in Dublin Castle during the War of Independence.

Dudley Carroll; he was in Boland's Bakery/Mills and Grand Canal Street.

Leo Casey; he was in Boland's Mills and on the Dublin and South Eastern Railway out to Lansdowne Road, and was seriously wounded on the railway line. Imprisoned at Frongoch.

Thomas Cassidy; he was at Boland's Bakery/Mills, Grand Canal Street and Horan's shop. Imprisoned at Frongoch.

William Christian; he was in St Stephen's Parochial Hall on Northumberland Road. He and Joe Clarke, Paddy Doyle and P.B. McGrath held off the Sherwood Foresters from their position as long as they could; they then fled to Percy Place, where they were captured. A Fianna member, he was imprisoned at Frongoch.[650]

Joseph (Joe) Clarke; he was in St Stephen's Parochial Hall on Northumberland Road. He and Patrick J. Doyle, William Christian and P.B. McGrath held off the Sherwood Foresters from their position as long as they could; they then fled to Percy Place, where they were captured. Imprisoned at Frongoch.

Peter Coates; he was in Boland's Bakery/Mills and Grand Canal Street. Imprisoned at Frongoch.

Daniel Colgan; he was in Boland's Mills and on the Dublin and South Eastern Railway between Westland Row and Lansdowne Road.

William Conroy; he was in Boland's Bakery. He evaded capture and went 'on the run'.

Robert Cooper; he was one of the four Volunteers (James [Séamus] Kavanagh, Denis

O'Donoghue and James H. Doyle were the others) originally in the schoolhouse opposite Clanwilliam House. They were withdrawn early in the week, then occupied Robert's Builders' Yard, providing covering fire for those in Clanwilliam House. He received a bullet wound to the chest and was treated in the dispensary in Grand Canal Street.

John Cosgrave; he was in Boland's Mills and Grand Canal Street. Imprisoned at Frongoch.

**2Lt John (Seán) Costello (23);[651] he was born in Athlone, Co. Westmeath, and he was one of the pallbearers at the funeral of O'Donovan Rossa. He was wounded in Grand Canal Street while carrying dispatches to Boland's Mills, and is buried in Deansgrange Cemetery.

Thomas Coyne; he was in Boland's Bakery and Grand Canal Street.

Capt. Michael Cullen; erected the decoy flag on the Ringsend Distillery tower. He 'watched over' de Valera when de Valera went to sleep, and Dev awoke and cried 'Set the Railway on fire'.[652] He was imprisoned at Frongoch. Shortly after his release from Frongoch, he and two other Volunteers from the Boland's Garrison, James Grace and Seán Cullen, went to Glasnevin Cemetery and fired a salute of three volleys over the grave of Michael Malone.[653]

John Christopher (Seán) Cullen; he was in Boland's Bakery and Grand Canal Street. Along with two other Volunteers from the Boland's Garrison, James Grace and Michael Cullen, he went to Glasnevin Cemetery and fired a salute of three volleys over the grave of Michael Malone.[654]

Joseph Michael Curran; he was in the Gas Works and on the Dublin and South Eastern Railway between Westland Row and Lansdowne Road.[655]

James Daly; he was in Robert's Yard on Grand Canal Street and on the Dublin and South Eastern Railway between Westland Row and Lansdowne Road.

Capt. Simon Donnelly; he became O/C of C Company.[656] He joined the IRB in 1914 and took part in the Howth gunrunning. He was one of the Volunteers who bought his own rifle, a Martini, in 1914. He noted that the Company was about 90 strong, but only a third reported on Monday. The Battalion Quartermaster, James Byrne, failed to muster, as did the Company Captain, Eddie Byrne, so Donnelly took charge. Donnelly led the men who took the disused distillery tower, and attracted the fire of the British by raising a green flag on it. When it was fired upon, de Valera was delighted, but the men in the tower did not share his enthusiasm—they wondered what would happen when the tower was demolished. In any case it never came to that, as the British inexplicably stopped after hitting the tower a dozen times.[657] Imprisoned at Frongoch and became O/C of H Company of the North Camp.[658]

Michael Donovan; he was in Boland's Bakery and Grand Canal Street.

David Doyle; he was in the railway station at Lansdowne Road.

James H. Doyle; he was one of the four Volunteers (Robert Cooper, James [Séamus] Kavanagh and Denis O'Donoghue were the others) originally in St Stephen's Parish School on Northumberland Road, across from St Stephen's Parochial Hall, opposite Clanwilliam House. They were withdrawn early in the week. On Tuesday morning he went with two others under the command of Lt George Murphy to the Tram Power Station on Ringsend Road and ordered it to close. On Wednesday he, along with Volunteers Bob Cooper and Séamus Kavanagh, under section commander Denis O'Donohue, occupied the premises of Robert's Builders' Yard in Clanwilliam Place; after heavy firing they returned to Boland's Bakery. He remained on guard duty on the railway until the surrender on Sunday. Imprisoned at Frongoch.[659]

James Joseph (Séamus) Doyle; he was a Clanwilliam House survivor. An explosion of ammunition in the house knocked him unconscious and smashed his Martini rifle; he finished the fight with a borrowed Howth Mauser.[660] He was imprisoned at Frongoch[661] and later became a member of Michael Collins's 'Squad'.

John William Doyle; he was in Boland's Bakery and Grand Canal Street.

Michael Doyle; he was in Boland's Mills and Grand Canal Street.

**Patrick Doyle (36);[662] Clanwilliam House detachment. He was a Volunteer musketry instructor. 'Did I ever think I'd live to see a day like this? … Shouldn't we all be grateful to God that He's allowed us to take part in a fight like this?'[663] Then he fell silent. His body was consumed in the flames of Clanwilliam House.[664] He left a wife and five young children.

Patrick Doyle; he was in the Hammond Lane Foundry and in Ringsend Road.

Patrick J. Doyle; O/C at St Stephen's Parochial Hall, Northumberland Road detachment. He and Joe Clarke, William Christian and P.B. McGrath held off the

Sherwood Foresters from their position for as long as they could and then fled to Percy Place, where they were captured. Imprisoned at Frongoch.

John Dunne (Seán Ó Duinn); he was in Boland's Bakery and Grand Canal Street. Imprisoned at Frongoch.

John Dunne; he was in Boland's Mills and Grand Canal Street.

Thomas Dunne; he was in B Company and is listed on the Roll of Honour.

**Edward Ennis (33);[665] he had been to the Fairyhouse Races on Monday and missed the mobilisation. He was supposedly killed 'on the railway' near the railway sheds, but the location is uncertain.[666]

James Fagan; he was in the Ringsend Distillery and the Hammond Lane Foundry.

Lt Timothy (Tim) Finn; he was in A Company and was imprisoned at Frongoch.

Lt James Fitzgerald; he was in Boland's Mills/Bakery and Grand Canal Street. Imprisoned at Frongoch.

Leo Fitzgerald; he was in Boland's Bakery and Grand Canal Street. He was killed in a battle with the Black and Tans on Great Brunswick Street [Pearse Street] in the War of Independence.

Theobald Wolfe Tone Fitzgerald (brother of Thomas and William, below); he was in Boland's Bakery.

Thomas Fitzgerald; he was in Boland's Bakery/Mills and Grand Canal Street. Imprisoned at Frongoch.[667]

William (Willie) Fitzgerald (15); he was in Grand Canal Street and on the railway line between Westland Row and Lansdowne Road. Imprisoned at Frongoch.

Patrick (Paddy) Flanagan; he was in Boland's Bakery and Grand Canal Street. He became a member of Michael Collins's 'Squad'.

Michael Fleming; he was in B Company and was imprisoned at Frongoch.

John A. Flynn; he is listed on the Roll of Honour.

Thomas Fulham (Fullam); he was in Boland's Bakery and in Westland Row Station and on the railway line.

James T. Gill; he was in Boland's Bakery and Grand Canal Street. Imprisoned at Wakefield and Frongoch.

Edward Gordon (Gorman?); he was at Boland's Bakery and on the Dublin and South Eastern Railway between Westland Row and Lansdowne Road.

Seán Goulding; he was in A Company and is listed on the Roll of Honour.

James J. Grace; he was in the 25 Northumberland Road detachment. Grace moved to the US in 1913 and then moved to Canada, where he joined a British Territorial Regiment to learn how to be a soldier. In 1914 he packed up his Lee-Enfield and moved back to Ireland to join the Volunteers.[668] In 25 Northumberland Road he came down the stairs and made it to the kitchen, then escaped out the back after the British had taken the house and killed Lt Michael Malone.[669] Shortly after his release from Frongoch he, along with two other Volunteers, Michael and Seán Cullen, went to Glasnevin Cemetery and fired a salute of three volleys over the grave of Lt Malone.

Owen Greene; he was at Boland's Bakery and Grand Canal Street. He was wounded on 28 April and taken to Sir Patrick Dun's Hospital and later to Dublin Castle Hospital. He was released from Kilmainham Military Hospital in July 1916.

Martin Griffin; he was at Boland's Bakery and Grand Canal Street and on the railway line between Westland Row and Lansdowne Road. Imprisoned at Frongoch.

Lt John (Seán) Guilfoyle; he tunnelled into a shop across from Beggar's Bush Barracks and harrassed the barracks with rifle fire.[670] At the surrender, he wanted to escape to the mountains and continue fighting.[671] He was imprisoned at Frongoch and became O/C of F Company of the North Camp.

Joseph Guilfoyle, brother of John (above); he guarded a bridge on the line to Harcourt Street Station. Imprisoned at Frongoch.

William Halpin; he was an ICA member and was wounded.

Augustine Hayes (Aoistin Ó hAodha, Aghuirain Ó hAosha); he was at Boland's Bakery and Grand Canal Street.

Michael Hemming; he is listed on the Roll of Honour.

James Henry; he was in Boland's Bakery/Boland's Mills and Grand Canal Street, and on the Dublin and South Eastern Railway Line between Westland Row and Lansdowne Road. Imprisoned at Frongoch.

Lt Michael Hickey; a member of A Company, he was imprisoned at Frongoch.

Samuel Patrick Irwin; he was at Boland's Mills/Bakery and Grand Canal Street.

Francis (Frank) Jackson; he lived at 26 South King Street and is listed on the Roll of Honour. He was detained at Wakefield Detention Barracks.

Joseph Jackson; he was in the distillery when it was shelled.[672] Imprisoned at Frongoch.

James (Séamus) Kavanagh; he was one of the four Volunteers (Robert Cooper, Denis O'Donoghue and James H. Doyle were the others) originally in St Stephen's Parish School on Northumberland Road, across from St Stephen's Parochial Hall, opposite Clanwilliam House. They were withdrawn early in the week, and then he was in the Robert's Builders' Yard outpost.[673] Imprisoned at Frongoch.

Michael Kavanagh; he was in C Company and is listed on the Roll of Honour.

Patrick Kavanagh; he was in C Company and is listed on the Roll of Honour.

Peter Paul (Peadar) Kavanagh; he was at Boland's Bakery and on Grand Canal Street. Imprisoned at Frongoch.[674]

William (Liam) Kavanagh; he was at Boland's Bakery and Grand Canal Street. Imprisoned at Frongoch.

Michael Kearney (Mícheál Ó Caomhanaigh ?); he was in C Company and is on the Roll of Honour.

Patrick Kelly; he was in C Company and was imprisoned at Frongoch.

Richard Kelly; he was at Boland's Bakery/Mills and Grand Canal Street.

Thomas Joseph Kelly (24); he was at the Westland Row Railway Station. He was wounded and received a wound pension. His brother Joseph was in the GPO. Imprisoned at Frongoch.

Charles Kenny; he was on Grand Canal Street and on the Dublin and South Eastern Railway line. Imprisoned at Frongoch.

John Kinsella; he was at the Catholic Club in Great Brunswick Street, in Clarence Street and at Boland's Bakery. Imprisoned at Frongoch.

Edward Kirwan; he was at Boland's Bakery and on the Dublin and South Eastern Railway line between Westland Row and Lansdowne Road.

Edward (Éamonn) Lalor; he was at Boland's Bakery and on the Dublin and South Eastern Railway line between Westland Row and Lansdowne Road.

Michael Lennon (O'Lennon) (Miceal Ó Laonnain); he was in B Company and is listed on the Roll of Honour.

Edward Leonard; he was at Boland's Bakery and Grand Canal Street.

Patrick Leonard; he was at Boland's Bakery and Grand Canal Street.

Leo Lifforoi (Laffoy, Laffroy?); he is listed on the Roll of Honour.

George A. Lyons (Seoirse A. Ó Liathain); he was a B Company officer and was in the Westland Row Railway Station detachment.[675] According to Lyons, de Valera 'decided they [the women] would probably be an encumbrance where an extremely mobile force was necessary, and that anyhow women should be spared, as far as possible, from witnessing the horrors of war, especially the class of war we expected to develop'.[676] Lyons felt that the waiting in Boland's Mills was having a deleterious effect on the men: 'You had a feeling that your comrades might go mad—or, what was even worse, that you might go mad yourself'.[677]

Peter (Owen) McArdle; he was in Ringsend Distillery, Westland Row Railway Station, the Gas Works, Tara Street Bridge, Boland's Bakery and Grand Canal Street.

Patrick McBride (Padraic Mac an Bhaird, Mac an Boird); he was at the Gas Works, Barrow Street Bridge, Boland's Bakery, Westland Row Railway Station and on the railway line to Lansdowne Road. Imprisoned at Frongoch.

Patrick McCabe; he was at 144 Great Brunswick Street, Barrow Street Bridge and on the Dublin and South Eastern Railway line. Imprisoned at Frongoch.

William A. (Liam) McCabe; he was at Boland's Bakery and on the Dublin and South Eastern Railway line between Westland Row and Lansdowne Road. Imprisoned at Frongoch.

Bernard McCarthy; he was at Boland's Mills/Bakery and on Grand Canal Street. Imprisoned at Frongoch.

Michael McCarthy; he was at Boland's Bakery and on the Dublin and South Eastern Railway line between Westland Row and Lansdowne Road. Imprisoned at Frongoch.

Patrick MacCormack; originally from Belfast. Imprisoned at Frongoch.

Joseph McCurran; he is listed on the Roll of Honour.

Joseph (Joe) MacDermott (McDermott); he was in Boland's Mills and Grand Canal Street, and on the railway line between Westland Row and Beggar's Bush.

Seán McDermott; he is listed on the Roll of Honour.

Lt Andrew (Andy) McDonnell; armed only with a pike, he was ordered to stop a tram outside de Valera's HQ. 'I was the proud possessor of a .22 revolver and a pike, both of which I kept at home well polished. I was all ready …'[678] While his pike was laid aside at first, it became a flagstaff for an Irish Republic flag.

Cathal (Charles) MacDowell; he was at Boland's Bakery and Grand Canal Street. He was imprisoned at Frongoch until July 1917.

Patrick McDowell (Padraig MacDubhaill); he was at Lansdowne Road and on the Dublin and South Eastern Railway line between Westland Row and Lansdowne Road.

Seán McEffoy; he is listed on the Roll of Honour.

Patrick McGill (Padraig MacGhaill, MacGiolla); imprisoned at Frongoch.

Charles McGowan; his brother Claude was in the 2nd Battalion, and his sister Josephine (Josie) was in Marrowbone Lane in the 4th Battalion. He was imprisoned in

Kilmainham during the War of Independence.

P.B. (James) McGrath; he was in the Parochial Hall on Northumberland Road. He and Paddy Doyle, William Christian and Joe Clarke held off the Sherwood Foresters from their position for as long as they could and then fled to Percy Place, where they were captured. Imprisoned at Frongoch.

Seán McGrath; he was in Boland's Bakery and on Grand Canal Street.

**Peadar Macken (37);[679] he was elected an alderman in the North Dock Ward in 1913.[680] An officer, he reprimanded a Volunteer who kept ignoring the order for silence.[681] The truculent Volunteer shot him through the heart.[682] His body was taken to the dispensary in Grand Canal Street where de Valera had his headquarters and was buried in the dispensary yard,[683] then later reinterred in Glasnevin Cemetery. At the time, the street on which he fought was named Great Clarence Street, but it was changed to Macken Street in his honour.

John (Seán) MacMahon; he was O/C of B Company and was in Boland's Bakery and on the Dublin and South Eastern Railway line between Westland Row and Lansdowne Road.[684]

Capt. John (Seán) McMahon; he was O/C of B Company and was imprisoned at Frongoch.

Seán MacTialaghoigh (?); he is listed on the Roll of Honour.

James Maguire; he was in the Gas Works, at 144 Great Brunswick Street, the Ringsend Distillery and Boland's Mills/Bakery.

Daniel Maher; a very young lad, he was sent home by George Reynolds, O/C in Clanwilliam House, on Monday because he was very ill.

James Mallon; he was in Boland's Bakery and Grand Canal Street. Imprisoned at Frongoch.

**Lt Michael Malone (28);[685] O/C of the 25 Northumberland Road detachment. He was the best marksman in the Company. 'We know what we are dying for, thank God the day has come.'[686] A little after midnight on Wednesday, Malone called James Grace aside: 'Look here, Jimmy, you know we haven't a chance … So I'd like to send the young [Paddy] Rowe and [Michael] Byrne away. They're not even sixteen yet …'[687] Malone and James Grace decided to make a last stand at the head of the stairs; while Grace made it to the kitchen and then escaped, Malone was shot as he came down the stairs.[688] De Valera ended up with his Mauser and kept it for the rest of his life. Malone's brother, William, had been killed in France serving as a sergeant with the 2nd Battalion of the Royal Dublin Fusiliers.

Robert Malone; he was in Boland's Bakery and Grand Canal Street. Imprisoned at Frongoch.

Joseph Patrick (Joe) Martin; he was in Camden Row, Boland's Bakery and Grand Canal Street.

Michael Meagher; he was at the Westland Row Railway Station and on the Dublin and South Eastern Railway line to Lansdowne Road.

Patrick Meagher; he was in Westland Row Railway Station, then Boland's Bakery/Mills.

Seán Merlahan; he is listed on the Roll of Honour.

Michael Merriman (Merrimon); he was in Boland's Bakery and Grand Canal Street.

Joseph Molloy; he was in C Company and was imprisoned at Frongoch.

Laurence Moore; he was in Westland Row Railway Station, then Boland's Bakery and Grand Canal Street.

Capt. Frank Mullen; he halted his company on Mount Street Bridge and told them: 'Any Volunteer who wishes may hand over his rifle and leave our ranks'. Only one did.

Martin Mullen; he was in Earlsfort Terrace and New Street, and then went to Jacob's. (Counted in the 2nd Battalion garrison.)

Patrick Mullen; he was imprisoned at Frongoch.

Charles Murphy; he was in B Company and is listed on the Roll of Honour.

Christopher J. (Christy) Murphy; in the middle of the week he was shot by a sniper from a height, the bullet entering his throat and coming out through his lung.[689] Despite the best efforts of doctors after the surrender, it proved impossible to remove

Diarmuid Lynch, GPO. He was a member of the Supreme Council of the IRB. During the War of Independence he organised Sinn Féin's blockade of food exports in 1918 and was deported to the US for doing so. (He was a US citizen.) While deported, he was elected TD for Cork South East. (Courtesy of the Trustees of the National Library of Ireland)

Seán McGarry, GPO. A great friend and confidant of Tom Clarke. Of Clarke he wrote: 'If one may hazard a guess, it is that history will write Tom Clarke as a great Irishman—great in his love for Ireland, great in his faith in her destiny, great in his purpose, great in his achievement, and great in his death'. (Courtesy of the Trustees of the National Library of Ireland)

Joseph McGuinness, 1st Battalion. He was in command of the first twenty Volunteers sent to take the Four Courts; they stormed the Chancery Street entrance. While imprisoned in Lewes Gaol, he won the South Longford election on 9 May 1917: 'Put him *in* to get him *out*' was the election slogan. (Courtesy of the Trustees of the National Library of Ireland)

Brian O'Higgins, GPO. He was unwell for several months prior to the Rising, and was one of those who were 'relegated in this way to the Reserve very much against their will … We called ourselves the "Lame ducks" and joked over our extreme military knowledge, but were very proud that we had not been passed over and we were to have our own special place in the great mobilisation.' (Courtesy of the Trustees of the National Library of Ireland)

Willie Pearse, GPO. The younger brother of Patrick Pearse, Willie idolised his older brother. They were inseparable. When Willie studied history as a young boy, he imagined his brother as the heroes about whom he was learning. He was the only one to plead guilty to all the charges at his court martial. (Courtesy of the Trustees of the National Library of Ireland)

Gearóid O'Sullivan, GPO. A cousin of Michael Collins, he was the youngest officer in the GPO. On 19 October 1922 he married Maud Kiernan, Kitty's sister, in what had been intended to be a double wedding with Kitty and Michael Collins. Kitty was a bridesmaid, but dressed all in black. He became Adjutant General of the Free State Army. (Courtesy of the Trustees of the National Library of Ireland)

Thomas Traynor, 3rd Battalion. The father of ten children, he was interned in Wakefield Jail and Frongoch. In the War of Independence Traynor was captured during an ambush of Auxiliaries in Brunswick Street. Tried on 5 April 1921 at City Hall, he was executed in Mountjoy on 25 April 1921. (Courtesy of the Trustees of the National Library of Ireland)

Louise Gavan-Duffy, GPO. She was a member of the initial Provisional Committee of Cumann na mBan and its Hon. Secretary. Sister of George Gavan-Duffy, later Minister for Foreign Affairs in the First Dáil, she founded Scoil Bhríde, Ireland's first Gaelscoil for girls.

On Easter Monday she came to the GPO and asked to see Pearse: 'I said to him that I wanted to be in the field but that I felt that the Rebellion was a frightful mistake, that it could not possibly succeed, and that it was, therefore, wrong'. Pearse suggested that she help out in the kitchens, and she agreed to this, since it was not active service. (Pearse Museum)

Dr Kathleen Lynn, City Hall, and **Madeleine ffrench-Mullen**, St Stephen's Green. Both members of the ICA, Dr Lynn and Miss ffrench-Mullen led the medical detachments in their respective garrisons. In 1919 they founded St Ultan's Children's Hospital (with £70 and two cots) 'for the medical treatment of infants under one year of age'. St Ultan's became the front line in the battle against infant mortality. (Multi-text, UCC)

Martin Kelly, City Hall. He was a member of the *Dublin Evening Mail*, 38–40 Parliament Street, squad. One of three brothers to take part in the Rising, Martin was a captain in the ICA. He married Elizabeth (Bessie) Lynch. He managed to avoid capture after the Rising and was to remain active. (Kelly family)

Mary Stephenson (née Kilmartin), 1st Battalion. Mary was known as 'Mamie' and was in the Four Courts garrison. She married Patrick Joseph (Paddy) Stephenson, who was in the GPO and the Mendicity Institute. (David Kilmartin)

Michael Malone, 3rd Battalion. O/C of the 25 Northumberland Road detachment, he was the best marksman in the Company. 'We know what we are dying for, thank God the day has come.' Malone was shot as he came down the stairs. His brother, William, had been killed in France serving as a sergeant with the 2nd Battalion of the Royal Dublin Fusiliers. (*Come here to me!—Dublin life and culture* blog)

Michael (Mick) Kelly, St Stephen's Green. He led a detachment of sixteen men, six of whom went to Charlemont Street and another ten to the railway bridge crossing the Grand Canal at Davy's public house. Upon returning to the Green, he was sent to set fire to houses at the top of Grafton Street, but the detachment was withdrawn before attempting their mission. (Kelly family)

Mary Teresa (Molly) O'Reilly, City Hall, GPO. On the Sunday before the Rising, the *Irish Republic* flag, with the harp but without the crown, was first raised over Liberty Hall. Connolly handed the flag to Molly and said: 'I hand you this flag as the sacred emblem of Ireland's unconquered soul'. He chose Molly to hoist the flag as a replacement for Countess Markievicz. (Courtesy of Constance Cowley)

Helena Molony, City Hall. Helena Molony (seated third from the left, second row, next to Maud Gonne MacBride) was an early member of Inghinidhe na hÉireann/Daughters of Ireland, which was founded by Maud Gonne MacBride in 1900. Molony was one of the founders of the Fianna, an ICA officer and an Abbey actress, and was the secretary of the Irish Women's Workers' Union. (*Irish Revolutionary Women*)

Seán T. O'Kelly (Ó Ceallaigh), GPO. An ICA member, he was Pearse's adjutant during the Rising. He was sent on missions throughout Dublin, as well as fighting in the GPO. He was president of Ireland from 1945 to 1959. (Kelly family)

all the bullet shrapnel. He continued to serve through the War of Independence, using his barber shop at Camden Row in Dublin as a safe house. During the Emergency he joined the Irish Army despite his ill health. He joined at Griffith Barracks in July 1940 at the age of 50, his enlistment documents noting as a distinctive mark 'Bullet wound scar on throat 1916'.

John J. (Seán) Murphy; he was in Westland Row Railway Station and then Boland's Mills. Imprisoned at Frongoch.

William P. (Liam) Murphy; he was in Grand Canal Street, at Beggar's Bush Barracks, Grattan Street and Boland's Bakery. Imprisoned at Frongoch.

**Richard (Dick) Murphy (24);[690] Clanwilliam House detachment. His body was consumed in the flames of Clanwilliam House.[691] He was engaged to be married the next week.

William P. (Liam) Murphy; he was in Grand Canal Street, at Beggar's Bush Barracks, Grattan Street and Boland's Bakery. Imprisoned at Frongoch.

Frank Murray; he was in Camden Row, Boland's Bakery and the Dublin and South Eastern Railway Works.

James (Séamus) Murray; 'We were lined up in the Bakery and the Commandant [de Valera] told us that it had been decided to surrender. This announcement met with general disapproval. Some of the men proceeded to smash their rifles. We were formed into fours and marched out through the Clarence Street entrance into Grand Canal Street and into Grattan Street where we were halted, and laid down our arms in Grattan Street outside Smyley House.'[692] He was attached as the Staff Quartermaster General in the War of Independence.

Michael Murray; he was in Clanwilliam Place, Boland's Bakery and on the Dublin and South Eastern Railway line between Westland Row and Lansdowne Road.

Arthur Nolan; he was a baker at Boland's and stayed when the Volunteers took over.

Patrick Nolan; he was at Boland's Bakery and on the Dublin and South Eastern Railway line between Westland Row and Lansdowne Road.

Peter Nolan; he ripped out rails on the line to Harcourt Street Station and dug a foxhole between the railway sleepers, where he slept at night.

John Nugent; he was in C Company and is listed on the Roll of Honour.

Joseph Nugent; he was in C Company and is listed on the Roll of Honour.

William (Liam) O'Brien (Ó Broin); he was at Boland's Bakery and Grand Canal Street. He was imprisoned at Frongoch and became O/C of C Company of the North Camp.

Lt Joseph Michael O'Byrne (Seosaimh Ó Broin); a Red Cross officer, he served as a doctor and was O/C of D Company. Imprisoned at Frongoch.

Lt Seán O'Byrne; a Red Cross man, de Valera left him to deal with the Cumann na mBan women who had been turned away from the garrison.[693]

Thomas Joseph O'Byrne; he was in Boland's Bakery and on Grand Canal Street. Imprisoned at Frongoch.

William O'Byrne; he was in D Company and is listed on the Roll of Honour.

Miceal Ó Caoinhanadh; he is listed on the Roll of Honour.

Capt. Joseph O'Connor; he was in Boland's Bakery/Mills.[694] He was O/C of A Company. Michael Malone said to him on Good Friday: 'Well, Joe, it's pretty close to hand. I know you'll come through, but I won't.' Imprisoned at Frongoch, he became O/C in charge of the 5th Dormitory.[695] He received the maximum pension of £350 per year.

Lt Thomas O'Connor (brother of William, below); he was O/C of F Company.[696] On Monday, while on his way to Carrisbrook House, Ballsbridge, he dismantled the telephone exchange in Dún Laoghaire and cut telephone wires at Merrion and Ballsbridge. After he and his men engaged in firing at Beggar's Bush barracks, they were ordered to evacuate Carrisbrook House and went on to dismantle a second telephone exchange at Blackrock. He was taken prisoner on 6 May and spent time in Wakefield prison and in Frongoch until September 1916.

William O'Connor (brother of Thomas, above); he was in Carrisbrook House, and left with the others to occupy grounds and fields nearby.[697] He was a dispatch rider operating in the Ballsbridge area.

Denis O'Donoghue; he was asked by de Valera whether he knew anyone who could drive a train engine, and he said that his brother could. For a while de Valera considered getting up steam in an engine and running it up and down the tracks to launch hit-and-run raids on the railway line.[698] O'Donoghue was one of the four Volunteers (Robert Cooper, James H. Doyle and James [Séamus] Kavanagh were the others) originally in St Stephen's Parish School on Northumberland Road, across from St Stephen's Parochial Hall, opposite Clanwilliam House. They were withdrawn early in the week. On Wednesday Volunteers Bob Cooper and Séamus Kavanagh, under section commander O'Donoghue, occupied the premises of Robert's Builders' Yard in Clanwilliam Place; after heavy firing they returned to Boland's Bakery. They remained on guard duty on the railway until the surrender on Sunday.[699]

Anthony O'Grady; he was a draper's porter living at 33b Nicholas Street and is listed on the Roll of Honour.

Séamus Ó Greargain; he is listed on the Roll of Honour.

John (Seán) O'Hanlon; he was in Boland's Bakery and Grand Canal Street. Imprisoned at Frongoch.

John (Seán) O'Keefe; he was in Boland's Bakery and the Dublin and South Eastern Railway works. He was badly wounded on Thursday night at Robert's Builders' Yard.[700] Imprisoned at Frongoch.

Michael O'Keefe; he was in Boland's Mills and on the Dublin and South Eastern Railway line between Westland Row and Lansdowne Road.

Patrick Anthony O'Kelly; he was in Boland's Bakery, Robert's Timber Yard in Grand Canal Street, and on the Dublin and South Eastern Railway line between Westland Row and Lansdowne Road.

Liam Ó Leroin; he is listed on the Roll of Honour.

Peter O'Mara (Peadar Ó Meadhra); he was in Boland's Bakery and on the Dublin and South Eastern Railway line between Westland Row and Lansdowne Road, and in Horan's shop near Beggar's Bush Barracks. Imprisoned at Frongoch.

Andrew O'Neill; he was in Westland Row Railway Station and Boland's Bakery, and on the Dublin and South Eastern Railway line between Westland Row and Lansdowne Road.

Christopher (Christy) O'Reilly; he was in Boland's Bakery and on Grand Canal Street.

Patrick O'Reilly; he was in A Company and was imprisoned at Frongoch.

Thomas O'Rourke; he was in A Company and is listed on the Roll of Honour.

John James (Seán) O'Shea; he was in Boland's Bakery and Grand Canal Street.

Séamus O'Treacy; he is listed on the Roll of Honour.

Richard Pearle (16); 'Go home, mother, this is no place for a woman'.[701] He was at Westland Row Railway Station, Boland's Bakery/Mills, Grand Canal Street, the Gas Works and the Dublin and South Eastern Railway line between Westland Row and Lansdowne Road. Imprisoned at Frongoch.

Thomas Peate; he was at Boland's Bakery/Mills, Grand Canal Street and the Dublin and South Eastern Railway line between Westland Row and Lansdowne Road. Imprisoned at Frongoch.

Denis Peelo; he was at Camden Row, Boland's Bakery/Mills and Grand Canal Street.

James Peely; he is listed on the Roll of Honour.

James Pender; he was at Boland's Bakery and Grand Canal Street. Imprisoned at Frongoch.

Eugene (Owen) Porter; he was at Boland's Bakery/Mills, Grand Canal Street and the Dublin and South Eastern Railway line between Westland Row and Lansdowne Road. Imprisoned at Frongoch.

Patrick Power; he was in B Company and was imprisoned at Frongoch.

James (John) Purfield (Purneld, Purfeld?); he was at Boland's Bakery/Mills, Grand Canal Street and the Dublin and South Eastern Railway line between Westland Row and Lansdowne Road.[702] An ICA member, he was wounded at Boland's Mills and received a wound pension.

Lt John (Seán) Quinn; he commanded B Company at Westland Row Station.[703] His company seized the station a few minutes after noon and had it under control before the staff or the public realised it.[704]

Thomas Quinn; he was imprisoned at Frongoch.

Liam Raftis; he was in B Company and is listed on the Roll of Honour.

James Redican; he was in C Company and was imprisoned at Frongoch.

Thomas Christopher Redican; he was at Boland's Bakery and Grand Canal Street.

Denis Joseph Redmond; he was at Boland's Bakery/Mills, Grand Canal Street and the Dublin and South Eastern Railway line between Westland Row and Lansdowne Road.

John Joseph (Seán) Reid; he was at Boland's Bakery/Mills, Grand Canal Street and the Dublin and South Eastern Railway line between Westland Row and Lansdowne Road. Imprisoned at Frongoch.

Patrick Reid; he was at Boland's Bakery/Mills, Grand Canal Street and the Dublin and South Eastern Railway line between Westland Row and Lansdowne Road.

**George Reynolds;[705] an ecclesiastical silversmith by trade, he was O/C in Clanwilliam House. Reynolds was born in Dublin and educated in the Synge Street Christian Brothers' School.[706] His body was consumed in the flames of Clanwilliam House.[707]

William Charles Roe; he was at Boland's Bakery and Missionary Hall in Northumberland Road.

William (Willie) Ronan (Rownan?); he was in Clanwilliam House and escaped with the Walsh brothers.[708] They escaped to the rear of the house and into a laneway. Then they crossed several garden walls and entered a house with an open door, where they asked a little girl for clothes to cover their uniforms. She told her mother about them, and her mother threw them out, claiming that 'We'd all be shot'. He is buried in Deansgrange Cemetery.

Patrick Joseph (Paddy) Rowe (Roe?); a member of the Fianna and under sixteen years of age, he was in No. 25 Northumberland Road up to 2.30 a.m. on Wednesday. Lieutenant Malone gave orders that he and another Fianna member, Michael Byrne, deliver dispatches. The boys guessed that this was a ruse to get them away from the battle and strenuously objected, but Malone, knowing the hopelessness of the situation, ordered them to go and not return.

Cornelius (Con) Ryan; he was at Boland's Bakery and Northumberland Road.

Thomas Scully (Tomas Ó Scolaige); he was in Boland's Bakery/Mills and Grand Canal Street.

Albert Smith; he was in Boland's Bakery and on the Dublin and South Eastern Railway line.

Liam Stanley; he was in A Company and is listed on the Roll of Honour.

John Joseph Stokes; he was at Boland's Bakery, the Ringsend Distillery and the Gas Works.

Michael Aloysius (Miceal) Tannam; he was at 144 Great Brunswick Street and Boland's Bakery/Mills. Imprisoned at Frongoch.

Alexander Thompson; he was at Boland's Bakery and the Dublin and South Eastern Railway line.

Thomas Traynor; a bootmaker from Tullow, Co. Carlow, and the father of ten children, he was later interned in Wakefield Jail, where he shared a cell with Seán MacEoin. He was also in Frongoch. During the War of Independence Traynor was captured during an ambush of Auxiliaries in Brunswick Street. He was badly beaten by the Igoe Gang before execution. Tried on 5 April 1921 at City Hall, he was executed in Mountjoy on 25 April 1921.

John Walker; he was imprisoned at Frongoch.

Leo Walpole; he was outside Beggar's Bush Barracks and at Boland's Bakery.

James Walsh (brother of Thomas, below); Clanwilliam House detachment.[709] He had a Howth Mauser with about 200 rounds of ammunition and a .45 revolver with 50 rounds.[710] He and his brother escaped Clanwilliam House with Willie Ronan. They escaped to the rear of the house and into a laneway. Then they crossed several garden walls and entered a house with an open door, where they asked a little girl for clothes to cover their uniforms. She told her mother about them and her mother threw them out, claiming that 'We'd all be shot'. Imprisoned at Frongoch.

Thomas Walsh (brother of James, above); Clanwilliam House detachment. On Tuesday the brothers, along with ten other men, were detailed to go to Clanwilliam

House to defend Mount Street Bridge. The party arrived at Clanwilliam House at about 3 p.m. and were admitted by George Reynolds, who was in charge of the position. Paddy Doyle, Jimmy Doyle, Dick Murphy and Willy Ronan were in the house when the group arrived. Tom had about 200 rounds of ammunition for his Mauser, and a .45 revolver with 60 rounds. On Wednesday morning their younger brother Leo arrived with a large parcel of food. While they were attempting to get the parcel into the house by hauling it up on a rope, they were fired on; Leo was forced to take cover, and in their haste to get the parcel in through the window the rope snapped and the food fell to the ground. Leo managed to secure the parcel to the rope and on the second attempt they managed to haul it into the house.[711]

Patrick Ward; he'd had pneumonia earlier in the year and moved to Sandyford. He did not receive notice of the Rising and so reported only on Tuesday morning. Imprisoned at Frongoch.[712]

James Watters (Waters); he was imprisoned at Frongoch.

****Patrick Whelan** (23);[713] he was a member of the Gaelic League and an accomplished hurler. He had been dispatched to Tralee, but returned with the discouraging news of Casement's capture and Robert Monteith's bitter denunciation of the Germans. Killed at Boland's Mills on Wednesday,[714] he was first buried under a mound of clinkers at the Mills and then later reinterred in Glasnevin Cemetery. He was shot just under the eye by a sniper and died instantly.

Patrick Williams; he was in B Company and was imprisoned at Frongoch.

William Joseph Woodcock; he was at Boland's Bakery and on the Dublin and South Eastern Railway line. Imprisoned at Frongoch.

VI. 4th Battalion

Commandant Éamonn Ceannt's 4th Battalion was assigned the unenviable task of securing the South Dublin Union, which was an urban battlefield within the larger Dublin urban battlefield. The strategic importance of the Union lay in the fact that it commanded the western and southern approaches to the city. It prevented the movement of troops from Richmond Barracks to the city centre and it overlooked army HQ at the Royal Hospital, Kilmainham, which was well within rifle range. Ceannt's task was to prevent the British in Islandbridge and Richmond Barracks from entering the city and coming to the relief of Dublin Castle. The Union was composed of almost a dozen large buildings, all of which were built with several wings, and was surrounded by twice that number of smaller buildings. The entire complex was a maze: each building and cul-de-sac was part of a labyrinth of open areas, streets and courtyards, as well as active hospitals and infirmaries housing over 3,000 patients and medical personnel at the time of the Rising. To compound Ceannt's problem, the 4th Battalion, like all the rest, was severely undermanned owing to the cancellation order, and some Volunteers recalled that they had seen three or four times as many men on manoeuvres as reported for the Rising. W.T. Cosgrave noted that, out of nominal battalion strength of about 700, only 120 men turned out.[715] Because his area of command was huge, the order probably adversely affected Ceannt more than any other commander. Since the Union covered over 50 acres, all the buildings within it made it a nightmare to defend; at the same time, it proved almost impossible for the British to determine where the Volunteers were posted, and they had to attack while under fire from almost every direction.

On Thursday afternoon the Sherwood Foresters, having overcome resistance at Mount Street Bridge, tried to force their wagons and infantry over the Rialto Bridge towards army HQ at the Royal Hospital but came under heavy fire from the South Dublin Union. The Foresters were forced to halt and carry out a major assault on the Union to clear the way over the bridge. Major Sir Francis Vane, who had come up from Portobello Barracks, joined them. He led a collection of 'Highlanders, sailors and policemen'. They, too, joined the attack on the Union. This time the attackers fought their way into close range and began to bore holes through internal walls. Both sides used rifles, small arms and grenades. Leading the attack for the British was Capt. Michael Martyn of the Foresters; when a grenade thrown by one of Martyn's men dropped short of its target and rolled back to the feet of the attackers, Martyn snatched it up and hurled it through an aperture above the door frame.

To his credit, Ceannt had an intimate knowledge of the entire Union and deployed his Volunteers to excellent advantage. He had conducted training manoeuvres in the exact positions the men were to occupy within the Union just days before the Rising,[716] and he also had drawings of the Union, so his defence was well planned.[717] The buildings offered cover and concealment to the Volunteers, and they maximised this by tunnelling from one building to the next. The battalion second-in-command, Cathal Brugha, assigned mutually supporting areas of responsibility with converging fields of fire.[718] These positions were manned throughout the week and posed an almost impenetrable barrier to the British. The Volunteers took advantage of their knowledge of the buildings to tunnel out of danger when they were attacked, 'reappearing' in another location to fire on the advancing British. This movement within the garrison convinced the British that they were facing a much larger force and was a prime part of Ceannt's tactical plan. Neither side knew precisely where the enemy was, nor were there any fixed battle lines. Ceannt masterfully placed his troops in positions where they could utilise covering fire and this also kept the British from being able to flank his positions. Soon the Union turned into an unnerving battle for both sides: men chased men from room to room, small parties of both sides were cut off in buildings held by the enemy, and each door and wall threatened death.[719]

On Friday the Volunteers saw British artillery spotters reconnoitring the Union. That evening Gen. Maxwell wrote to Lord French, promising that any strong points that continued to hold out would be 'blown off the face of the earth'.[720] The battle at the Union ended in a stalemate, as the British were unable to breach the Volunteers' well-chosen positions. Because of Ceannt's deployment and movement of Volunteers, the garrison were never beaten but only surrendered on Pearse's orders on Sunday.

4TH BATTALION: MEN

South Dublin Union Workhouse, mustered in Emerald Square, Dolphin's Barn. Mostly owing to Eoin MacNeill's cancellation order, only approximately 120 mustered on Monday out of a battalion strength of about 1,000—it was one of the battalions most badly affected by the order. Garrison total about 255 men and women; two executed, seven killed.

Fairbrother's Field, James's Street, Jameson's Distillery, Marrowbone Lane, Roe's Distillery, Mount Brown, South Dublin Union Workhouse, Watkins's Brewery, Ardee Street.

(This is not the famous John Jameson and Sons Distillery. John's son, William, went into business with his father-in-law, John Stein, around 1800. Stein owned the Marrowbone Lane distillery. William died shortly afterwards, and his share passed to his

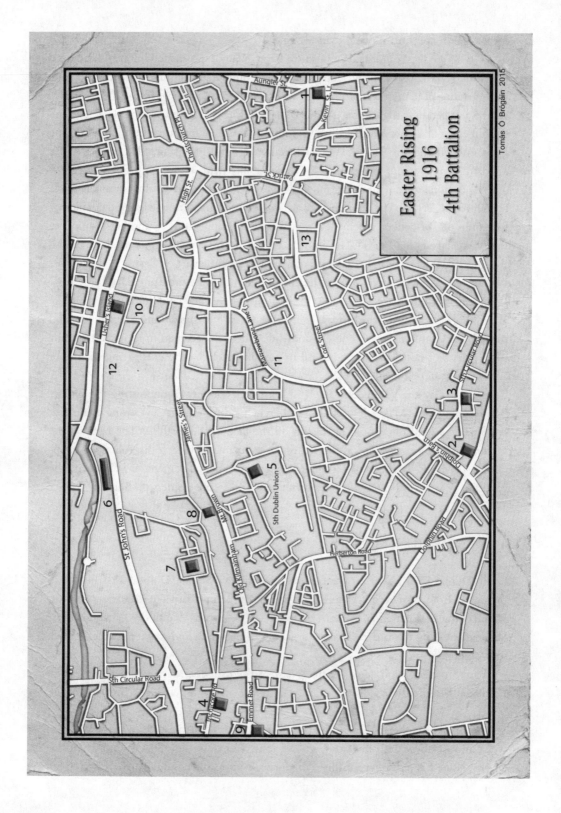

Easter Rising
1916
4th Battalion

Tomás Ó Brógáin 2015

No.	Address	Site	Description
1	26–50 Bishop Street, at corner of Peter Street and Aungier Street	Jacob's Biscuit Factory	HQ of 2nd Battalion. The front entrance, on Peter Street, is in Dublin 2.
2	Dolphin's Barn		Where James Connolly was taken for 'consultation' in January 1916.
3	2 Dolphin's Terrace, off South Circular Road and Herberton Road	Home of Éamonn and Áine Ceannt	He was OC of the 4th Battalion, and many meetings were held here prior to the Rising.
4	Inchicore Road	Kilmainham Gaol	The Rising's leaders were executed here. Many men and women were imprisoned here after the Rising.
5	James's Street	South Dublin Union	Major position of the 4th Battalion.
6		Kingsbridge Railway Station	Never taken by the Volunteers, it was a major conduit for the British reinforcements from the west. Now Heuston Station.
7	Kilmainham	Royal Hospital, Kilmainham	Administrative HQ of the British Army during the Rising.
8	Mount Brown	Roe's Distillery	Major position of the 3rd Battalion.
9	Inchicore	Richmond Barracks	Courts martial were held here after the Rising.
10	Usher's Island	Mendicity Institute	Held by 35 Volunteers during the Rising.
11	Marrowbone Lane	Jameson's Distillery	A major position of the 4th Battalion.
12		Guinness's Buildings	
13	Ardee Street	Watkins's Brewery	A major position of the 4th Battalion.

brother James, who purchased Stein's share in 1820, and thenceforth it was called Jameson's Distillery.)

*Cmdt Éamonn Ceannt (executed 8 May 1916, aged 34).[721] Ceannt was quite tall—about 6ft—and was an excellent musician, playing the uilleann pipes before Pope Pius X in Rome in 1908. The family was originally from County Galway, though they moved to Dublin when Éamonn was very young. His father was a member of the RIC. Éamonn was born on 21 September 1881, reputedly in the RIC barracks in Ballymoe, and christened Edward [Edmund] Thomas Kent. He taught at St Enda's and was an official in the City Treasurer's Office of Dublin Corporation.[722]

In Kilmainham he was in cell no. 88 (upper floor) and was moved to cell no. 20. He was seen by his wife Áine[723] and Lily O'Brennan (Áine's sister), and was attended by Fr Augustine.[724]

Áine wrote:

Thursday morning's paper brought the news of the execution of Pearse, MacDonagh and Clarke, and I believe in that same paper it said that it was stated in the House of Commons that a sentence of three years' penal servitude had been imposed on Éamonn and three others. I do not know who the other three were. When I read this I was delighted, but at the same time I thought it very hard that MacDonagh, who to my mind had not been so deeply involved until the last moment, should have suffered execution …

During this period I was labouring under the delusion that my husband had been sentenced to three years, but my sister-in-law, who lived in Drumcondra, traced me to Mrs Brugha's home and told me that I need not believe what I saw in the papers, that four more had been executed, Willie Pearse, Ned Daly, Michael O'Hanrahan and Joe Plunkett. She suggested that I come over with her and call down to the priests in Church Street, where the only reliable information could be obtained. She also told me that the military escort sent for Mrs MacDonagh had failed to reach her, so that Mrs MacDonagh had no final interview with her husband before his execution. Bearing this in mind I decided to stay up all night …

That evening I went down with my sister-in-law to Church Street, and for the first time met Father Albert. He warned me to take no counsel with anyone I met, and to be very discreet in all I said. I stayed in Drumcondra that night as it was too late to cross the bridges …

I arrived at Kilmainham, was shown in, and found Éamonn in a cell with no seating accommodation and no bedding, not even a bed of straw. The first thing I noticed was that his Sam Brown belt was gone, and that his uniform was slightly torn. A sergeant stood at the door while we spoke, and we could say very little, but I gathered from Éamonn that he had heard about the supposed three years' sentence and he felt it would worry me. I said to him that the Rising was an awful fiasco, and he replied, 'No, it was the biggest thing since '98. They told me here that the railway lines were up.' Those were Éamonn's words …

He gave me Cathal Brugha's watch to give to Mrs Brugha, and some money which he had on him …

I left Éamonn after getting a promise that he would send for me no matter what was going to happen …

… an Army officer arrived with a note to say that my husband would like to see myself and his sister. We went out to the car and there we found that this soldier had already collected Richard Kent and Michael Kent, brothers.

We reached Kilmainham and had about twenty minutes' interview with my husband. He was in a different cell, and had been given a couple of boards, on which I presume he rested. He also had a soap box, a chair, a candle and pen and ink.

No executions had taken place for some days, I think MacBride's execution had taken place on Friday, and the soldiers were coming in and out in a jocose manner, saying such things as, 'It's a long way to Tipperary', and, 'You never know what will happen'. Éamonn said his mind had been disturbed. He said, 'I was quite prepared to walk out of this at a quarter to four in the morning, but all this has upset me'. He told me he had sent for Father Augustine to come to him …

As I was still in doubt as to the outcome of the morning, I remained up all night with my sister-in-law, and each hour we knelt down and said the Rosary. From three o'clock I remained praying until about half past five, when I knew that everything would be over if the executions were to take place.

At six o'clock curfew was lifted, and we made our way down to Church Street. It was a glorious summer morning, and when we arrived at the Priory I asked for Father Augustine.

He sent down another Friar who told me that Father Augustine had only come, celebrated Mass and had gone to his room, but that if I wished he would get up and come down to me. I said no, that I only wanted to know the truth, and this priest said, 'He is gone to Heaven'.

At about ten o'clock on 8th May my sister-in-law accompanied me to Church Street, where we met Father Augustine.

He gave me full details of Éamonn's last moments, and I think enough praise could not be given to both Father Augustine, O.F.M. Cap., and to his comrade Father Albert, for all they did for the executed men.

Father Augustine told me that Éamonn had held his, Father Augustine's, crucifix in his hands, and the last words he spoke were, 'My Jesus, mercy'.

In every case it would appear as if it was necessary for the officer in charge of the firing party to dispatch the victim by a revolver shot. Father Augustine thought that this was a dreadful thing. He gave me two letters which he had brought from the jail; one was my husband's personal letter to me, and the other was a letter which he left more or less for the Irish nation.[725]

On 7 May, Ceannt wrote a letter to the Irish people:

I leave for the guidance of other revolutionaries, who may tread the path which I have trod, this advice, never to treat with the enemy, never to surrender to his mercy, but to fight to a finish. I see nothing gained but grave disaster caused, by the surrender which has marked the end of the Irish Insurrection of 1916—so far at least as Dublin is concerned. The enemy has not cherished one generous thought for those who, with little hope, with poor equipment, and weak in numbers, withstood his forces for one glorious week. Ireland has shown she is a Nation. This generation can claim to have raised sons as brave as any that went before. And in the years to come, Ireland will honour those who risked all for her honour at Easter in 1916. I bear no ill will against whom I have fought. I have found the common soldiers and the higher officers human and companionable, even the English who were actually in the fight against us. Thank God soldiering for Ireland has opened my heart and made me see poor humanity where I expected to see only scorn and reproach. I have met the man who escaped from me by a ruse under the Red Cross. But I do not regret having withheld my fire. He gave me cakes!

I wish to record the magnificent gallantry and fearless, calm determination of the men who fought with me. All, all were simply splendid. Even I knew no fear nor panic and shrank from no risk as I shrink not now from the death which faces me at daybreak. I hope to see God's face even for a moment in the morning. His will be done. All here are very kind. My poor wife saw me yesterday and bore up—so my warden told me—even after she left my presence. Poor Áine, poor Ronan. God is their only shield now that I am removed. And God is a better shield than I. I have just seen Áine, Nell, Richard and Mick and bade them a conditional good-bye. Even now they have hope.

*Cornelius (Con) Colbert (Conchubhair Ó Colbaird) (executed 8 May 1916, aged 28).[726] He was in command at Watkins's Brewery/Ardee Street Brewery, and the entire Marrowbone Lane post.

In Kilmainham he was in cell no. 17 and was seen by Rose McNamara, wife of Capt. James McNamara (Séamus O'Murchadha), who was also a prisoner. Fr Augustine attended him: 'Perhaps I'll never again get the chance of knowing when I was to die, and so I'll try and die well'.[727] As he was being led to his death, accompanied by Fr Augustine, Colbert's hands were tied behind his back and a cloth tied over his eyes. When the soldier pinned a small piece of white paper, about four or five inches square, on to his coat over his breast, Colbert said: 'Wouldn't it be better to put that a little higher, nearer the heart?' Fr Augustine said: 'It was not irreverent but it was Colbert. He was one of the finest of them all. On Good Friday he was in a friend's house. They offered him food and all he would take was a bit of dry bread and a cup of black tea in memory of the sufferings of Christ.'

His sister, Elizabeth (Lila) Colbert, did not hear of his execution until later. 'I did not hear of his execution until late in the evening of 8th May. It was announced in the papers but I was working at Lafayette's, the photographers, as usual and my fellow workers kept the papers from me. I got a message that Fr Albert wanted to see me, and I went up to the Capuchin Friary in Church St. not suspecting anything tragic. He broke the news to me. He had no written message to me from Con. Afterwards I got a long letter from Con and his prayer-book as a token. I have a copy of that letter and of the others that he wrote to my brothers and sisters.'

Con Colbert and Thomas (Tom) Byrne were rivals for the affections of Lucy Smyth. (Both Thomas and Lucy served in the GPO.) The night before Colbert was executed at Kilmainham he sent Lucy a message through Fr Albert. Lucy even kept a lock of Con's hair somewhere in her house in the Phoenix Park area. There was the hint of an engagement between Con and Lucy, according to Con's sister Elizabeth: 'I went to a *céilidhe* with Con shortly before the Rising. There were a lot of prominent people in the movement at it and many of them have since become well known. In the course of the evening he said to me "I'll show you the nicest girl in Dublin". He introduced me to Lucy Smith [*sic*]. I think he was in love with her and would probably have married her if he had lived. She was a nice, gentle, refined girl, a member of Cumann na mBan and a great worker in the movement. She afterwards married Tom Byrne of Boer War fame who was also keen on her at the same time. He was Con's rival.'[728]

Later, Fr Augustine felt compelled to write to the *Herald* to clear up any misconceptions about Colbert's execution:

DEAR SIR,

In last evening's issue of your paper, towards the end of the second news column of the front page, under the heading 'Last Moments of Volunteer Leader,' it is stated that Cornelius Colbert 'died joking the men who were preparing him for death'. It is also asserted that when one of the soldiers was fixing the white cloth on his breast, to indicate his heart, he told them 'his heart was far away at the moment'.

This version is quite inaccurate and fanciful, and I owe it to his memory to give the true one. There was no joking, not even the semblance of it. Poor Colbert was far too beautiful and too reverent a character to joke with anyone in such a solemn hour.

I know very well where his heart was then. It was very near to God and to the friends he loved. What really happened was this. While my left arm linked the prisoner's right, and while I was whispering something in his ear, a soldier approached to fit a bit of paper on his breast. While this was being done he looked down, and addressing the soldier in a perfectly cool and natural way said: 'Wouldn't it be better to pin it up higher—nearer the heart ?'

The soldier said something in reply, and then added: 'Give me your hand now'. The prisoner seemed confused and extended his left hand. 'Not that', said the soldier, 'but the right'. The right was accordingly extended, and, having shaken it warmly, the kindly human-hearted soldier proceeded to bind gently the prisoner's hands behind his back, and afterwards blindfolded him.

Some minutes later, my arm still linked in his, and accompanied by another priest, we entered the dark corridor leading to the yard and, his lips moving in prayer, the brave lad went forth to die.[729]

John Adams; he was in Jameson's Distillery in Marrowbone Lane.

James Arnold; he was in the South Dublin Union. Imprisoned at Frongoch.

Patrick J. Bailey; he was in Jameson's Distillery, Marrowbone Lane.

William Patrick Bowles; he was in James's Street, Bow Lane and Roe's Distillery.

Joseph Bowman; he was in Jameson's Distillery, Marrowbone Lane. Imprisoned at Frongoch.

William Bowman; he was in Jameson's Distillery, Marrowbone Lane.

Thomas J. Boylan; he was in the South Dublin Union.

Michael Brady; he was in the South Dublin Union.

Cathal Brugha, Vice-Commandant of the Battalion; South Dublin Union. Running down the main staircase of the nurses' home, he charged directly into a grenade blast. He suffered 25 wounds in the Union: five were considered 'very dangerous', nine were 'very serious' and eleven were 'superficial'. His condition was so grave that he was attended by Fr Gerhard and taken to one of the Union medical wards, then transferred to Dublin Castle Hospital.[730] The British deemed that he would not survive and released him to his family.[731] His wounds bothered him greatly for the rest of his life, and he was never able to walk well again.

In 1919 he was the first president pro tem of Dáil Éireann, then Minister for Defence. Extremely anti-Treaty, he was killed in Findlater Place in the opening days of the Civil War.

James Joseph Burke; South Dublin Union. With two other Volunteers, James and Paddy Morrissey, he managed to enter the South Dublin Union, which had already been partially occupied by the Volunteers. With a small group of Volunteers he occupied a hut at the back of the Union, and at about 12 noon a large body of British troops approached down Mountshannon Road; they opened fire on the British, who retreated in all directions. Because the Volunteers were in a disadvantageous position, they sent Paddy Morrissey back to the main body of Volunteers to get orders as to what to do. No sooner had Paddy left when they heard a volley of shots and Paddy crawled back injured; they were surrounded. They moved to the back of the building and attempted to barricade the windows. It was during this operation that Volunteer John Traynor was shot dead. The hut came under heavy fire from the British troops; soon after, there was a cry of 'Put your hands up', and before the Volunteers could react the British had entered the hut. The group of Volunteers were taken prisoner and their fight was over. Of the six Volunteers taken prisoner in the hut five were sentenced to death and one, the wounded Paddy Morrissey, escaped because he was in hospital.[732]

Matthew Burke; he was in Marrowbone Lane. Imprisoned at Frongoch.

**William Francis (Frank) (Goban) Burke;[733] section commander of C Company, South Dublin Union. Burke was on sentry duty in the corridor of the nurses' home, and they were constantly under fire from machine-guns in the Royal Hospital.[734] As Burke leaned over to light a cigarette from James Fogarty's pipe, a shot hit him in the neck, killing him instantly.[735] His death had a profound effect on his step-brother, W.T. Cosgrave, who blamed himself in later years for involving Burke in the fighting.[736]

Christopher Butler; he was in Jameson's Distillery, Marrowbone Lane.

Con Butler; he was in Jameson's Distillery, Marrowbone Lane.

James Butler; he was in Watkins's Brewery, Ardee Street.

Alphonsus (Alfie) Byrne; Marrowbone Lane. He berated Volunteer James Fogarty for the death of Frank Burke, and Fogarty was so distraught that he lost control of himself and remained in that state for many weeks.[737]

Charles Byrne; he was in the South Dublin Union.

Christopher Byrne; he was in the Ardee Street Brewery.

Denis Byrne; he was in Jameson's Distillery, Marrowbone Lane.

Frank Byrne; he was in Jameson's Distillery, Marrowbone Lane. Imprisoned at Frongoch.

George Byrne; he was in Roe's Distillery, Mount Brown.

James Byrne (Séamus Ó Broin); he was in Jameson's Distillery, Marrowbone Lane. Imprisoned at Frongoch.

John Joseph Byrne; he was in Jameson's Distillery, Marrowbone Lane.

Joseph P. Byrne; he was in the South Dublin Union. Imprisoned at Frongoch.[738]

Liam Byrne; he was in the South Dublin Union.

Michael Byrne; he was in Jameson's Distillery, Marrowbone Lane.

Michael Byrne; he was in Jameson's Distillery, Marrowbone Lane.

Patrick Byrne; he was in Watkins's Brewery, Ardee Street.

Patrick Byrne; he was in Roe's Distillery and Mount Brown, then Marrowbone Lane.

Thomas Carty; he was in Jameson's Distillery, Marrowbone Lane. Imprisoned at Frongoch.

Bartholomew Leo Carroll; he was in the South Dublin Union and was interned until July.

James Carroll; he was in the South Dublin Union.

Joseph Clarke; he was in Jameson's Distillery, Marrowbone Lane. Imprisoned at Frongoch.

William Coady; he was in the South Dublin Union. Imprisoned at Frongoch.

William (Liam) Condron; in the South Dublin Union. Imprisoned at Frongoch.

Brother Joseph Louis Corcoran, OFM; he was in Jameson's Distillery.

James Corrigan; he was in Jameson's Distillery, Marrowbone Lane.

William P. (Willie) Corrigan; South Dublin Union. He was a solicitor and the brother of Michael Corrigan, who became the chief state solicitor in 1922. William was captured and taken to Kilmainham police station. 'Before going into the room in which the Court Martial took place I was seen by Mr W.E. Wylie K.C. (afterwards Judge Wylie) who was acting as Prosecutor, he having a Commission and being attached to Dublin University O.T.C. We were both surprised to see each other in our respective capacities. He said to me, "Remember if you do not consider you are being fairly treated you can call on me".'[739]

Philip Cosgrave (brother of William, below); he was in Marrowbone Lane and the South Dublin Union.

Lt William T. Cosgrave (brother of Philip, above); Adjutant and Brugha's deputy, he was detailed to the front of the building, where he and other Volunteers waited for the British troops to attack.[740]

The Cosgraves grew up across from the Union and were very familiar with its grounds. Upon entering the Union, he approached Brugha: 'Look, isn't this hopeless? Surely we can't hope to hold the whole Union, we haven't got the men.' Brugha asked him what he suggested and Cosgrave said to take the night nurses' home. 'It's the strongest building in the Union and it's in the right position. From the back we could control MacCaffrey's, Mount Brown, Brookfield Road, and even the Rialto Gate.' Brugha was so impressed that he ordered Cosgrave: 'Get the men at once. Ceannt will want to make that headquarters.'[741]

A Sinn Féin councillor on Dublin Corporation, he was the first Irish Minister for Local Government, and then succeeded Arthur Griffith and Michael Collins as the head of the Free State government.

James John Coughlan; he was a member of C Company. He brought in many wounded Volunteers in McCaffrey's Estate while under constant fire. Imprisoned at Frongoch.[742]

John Cullen; he was in Jameson's Distillery, Marrowbone Lane. Imprisoned at Frongoch.

Thomas Cullen; South Dublin Union. Imprisoned at Frongoch. He became one of Michael Collins's most trusted lieutenants.

Michael Cunningham; he was in the South Dublin Union and Roe's Distillery.

William Curran; he was in the South Dublin Union.

John Francis Darcy; he was in the South Dublin Union.

William Dempsey; he was in Jameson's Distillery, Marrowbone Lane.

John Joseph (Jack) Doherty (O'Doherty); he was in the South Dublin Union. He and Douglas ffrench–Mullen returned the fire from British troops outside the nurses' home.

★★Brendan Donelan (Donnelan, Donolan) (18);[743] a Fianna member from Galway, he was killed on the very first day of the Rising. A native of Loughrea, he was employed as a draper. With other Volunteers, he was retreating under fire from machine–guns at the Royal Hospital. Apparently he was killed while he lay wounded in the field.[744]

Joseph (Joe) Doolan; he was in the South Dublin Union. He attempted to dress Cathal Brugha's wounds.[745]

John (Seán) Dowling; he was in Roe's Distillery. He was captured and taken to Kilmainham police station.

John (Seán) Downey; he was in the South Dublin Union.

Joseph Downey; he was in Jameson's Distillery, Marrowbone Lane. 'My late father, Joseph Downey, died about twelve years ago. He took part in the 1916 Rising in Marrowbone Distillery. Following the Rising he was arrested and removed to Richmond Barracks. Before he died he related to me that he had been suffering from ptomaine poisoning while a prisoner in Richmond Barracks. During this illness he was nursed by Joseph Plunkett, who was then a prisoner there.'[746]

Christopher Doyle; he was in Jameson's Distillery. Imprisoned at Frongoch.

Gerald Doyle; he was in the South Dublin Union.

Joseph Francis Doyle; he was in Jameson's Distillery, Marrowbone Lane.

Alderman Peadar Seán Doyle; South Dublin Union. An inhabitant of the Union, he was Ceannt's orderly and Battalion Quartermaster, and was sent to the convent in the centre of the Union. He was imprisoned at Lewes Jail. Later he was a TD and lord mayor of Dublin. His son, Seán, died fighting the British in 1920.[747]

Thomas J. Doyle; he was in Marrowbone Lane, and was imprisoned at Frongoch. 'I remember clearly that somebody said "What about Guinness's Brewery?", which was in the 4th Battalion area. Éamonn Ceannt said there were two reasons against taking Guinness's brewery, one was the vastness of the place, it would be nearly impossible to garrison it, and the other reason was that there was no food in it. I can always remember that the late Hugh Byrne said to the group around, "Is the man mad? The most magnificent food in Ireland is in Guinness's".'[748]

Denis K. Dunne; he was in Jameson's Distillery, Marrowbone Lane. Imprisoned at Frongoch.

Patrick Joseph Dunne; he was in Jameson's Distillery, Marrowbone Lane. Imprisoned at Frongoch.

Peter Dunne (Peadar Ó Duinn); he was in Jameson's Distillery, Marrowbone Lane. Imprisoned at Frongoch.

Michael Dwyer; he was in Jameson's Distillery, Marrowbone Lane. Imprisoned at Frongoch.

John Edwards; he was in Jameson's Distillery, Marrowbone Lane. Imprisoned at Frongoch.

Patrick Egan; he was in Roe's Distillery. Egan's section was detailed to take over Roe's. 'As for arms, we had about four modern rifles, one (?) shotgun, three revolvers, a few bayonets. The Captain and I, in addition to the revolvers already mentioned, carried swords, and O'Grady his pike. I think there were one or two unarmed men. The remainder of the men had Howth guns. I reckon we had a little over 300 rounds of ammunition. These were the only type of weapons the section possessed'. As the Volunteers attempted to erect a barricade across Bow Bridge, they were jeered at and spat at by a large crowd; when some of the men in the crowd attempted to destroy the barricade, they had to be prevented by the use of rifle butts, and Volunteer John O'Toole knocked two of the men out. The Volunteers remained at Roe's until late Tuesday night/early Wednesday morning, when it was decided that remaining at their post was impossible. Although many attempts had been made to contact the main garrison in the South Dublin Union, all had failed. Any Volunteers in uniform were given civilian clothes and they left Roe's in small groups and escaped.[749] Egan eventually managed to make it to his home. He joined the Garda Síochána.

Robert J. Evans; he was in the South Dublin Union. He was wounded and placed in one of the hospital's wards, where he remained for the duration of the battle.

Brian Fagan; he was in the South Dublin Union.

William Fagan; he was in Roe's Distillery, Mount Brown.

Michael Farrell; he was in the South Dublin Union.

James Feehan; he was in Jameson's Distillery, Marrowbone Lane.

Capt. Douglas ffrench-Mullen; a talented musician, he was wounded at the South Dublin Union.[750] He led a group of six Volunteers at the back of the Union, and they prepared the area for an assault through the canal gate.

James Fitzpatrick; he lived in McCaffrey's Estate in Mount Brown and worked as a coachbuilder for the Great Southern Railways. He was in Jameson's Distillery, Marrowbone Lane, and was the one who raised the flag over the distillery. Imprisoned at Frongoch, he took the Republican side in the Civil War.

James Flaherty (O'Flaherty) (Séamus Ó Florbheartaigh, Ó Flaithbertaigh?); South Dublin Union.

William (Liam) Flaherty (O'Flaherty) (Ó Florbheartaigh); he was in the South Dublin Union. He was sent with John Murphy to try to make contact with Capt. McCarthy's section in Roe's Distillery. They found that McCarthy had abandoned the position and that the flank of the Union had been left exposed.[751] He was imprisoned at Frongoch.

James Fogarty; he was in the South Dublin Union. He lit his pipe and Frank Burke leaned over to light a cigarette from it; a shot hit Burke, killing him instantly.[752]

William Foley; he was in Jameson's Distillery, Marrowbone Lane.

James Foran; South Dublin Union. Ceannt put him in charge of the front gate of the Union. He raised an improvised flag from a window, an emerald harp painted on a window blind. He and William Cosgrave met Thomas MacDonagh to get the terms of surrender. Imprisoned in Knutsford Prison.[753]

Laurence Gannon; he was in the South Dublin Union.

Francis Gaskin; he was in Jameson's Distillery, Marrowbone Lane.

Henry Gaskin; he was in Roe's Distillery, Mount Brown.

Thomas Gaskin; he was in Roe's Distillery, Mount Brown.

Thomas (Tomás Ernán) B. Gay; he was attending the races at Fairyhouse with some of his family and his fiancée on Easter Monday when he heard what he described in his witness statement as 'greatly exaggerated rumours' of the fighting in Dublin. On Tuesday morning he reported to Jameson's Distillery in Marrowbone Lane, where he was given the duty of maintaining communications with other garrisons around the city. An intelligence officer, he monitored the movements of the Sherwood Foresters on South Circular Road, and reported directly to Colbert. He learned of the surrender on Sunday morning when he went to Jacob's Factory to obtain supplies for the Marrowbone Lane garrison; he was told that Cmdt MacDonagh was in Dublin Castle discussing terms for surrender. He was not captured after the Rising, and helped Jack O'Shaughnessy, who had received a bullet wound to the foot in the fighting at the South Dublin Union, to evade capture by hiding and caring for him.[754] During the War of Independence he was the librarian at the Dublin Municipal Library at 106 Capel Street. Michael Collins and his men used the premises as a 'drop'.

Edward (Edmund) Gibson; he was in the South Dublin Union and was imprisoned at Frongoch. He was a 'master' of the Dublin Silk Weavers' Trade Society.

Michael Gibson; he was in the South Dublin Union. Imprisoned at Frongoch.

James Glynn; he was in the South Dublin Union and Roe's Distillery, Mount Brown. Imprisoned at Frongoch.

John Gerard Gogan; he was in Roe's Distillery, Mount Brown.

Thomas Graham; he was in the South Dublin Union.

James Grehan; he was in Jameson's Distillery, Marrowbone Lane. Imprisoned at Frongoch.

D. Haran; he was in Roe's Distillery, Mount Brown.

Patrick Harbourne; he was in Jameson's Distillery, Marrowbone Lane.

Seán Harbourne; he was in Jameson's Distillery, Marrowbone Lane.

Patrick Joseph Harmon; he was in Jameson's Distillery, Marrowbone Lane.

Daniel (Dan) Holland, brother of Frank, Robert and Walter (below); he was in Jameson's Distillery, Marrowbone Lane. Imprisoned at Frongoch.

Francis Michael (Frank) Holland (brother of Daniel, Robert and Walter); he was in the South Dublin Union. Frank was the eldest son and called a meeting of the brothers. He made a decision that the four sons would go out if their father stayed at home. Frank had already posted the other brothers and he pointed out that their mother was a cripple and they had a young sister then about seven years of age. Their father kicked up a row about this decision; he said that he had spent all his life in both the Fenians and the IRB and that he would go out whether the sons went or not. They could not persuade him to stay at home and left it at that.[755] Imprisoned at Frongoch.

Robert (Bobby) Holland; he was in Jameson's Distillery, Marrowbone Lane. He shot an English sniper who appeared at a window dressed as a woman; when he was shot, the man fell out of the window and the hat and shawl he had been wearing fell off, revealing a British soldier in shirtsleeves.[756] His birthday was 25 April, and Walter brought him a cake. Imprisoned in Frongoch.

Walter Leo (Watty) Holland (15); he was in Jameson's Distillery, Marrowbone Lane. Imprisoned at Frongoch.

Daniel Horan; he was in Roe's Distillery, Mount Brown.

George Howard; he was in the South Dublin Union.

Capt. George Irvine; an IRB centre, he was in the South Dublin Union.[757]

> I was a member of the Gaelic League, which I joined in the year 1905. I was approached by Séamus O'Connor, in or about the year 1907, to join the I.R.B. I refused at that time to do so. A few months later I was again approached, this time by Séamus Deakin, and I then joined and was attached to the Teeling Circle, which met at 41 Parnell Square, Dublin. Later I became Centre of the Clarence Mangan Circle, an offshoot of the Teeling Circle. Sometime before 1913 I was appointed Secretary to the Dublin Centres' Board and a member of the Leinster Council of the I.R.B. Bulmer Hobson was at this time Chairman of the Leinster Council and also Chairman of the Dublin Centres' Board. He remained

Chairman and I remained Secretary of the Dublin Centres' Board up to the Rising in 1916. I remember the following Dublin Centres—Bulmer Hobson, George Lyons, Tom Hunter, Con Colbert, Frank Gaskin, Seán Murphy, Séamus O'Connor, P.J. Farrell, Peadar Kearney, Seán Tobin, Séamus Deekin, Greg Murphy, Cathal Kickham, Val Jackson, Martin Conlan, Seán Farrelly and Seán MacDermott.[758]

He was part of a small group of Volunteers who occupied an outbuilding at the back of the South Dublin Union on Easter Monday. Irvine was one of those men who had little prior notice of the Rising—a few days before Easter Monday he had actually issued invitations to a *ceilidhe*, to take place on 30 April. With Irvine were seven men: John Downey, John Traynor, Patrick and James Morrissey, Gerald Doyle, James Burke and William Corrigan. This group opened fire on a large body of British troops coming down Mountshannon Road; the troops initially retreated but then regrouped and attacked the hut, killing Traynor. The hut was soon taken by the British troops and the six Volunteers were arrested. Patrick Morrissey was removed to hospital and the other Volunteers, including Irvine, were taken first to Kilmainham police station and then to Richmond Barracks.

John Vincent Joyce; South Dublin Union. He was a section commander, and he led an ambush of troops of the 3rd Royal Irish Regiment.[759]

John Patrick Judge; he was in Jameson's Distillery, Marrowbone Lane.

James Joseph Kavanagh, brother of Martin and Thomas (below); he was in Jameson's Distillery, Marrowbone Lane. Imprisoned at Frongoch.

Martin Kavanagh, brother of James and Thomas; he was in the South Dublin Union and Jameson's Distillery, Marrowbone Lane.

Thomas (Tom) Kavanagh, brother of Martin and James; he was in the Ardee Street Brewery and Jameson's Distillery, Marrowbone Lane.

Liam Keane; he was in Jameson's Distillery, Marrowbone Lane.

Thomas Kearney (Tomás Ó Caomhanaighe ?); he was in Marrowbone Lane. Imprisoned at Frongoch.

Edward Laurence (Éamonn) Keegan; he was in the South Dublin Union. He was shot through the lung; though he survived the wound, he never really recovered.[760]

Joseph Francis Kelly; he was in the South Dublin Union.

Seán Kelly; he was in Roe's Distillery, Mount Brown.

William (Bill) Kelly; he was in Watkins's Brewery, Marrowbone Lane. Imprisoned at Frongoch.

Joseph P. Kennedy; he was in Jameson's Distillery, Marrowbone Lane.

James Kenny; he was in Jameson's Distillery, Marrowbone Lane. Imprisoned at Frongoch.

James Kenny; South Dublin Union. With Dan McCarthy, he played 'hide and seek' with English soldiers in Hospital 2–3.[761]

Kieran Kenny; he was in Jameson's Distillery, Marrowbone Lane. Imprisoned at Frongoch.

John Keogh; he was in Jameson's Distillery, Marrowbone Lane. Imprisoned at Frongoch.

Martin Keogh; he was in Roe's Distillery, Mount Brown.

Patrick Keogh; he was in Jameson's Distillery, Marrowbone Lane.

Michael Kerr; he was in the South Dublin Union. Imprisoned at Frongoch.

Sgt Owen Kerrigan; he was in Jameson's Distillery, Marrowbone Lane. Imprisoned at Frongoch.

John Keys; he was in Jameson's Distillery, Marrowbone Lane.

Patrick Lamb; he was in Jameson's Distillery, Marrowbone Lane.

James Leigh; he was in Jameson's Distillery, Marrowbone Lane.

Michael (Mick) Liston; known as 'Supersniper', he was the best shot in the battalion. He was in Jameson's Distillery, Marrowbone Lane; he was wounded in the head, but continued firing at his post.

We got word that Mick Liston was wounded up in the 'Crow's Nest', a name that we had put on the air vent that ran along the length of the wing in our section. This vent had no cover or protection and only consisted of wooden louvers. Liston was wounded in the head and was taken down and dressed. It was the first time I realised that I could be killed …

Liston was not long away getting dressed when he was back with a piece of black coat lining stitched round his head like a cap. We asked him not to go up again, but he insisted. I might mention that Mick Liston was the best rifle shot in 'F' Company at any rate—in fact the best rifle shot in the whole 4th Battalion. We all had a great affection for him, and his wounding brought out the first bit of bitterness in us. We all set our teeth to get revenge …

Mick was no sooner up in position when he was down again with another head wound, this time more serious. As he passed me I saw blood running down his face. He said he was alright but I got a chilly feeling in my stomach. He was about 20 years of age. Our hearts sank and I saw the tears run down Rosie McGowan's face and Josie O'Keeffe's as they brought him down.[762]

Michael Joseph Lynch; he was in the South Dublin Union and was interned at Knutsford and Frongoch.

Edward McCabe; he was in Marrowbone Lane. Imprisoned at Frongoch.

John McCabe; he was in the South Dublin Union.

Michael B. McCabe; he was in Roe's Distillery, Mount Brown, and the Bow Lane Distillery.

Peter McCabe; he was in Jameson's Distillery, Marrowbone Lane. Imprisoned at Frongoch.

William McCabe; he was in Jameson's Distillery, Marrowbone Lane. Imprisoned at Frongoch.

Daniel (Dan) McCarthy; he was in the South Dublin Union. He played 'hide and seek' with English soldiers in Hospital 2–3, where he was wounded in the stomach. While in the Union hospital, he hid a revolver under his pillow and the English soldiers took it when they found it; then he was transferred with Cathal Brugha to Dublin Castle Hospital.[763] Imprisoned at Frongoch.

Patrick McCarthy; he was in Jameson's Distillery, Marrowbone Lane.

Capt. Thomas (Tommy) McCarthy; he brought in a load of ammunition.

> We occupied Roe's Distillery from Monday morning. We did not anticipate any hindrance in our ingress into the building. … I then gave orders to my Company to get their trench tools, and we had to bash in the gate. During all this delay we were being exposed to the tower of the old men's Home, and they had a commanding view from which we were directly under fire in our present Position. We had to smash the gate in and also some of our lads scaled the wall, which was covered with glass, and got in and opened the gate. I went up afterwards and demanded every key of the place from Boyd. He was a bit hesitant at first, but I said, 'If you don't deliver the keys I'll have to take them off your corpse'. He delivered up the keys then. During the time we were trying to knock down the gate we were practically attacked by the rabble in Bow Lane, and I will never forget it as long as I live. 'Leave down your —— rifles,' they shouted, 'and we'll beat the —— out of you.' They were most menacing to Our Lads.

He left his post in Roe's Distillery on Thursday. He didn't tell Ceannt but just withdrew, leaving the flank of the Union exposed.[764]

> After withdrawing it was a case of every man for himself. Some of them succeeded in getting into other posts. After our withdrawal from this post there was no reaction except that I was a much maligned man, but I still say that under similar circumstances I would adopt the same attitude, and I have never yet apologized for our action.[765]

Louis Bernard McDermott (Lughaidh MacDuirmuid); he was in Jameson's Distillery, Marrowbone Lane.

**William McDowell (MacDowell) (44, 46?, 49?);[766] South Dublin Union. A long-time Gaelic League member, he said that he would die happy if only he had a chance to strike a blow for Ireland. He joined the Volunteers only the week before the Rising. On the day, Cathal Brugha asked for volunteers, and James Coughlan and McDowell went forward. He brought in many wounded Volunteers in McCaffrey's Estate while under constant fire. He was killed on Monday in a field between the nurses' home and the convent.[767]

Christopher McEvoy; he was in Watkins's Brewery, Ardee Street.

Christopher James McEvoy; he was in Jameson's Distillery, Marrowbone Lane.

Capt. John (Seán) McGlynn; in the South Dublin Union, he was pinned down on the rooftop by machine-gun fire from the Royal Hospital, Kilmainham. He was imprisoned at Frongoch.

Joseph (Joe) McGrath; Marrowbone Lane. He escaped after the surrender: 'Toor-a-loo, boys, I'm off'. He was the first secretary of the Irish National Aid and Volunteers' Dependants' Fund. He became a TD and a minister, and later started the Irish Sweepstakes.

Patrick McGrath; he was in Jameson's Distillery, Marrowbone Lane. Imprisoned at Frongoch.

Patrick McGrath; he was in Jameson's Distillery, Marrowbone Lane.

Seán McGrath; he was in Jameson's Distillery, Marrowbone Lane.

Bernard McKenna; he was in Jameson's Distillery, Marrowbone Lane. Imprisoned at Frongoch.

John (Seán) McKenna; he was in the South Dublin Union.

Daniel Joseph McMahon; he was in the South Dublin Union. Imprisoned at Frongoch.

James Kevin McNamee; he was in Jameson's Distillery, Marrowbone Lane, and Watkins's Brewery, Ardee Street.

Dermot John (Diarmuid) MacNeill; he was in Jameson's Distillery, Marrowbone Lane.

James McVeigh; he was in Jameson's Distillery, Marrowbone Lane.

James Maguire; he was in the South Dublin Union. Imprisoned at Frongoch.

Edward Marrinan; he was in Jameson's Distillery, Marrowbone Lane.

D.H. Mason; he was in Jameson's Distillery, Marrowbone Lane.

Patrick Mason; he was in Jameson's Distillery, Marrowbone Lane.

Daniel Meade; he was in Jameson's Distillery, Marrowbone Lane.

Edward Merriman; he was in Jameson's Distillery, Marrowbone Lane.

John Joseph Moloney; he was in Jameson's Distillery, Marrowbone Lane.

Patrick Moloney; he was in the South Dublin Union.

John Morgan; he was in Jameson's Distillery, Marrowbone Lane, and Roe's Distillery, Mount Brown. Imprisoned at Frongoch.

James (Jimmy) Morrissey (brother of Patrick, below); South Dublin Union. He was part of a small group of Volunteers who occupied an outbuilding at the back of the South Dublin Union on Easter Monday. This group opened fire on a large body of British troops coming down Mountshannon Road. The British troops initially retreated but then regrouped and attacked the hut. The hut was soon taken, and the six Volunteers in it were arrested. Patrick Morrissey was removed to hospital and the other Volunteers, including Jimmy Morrissey, were taken first to Kilmainham police station and then to Richmond Barracks.[768]

Patrick S. (Paddy) Morrissey (brother of James, above); South Dublin Union. He went back and forth all over the Union as a messenger. He was part of a small group of Volunteers who occupied an outbuilding at the back of the South Dublin Union on Easter Monday. This group opened fire on a large body of British troops coming down Mountshannon Road. The British troops initially retreated but then regrouped and attacked the hut. Patrick Morrissey was sent to the main group of Volunteers occupying the South Dublin Union to get orders as to what they should do. No sooner had Morrissey left the hut than he returned, having been shot in the leg. The hut was soon taken and the six Volunteers in it arrested. Morrissey was taken to hospital, his leg badly shattered by the bullet. He escaped from the hospital a few days later in a milk cart, and was never formally arrested by the British.

Patrick Mulcahy; he was in Jameson's Distillery, Marrowbone Lane.

Martin Mullen; he was in Jameson's Distillery, Marrowbone Lane. Imprisoned at Frongoch.

Patrick Mullen; he was in Jameson's Distillery, Marrowbone Lane. Imprisoned at Frongoch.

Francis (Frank) Murphy; he was in Jameson's Distillery, Marrowbone Lane, and Roe's Distillery, Mount Brown. Imprisoned at Frongoch.

Capt. James Murphy (Séamus Ó Murchadha); he was in Jameson's Distillery in Marrowbone Lane and in Roe's Distillery.[769] He participated in a scheme to acquire rifles in which each man contributed one shilling per week towards the purchase of a weapon. Imprisoned at Frongoch.

John Christopher (Seán) Murphy; South Dublin Union. He was sent with William (Liam) Flaherty to try to make contact with Capt. McCarthy's section in Roe's Distillery. They found that McCarthy had abandoned the position, leaving the flank of the Union exposed.[770] Imprisoned at Frongoch.

Michael Murphy; he was in Jameson's Distillery, Marrowbone Lane.

Thomas Murphy; he was in Jameson's Distillery, Marrowbone Lane.

William Murphy; he was an official at the South Dublin Union. Ceannt requested a short cease-fire so that both the Volunteers and the British could recover their wounded, but the British refused. The British O/C, Major Ramsey, had been killed and his second in command would give no terms. When the Volunteers heard that the British O/C had been killed, they cheered.[771]

Edward Joseph Murray; he was in Jameson's Distillery, Marrowbone Lane.

Gabriel B. Murray; he was in Jameson's Distillery, Marrowbone Lane.

Lt Henry S. (Harry) Murray; he was in Jameson's Distillery, Marrowbone Lane. Imprisoned at Frongoch.

Fr Eugene Nevin; he acted as chaplain at Marrowbone Lane.[772]

George Leo Nolan; he was in Marrowbone Lane. 'On the last day of the Surrender Con Colbert came up to me and asked me would I take two letters to Fathers Kiernan and Eugene at Mount Argus and that when I had delivered these letters I need not return to my post. I did not know what the letters contained but I delivered them to the two priests concerned and then made my way home as best I could. I learned that evening that the Marrowbone Lane garrison had surrendered.'[773] He became a member of Michael Collins's 'Squad'.

Thomas Nolan; he was in Jameson's Distillery, Marrowbone Lane.

John Nugent; he was in Jameson's Distillery, and Roe's Distillery, Mount Brown.

Denis O'Brien (Donncada Ó Briain); he was in Jameson's Distillery, Marrowbone Lane. He married Anne Cooney, who was in Jameson's Distillery.[774]

Denis O'Brien; he was in the South Dublin Union. Imprisoned at Frongoch.

Laurence (Larry, Lorcan) O'Brien; he was in Roe's Distillery and Marrowbone Lane.[775] 'On arrival at Marrowbone Lane I was questioned closely by Captains S. Murphy, Con Colbert and Lieut. Jos. McGrath regarding the evacuation of Roe's Distillery. Lieut. McGrath was inclined to doubt the statement that Capt. McCarthy had evacuated Roe's Distillery. Capt. Colbert, however, declared unequivocally that he was prepared to accept the statement and the small party was admitted to the Marrowbone Lane garrison, where we remained until the surrender which took place the following Sunday.'[776] Imprisoned at Frongoch.

Liam O'Brien; South Dublin Union. He worked at O'Reilly's Printing Works and was one of the printers of the 1916 Proclamation.[777]

Patrick O'Brien; he was in Jameson's Distillery, Marrowbone Lane.

Patrick O'Brien (Padraig Ó Broin); he was in the South Dublin Union and Jameson's Distillery, Marrowbone Lane.

Peter (Peadar) O'Brien; he was in Jameson's Distillery, Marrowbone Lane. Imprisoned at Frongoch.

Stephen L. O'Brien; he was in the South Dublin Union. Imprisoned at Frongoch.

Lt William (Liam) O'Brien; he took up an advance position at the junction of Mount Brown and Brookfield Road.[778]

Hugh O'Byrne; he was in Jameson's Distillery, Marrowbone Lane. Imprisoned at Frongoch.

John (Seán) O'Byrne; he was in Jameson's Distillery, Marrowbone Lane. Imprisoned at Frongoch.

William (Liam) O'Byrne; he was in the South Dublin Union.

Michael (Mick) O'Callahan; he was imprisoned at Frongoch.

Joseph O'Carroll; he was in Jameson's Distillery, Marrowbone Lane.[779]

James O'Connell; he was in Jameson's Distillery, Marrowbone Lane, and Roe's Distillery, Mount Brown. Imprisoned at Frongoch.

Bernard O'Connor; he was in Jameson's Distillery, Marrowbone Lane.

Martin O'Flaherty; he was in the South Dublin Union and was interned until September.

John J. O'Gorman; he was in Jameson's Distillery, Marrowbone Lane.

John Patrick O'Gorman; he was in the South Dublin Union and Jameson's Distillery, Marrowbone Lane.

Joseph O'Gorman; he was in Jameson's Distillery, Marrowbone Lane, and the South Dublin Union. Imprisoned at Frongoch.

Charles Joseph O'Grady; he was in Roe's Distillery, Mount Brown.

James O'Hagan; he was in Roe's Distillery, Mount Brown.

Cornelius (Con) O'Halloran; he was in Jameson's Distillery, Marrowbone Lane.

Patrick O'Loughlin; he was in the South Dublin Union. Imprisoned at Frongoch.

Sgt Edward (Ned) O'Neill; he was in Jameson's Distillery, Marrowbone Lane.[780] He was a courier for Michael Collins during the War of Independence.[781]

Joseph O'Neill; he was in Jameson's Distillery, Marrowbone Lane. Imprisoned at Frongoch.

Michael O'Neill; he was in the Ardee Street Brewery and Jameson's Distillery, Marrowbone Lane. Imprisoned at Frongoch.

Thomas O'Neill; he was in the Ardee Street Brewery and Jameson's Distillery, Marrowbone Lane.

John O'Reilly (brother of Richard, below); he was in the South Dublin Union and was sent to prison in England but released because of his youth. He had two other brothers serving in the British Army in France, and later he remarked that 'that day there were two of us fighting for England and two of us against'.[782] Almost immediately after his release he was re-arrested and was sent to prison in Scotland, where he heard of his brother Richard's death.[783]

Patrick O'Reilly; he was in the South Dublin Union. Imprisoned at Frongoch.

⋆⋆Richard O'Reilly (brother of John, above); he was in the South Dublin Union.[784] He was shot and killed while crossing McCaffrey's Orchard field between the nurses' home and the convent.[785] Two other brothers were in the British Army and one of them was killed in France.

Michael O'Riordan; he was in Jameson's Distillery, Marrowbone Lane.

Patrick O'Rourke; he was in Jameson's Distillery, Marrowbone Lane.

John (Seán) O'Shaughnessy; he was in the South Dublin Union.

Theobald O'Shaughnessy (Ó Seachnasaigh); he was in Jameson's Distillery, Marrowbone Lane.

John O'Toole; he was in Roe's Distillery, Mount Brown, and Jameson's Distillery, Marrowbone Lane.

> As the Volunteers attempted to erect a barricade across Bow Bridge they were jeered and spat at by a large crowd; when some of the men in the crowd attempted to destroy the barricade and had to be prevented by the use of rifle butts, Volunteer John O'Toole knocked two of the men out. The Volunteers remained at Roe's until late Tuesday night/early Wednesday morning, it was decided the remaining at their post was impossible and although many attempts had been made to contact the main Garrison in the South Dublin Union all had failed. Any Volunteers in uniform were given civilian clothes and in small groups they left Roe's and escaped.[786]

⋆⋆John (Seán) Owens (24);[787] South Dublin Union. He was from the Coombe and made artificial limbs for Fannin and Co. There was an area of the fields that was known as McCaffrey's Orchard, and it became known as Ceannt's Fort. About a dozen Volunteers were stationed there under the cover of trees. Owens was sent with a unit towards Mount Brown, where they repulsed an attack, but while the English were retreating their cover fire killed Owens.[788] He is interred in the grounds of Dr

Steevens's Hospital, along with Peter Wilson, who was killed at the Mendicity Institute.

Seosamh Pairceir (Joseph Parker?); he was in Jameson's Distillery, Marrowbone Lane.

Henry Pender; he was in Jameson's Distillery, Marrowbone Lane.

William Phelan; he was in Jameson's Distillery, Marrowbone Lane.

John Phillips; he was in Jameson's Distillery, Marrowbone Lane.

Matthew Phillips; he was in Jameson's Distillery, Marrowbone Lane.

Arthur Power (brother of William, below); he was in Jameson's Distillery, Marrowbone Lane.

Joseph Power; he was in the Ardee Street Brewery and Jameson's Distillery, Marrowbone Lane.

William (Liam, Billy) Power (brother of Arthur, above); he was in the Ardee Street Brewery and Jameson's Distillery, Marrowbone Lane.

Charles Quinn; he was in the South Dublin Union.

George J. Quinn; he was in Roe's Distillery, Mount Brown. Imprisoned at Frongoch.

**James Joseph Quinn (42);[789] South Dublin Union. He was a painter by trade and was a member of the Colmcille Hurling Club. 'I won't trade my caman for nothing but a rifle.'[790] He was killed holding the back entrance of the Union on Monday. Originally buried in the Union, he was reinterred (under the name *Joseph* Quinn) in Glasnevin Cemetery.

Patrick Joseph (Paddy) Rigney; he was in Jameson's Distillery, Marrowbone Lane, and the South Dublin Union.

William Roche; he was in Marrowbone Lane. Imprisoned at Frongoch.

James Russell; he was in the South Dublin Union. Imprisoned at Frongoch.

Frank Saul; he was in Jameson's Distillery, Marrowbone Lane, with his brother Jack (below).

John (Jack) Saul; he was in Roe's Distillery, Mount Brown, and Jameson's Distillery, Marrowbone Lane. Imprisoned at Frongoch.

David Sears; South Dublin Union. He was the youngest in the garrison. He and his father were journalists, and his father became a TD in the first four Dáils.

Michael Smith; he was in Jameson's Distillery, Marrowbone Lane.

Michael Sweeney; he was in the South Dublin Union.

James Teehan; he was in Jameson's Distillery, Marrowbone Lane.

John (Seán) Tracey; he was in the South Dublin Union.

⋆⋆John (Seán) Joe Traynor (17);[791] South Dublin Union. He lived only 200 yards away in Shannon Terrace and was the best shot in his Company.[792] He was killed in Dormitory 6, one of the corrugated tin sheds nearest the Rialto Gate of the Union,[793] which was occupied by a small group of Volunteers. At about 12 noon a large body of British troops approached down Mountshannon Road. The Volunteers opened fire on the British, who retreated in all directions. Being in a disadvantageous position, the Volunteers sent Paddy Morrissey back to the main body to get orders as to what to do. No sooner had Paddy left than they heard a volley of shots and Paddy crawled back injured; the group of Volunteers was surrounded. They moved to the back of the building and attempted to barricade the windows. It was during this operation that Traynor was shot in the eye.[794] He had been employed at the Guinness Brewery, very close to where he was killed. He was originally buried in Richmond Barracks and later reinterred in Glasnevin Cemetery.

Daniel (Dan) Troy; he was in Jameson's Distillery, Marrowbone Lane. Imprisoned at Frongoch.

Paddy Troy; Marrowbone Lane. He was a brother of Dan (above) and was imprisoned at Frongoch.

Thomas Venables; he was in Jameson's Distillery, Marrowbone Lane. Imprisoned at Frongoch.

James Walsh (Séamus Breathnach); he was in Jameson's Distillery, Marrowbone Lane. Imprisoned at Frongoch.

James Walsh; he was in Jameson's Distillery, Marrowbone Lane.

Patrick Joseph Walsh; he was in Jameson's Distillery, Marrowbone Lane. Imprisoned at Frongoch.

Bernard Ward; he was in Roe's Distillery, Mount Brown.

Patrick Ward; he was in the South Dublin Union and Roe's Distillery, Mount Brown. Of the founding of the Fianna he wrote:

> Éamon Martin and I belonged to Father Anderson Branch of the Gaelic League, 44 Sandwich St. I was secretary of that Branch at the time. That would be 1909. Éamon Martin came to a class meeting in the usual way early in 1909, certainly before April, and he told me on our way home that he had been talking to his old headmaster, Mr William O'Neill, who, at that time, lived on lower Kimmage Road. In fact, his old head schoolmaster sent for him …
>
> Mr O'Neill told Éamon that Countess Markievicz had called into the school during the week and told him that she was engaged with others in starting a Boy Scout Movement which would be run on national, patriotic lines, and would he use his influence to have the boys join the scout movement. Mr O'Neill told Éamon that he put some questions to Madame Markievicz because he thought that he ought to know what kind of Movement it was likely to be; and from what she said he thought that the Movement would be good. But, at all events, he had promised to mention it to a couple of older pupils and that was the reason he was giving Éamon the information. Well, we had a chat about this (Éamon and I) and we decided to go along. The schoolmaster had the address of Madame Markievicz, 34 Lower Camden St., and we decided we would go along and see for ourselves. Although Madame Markievicz probably was very well known in Dublin at the time we had never heard of her before. A day or two after this conversation, having decided on the day we'd go, we did go to Camden St. and found a small number of people in the hall. Acting as a sort of committee was Madame herself, Bulmer Hobson, who was always at her right hand, and Padraig Ó Riain.[795]

He was imprisoned at Frongoch.

Patrick Joseph Ward; he was in the South Dublin Union and Roe's Distillery, Mount Brown.

Peter Ward; he was in the South Dublin Union. Imprisoned at Frongoch.

Michael Whelan; he was at McCabe's public house, Ballybough Bridge.

Richard Whelan; he was in the South Dublin Union. Imprisoned at Frongoch.

Michael (Mick) White; he was in the South Dublin Union and Jameson's Distillery, Marrowbone Lane.

Éamon Christopher Young; he was in the Ardee Street Brewery and Jameson's Distillery, Marrowbone Lane.

Patrick John Young; he was in the Ardee Street Brewery and Jameson's Distillery, Marrowbone Lane.

Robert Martin Young (brother of Thomas, below); he was in the Ardee Street Distillery and Jameson's Distillery, Marrowbone Lane. Imprisoned at Frongoch.

Thomas (Tom) Young (brother of Robert, above); on Holy Thursday he was instructed by Con Colbert to reconnoitre the area around Wellington Barracks and produce a detailed map of the area. After the cancellation of the Easter Sunday mobilisation, Colbert, who ordered him to assemble his company and parade in Emerald Square at 10 a.m., awakened him at 9 a.m. on Easter Monday morning. With six other men, Young was instructed to take up a position with a view of the main entrance to Wellington Barracks and to prevent troops from leaving the barracks. He was to maintain this position until noon, after which they went to the Marrowbone Lane Distillery area. As his small group was going towards Forbes Lane, they met a party of unarmed British soldiers accompanied by their families. Several of the soldiers' wives attacked the Volunteers, pulling them off their bicycles, and the Volunteers were forced to use their rifle butts to repel the attack. He remained at Marrowbone Lane until the surrender. He also led a patrol to scout the Ardee Street Brewery for Colbert.[796] Imprisoned at Frongoch.

4TH BATTALION: WOMEN

The women's HQ was in Marrowbone Lane, where they helped guard the rear of the South Dublin Union.

Ellen Sarah Bushell; she was involved for four days, during which she served in a variety of supporting roles, mostly as a courier for Con Colbert.

Catherine (Katie) Byrne; she was in Jameson's Distillery, Marrowbone Lane. She was imprisoned.

Mary (May) Byrne (Doyle), sister of Winnie (below); she was in Jameson's Distillery, Marrowbone Lane. Like all the women, she was trained in first aid and they were responsible for procuring and preparing food.[797]

Winifred (Winnie) Byrne (Somerville), sister of Mary (above); she was in Jameson's Distillery in Marrowbone Lane.

Áine Cooney (O'Brien) (22), sister of Eileen and Lily (below); she was in Jameson's Distillery, Marrowbone Lane, and was subsequently imprisoned.[798] From a very nationalist family, her first job was selling souvenir programmes at the funeral of Jeremiah O'Donovan Rossa. She recalled that, when being marched to Kilmainham Gaol, women who had men serving in France taunted her and the other women prisoners. These women had been deprived of their 'separation allowance' when the GPO was occupied, and as a result many families faced hunger and hardship until things were sorted out. Before he was executed, the sisters saw Con Colbert for the last time in Kilmainham Gaol. He wrote to Áine and Lily and left them his gloves and rosary beads.[799]

Eileen Cooney (Harbourne) (16), sister of Áine (above); she was in Jameson's Distillery, Marrowbone Lane. Later she was imprisoned.

Lily Cooney (Curran) (20), sister of Áine (above); she was in Jameson's Distillery, Marrowbone Lane. Later she was imprisoned.

Marcella Cosgrave; Quartermaster and second in command.[800] While she was imprisoned in Kilmainham, her brother-in-law approached a British officer and arranged to have her released, but she refused to leave.

Bridget Hegarty (Harmon); she was in Jameson's Distillery, Marrowbone Lane.

Josephine Kelly (Greene); she was in Jameson's Distillery, Marrowbone Lane. She was mainly involved in nursing and was imprisoned.

Margaret Agnes Kennedy (Hennessey); she was in Jameson's Distillery, Marrowbone Lane.

On Sunday, about 3 or 4 o'clock p.m., Father Augustine from Church Street and a British Officer came along to the Distillery & as far as I know it was the Priest mentioned who first contacted Con Colbert concerning the surrender. My impression is that the Priest and the Officer went away and came back later on with Ceannt, who was not wearing either sam-brown belt or sword. The whole garrison then surrendered. Miss McNamara ordered that we were to surrender with the men, and we all did with one exception. We marched behind the men from the Distillery to Ross Road. On our way through the Coombe I picked up a rifle and carried it the rest of the way but I had to surrender it on orders from the British Officer. The men had to turn everything out of their pockets as well as laying down their arms. We marched under escort behind the Volunteers to Richmond Barracks. When we arrived there we were put into two rooms in the Married Quarters and locked up there for the night. The following morning, 1st May, we were marched to Kilmainham Jail and kept there until 8th May. I have no complaints concerning my treatment while in jail.[801]

Later she was elected a senator.

Josie McGowan (Mac Gabhan) (on the Roll of Honour she is listed as 'McGavan') (18); she was in Jameson's Distillery in Marrowbone Lane. Her brother Charles was in the 3rd Battalion, and another brother, Claude, was in the 2nd Battalion.

Rose McNamara (Mrs Séamus Murphy [Ó Murchadha]); Marrowbone Lane. Her husband was Capt. Murphy.

On Good Friday 1916, I spent the day making field dressings in No. 2 Dawson Street, having previously purchased the materials. There was a big crowd of us there and we worked very hard to ensure that there would be enough dressings for the Volunteers for the manoeuvres that were soon to take place. I had nothing to do on Saturday. That night we were given our instructions for the Sunday mobilization and what followed is fully described in a memorandum I wrote in the beginning of June, 1916, when the events were still fresh in my memory, and which you may have copied for the Bureau.

(Easter Sunday, April 23rd 1916) Craobh Inghinidhe, Cumann na mBan, was mobilised to parade at Mount Street. Waited there for further orders. We were dismissed to attend at 6 Harcourt Street. We waited there for some time and there were all sorts of rumours about. Finally, our Commandant dismissed us with orders to be ready for a further mobilization and not to leave the city during the week end …

On Easter Monday, April 24th, I was mobilised for Weaver's Hall, Cork Street, full uniform and equipment, for 10 o'clock a.m. We formed up outside the hall, 25 in number, where we marched to Emerald Square for orders from Commandant E. Ceannt; got orders to follow Company of Volunteers just forming up …

We marched behind until we reached the Distillery in Marrowbone Lane (used as forage stores for the British Government) at 12 o'clock. I next saw Captain Murphy who was in charge of Volunteers, 4th Battalion, knock at small gate and demand same to be opened in the name of the Irish Republic. As soon as we got in prisoners were made of the Lodgekeepers, also a soldier in khaki. We remained in an old cellar all day, waiting for work to do. We heard heavy firing from both sides all the day. There were four workmen on the premises who were also made prisoners but were later blind-folded and were let out at dark. One slight casualty P. McGrath which we dressed with success.

Firing continues till dark. Reinforcements of 60 men arrive in the evening; towards evening two women bring us in some food, tea, etc., which we needed badly. We divided up into squads and posted ourselves in close touch with the different firing lines, and lay on sacks of oats or grains which was very uncomfortable. M. Cosgrave, the Q.M., and self were up very early to prepare some sort of breakfast for the men.

She cooked for the Marrowbone Lane garrison, and was the leader of the women there. In addition to providing first aid to the men, Rose and the women loaded the rifles for them and acted as spotters for snipers—many times in full view of the British. Then Rose led several women and appropriated a cow with her two calves, and made bread and butter for the entire garrison with the milk. There was such a strong feeling of camaraderie among the women and the rest of the garrison that Rose planned a victory *céilidhe* to be held on Sunday, blissfully unaware of the defeat of the Rising.[802]

When the garrison surrendered, the women could have evaded capture, but Rose would have none of it. She went to a British officer and curtly informed him that the women were part of the garrison. Then they proudly marched along with the men and were imprisoned in Kilmainham. Later, at Kilmainham Gaol, she met John MacBride, who told her, 'You'll be all right, you'll be out tomorrow'. Of himself he said, 'Ah no, we won't be out, we'll be shot'.[803]

Sarah McNamara (MacNamara); she was in the Michael Dwyer Club in Skipper's Alley, off Merchant's Quay.

Agnes MacNamee; she was in Jameson's Distillery, Marrowbone Lane.

Lizzie Mulhall; she was imprisoned.

Rosanna (Rose) Mullally (Farrelly); she was in Jameson's Distillery in Marrowbone Lane and later was imprisoned.

Kathleen (Kate) Murphy; she joined Cumann na mBan on the day of the Rising. She went with her husband to the mobilisation of the 4th Battalion at Dolphin's Barn on Monday and was sent home to get some ammunition; she brought it back to Jameson's Distillery in Marrowbone Lane, where she stayed until the surrender. She was arrested, detained in Kilmainham and released owing to ill health.

Elizabeth (Lily) M. O'Brennan; she was in Jameson's Distillery, Marrowbone Lane. She was Áine Ceannt's sister.[804]

> On Easter Monday morning, the 24th April, the sun rose warm and splendid, stealing softly over the green hills of Tallaght until it streamed into the old-fashioned streets of the little village of Dolphin's Barn …
>
> I was due at Cleaver Hall at 10.30 o'clock. I had no Cumann na mBan uniform. They were the exception not the rule in those days but I had put on a coat and skirt I used for mountain walks. The coat had a belt and fine pockets.
>
> I strapped my knapsack on my back, and tied my waterproof to the bicycle which I had ready in the hall. I looked back at my mother, who had helped me get my sandwiches.
>
> I waved a merry 'good-bye' to her and my sister, and bent down to kiss my little nephew who was near me.
>
> Then I wheeled the bicycle down the garden path. At the kerb I mounted it and rode away without even giving one look back at the home which was never to be home to me again.

She was imprisoned in Kilmainham after the Rising when Ceannt was there. She and Áine saw him before his execution.[805] She kept a diary of her week in the Distillery, but when she was captured she decided to destroy it while marching to Richmond Barracks.[806]

Cissie O'Flaherty, sister of Margaret (below); she was in Jameson's Distillery in Marrowbone Lane.

Margaret O'Flaherty (Timmons), sister of Cissie (above); she nursed the wounded in Jameson's Distillery in Marrowbone Lane and was later imprisoned.

Mary (Molly, Máire) O'Hanlon; she was in Jameson's Distillery, Marrowbone Lane. On Thursday Con Colbert sent her out to Éamonn Ceannt's home and to another house on Reuben Street, but she was unable to return.

Sheila (Sighle) O'Hanlon (Lynch); she was in Jameson's Distillery in Marrowbone Lane and was imprisoned.

Emily O'Keefe (Hendley), sister of Josie (below); she was in Jameson's Distillery, Marrowbone Lane, and was imprisoned.

Josephine O'Keefe (McNamara); she was in Jameson's Distillery, Marrowbone Lane.

Josephine (Josie) O'Keefe, sister of Emily (above); she was in Jameson's Distillery, Marrowbone Lane. She loaded two rifles in turn for Robert Holland, and from their position in one of the grain storerooms they commanded the view to the west for four days of fighting. She was subsequently imprisoned.

Maria (Mary) Quigley (Clince), sister of Priscilla (below); she was in Jameson's Distillery in Marrowbone Lane and was imprisoned.

Priscilla (Cilla) Quigley (Kavanagh), sister of Maria (above); she was in Jameson's Distillery, Marrowbone Lane, and was imprisoned.

Josephine Spicer; she was in Jameson's Distillery, Marrowbone Lane, and was imprisoned.

VII. North County Dublin—5th Battalion or Fingal Battalion

Commandant Thomas Ashe led the Volunteers in north County Dublin and County Meath. This was known as the 5th Battalion, but after the Rising it was referred to as the 'Fingal Battalion'. The 5th Battalion carried out a series of raids and reconnaissance movements throughout north County Dublin from Easter Monday to Friday.[807] Volunteers came from companies in Lusk, Skerries and St Margaret's. The Swords and Lusk contingents were the largest, with about 30 men on their rolls who reported. James V. Lawless commanded the St Margaret's men, Dick Coleman commanded Swords, Edward Rooney commanded Lusk, and Joe Thornton and Jim McGuinness commanded Skerries.

Most of the men who reported on Easter Monday did so on bicycles. The raids upon RIC barracks and communications in the area were undertaken with the purposes of collecting arms, hampering enemy movements and drawing some enemy attention away from the Volunteers fighting in Dublin.

On Monday afternoon they moved off towards Finglas under the command of Ashe. The convoy consisted of one automobile driven by Dr Dick Hayes, one motor bike and one horse and cart. The battalion took up position for the night at a farm where the Premier Dairies were later located. That night, on James Connolly's instructions, Coleman was sent with twenty men towards Blanchardstown to create a disturbance, to try and distract some of the military forces from Dublin.[808]

At 10 a.m. on Tuesday, Ashe received instructions from Connolly to send 40 men into Dublin. Ashe, however, decided to send only half that number. Having selected the men, he sent Capt. Coleman into the city in charge of them. Coleman, one of the few wearing uniform, entered the GPO with his men and reported to Connolly.

Ashe followed James Connolly's orders to act in the area 'with a view to aiding in the dispersal of enemy forces'. Some claim that this 'dispersal' was to allow the Dublin Volunteers an escape route to the north, but there is no definitive evidence of this.[809] On Friday Ashe split his 50 Volunteers into four 'columns' and set out to cut the railway line of the Midland and Great Western Railway, thus forestalling the entry of some British troops into Dublin from the north. The sections were diverted near the RIC barracks at Rath Cross and attacked it. During a five-hour battle, the RIC suffered eight killed, fifteen wounded and 80 subsequently surrendered, while the Volunteers lost two and had six wounded.

Though the battalion's activities presaged the 'hit and run' tactics of flying columns in the War of Independence, they had no direct effect on the Rising in Dublin. On Sunday, Ashe and Vice-Commandant Richard Mulcahy went to Dublin to confer with Pearse, who ordered them to surrender.[810]

5TH BATTALION: MEN

North County Dublin, Rath (Rathbeal, Ratoath) Cross Roads.

RIC barracks at Ashbourne, Swords, Donabate and Garristown (Co. Meath).[811]

Garrison total about 80 men and women (including approximately twenty Volunteers who were sent to the GPO on Tuesday 25 April); none executed, two killed; eight RIC men killed.

Known after the Rising as the 'Fingal Battalion', it foreshadowed the flying columns and barracks attacks of the 1920 campaigns.[812] Each of the 48 men who reported on Monday had a bicycle as well as a rifle.

Cmdt Thomas Ashe; a native of Dingle, Co. Kerry, he was previously a schoolteacher at Corduff, Co. Dublin.[813] He was known as an inspirational but somewhat impractical leader, and was the great-uncle of actor Gregory Peck. In 1917 Ashe was imprisoned for sedition as a result of an incendiary speech, and he led a hunger strike in Mountjoy Prison. During force-feeding by Dr Lowe on 23 September, Ashe's lung was pierced and he was taken to the Mater Hospital, where he died on 25 September 1917 of 'heart failure and congestion of the lungs'.[814] Ashe had been arrested on 20 August, just before he was to travel to Skibbereen with Michael Collins. Upon hearing of his arrest, Collins wrote to his sister Hannie: 'Tom Ashe has been arrested so that fixes him'.

Richard (Dick) Aungier; he was one of the first men to come under fire from the RIC. Interned until December.

Peter (Peadar) Blanchfield (brother of Thomas, below); he was a member of the 1st Battalion and had escaped capture in Phibsborough, fleeing to the 5th Battalion. He became the 'official grenadier', as he was the only one with experience with bombs.

Thomas (Tom) Blanchfield (brother of Peter, above); he was a member of the 1st Battalion and escaped capture in Phibsborough, fleeing to the 5th Battalion.

Patrick Birney; he came from the 2nd Battalion.

Paddy Brogan; a member of the Lusk Company, he was one of the squad that attacked the police convoy from the rear.

#[815] Daniel (Dan) Brophy; he was sent to the GPO on Tuesday. Interned until July.

 # Patrick Caddell; a member of the Lusk Company, he was sent to the GPO on Tuesday.

 # John Clarke; a member of the Lusk Company, he was sent to the GPO on Tuesday.

 # Richard (Dick) Coleman (25); Captain of the Swords Company, he was sent to the GPO on Tuesday. He died of influenza in Usk Prison, Wales, on 9 December 1918 while a candidate for parliament. (See also GPO and 1st Battalion at Mendicity Institute.)

James (Jimmy) Connor; a member of the Lusk Company, he was one of the squad that attacked the police convoy from the rear.

 # James Crenigan (brother of John, below); a member of the Roganstown Company, he was sent to the GPO on Tuesday.

> We remained in the Gym at Arbour Hill until we were tried at Richmond Barracks. I think that was about one week later, after our trial we were brought to Kilmainham Jail and put in the cells. We had one blanket there also and again had to lie on the floors. We were all in single cells and were only allowed out to wash. After about two days we were told the findings of our court martial which in my case was 3 years penal servitude, mitigated to one on account of my age (young). Next day we were removed to Mountjoy. It was while out exercising there that Frank Lawless was able to tell me that my brother had been killed at Ashbourne.[816]

**John (Jack) Crenigan (21);[817] a member of the Swords Company, he formerly worked for the Dublin Tramways Company. He was one of the Volunteers who went up the road to Hamilton Hill and he was killed at his position there on Friday[818] by District Inspector H. Smith, who had been exhorting his men and calling out to the Volunteers to stop 'skulking in the brush'; Smith shot at Joseph Lawless but missed and hit Crenigan in the head.[819]

Francis (Frank) Daly; he was an IRB centre[820] and was imprisoned at Frongoch.

John (Johnny) Devine; a member of the Lusk Company, he was one of the squad that attacked the police convoy from the rear. Imprisoned at Frongoch.

Patrick (Paddy) Doyle; he took part in the attacks on RIC barracks in Ashbourne, Swords and Donabate.

 # William Doyle; a member of the Swords Company, he was sent to the GPO on Tuesday.

Richard Duke; St Margaret's Company. He and his brother, Thomas (below), were sent to Wandsworth Detention Barracks.

Thomas Patrick Duke; St Margaret's Company. He was involved in attacks on RIC barracks in Swords, Donabate and Garristown.

Patrick Joseph Early; Swords Company. He was involved in attacks on RIC barracks in Swords, Donabate and Garristown.

Walter Farrelly; no information available.

Michael (Mick) Fleming; a Volunteer, he arrived after fleeing the British in Drumcondra. He was involved in attacks on RIC barracks in Swords, Donabate and Garristown.

Peter Ganley; he arrived late, on Wednesday.

Gerry Golden (Jeremiah Golden, James Barry); he was a member of the 1st Battalion and escaped capture in Phibsborough, fleeing to the 5th Battalion.

> On my arrival in 5 Blackhall Street I found about 250 men gathered in the hall and rooms on the ground floor, while upstairs a Battalion Council Meeting was being held … When the B.C. Meeting was over I saw Comdt. [Daly] and other officers come down, and on my speaking to the Comdt. I asked him if I would be sent down the country. He replied 'No', as the Countermanding Order of Sunday had upset all the plans. He then enquired about my mother and I informed him that she had left for Longford on the 9 a.m. train. He said he was glad she had got out of town in time and then asked me what arms I had brought with me. I replied, 'Everything I had in the house'. I also told him I was keeping the Service Rifle, but that all the others could be given to anyone who had no arms or ammunition only small arms. He then told me to take my place with 'B' Co. men, as he was about to make a very important announcement. On my taking my place in the ranks of 'B'

Co. in the Hall, I saw the Comdt. come out to the back room and he called all the men to take their places in their Cos. When all had got into the ranks he called the men to attention, and spoke to them about the training they had gone through for the past 16 months, and that he was glad to see such a muster of the Batt. While he was speaking he was handed a written message. When he read it he looked earnestly at the men, and then told them that 'The Irish Republic' had been proclaimed at 12 noon by Comdt. Gen. Patrick Pearse who had, with some of the Kimmage Garrison and Head Quarters staff, and Comdt. James Connolly with the Irish Citizen Army, taken over the G.P.O. and were preparing to defend the Republic with their lives. The Comdt. then said that if any man present did not agree with the opinions of the Supreme Council of the Irish Republic he was at liberty to return home, but if anyone did so, he would ask him to leave his arms, ammo., and equipment behind as some of the men present were not fully armed. No man left the ranks, and the Comdt. said he was glad he had the men 100 per cent behind him and the officers of the Supreme Command.[821]

On Tuesday he came to Finglas.

James Gough; he was involved in attacks on RIC barracks in Swords and Donabate.

Jack Gowan; he was sent home on Thursday because he was too young.

Patrick (Paddy) Grant; he came from Dublin with Richard Mulcahy and was involved in attacks on RIC barracks in Swords, Donabate and Garristown.

Dr Richard Hayes; he was the medical officer and intelligence officer. He had formerly been the O/C but resigned in favour of Ashe owing to the pressures of his medical practice. He was involved in attacks on RIC barracks in Swords, Donabate and Garristown. He later became a TD.[822]

Paddy Holohan (his brother Hugh was in the GPO, and his cousins Garry and Patrick were in the 1st Battalion); he was a member of the 1st Battalion and escaped capture in Phibsborough, fleeing to the 5th Battalion, then later went back to North King Street. Imprisoned at Frongoch. (Counted in the 1st Battalion garrison.)

 # John Francis (Jack) Hynes; a member of the Lusk Company, he was sent to the GPO on Tuesday.

 # John J. (Jack) Kelly; a member of the Swords Company, he was sent to the GPO on Tuesday.

James (Jimmy) Kelly; he arrived late, reporting on Wednesday. He was involved in attacks on RIC barracks in Donabate and Ashbourne.

Joseph Patrick Kelly; he was involved in attacks on RIC barracks in Swords, Donabate and Ashbourne.

Matthew Kelly; a member of the Corduff Company, he was involved in attacks on RIC Barracks in Swords, Donabate, Ashbourne and Garristown. He was wounded and was imprisoned at Frongoch.

 # Patrick Kelly; he was sent to the GPO on Tuesday.

Peter Kelly (Peadar Ó Cellaigh); he was involved in attacks on RIC barracks in Swords, Donabate and Ashbourne.

 # Richard (Dick) Kelly; a member of the Corduff Company, he was sent to the GPO on Tuesday.

Colm Lawless; he was sent home on Thursday because he was too young.

 # Edward Lawless; he was sent to the GPO on Tuesday.

Frank Lawless Snr; Battalion QM. He became a TD.

Capt. James Vincent (Jim) Lawless; Captain of the St Margaret's Company. He was involved in attacks on RIC barracks in Swords, Donabate, Ashbourne and Garristown. Imprisoned at Frongoch.

Joseph Vincent Lawless; he was one of the section leaders, as well as assisting his father, Frank, as QM.[823] He was involved in attacks on RIC barracks in Swords, Donabate, Ashbourne and at Rogerstown Bridge. Imprisoned at Frongoch,[824] he later became a colonel in the Free State Army.[825]

Thomas Leaver (Seaver?); he was involved in attacks on RIC barracks in Swords, Donabate, Ashbourne and Garristown.

Capt. Bernard (Bennie) McAllister, brother of John and Michael (below); he was involved in attacks on RIC barracks in Swords, Donabate and Ashbourne. Imprisoned at Frongoch.[826]

John McAllister, brother of Bernard and Michael; he attacked the police column from the road at Rath Cross.

Michael (Mick) McAllister; brother of Bernard and John.

> The late Thomas Ashe was a frequent visitor to our house, where he used to play cards. On one occasion I mentioned to him that we in this country should have some kind of an intelligence organisation to counteract the propaganda about this country in the English Press. He said we had such an organisation here and asked me if I would like to join. I said I would. The organisation that I visualised was quite different from the one which I discovered that Ashe belonged to. He took me to a meeting of this organisation, which was the I.R.B.[827]

McAllister fired the shot that killed Constable James Gormley.

James McArdle (brother of Patrick and Thomas); he was imprisoned at Frongoch.

Patrick McArdle (brother of James and Thomas); he was imprisoned at Frongoch.

Thomas McArdle (brother of James and Patrick); he was involved in attacks on RIC barracks in Swords, Donabate, Ashbourne and Garristown.

John McCann; a quarryman with experience in explosives, he was detailed to lead an attempt to destroy the railway bridge at Rogerstown between Donabate, Rush and Lusk stations. The explosion failed to destroy the bridge, however.

Jack McGowan; he arrived late, reporting on Wednesday.

Capt. Jim McGuinness; he was Captain of the Skerries men.

 # John McNally; a member of the Swords Company, sent to the GPO on Tuesday.

 # James Marks; a member of the Swords Company, he was sent to the GPO on Tuesday, and from there to the Mendicity Institute.

James Masterson; he was involved in attacks on RIC barracks in Swords, Donabate and Ashbourne.

Thomas (Tom) Maxwell; he came from Dublin with Richard Mulcahy and was involved in attacks on RIC barracks in Swords, Donabate, Ashbourne and Garristown.

 # William Meehan; a member of the Lusk Company, he was sent to the GPO on Tuesday.

Christopher Moran; he was involved in attacks on RIC barracks in Swords, Donabate, Ashbourne and Garristown.

Peter Moran; he was involved in attacks on RIC barracks in Swords, Donabate, Ashbourne and Garristown.

Richard Mulcahy; Vice-Commandant. On Sunday evening James Connolly sent him to Howth to cut the undersea telephone wires between Dublin and London. It was impossible to return to Dublin, so he went to Ashbourne and Ashe appointed him Vice-Commandant for the Rising. Imprisoned at Frongoch, he became O/C of D Company of the North Camp. Succeeded Collins as commander in chief of the Free State Army.[828]

Éamonn Murphy; no information available.

Francis Ciaran Murphy; he was involved in attacks on RIC barracks in Swords, Donabate, Ashbourne and Garristown.

 # Joe Norton; he was sent to the GPO on Tuesday.

William (Bill) Norton; he was sent home on Thursday because of his age.

Christopher (Christy) Nugent; he fired a single shot from his Martini rifle to alert the other Volunteers of the approaching vehicles carrying the RIC to Rath Cross.

James O'Connor; he was a member of the St Margaret's Company.

> Saturday morning found everybody in good spirits and looking forward to further action. About 2 p.m. on that date Ashe told us that it was all over, that they had surrendered in Dublin and that it would be ridiculous for us to hold out. He seemed very disappointed and naturally we were very disappointed too. He told me to go home and make the best of it. A few others who were the youngest also went home.[829]

He was imprisoned in Wakefield Prison.

Anthony (Arthur?) O'Reilly; he was a member of the 1st Battalion and escaped capture in Phibsborough, fleeing to the 5th Battalion.

Thomas Peppard; a member of the Lusk Company, he was sent to the GPO on Tuesday. He was the Intelligence Officer for the Brigade.[830]

John (Jack) Rafferty; a member of the Lusk Company, he was involved in attacks on RIC barracks in Swords, Donabate, Ashbourne and Garristown. He was wounded and was imprisoned at Frongoch.

**Thomas (Tommy) Rafferty (22);[831] an accomplished hurler, he died of his wounds after the Rising. He was among the Volunteers who attacked the RIC barracks from the rear, and was shot when he rose from his position to see whether any RIC men had escaped to the fields.[832] He was wearing a brightly coloured bandolier and this may have attracted enemy fire.[833]

Thomas Reilly; he is listed on the Roll of Honour.

James Rickard; he was involved in attacks on RIC barracks in Swords, Donabate, Ashbourne and Garristown.

Capt. Edward N. (Ned) Rooney; Captain of the Lusk Company. He was wounded in the eye and was imprisoned at Frongoch.

James Rooney; a farmer from Lusk, he is listed on the Roll of Honour.

Patrick Joseph Ryan; he was involved in attacks on RIC barracks in Swords, Donabate, Ashbourne and Garristown.

Patrick (Paddy) Sherwin; he was involved in attacks on RIC barracks in Swords, Donabate, Ashbourne and Garristown.

Edward (Ned) Stafford; a butcher's assistant from Swords, he is listed on the Roll of Honour.

Joseph (Joe) Taylor; he was a member of the Swords Company and was wounded. A butcher, he slaughtered a sheep on Tuesday morning and the men feasted.

Thomas Taylor; he was involved in attacks on RIC barracks in Swords, Donabate, Ashbourne and Garristown.

Nicholas Teeling (Teehan?); a member of the St Margaret's Company. At Rath Cross he was one of the squad that attacked the police convoy from the rear.

Capt. Joseph (Joe) Thornton; he was Captain of the Skerries Company. Imprisoned at Frongoch.

Willie Walsh; a Volunteer from Liverpool, he was a member of the 1st Battalion and had escaped capture in Phibsborough, fleeing to the 5th Battalion. He was wounded in the hand.

Bartholomew (Bartle) Weston, brother of Charles and Thomas (below); he attacked the police column from the road as a member of his brother's section. He was involved in attacks on RIC barracks in Swords, Donabate, Ashbourne and Garristown.

Charles Weston, brother of Bartholomew and Thomas; one of the section leaders, he was involved in attacks on RIC barracks in Swords, Donabate, Ashbourne and Garristown. He was detailed to blow up the bridge at Rogerstown Viaduct:

> Ashe called me aside and gave me instructions about the Bridge again. We tied the gelignite fuses and detonators on Ashe's motor cycle. The quarry men from Lusk who were to come with me on this job had not mobilised. Ashe told me I would meet them on my way and to bring them with me. Joe Lawless rode the motor cycle and I was on a push bicycle. On leaving Knocksedan Dr Hayes gave me two strips of red bunting. These were to be tied a distance away from the ends of the bridge to warn oncoming trains. We met the Lusk Coy at Rogerstown with Ned Rooney in charge. I took the Quakey EW men with me and told Ned Rooney I was going to blow the bridge, and that the fight was on. There was a great buzz of excitement amongst the Lusk men on hearing the news. When we got to Rogerstown the tide was flowing very strong through the arches and it was impossible to get the charges placed at the buttresses. Joe Lawless was cutting the telephone wires at this time. A man of mine who was posted down the line halted the Stationmaster who became abusive and he had to be threatened to keep him from going on the bridge. We put the charges between the girders of the bridge. We set the fuses off and the resultant explosion blew the rails out of position and made the line unserviceable. This was only of a temporary nature and it was easily repaired by railway engineers during the week.[834]

Imprisoned at Frongoch.

Thomas Weston, brother of Bartholomew and Charles; he was involved in attacks on RIC barracks in Swords, Donabate, Ashbourne and Garristown.

 # James Wilson; he was sent to the GPO on Tuesday.

 # Peter Wilson; he was sent to the GPO on Tuesday.

 # William (Beck) Wilson; he was sent to the GPO on Tuesday.

 # William (Cody, Cooty) Wilson; a member of the Swords Company, he was sent to the GPO on Tuesday.

5TH BATTALION: WOMEN

Molly (Mollie) Adrian; she was a messenger and bicycled from the GPO several times during the week. (Counted in the GPO garrison.)

Monica (Dot) Fleming (Lawless); she married Joseph Lawless.

Eileen Lawless; she became one of Michael Collins's secretaries.[835] Later she entered the religious order of Our Lady of Refuge in Gloucester Street as Sr Eithne.

Kathleen Lawless (McAllister); she assisted in the removal of arms to her father's (Frank Lawless) house in Saucerstown, Co. Dublin. During the Rising she carried dispatches, assisted in the acquisition and delivery of supplies for the Volunteers and carried out first aid. Although briefly detained for one day following the surrender, she was not interned.

Thomasina Lynders (Weston); her main activities involved gathering information about military and RIC movements, carrying dispatches, collecting funds and carrying arms from Portrane.

Mary Julia Weston; she was involved in intelligence-gathering in the Finglas and Swords areas.

VIII. Irish Citizen Army at Dublin Castle and in City Hall

Immediately after falling in at Liberty Hall, Capt. Seán Connolly led about 30 Citizen Army men and women down Dame Street to the entrance of Dublin Castle.[836] When the Rising began, the Castle was quite empty of British troops; it was a bank holiday and many had gone to the Fairyhouse Races. It was reported that 'an attempt was made to seize Dublin Castle but this failed. The Rebels then took possession of the City Hall and the *Dublin Daily Express* office. During these operations a soldier and policeman were shot dead', but there was no real attempt to take the Castle.[837] There has never been consensus on the intent of the Volunteers in attacking Dublin Castle.[838] Many have contended that it was never the intent of the Volunteers and ICA to seize the Castle, as they did not believe that it would be easy to take and it would be very difficult, if not impossible, to hold.[839] Others hold that attempts to take the Castle were a designed part of the Rising but were unsuccessful.[840] Finally, still others conclude that the reduced strength as a result of the countermanding order precluded its capture.[841] Connolly did take his force to the gate of Dublin Castle and a guard there was killed—the first casualty of the Rising.

Though some of Connolly's men took over the Castle's guardhouse, they quickly retreated to the City Hall next door and occupied it.[842] On the first afternoon of the Rising Capt. Seán Connolly was killed, becoming the first rebel casualty. While the Castle was very lightly defended when Connolly held the guardroom, it was the first British position to be reinforced, and by nightfall on the first day over 300 British troops were within the Castle grounds. Whatever chance the rebels had to take the Castle was lost in the first few hours of the Rising. The small City Hall garrison did occupy the *Evening Mail* office, as well as the Nicholas Street graveyard, Synod House and Henry & James at the corner of Cork Hill and Parliament Street.

CITY HALL: MEN

Mustered at Liberty Hall; all Irish Citizen Army unless otherwise designated. Dublin Castle/City Hall; garrison total ten in City Hall and about 40 others spread over the other posts; nine women accompanied the men from Liberty Hall; none executed, six killed.

**Capt. Seán Connolly (33), Commandant;[843] a brother of Éamonn, George and Matt. His sister Katie was also in the garrison. He was employed in the motor tax office of Dublin Castle. James Connolly had told him: 'Good luck, Seán, we won't meet again'. He was ordered to take City Hall and contain any British forces within Dublin Castle. He was the first to fire a killing shot and the first Volunteer/ICA to die in the Rising. It seems that when Constable James O'Brien tried to prevent the men from entering Dublin Castle, Connolly shot O'Brien in the head.[844] Connolly himself was killed on the roof at about 3.15 p.m., becoming the first rebel casualty. Kathleen Lynn wrapped him in the green flag from the play *Under Which Flag* in which he had starred only a week before. As she did so, she recalled his final speech from the play: 'Under this flag only will I serve. Under this flag, if need be, I will die.'[845]

Christopher (Christy) Brady; he was in the detachment that seized the guardroom and went into the Upper Yard of Dublin Castle. The six men who took the guardroom were Brady, Philip O'Leary, Tom Daly, George Connolly, James Seery and Lt Tom Kain.

John (Seán) Byrne; a member of the 123 Parliament Street squad, he occupied the roof of Henry & James, outfitters. Imprisoned at Frongoch.[846]

John Byrne; a Volunteer, he was with the men who occupied the roof of Henry & James on Parliament Street.

**Louis Byrne (46);[847] he was one of the reinforcements sent to City Hall from the GPO. He was treated in the Dublin Castle Red Cross hospital and then was buried in the Castle Yard, before being reinterred in Glasnevin Cemetery. Not on the list issued by the Irish National Aid and Volunteers' Dependants' Fund as 'men who were killed whilst fighting for Ireland during Easter Week, 1916'. His son, also Louis (15), was with him in the GPO.

Patrick Byrne; he garrisoned the Synod Hall in High Street. Imprisoned at Frongoch.

Thomas Francis (Tom) Byrne; he was in command in Shortall's in Parliament Street and at the Capel Street Bridge.[848] (He came from the GPO and is counted in that garrison.)

Éamonn (Edward, Eddie) Connolly, brother of George, Matt and Seán; he was a member of the 123 Parliament Street squad. He occupied the roof of Henry & James.

George Connolly, brother of Éamonn, Matt and Seán; a Volunteer, he was in the detachment that seized the guardroom and went into the Upper Yard of Dublin Castle.

The six men who took the guardroom were Connolly, Christopher Brady, Philip O'Leary, Tom Daly, James Seery and Lt Tom Kain.

Matthew (Mattie) Connolly (14); a brother of Seán, he was on the roof and saw his brother die in the arms of Dr Lynn.[849]

John (Thomas) Coyle; a Volunteer, severely wounded and imprisoned at Frongoch.

Thomas (Tom) Daly; he was in the detachment that seized the guardroom and went into the Upper Yard of Dublin Castle. Imprisoned at Frongoch. The six men who took the guardroom were Daly, George Connolly, Christopher Brady, Philip O'Leary, James Seery and Lt Tom Kain.

**Charles (Charlie) Darcy (D'Arcy, Darcey) (15);[850] 'I'm ready, lads, where do you need me?' He was a Lt of the boys' section. When he left home to fight, his father told him that he had to choose 'between Liberty Hall and his family'. A member of the 123 Parliament Street squad, he was killed on the roof of the Henry & James store on Parliament Street across from City Hall on Tuesday.[851]

Michael Delaney; he was with the section that held the Huguenot graveyard in Nicholas Street.

James Donnelly; a Volunteer and a member of the 123 Parliament Street squad, he occupied the roof of the Henry & James store.[852]

Francis Devine; he was in Parliament Street. He came from the GPO and is counted in that garrison.

Peter Doyle; he came from the GPO and is counted in that garrison.

James Dwyer; he is listed on the Roll of Honour.

Sgt Elliot (Ellett) Elmes (Ellems); a member of the 123 Parliament Street squad. A Protestant, he was imprisoned at Frongoch.

Denis Farrell; a Volunteer, he was one of the reinforcements sent to City Hall from the GPO. Imprisoned at Frongoch.

John Finlay (Finley, Findlay); he was wounded and was carried to the Red Cross hospital in Dublin Castle. Imprisoned at Frongoch.

Francis (Frank) Fitzpatrick; a Volunteer, he was a member of the *Dublin Evening Mail*, 38–40 Parliament Street, squad.

**George Geoghegan (36);[853] he was from Kildare and was employed in the railway works at Inchicore. A Volunteer, he was in the City Hall garrison; some claim that he was killed in the grounds of Dublin Castle while escaping,[854] but in a letter to the National Graves Association J. O'Connor wrote that Geoghegan was killed in City Hall. He was brought into the Castle grounds on Wednesday and initially buried in the Castle Yard before being reinterred in Glasnevin Cemetery. When he left on Monday he wrote to his wife: 'Goodbye dear wife and children … If I am killed you will know I have died fighting in a sacred cause and I trust it will benefit you and the children of every good Irishman for years to come'.[855]

William Halpin; a member of the 123 Parliament Street squad, he occupied the roof of Henry & James. Imprisoned at Frongoch. (Counted in the GPO garrison.)

William Thomas Halpin; he tried to hide in a chimney when the Hall fell but was captured and was imprisoned at Frongoch.

Thomas Healy; he garrisoned the Synod Hall in High Street.

Lt Thomas (Tom) Kain (Kane?); ICA Secretary to the Army Council and Director of Mobilisation. He took part in the attack on Dublin Castle on Monday and was one of a small group (the others being Philip O'Leary, Tom Daly, George Connolly, James Seery and Christopher Brady) who occupied the guardroom of the Castle, taking the guards prisoner. After some time the position became untenable on account of the advancing British troops and the group were forced to retreat by way of a side door into Castle Street. The men made it as far as Lahiff's shop and occupied the basement, where they remained for some time. They managed to obtain a supply of fresh water by boring a hole in a lead pipe; the hole was plugged with a matchstick when water was not required. As chief mobilisation officer, Kain had in his possession a complete list of membership of the Citizen Army. When surrender became inevitable, a suitable hiding place was found for the list. Kain and Frank Robbins returned to the shop eleven years later and recovered it.[856] Imprisoned at Frongoch.

Martin Kelly; he was a member of the *Dublin Evening Mail*, 38–40 Parliament Street, squad. One of three brothers to take part in the Rising, Martin was a captain in the ICA. He married Elizabeth (Bessie) Lynch. He managed to avoid capture after the Rising and was to remain active.

Arthur King; he and Andy Fitzpatrick cut the telephone cables in Talbot Street.[857] He was a member of the *Dublin Evening Mail*, 38–40 Parliament Street, squad.

Mick King; he was a brother of Arthur, Martin and Sam. Martin was in the College of Surgeons.

Samuel (Sam) King; a member of the 123 Parliament Street squad, he occupied the roof of Henry & James.

Patrick Kirwan; he was in the *Dublin Evening Mail* office. He came from the GPO and is counted in that garrison.

James Lambert; he was a Volunteer.

Thomas Lambert; he was sent from the GPO to the City Hall on Monday evening and is counted in this garrison.

James McDonnell; a Volunteer, he was a member of the *Dublin Evening Mail*, 38–40 Parliament Street, squad. Imprisoned at Frongoch.

Seán Milroy; he was in Parliament Street. He came from the GPO and is counted in that garrison.

Michael Mullally (Mullaley); a Volunteer from the 1st Battalion, he reported here because the fighting had already started.

Frederick (Fred) Murphy; he lived on the North Wall, very near Liberty Hall, and was imprisoned at Frongoch.

Thomas Nelson; after the guardroom was seized, he went into the Upper Yard of Dublin Castle. Imprisoned at Frongoch.

Shaun (John Michael) Nolan; a Volunteer, he came from the GPO and is counted in that garrison.

Sgt Alfred George Norgrove; he led a group of twelve reinforcements sent to City Hall from the GPO and is counted in that garrison.[858]

James O'Dwyer; a Volunteer.

John Christopher O'Keefe (O'Keeffe); a Volunteer, he garrisoned the Synod Hall in High Street. Imprisoned at Frongoch.

Edward (Éamonn) O'Kelly; he was in the *Dublin Evening Mail* office. He came from the GPO and is counted in that garrison.

Philip (Phil) O'Leary; he was in the detachment that seized the guardroom and went into the Upper Yard of Dublin Castle. The six men who took the guardroom were O'Leary, Tom Daly, George Connolly, Christopher Brady, James Seery and Lt Tom Kain. Imprisoned at Frongoch.

William Edward (Willie) Oman (16); he was the ICA bugler and after about six months joined the Citizen Army. On Monday morning he was sent to Royal Barracks to watch and report any troop movements. He was part of a group of four who took up position at the viaduct with a commanding view of Upper and Lower Ship Street. About 5 p.m., the risk of being surrounded by troops coming to reinforce the Castle forced him to leave his position. Because of the hostile crowd that gathered to cheer the advancing troops, he was forced to abandon his rifle and cover his uniform with his overcoat. When he reached Christchurch Place one of the mob spotted his uniform and, with the shout of 'There's one of them', they chased him, and he was forced to take refuge in his own home in High Street. He changed into civilian clothes and spent the night in his grandmother's house in Blackpitts. On Tuesday morning he reported to Jacob's, where he was appointed as orderly to Cmdt MacDonagh. On Wednesday, Jacob's received a message from the College of Surgeons that they were low on food. Late on Wednesday night, along with fourteen or fifteen others, Oman took a supply of flour and other provisions to the College. He was posted to the lower lecture hall with the main garrison. He remained at the College until the surrender on the Saturday. While they marched under escort to Dublin Castle, the British officer in charge was forced to threaten the mob with a bayonet charge when they attempted to attack the rebels on Grafton Street. After being held in Dublin Castle for about an hour, he was taken to Richmond Barracks. He was one of 121 boys deemed to be under age and released from Richmond Barracks.[859] (Counted in the St Stephen's Green garrison.)

John O'Reilly; he lived at 3 Ballybough Lane and is listed on the Roll of Honour.

**Lt Seán (John, Jack) O'Reilly (30);[860] he succeeded Seán Connolly in command but was killed on Monday afternoon, not long after Connolly. He was originally buried in the Castle Yard, but was later reinterred in Glasnevin Cemetery. A very tall man, his coffin was almost 7ft long.

John Poole (brother of Pat, below); he was one of the reinforcements sent to City Hall from the GPO. Imprisoned at Frongoch.

Pat Poole (brother of John, above); a Volunteer, he was imprisoned at Frongoch.

Oliver Ryan; he was in the Royal Exchange Hotel in Parliament Street. He came from the GPO and is counted in that garrison.

James Seerey (Seery); he was in the detachment that seized the guardroom and went into the Upper Yard of Dublin Castle. The six men who took the guardroom were Seerey, Philip O'Leary, Tom Daly, George Connolly, Christopher Brady and Lt Tom Kain. Imprisoned at Frongoch.

Michael Sexton; a Volunteer, he was imprisoned at Frongoch.

Christopher Walsh; he came from the GPO and was in Shortall's in Parliament Street. Son of Edward (below), he saw his father killed and was sent home because of his age.[861]

★★Edward (Ned) Walsh (43);[862] the only member of the Hibernian Rifles to be killed in the Rising. He was sent from the GPO to the Dolphin Hotel, and then to the Exchange Hotel in Parliament Street. Some reported that he was killed in the Exchange Hotel,[863] but others maintained that he was killed getting through a skylight in Shortall's in Parliament Street.[864]

Thomas Walsh; a Volunteer, he was imprisoned at Frongoch.

Patrick Joseph Williams; a Volunteer, he was in the Huguenot graveyard in Nicholas Street. Imprisoned at Frongoch.

Henry Winstanley; a Volunteer, he was in the *Dublin Evening Mail* office and Cochrane's tailors in Parliament Street.

CITY HALL: WOMEN

Teresa Byrne; a member of the Hibernian Rifles, she reported here and carried dispatches. Later in the week, she was sent to Church Street where she helped with nursing the wounded.

Brigid (Bridget) Brady (Murphy); she joined the ICA in 1913 and was mobilised a month before Easter Week 1916. She was in Liberty Hall on the Sunday and marched to City Hall on Monday. She was arrested in City Hall and was brought to Ship Street Barracks, and from there to Kilmainham. During the time she was present in Liberty Hall and City Hall she helped with cooking, bandages, making first-aid kits and collecting cans for bombs.

Kathleen (Katie, Kitty) Connolly (Barrett); she was Seán Connolly's sister. She played a role in James Connolly's play *Under Which Flag*, in which Seán played the leading role.[865] She was also a poet, and several of her poems—the most noted of which was *Call to Arms*—were published in *Workers' Republic*.

Brigid Davis (O'Duffy); a medic, she was the first to reach Seán Connolly when he was shot. Brigid helped Dr Lynn with the wounded in the City Hall garrison and was with her in Kilmainham. She said that one of the British soldiers sensed the anxiety of the women and comforted them when he told her, 'You have nothing to worry about, we have sisters of our own'.

Elizabeth (Bessie) Lynch (Kelly); she worked for Countess Markievicz at her home, Surrey House. When Markievicz was imprisoned, she arranged for a weekly payment to Bessie.[866]

Dr Kathleen F. Lynn; 'On Holy Thursday, (James) Connolly and the Citizen Army made me a present as a token of gratitude for the help I had given in connection with medical preparations for the Rising, providing first aid equipment, medical dressings and so on. It was a gold brooch in the form of a fibula and it is still my most treasured possession.'

An ICA Captain, she and Madeleine ffrench-Mullen, Helena Molony and Countess Markievicz delivered arms to City Hall early in the afternoon. Lynn and Molony stopped at City Hall, while Markievicz drove on to the Green. As the Medical Officer and the highest-ranking officer after the deaths of Connolly and Seán O'Reilly, she surrendered the garrison, causing a minor flurry among the British, as they did not know whether they could accept a surrender from a woman.[867]

Her diary entry for that date is typically understated:

Easter Monday. Emer [Molony] & I in City Hall. Seghan Connolly shot quite early in day. Place taken in evening. All women taken to Ship St. about 8.30. Emer, Mrs Barrett, 2 Norgroves, B. Davis & I, joined later on by B. Lynch, J. Shanahan & B. Brady. We were locked up in a filthy store, given blankets thick with lice & fleas to cover us & some 'biscuits' to lie on, not enough to go around.[868]

When I got to City Hall, say some time before 12, it was already occupied by Seán Connolly, and his section of the Citizen Army. As I arrived there I saw the dead body of a big policeman lying on the ground—it seemed to be in front of the Castle gate. Just then, Sir Thomas Myles came up, evidently going into the Castle, and I still remember the look of horror on his face when he saw the body. I don't think he noticed me. He rushed off. I heard afterwards it was to get first aid equipment.

The gate of the City Hall was locked and I had to climb over it though I don't know how I did it. Finally somebody came out and helped me in with my things. When I got in Seán Connolly said it would be better if some of us went up on the roof in case an attack might take place there.

It was a beautiful day, the sun was hot and we were not long there when we noticed Seán Connolly coming towards us, walking upright, although we had been advised to crouch and take cover as much as possible. We suddenly saw him fall mortally wounded by a sniper's bullet from the Castle. First aid was useless. He died almost immediately; that, I think, was in the early afternoon.

We had another casualty on the roof. A young boy, whose name I don't remember, got a wound in the shoulder which I dressed immediately. His condition was not very serious, but he was nervous. He was brought downstairs and remained there until the evacuation. When he heard the others talk of trying to get out, he was afraid they would leave him behind.

Shortly afterwards, a regiment of British soldiers arrived at the Castle, and after Connolly's death the rebel garrison lacked leadership.

I often thought afterwards that it was surprising that those soldiers were allowed to enter the Castle yard unmolested by our men. I think that Seán Connolly's death had a demoralising effect on the City Hall men. It was a pity some attack was not made on them because immediately after their arrival the fusillade started.

The bullets fell like rain. The firing came from all sides and continued till after darkness fell. There was no way of escape although we discussed all possibilities. There was no electric light but there was a moon and we could see things where a beam of moonlight fell.

Lynn was among those held at Kilmainham Gaol.

It was a very trying time for us because Madame Markievicz was overhead in the condemned cell and we used to hear reports that she was to be executed. We could hear shootings in the mornings, and we would be told afterwards who it was. It was a very harrowing experience.

Helena Molony;[869] when she was in America in 1907, she encouraged James

Connolly to return to Ireland as a union organiser.[870] She was one of the founders of the Fianna, an ICA officer and an Abbey actress, and was the secretary of the Irish Women's Workers' Union.[871] She was in Liberty Hall on Sunday when news of the countermanding order came out:

> I saw Eoin MacNeill's countermanding order in the paper and heard the discussion in Liberty Hall. Connolly was there. They were all heartbroken and when they were not crying they were cursing. I kept thinking "does this mean that we are not going to go out?" There were thousands like us. It was foolish of MacNeill and those to think they could call it off. They could not. Many of us thought we would go out single-handed, if necessary.[872]

She was always surprised that others could not understand how the women got involved in the Citizen Army and then the Rising. She wrote: 'It is part of our military duty to knit and darn, but also to march and shoot, to obey orders in common with our brothers in arms'.

She was on the roof of the City Hall when Seán Connolly was shot, and immediately sent downstairs for Dr Kathleen Lynn to try and render first aid. Molony cradled the dying Connolly in her lap and whispered the Act of Contrition in his ear.[873]

While Molony was imprisoned in Kilmainham Gaol after the Rising, she attempted to escape by using a spoon to dig a tunnel. She failed, but as a result the female prisoners were not allowed to eat with utensils for a while.[874] She was transferred from Kilmainham to Lewes Prison and then to Aylesbury Prison, and was released on 23 December 1916.

Annie Norgrove (Grange) (16), sister of Emily (below); a daughter of George and Mrs Norgrove, she crawled on her hands and knees trying to bring water to Volunteers pinned down on the roof. She was arrested and taken to Ship Street Barracks, and then to Kilmainham.

Emily Norgrove (Hanratty), sister of Annie (above); she was a daughter of George and Mrs Norgrove and was a member of the Liberty Players. When the women were trying to get into City Hall, their long skirts hampered them in climbing the fence. Like the other women, Emily just picked up her skirt and climbed over—but in so doing she split her skirt.

Mary Teresa (Molly) O'Reilly (Corcoran) (16); on the weekend prior to Palm Sunday in 1916, Molly was at a dance in Liberty Hall and broke a window while swinging around. On the Sunday before the Rising, the *Irish Republic* flag, with the harp but without the crown, was first raised over Liberty Hall.[875] When Connolly sent

Liberty Hall. Following the Rising, members of the Irish Citizen Army and their families were pictured in front of Liberty Hall, which still bore the scars of the artillery bombardment during the Rising.

Patrick (Paddy) Kilmartin, GPO. Prior to the Rising he was very adept at acquiring weapons from British soldiers, and many of these were stored at his home. Upon capture, Paddy was sent to Richmond Prison, then to Kilmainham Gaol and Arbour Hill Prison, and finally to Wakefield Prison in Yorkshire. (David Kilmartin)

Patrick Joseph (Paddy Joe) Stephenson, GPO, 1st Battalion. Taking his position at the windows of the Mendicity Institute, he was challenged by a DMP man who told the Volunteers to 'quit going so far with this playing of soldiers'. After the policeman was told to 'get the hell off' but didn't move, Stephenson fired a shot in his general direction and the policeman 'shot off down the quays so quickly that his helmet fell off his head'. (David Kilmartin)

Patrick Carroll (front right), GPO, St Stephen's Green. He was a member of the Fianna. After reporting to the GPO he was sent to St Stephen's Green. He was a member of the Volunteers in both the War of Independence and the Civil War. (Kathleen Brady)

Irish Citizen Army Parade. The Irish Citizen Army often paraded through College Green. Patrick Carroll is seen, circled, in the centre of the photograph. (Kathleen Brady)

CON O'DONOVAN

Returned prisoners, 1917 (Mansion House). Following their release from English jails, over 100 of the men met in June 1917 at the Mansion House, where this photo was taken (presented to the Bureau of Military History by Lieutenant Colonel Seán Brennan, BMH P 17, Military Archives). (Photo Album of Ireland)

1st Row (sitting on ground, left to right): Fionán Lynch; John J. Byrne; Séamus Doyle; John Carrick; Conor McGinley; John Tompkins; J.J. Walsh; Tommy Walsh; Seán McDuffy; Con Donovan; J.F. Cullen; Séamus MacLynn; Fergus O'Connor.

2nd Row (kneeling, left to right): Tommy Bevin; Mick de Lacy; Peter Slattery; Con Collins; —; J.F. Cullen; Peadar Clancy; Richard Donoghue; Thomas Doyle; Seán Etchingham; Dick Coleman; John J. Reid.

3rd Row (seated on bench, left to right): John Williams; P.B. Sweeney; J.J. Burke; John Quinn; — Fury; Patrick Flanagan; J.J. Brookes; — Corcoran; Frank Martin; Thomas Ashe; Eoin MacNeill; Éamon de Valera; Tom Hunter; Piaras Béaslaí; — Corcoran; Michael Scully; John McArdle; Jack Shouldice; Austin Stack; John Lawless; — Gallagher/Doherty.

4th Row (left to right): Dennis O'Callaghan; Phil Cosgrave; Seán MacEntee; Frank Thornton Brennan; — Wilson; Mark O'Hehir; Colm O'Geary; Pádraig Fahy; — O'Toole; William O'Dea; Joe McGuinness; David Kent; Liam Tobin; John Darrington; — Darrington; Charlie Bevin; Henry O'Hanrahan; James Kiely; Dick King; Desmond Fitzgerald; Harry Boland; —.

5th Row (left to right): Willie Corrigan; Phil McMahon; Bob Brennan; Dick Kiely; John Downey; Frank Fahy; Séamus Hughes; — Wilson; Maurice Brennan; Patrick [Kelly]; Joseph Norton; John Clarke; Gerald Doyle; Michael Brady; Frank Lawless; George Irvine; Joseph Morrissey; J. O'Brien; Jack Plunkett; Mick Staines; — Kent.

6th Row (left to right): D. Lynch; — Corcoran; Brian Molloy; John Fogarty; Christie Carrick; Tadhg Brennan; Patrick McNestrey; William Meehan; — Peppard; Michael Mervine; George Levins; Séamus Rafter; James Joyce; — Fury; John Falkner; James Loughlin.

7th Row (left to right): Richard Davis; Jack Dempsey; Michael Higgins; Mick Fleming; Peter Paul Galligan; Michael Reynolds; Joseph Burke; Peadar Doyle; William T. Cosgrave; William Hussey; James Brennan; Dennis Leahy; James Sully; — Wilson.

Patrick (Paddy) Moran, 2nd Battalion. Moran was hanged at Mountjoy Prison on 14 March 1921 for his 'participation' in the Bloody Sunday killings at 38 Upper Mount Street, though he was not there. However, the Volunteers at the Gresham Hotel on Bloody Sunday were actually under his command. (May Moran)

Richard (Dick) McKee, 2nd Battalion. He was born in 1893 in Finglas, and after the Rising he was imprisoned at Frongoch. He became O/C of the Dublin Brigade and was murdered on Bloody Sunday. Marlborough Barracks in Phoenix Park was renamed McKee Barracks in his honour. (Glasnevin Trust)

Rosana (Rosie) Hackett, St Stephen's Green. One of the founders of the Irish Women's Workers' Union, she went to work full-time as the clerk of the ITGWU. She helped with the printing of the *Proclamation*. At St Stephen's Green she was in charge of a Red Cross station in the College of Surgeons and was imprisoned. She devoted the rest of her life to labour causes, and died in 1976. In 2014 a bridge across the Liffey was named in her honour. (Labour Youth of Ireland)

Margaret Skinnider, St Stephen's Green. A mathematics teacher from Glasgow, she joined Cumann na mBan and was involved in smuggling weapons and explosives to Ireland. She would carry the detonators in her hat and wrap the wires around her body. She took holidays from her teaching position in Scotland in order to take part in the Rising. Skinnider was wounded three times on a mission to set fire to the Russell Hotel. (Glasnevin Trust)

Michael Staines, GPO. He became QM of the Dublin Brigade after returning from Frongoch, and was a TD in the first three Dáils. He was the first Commissioner of the Garda Síochána, then retired from politics. Subsequently he became director of the New Ireland Insurance Company, with offices on Bachelor's Walk formerly occupied by the Kapp and Peterson and 'Kelly's Fort' premises. (Staines family)

Michael Joseph (The Ó Rahilly) O'Reilly, GPO. Michael Joseph O'Reilly was the Brigade munitions officer, and travelled throughout the south-west on Sunday to distribute MacNeill's cancellation order. When he went to Liberty Hall he is credited with one of the most famous quotations of the Rising: 'I've helped to wind up the clock, I might as well hear it strike'. He left the GPO about 8.00 p.m. on Friday night to find a way to Williams and Woods: 'It will either be a glorious victory or a glorious death'. (Proinsias Ó Rathaille)

for her to raise the flag, Molly thought that she was in trouble for breaking the window. Connolly handed the flag to Molly and said: 'I hand you this flag as the sacred emblem of Ireland's unconquered soul'.[876] Connolly chose Molly to hoist the flag as a replacement for Countess Markievicz, as he feared that Markievicz would be the target of a British assassination attempt.

Instead of going to Irish dancing classes in Liberty Hall, Molly would go and hear Connolly speak. Despite her youth, she was very aware that her family enjoyed better conditions than those who lived in abject poverty all around her. She went to work in the food kitchens during the Lockout and collected money for the families. Molly's father was a stonemason and pro-British. Her mother was outside their family home one day when Molly appeared with two young men and a cart with sacks on top. Inside the sacks were the unassembled guns from the *Asgard* that had been landed at Howth. Her mother asked what was in them and Molly replied, 'That is of no concern, Mother; Mr Connolly would like you to mind these for him for a while'. Her mother asked her where she would put them and Molly replied that she would put them under her father's bed, and that is where they remained. Later, British soldiers searched the house, looking for her; Molly's father was in his bed, but they considered him a pro-British sympathiser, wished him good evening and never searched under the bed. (Her parents were so opposed to her republican activities that she finally left home.)

Molly was at Liberty Hall on Easter Monday, standing in line with the Citizen Army, when her mother ran up to her and tried to drag her home. Molly told her to go home and mind the children, that she had work to do for Mr Connolly. She was assigned as a dispatch runner, carrying messages between City Hall and the GPO. One of her dispatches was taken to James Connolly in the GPO, telling him that Seán Connolly had been killed in City Hall.[877]

Jane (Jenny, Jennie, Jinny) Shanahan; she was not in uniform, and when she passed by the British as she was walking away from City Hall it was assumed that she had been a prisoner. When asked 'How many rebels are on the roof?' she answered, 'There must be hundreds of them still on the roof—big guns and everything'. So the British left it for the morning.[878] When she was taken to 'identify' some 'rebels', however, she was recognised instead and welcomed by her friends, who called out, 'Hullo, Jenny, are you all right?', and the British then confined her.[879]

Mary Shannon; a machinist at the Liberty Hall shirt-making cooperative, she made the *Irish Republic* flag that was raised over the Hall in the ceremony on 16 April.[880]

IX. Liberty Hall

Peter Ennis; he was the caretaker. He stayed in the Hall until the HMY *Helga* bombarded it on Wednesday.

Séamus McGowan; he commanded the rear party after the Volunteers marched to the GPO. He was on the first Army Council of the ICA, and would serve on the last in 1935.[881] He was in the GPO.

William (Willie) Edward Oman (16), bugler; he sounded the bugle to fall in at 11.45 a.m. on 24 April. He had played *The Last Post* at the funeral of O'Donovan Rossa on 1 August 1915.[882] He served in both City Hall and St Stephen's Green.

X. Irish Citizen Army in St Stephen's Green

Commandant Michael Mallin assembled the Citizen Army detachment at Liberty Hall and marched about 100 Citizen Army men and women to St Stephen's Green, sending forward detachments to positions in Harcourt Street Railway Station and Davy's public house, controlling the Portobello Bridge. Mallin's command was placed to block British troop movements into Dublin from the south, generally, and to counter attempts by British troops coming from Portobello Barracks to support Dublin Castle.

Upon arriving at St Stephen's Green, Mallin immediately set up barricades in the streets surrounding it and began to dig trenches at its four corners to cover the entrances. Digging trenches in the Green was one of the Rising's least realistic tactics, and taking the Green at all, rather than the tall buildings that surround it, was inexplicable and disastrous.[883] Although a dozen streets converge at the Green, it has always been questioned why Mallin took the Green first, rather than taking the buildings that overlooked it.[884] On the first night of the Rising, British troops occupied the Shelbourne Hotel, which commanded the Green. Machine-gun fire immediately overwhelmed the Citizen Army personnel, and they beat a hasty retreat to the Royal College of Surgeons on St Stephen's Green West, where they remained for the duration. Unfortunately, Mallin also withdrew his troops from their forward positions, and they remained with the larger detachment in the College of Surgeons until their surrender.

James Connolly led the Citizen Army on mock manoeuvres around St Stephen's Green a few weeks before the Rising and commented that the Shelbourne would be a suitable barracks, with a plentiful supply of food and beds. It was also the highest building of those surrounding the Green and it is unclear why it was not taken instead; that failure was probably due to lack of personnel and an inability to adapt plans to changing circumstances. Certainly the Green became indefensible once the British occupied the Shelbourne.

ST STEPHEN'S GREEN/COLLEGE OF SURGEONS: MEN

Mustered at Liberty Hall, all Irish Citizen Army unless otherwise designated; garrison total about 150 men and women, largely augmented by men from the 2nd Battalion garrison at Jacob's Biscuit Factory; one executed, seven killed; 109 men and ten women surrendered.

*Major Michael Mallin** (executed 8 May 1916, aged 42), Commandant.[885] He was ICA Chief of Staff under Connolly. He served twelve years in the Royal Fusiliers. In Kilmainham he was in cell no. 18, and was seen by his two brothers, Tom[886] and Bart, his sister Kate, his wife, Agnes, and his children—Séamus (12), Seán, Una (6) and Joseph (2 years and 6 months). The Dominican novice master, Fr Patrick Browne,[887] and Fr Albert[888] also attended him.

When the military lorry came to take Mrs Agnes Mallin to see her husband before execution, she brought the children with her. Near the time for departure, she returned to the cell to say a final goodbye to her husband, leaving the children in the guardroom. One of them, Una, was frightened and had no clear idea of what was happening. But she remembers one of the British soldiers going to her, putting his arms around her and saying, 'My poor little child'. Mallin wrote to his wife, 'I would like you to dedicate Una to the service of God and St Joseph', and again he wrote, 'Una my little one be a nun'. Una did so and became Mother Dolores, a Loreto sister in Spain.

Mallin expressed similar sentiments concerning the future of his sons, and two became Jesuits. 'Joseph, my little man, be a priest if you can. James and John, do you take care of your Mother. Make yourselves good strong men for our sake ...'[889]

His son Joseph *did* become a priest and lives in Hong Kong, China, where he works at the Wah Yan College, a Roman Catholic secondary school for boys run by the Society of Jesus, Ireland. Fr Joseph Mallin is the last surviving child of the Rising leaders. In a 2011 letter, Fr Joseph, who was just two years old in 1916, recounted what he remembered of 1916 and the aftermath. He also described a 2009 visit home to Ireland and to Kilmainham Gaol, scene of his father's execution:

> The young lady at the entrance mentioned the entrance fee. I couldn't refrain from a wee joke. I said, 'The first time I came here I didn't have to pay an entrance fee'—but went on—'Ah, that time I was only two and a half years of age—and I was asleep'.
>
> Later, when she [was] leading [us] round the prison and the group had dispersed, I told her who I was.

As he was just an infant then, Fr Joseph remembers little of the year 1916 or the day he was first brought to Kilmainham.

> As I said to the young lady in Kilmainham, 'I was asleep'. I know I was asleep on the metal stairway in the main hall. My sister told me that. A soldier came over and said he was very sorry for me. My first memory comes later.

Fr Joseph said that his father and the events of Easter week were not common topics of conversation in the years that followed the executions, as his mother did not want to burden him. 'Perhaps it was wise of my mother in those years not to speak of my father. She was very wise. Mrs Pearse and Mrs Austin Stack held her in a certain sort of reverence,' he said.

Educated at UCD, Fr Joseph has spent his life devoted to religion and the pursuit of social justice. It has led him from Ireland to Tiananmen Square and beyond. And he believes that those who fought in the Rising did so for justice and Ireland:

> 'You know before 1916 there was rather despair—you feel it in Yeats, Conor Sheehan [sic; Canon Patrick Augustine Sheehan?] and others,' he said, maintaining that their legacy helped to mould modern Ireland.
>
> 'They did shape the country. What is gained with little or no effort is not valued. 1916 did set an ideal.'[890]

Michael Mallin was survived by his wife Agnes, three sons (including Joseph) and two daughters, the youngest of whom was not born until four months after his death. Joseph explained: 'The 1916 event took a toll on my mother's health. I accidentally heard Surgeon Stokes say her breakdown in health was a "direct" result of 1916.'

**John Francis Adams (38);[891] he was wounded and died on the west side of St Stephen's Green, opposite King Street.[892]

Nicholas Alexander; he came from Jacob's and was in the Turkish Baths. He was a 'master' of the Dublin Silk Weavers' Trade Society. Imprisoned at Frongoch.[893]

John Bannon; he was in Harcourt Street Railway Station.

John Barry; he was in Little's public house in Harcourt Street.

Joseph Patrick Begley; he came from Jacob's and was in the Turkish Baths. (Counted in the Jacob's garrison.)

Peter Bermingham; he evaded capture and later joined the Volunteers in the War of Independence.

Luke Bradley; he came from Jacob's. (Counted in the Jacob's garrison.)

Patrick Bradley; a member of the IRB, he was involved in the 1913 Lockout and was an experienced ITGWU member. He was one of the first to join the ICA. He reported to Boland's Mills and then was in Little's public house in Harcourt Street. He was imprisoned at Stafford Prison, then in Wormwood Scrubs, and finally was sent to Frongoch.

Patrick Brady; he came from Jacob's. (Counted in the Jacob's garrison.)

James Brennan; he came from Jacob's. (Counted in the Jacob's garrison.)

James Brougham; he came from Jacob's and was in the Turkish Baths. (Counted in the Jacob's garrison.) Imprisoned at Frongoch.

Thomas Bryan; he lived at 31 Guild Street.

Edward Burke; he was in Leeson Street. Imprisoned at Frongoch.

Matt Burke; he was an ICA member.

Thomas Burke; he was in Leeson Street and York Street. He came from Jacob's. (Counted in the Jacob's garrison.)

Patrick (Paddy) Buttner (15); he ran across the open areas of the Green, evading the machine-gun fire, and made it to the College of Surgeons.

Christopher Byrne (O'Byrne); he was sent to St Stephen's Green and was interned until August.

Denis Byrne; he came from Jacob's. (Counted in the Jacob's garrison.) He was in Little's public house.

James Byrne; he was imprisoned at Frongoch.

Joseph Byrne; he was in Strahan's and the School of Music. He was a dock labourer and joined the Irish Citizen Army, becoming a Captain. Previously, Byrne joined the British army in 1909. In 1914 while on leave he was recalled to his regiment for the First World War. After boarding a ship for Liverpool he removed his army uniform. Byrne returned to Dublin in 1915 and became active in the ICA again. It is believed that Mallin suggested to those who had been in the British army that they should consider leaving the College of Surgeons before the surrender to avoid being arrested as deserters and be treated differently and worse than their comrades. Byrne did so because his wife was seven months pregnant, and they moved to Glasgow.

George Campbell; he was an ICA member.

Francis Joseph Carney; he came from Jacob's. (Counted in the Jacob's garrison.)

Michael Carroll; he was in Harcourt Street Railway Station and at the Leeson Street Bridge.

Eugene (Owen) Carton; he was at Davy's public house and the Portobello Bridge. Imprisoned at Frongoch.

Henry Cassidy; he was an ICA member.

Daniel Francis Chambers; he came from Jacob's. (Counted in the Jacob's garrison.)

Patrick Chaney; he was interned until June.

William Chaney; he was interned until June.

Michael Charlton (Charleton); he was imprisoned at Frongoch.

Peter Christie; he came from Jacob's. (Counted in the Jacob's garrison.)

**Philip Clarke (36, 40?);[894] he was from Slane, Co. Meath. On Monday he sent a little girl, Alice MacThomais, on his bicycle with a message to his wife in Cork Street. 'If necessary, say goodbye from me to your mother and to all the children and tell her to be of good heart for there are good times coming.' When Alice returned the next day with some cigarettes from his wife, he was already dead, leaving her a widow with eight children.[895] He had been killed on Tuesday morning.[896] Along with Johnnie McDonnell, he was building a barricade in front of the Shelbourne Hotel, chaining it together. At 4.00 a.m. Lt Thomas O'Donoghue heard the British in the Shelbourne and ordered Clarke and McDonnell back into the Green, but it was too late: Clarke was cut down by the British machine-guns.

Alice (15) was very small and had been to St Stephen's Green on Monday, but she was sent home because she began to cry when she saw an ICA man threatening to shoot a man pulling down a barricade on Kildare Street. As she was leaving, another man came up to her and said, 'Don't cry, little girl, we won't shoot him. Go on down to help the men in Jacob's', so Alice spent the rest of the day going on messages for the men in Jacob's. When she reached the Green on Monday Clarke asked her to take a message to his wife and to take his bike home. His wife told her that she was very brave, but Alice said, 'I don't know about that, they sent me home yesterday for crying'.[897]

Thomas (Tom) Clifford; he was in the College of Surgeons and was interned until July.

Peter Coates; he was one of the first into the College of Surgeons.

Joseph Connolly; a brother of Seán Connolly, who was killed in City Hall, he led rebel songs at night. He was a member of the Dublin Fire Brigade, stationed at Tara Street—he had just finished his shift before he reported to Liberty Hall on Monday. He and Margaret Skinnider proposed a plan to lob a bomb through the windows of the Russell Hotel. One ICA soldier, Freddie Ryan, was killed and Skinnider was wounded three times in the effort. Connolly dragged Mick Doherty off the roof after Doherty had been hit. Connolly became chief of the Dublin Fire Brigade.

John (Seán) Conroy; he was imprisoned at Frongoch.

**James Corcoran (33);[898] from Gorey, Co. Wexford, he joined the ICA when the Rising began. He was killed on Tuesday in a trench in St Stephen's Green on the east side, facing Hume Street. He was buried in Glasnevin Cemetery and shares a headstone with Michael Malone.

Joseph Alphonsus Patrick Cotter; he came from Jacob's and was in the Turkish Baths. (Counted in the Jacob's garrison.)

Bernard Courtney (Courtnay); his brother, Daniel, was in the GPO and they were both imprisoned at Frongoch.

Barney Craven; he is listed on the Roll of Honour.

Christopher Crothers (Carruthers);[899] ICA. He is listed as a 'boy' in the ICA list compiled by R.M. Fox.[900] He was a Volunteer during the War of Independence.[901]

Patrick Cullen; he was in Harcourt Street Railway Station.

Henry (Harry) Daniels; imprisoned at Frongoch.

Richard Patrick Davys; he came from Jacob's. (Counted in the Jacob's garrison.)

Lt Robert (Bob) De Coeur; an original member of the ICA.[902] He called out, 'If you are any bloody good, come in and fight for Ireland', and Liam Ó Briain and Harry Nichols jumped the fence into St Stephen's Green. Imprisoned at Frongoch.

Pte Michael (Mick) Doherty; he was wounded fifteen times on the roof of the College of Surgeons. ('I'm afraid you're a goner, Mick, may the Lord have mercy on your soul.') Joseph Connolly, a fireman, dragged Doherty off the roof while bullets were hitting all around them. He survived, however, only to die in the 1918 influenza epidemic.

Peter Dolan; he came from Jacob's. (Counted in the Jacob's garrison.)

James Donnelly; he was in the College of Surgeons.

Lt Michael Donnelly; he was in Harcourt Street Railway Station and was imprisoned at Frongoch. He approved the occupation of his home during the Rising. He pressed for greater involvement of the ICA in the War of Independence. In July 1920 he initiated a railwaymen's strike against carrying British soldiers who were under arms, and against carrying any munitions on trains. The strike lasted until December.[903]

Denis (Dennis) Doyle; he is listed on the Roll of Honour.

Joseph Doyle; he is listed on the Roll of Honour.

Sgt Joseph Doyle (Daly?); he was in Harcourt Street Railway Station and led seven men to Davy's pub at Portobello Bridge. Imprisoned at Frongoch.

Sylvester Joseph Doyle; he was in the College of Surgeons.

Thomas Doyle; he came from Jacob's. (Counted in the Jacob's garrison.)

Thomas Drumm; he came from Jacob's. (Counted in the Jacob's garrison.)

Joseph Duffy; he lived at 11 Emerald Street and is listed on the Roll of Honour.

Patrick Duffy (O'Duffy); he was in the College of Surgeons and was interned until August at Frongoch.

Andrew (Andy) Dunne; he was in Cuffe Street. Imprisoned at Frongoch.

James Dwyer; he was in Harcourt Street Railway Station. Imprisoned at Frongoch.

Michael Dwyer; he was in Harcourt Street Railway Station, in the GPO and then in Moore Street at the surrender. (Counted in the GPO garrison.)

Christopher Dynan; he was in the Merrion Street Post Office and the College of Surgeons.

William Egan; he was in the College of Surgeons and was interned until June.

James Farrell; he was in the College of Surgeons and was interned until December.

John J. Fitzharris; he was sent to the GPO and is counted in that garrison.

James (Séamus) Fox; he was in the College of Surgeons. Imprisoned at Frongoch.

**James Joseph (Jimmy) Fox (16);[904] a member of the Fianna, he was an only child. His father, Pat, told Sgt Frank Robbins, 'I am too old to fight, but here is my son. I give him into your charge. Look after him, he's all I have.'[905] Early on Tuesday morning Jimmy was shot when he fled from a trench on the north side of the Green, opposite the United Services Club.

Martin Foy (Fay?); he was in Cuffe Street and was imprisoned at Frongoch.

George Fullerton; he was wounded while fleeing the Green for the College of Surgeons. Imprisoned at Frongoch.

Tadgh Gahan; he came from Jacob's. (Counted in the Jacob's garrison.)

Eugene Geraghty; he is listed on the Roll of Honour.

Thomas Gleeson; he was imprisoned at Frongoch.

William Gleeson; he was imprisoned at Frongoch.

James (Jim) Gough; he was in Davy's public house, Little's public house and the College of Surgeons. Imprisoned at Frongoch.

John Gregory; he came from Jacob's. (Counted in the Jacob's garrison.)

William Halpin; he was imprisoned at Frongoch.

James Hampton; he was in Strahan's and the College of Surgeons. Imprisoned at Frongoch.

Matthew Hand; he was in the College of Surgeons.

John Joseph Hendrick; he reported to St Stephen's Green when he couldn't locate his assigned section. He was in the detachment sent to check out the College of Surgeons and was assigned to an observation post on the roof of the College.

Francis Henry; he was in Harcourt Street Railway Station. Imprisoned at Frongoch.

Frederick (Fred) Henry; he was in Davy's public house.

James Heron; he was imprisoned at Frongoch.

James Patrick Holden; he was in the College of Surgeons.

Robert Humphreys; he came from Jacob's and was in the Turkish Baths. (Counted in the Jacob's garrison.)

James Hyland; he was in the College of Surgeons and was interned until July.

Lt Peter Jackson; he produced a key that opened the gate at the Fusilier's Arch. Imprisoned at Frongoch.

Thomas Michael Jennings; he came from Jacob's. (Counted in the Jacob's garrison.)

Edward Joyce; he was in Harcourt Street Railway Station.

James Joyce (35); he came to St Stephen's Green from Jacob's and went to Davy's public house and then Little's public house.

Joseph James Joyce; he came from Jacob's. (Counted in the Jacob's garrison.)

John Kavanagh; he came from Jacob's. (Counted in the Jacob's garrison.)

Séamus Kavanagh; he was the leader of the reinforcements sent from Jacob's by Thomas MacDonagh. As a 'mobiliser' he was to contact seven or eight men prior to mobilising. Imprisoned at Frongoch. (Counted in the Jacob's garrison.)

Joseph Keeley; an ICA member, he is listed as a 'boy'.[906]

Tommy Patrick Keenan (12); after Jimmy Fox was killed, Mallin sent him home and his parents locked him in his room, but he 'escaped' and returned to the Green.[907] He was one of two twelve-year-olds who were the youngest to fight in Dublin. (Charles MacMahon, in the GPO, was the other.)

Francis Kelly; he came from Jacob's and was in Byrne's public house and Little's public house. (Counted in the Jacob's garrison.)

Sgt James Kelly; he was in Little's public house and Harcourt Street Railway Station.

John Kelly; he was in Davy's public house.

Joseph Kelly; he was at Portobello Bridge.

Hugh Kelly; he came from Jacob's and was in Davy's public house. (Counted in the Jacob's garrison.)

Lt Michael Kelly; just promoted to the rank of lieutenant on the morning of 24 April, he led a detachment of sixteen men, six of whom went to Charlemont Street and the other ten to the railway bridge crossing the Grand Canal at Davy's public house. Upon returning to the Green, he was sent with a detachment to set fire to houses at the top of Grafton Street, but they were withdrawn before attempting their mission. Imprisoned at Frongoch, upon his release he was very active, including taking part in the assassination of members of the Cairo Gang in the Gresham Hotel on Bloody Sunday. He married Mary Hyland, who was also in the garrison. Mick and Mary were to live in Liberty Hall during the '20s and '30s.

William Kelly; he was in the College of Surgeons.

James Joseph Kenny; he came from Jacob's. (Counted in the Jacob's garrison.)

Cyril Aloysius Keogh; he was at Leeson Street Bridge and was imprisoned at Frongoch.

Edward Patrick (Ned) Keogh;

> On Easter Monday, I was sent with a section to Stephen's Green and dug trenches inside the park (Green) railings. I fought till surrender on Sunday 30th April 1916. On Easter Monday night, I was sent out with a section under Capt. R. McCormack and we attacked Portobello Barracks. On our return, a British Soldier was held up and searched as he was coming out of Harcourt Street

Station. When the section returned to the Green (on return from Portobello), I spent the night in the Green which was evacuated the next morning (Tuesday) and we entered the College of Surgeons ...

On Tuesday night, I was in a party under Capt. McCormack which kept up continuous firing on the British who were in the buildings on the other side of the Green. This attack on the British was I believe to cover the advance of another party of the Citizen Army who were leaving the College for some operation. During the week, I was in other buildings including the Turkish Baths and the Athletic Stores from which we removed stuff for bedding in the College. We surrendered on Sunday the 30th and were brought as prisoners to the Castle. After an hour or two there, we were sent to Richmond Barracks and the same night (Sunday 30th) we were removed to North Wall and put on a boat and deported.[908]

James Keogh; he was in the College of Surgeons. Imprisoned at Frongoch.

Martin King; ICA.[909] On Good Friday he and Andy Fitzpatrick went on a tour of the principal trunk line centres with a view to disrupting communications on Sunday.[910] King was in command of the ICA contingent that was supposed to capture the telephone exchange in Crown Alley, but the Volunteers detailed for the job were turned away.[911] Because the Volunteers did not wait, King, who was detailed to cut the wires, could not find them and he reported to his post at St Stephen's Green. The exchange remained in operation all Monday afternoon with no guards and the rebels could easily have taken it. It could have been occupied early in the Rising, but the few ICA men were also deterred by a 'shawlie' who yelled, 'Go back, boys, the place is crammed with military'. Finally, it was taken over by the British about five hours later. King's brothers Arthur, George and Sam were in the City Hall Garrison.

Seán Joseph Francis King; he came from Jacob's. (Counted in the Jacob's garrison.)

Philip Lacey; he was wounded on Tuesday, subsequently hospitalised and interned until July.

Patrick Joseph Lalor (Lawlor); he was at Harcourt Street Railway Station.

J. Lambert; he is listed on the Roll of Honour.

Michael J. Lawless;

In Easter Week I served in the College of Surgeons with the Citizen Army, on the Monday at the Shelbourne Hotel gate, for the rest of the week on guard at a window overlooking Glovers Alley and in the houses occupied in the Grafton St. direction. On the Saturday night I was sent with a party to Jacob's for food and brought back supplies to the Surgeons. Then some of us E Coy men who had been in the Surgeons during the week, rejoined, by permission of Commandant Mallin, our Company which was in Jacob's. On the surrender next day, I got away accompanied by John O'Rourke of Seville Place. I arrived home next day, Monday, but was arrested almost immediately and brought to the L.N.W.R. station North Wall where a British post held various prisoners. I was brought before a Major Somerville there, about a fortnight later and released. That was the only imprisonment I ever experienced.[912]

Peter Leddy; he was in Merrion Row, and engaged in a shoot-out with British troops in the Shelbourne Hotel and Baggot Street.

James (Jem) Little; he was in the College of Surgeons. Imprisoned at Frongoch.

Seán Lynch; he came from Jacob's. (Counted in the Jacob's garrison.)

Edward Luke (Juke, Tuke?); he lived at 83 Queen Street and was interned until December.

Daniel McArt; he is listed on the Roll of Honour.

★★James McCormack;[913] born in County Meath, he was employed at the racecourse at Baldoyle. There is controversy about the place of his death: some say on Talbot Street, some in Fairview, but it is generally accepted that he died at the College of Surgeons. Liam Ó Briain stated that he was a sniper upstairs in the College of Surgeons and was killed there.[914] Fox lists him as killed in action.[915] He is not on the list issued by the Irish National Aid and Volunteers' Dependants' Fund as 'men who were killed whilst fighting for Ireland during Easter Week, 1916'. He is buried in Glasnevin Cemetery in his Volunteer uniform.

Thomas McCormack; he was in College Green and the College of Surgeons and was wounded.

Capt. Richard McCormick; there is disagreement in his pension application file as to whether McCormick or Christopher Poole was the senior ICA officer serving under Mallin. McCormick was sent with a 45-man section of the Citizen Army to take Harcourt Street Railway Station. He was to impede British troop movements until the Green had been secured, then fall back and reinforce those in the Green. Later he was in Davy's public house. He was the one who lowered the tricolour and raised the white flag at the College of Surgeons. Imprisoned at Frongoch.

Owen McDermott; he came from Jacob's. (Counted in the Jacob's garrison.)

John (Johnnie) Bernard McDonald; he came from Jacob's. (Counted in the Jacob's garrison.) Along with Philip Clarke, he was building a barricade in front of the Shelbourne Hotel, chaining it together. At 4.00 a.m. on Tuesday morning, Lt Thomas O'Donoghue heard the British in the Shelbourne and ordered Clarke and McDonnell back into the Green, but it was too late and Clarke was cut down by the British machine-guns. Imprisoned at Frongoch.

Matthew McDonnell; he came from Jacob's. (Counted in the Jacob's garrison.)

Patrick McDonnell; he came from Jacob's. (Counted in the Jacob's garrison.)

William McDonnell; he came from Jacob's and was in Harcourt Street Railway Station and the Turkish Baths. (Counted in the Jacob's garrison.)

Michael McGinn; he was imprisoned at Frongoch.

Thomas McGrane; he came from Jacob's. (Counted in the Jacob's garrison.)

Peter Paul MacGrath (McGrath); he was from Wexford and was at the Leeson Street Bridge and the College of Surgeons.

John MacMahon; he is listed on the Roll of Honour.

Peadar MacMahon (Peadar MacMathghamhna); he came from Jacob's. (Counted in the Jacob's garrison.)

Henry Russell MacNab; he was a medical doctor and went back and forth to other garrisons. He was captured but never interned.

James Maguire (McGuire); he came from Jacob's and was in the Harcourt Street Railway Station. (Counted in the Jacob's garrison.) Imprisoned at Frongoch.

John Mahon (Maher?); he is listed on the Roll of Honour, and was imprisoned at Frongoch.

Edward Mannering; he was imprisoned at Frongoch.

John William Meagher; he was in Leeson Street and the College of Surgeons.

Patrick Mitchell; he was imprisoned at Frongoch.

Michael J. Molloy; he came from Jacob's. (Counted in the Jacob's garrison.) He was one of the printers of the *Proclamation* and was chosen by James Connolly to oversee the printing, as he was an experienced compositor.[916] He carried with him the piece of paper signed by the signatories to the *Proclamation* until he found himself in Richmond Barracks after the surrender, when he chewed it up and spat it out to prevent its discovery. He was sent to Knutsford Prison, and thence to Frongoch.[917] He was released in August 1916.

Andrew Monks; he came from Jacob's and was in the Turkish Baths. (Counted in the Jacob's garrison.) Imprisoned at Frongoch.

Frederick Murphy; he came from Jacob's and was in Harcourt Street Railway Station and Little's public house. (Counted in the Jacob's garrison.)

Patrick Murphy; he was imprisoned at Frongoch.

James Joseph Murran; he came from Jacob's. (Counted in the Jacob's garrison.)

**Daniel Murray (27, 32?);[918] he was a member of the Gaelic League and the GAA. A Volunteer, he was wounded in the College of Surgeons and died in St Vincent's Hospital.[919]

Bernard Murtagh; he came from Jacob's and was in Little's public house. (Counted in the Jacob's garrison.)

James Nelson; he was in the College of Surgeons. Imprisoned at Frongoch.

Capt. Henry (Harry) Nicholls; he was a member of the 4th Battalion, Volunteers. He jumped the St Stephen's Green fence with Liam Ó Briain. He was an Ulsterman and a Protestant, and was imprisoned in Frongoch.

> ... [I] met Liam Ó Brien who told me he had been down in the country conveying the countermanding order on the previous day. He told me that the Citizen Army had seized the Green. As he belonged to one of the north side

battalions, he was in doubt as to what was the best thing to do. I said we better go along to the Green and join in and we could afterwards move over to join our own battalions if it were possible, and if we were not specially wanted there. We walked down to the Green, found the gates locked. A Citizen Army man came up with a gun in his hand. We told him we were Volunteers, had missed our battalions, and thought of joining in there. So he said 'Right Oh' and we climbed over the railings and got in. We were brought up to the Commander, Commandant Mallin, and I told him that I was in the Volunteers and that I was at his disposal if he wanted me, and Liam did the same. This would have been about 2 o'clock p.m. He detailed me to take up position facing Cuffe St. in the garden of the Greenkeeper's Lodge.[920]

Patrick Nolan; he came from Jacob's. (Counted in the Jacob's garrison.)

Liam Ó Briain (O'Brien); a Volunteer in the 1st Battalion, he cycled around Dublin trying to get information for Eoin MacNeill, and carried cancellation messages from MacNeill in the days before the Rising. He was first at Davy's public house at Portobello Bridge on his way to St Stephen's Green, and then just stayed at St Stephen's Green.[921] 'Yet among all was a vast elation. We seemed to breathe a purer air and dwell in sublime heights. It was a unique experience to feel that, once again, after a hundred years or more, the foreign yoke had been cast off, and that men in their own capital, with their own flag above them, should be standing at bay before their own race.'[922] He was imprisoned at Frongoch. Arrested as a Dáil/Republican judge early in 1920, he remained in prison for the remainder of the War of Independence. He took the Treaty side in 1922, and became a well-known writer and professor of Romance Languages at the National University.[923]

Francis (Frank) O'Brien (Ó Briain); he was seriously wounded on Monday and was evacuated from St Stephen's Green.

Dominick O'Callahan; he was interned until July.

John O'Callahan; he lived at 20 Leinster Street, Phibsborough. 'I stuck my sandwiches in one pocket of my coat, the bullets in the other, and my rifle down my pants, got on my bicycle and went off to declare war on the British Empire. And you know what? In the end we beat 'em.' Imprisoned at Frongoch.

James Joseph O'Carroll; he came from Jacob's. (Counted in the Jacob's garrison.)

John O'Connor; he was in the College of Surgeons.

Michael O'Doherty; he was in the College of Surgeons and was wounded. Imprisoned at Frongoch.

Henry Vincent O'Donoghue; he was in the College of Surgeons.

Sgt Thomas O'Donoghue (Tomás Ó Donnchadha); he was interned until December.

Patrick O'Duffy; he was a Volunteer who joined the ICA men at St Stephen's Green.

John O'Grady; he came from Jacob's. (Counted in the Jacob's garrison.)

Joseph John O'Hanrahan; he came from Jacob's. (Counted in the Jacob's garrison.)

Michael O'Kelly; he was in Harcourt Street Railway Station. Imprisoned at Frongoch.

David O'Leary; he was in the detachment sent to check out the College of Surgeons, and he assisted Robbins in raising the tricolour over the building.

William (Willie) Oman (16); he was the ICA bugler. He played the bugle to fall in the ICA and Volunteers outside Liberty Hall, and at the funeral of Jeremiah O'Donovan Rossa in 1915. Oman's involvement with the Rising was preceded by an operation for appendicitis, performed by Dr Kathleen Lynn. On Easter Monday he was posted to Castle Street, just beside City Hall, but came under fire from British troops and escaped, just ahead of a hostile mob, to his home in High Street. Next day he joined the Jacob's garrison, but was sent later that week to bring supplies to the College of Surgeons, and stayed there with his Citizen Army comrades. He recalled that the Citizen Army nickname for Countess Markievicz was 'Lizzie'.[924] Imprisoned at Frongoch. (See City Hall garrison, but counted in St Stephen's Green garrison.)

Capt. John J. O'Neill; his men supported Michael Kelly's men, and they were assigned to the railway bridge overlooking South Circular Road. Imprisoned at Frongoch.

Timothy (Tim, Jim) O'Neill; he was in the College of Surgeons. Imprisoned at Frongoch.

Joseph Lewis O'Reilly; he was in the College of Surgeons and was interned until August.

Patrick O'Reilly; he was imprisoned at Frongoch.

Frederick (Fred) O'Rorke (16); he was in the Turkish Baths and was imprisoned at Frongoch. (He came from Jacob's and is counted in the 2nd Battalion garrison.)

John O'Rorke (O'Rourke); he was sent with a party to Jacob's for food and brought back supplies to the College of Surgeons. 'Then some of the E Coy men who had been in the Surgeons during the week, rejoined, by permission of Commandant Mallin, our Company which was in Jacob's.'[925] (He is counted in the 2nd Battalion garrison.)

John Joseph O'Rourke; he came from Jacob's and his officer told him to escape at the surrender, as he was in civilian clothes. (Counted in the Jacob's garrison.)

Albert O'Shea; he was imprisoned at Frongoch.

James O'Shea; he was an ICA member, and was interned until December.

Sgt James O'Shea; he had been a member of the ICA since its inception.[926] He came from Jacob's. (Counted in the Jacob's garrison.)

> In a conversation I had with him [Mallin] afterwards he told me his reason and Connolly's for Stephen's Green. This was his plan. It was intended that at least 500 men would take over this area. It would be barricaded at different entrances, such as Merrion Street and the street at Shelbourne Hotel and all streets leading to Green. It was to be a base as it had all the necessaries for a base. It had plenty of water; as he remarked water could be cut off if there was a long fight. It had hotels with plenty of food and beds. It also had a hospital—St Vincent's. It was intended also for prisoners. Now this is a rough plan of the 'scrap'. When the fight was on for a day or two it was assumed that most of the barracks would fall as they would be attacked from two sides. The men in the city would move out and the men in Wicklow and Kildare move in. Of course this was fixed on the assumption that there would be about 5,000 men in Dublin. It was the published number in Volunteer papers at the time and the rough plans were made on that number. Now you can see how well Connolly and Mallin planned Stephen's Green base; Jacob's controlling the Castle, Boland's an outpost for the searoads, Jacob's having outposts along Camden Street, Kevin Street, New Street and the Coombe to stop reinforcements for the Castle; Marrowbone Distillery in touch with South Dublin Union and it holding the roads from Richmond Barracks. The Mendicity Institute controlling Royal Barracks and Four Courts holding roads from Arbour

Hill, Marlboro barracks. Also a post at Phibsboro—its job was to hold roads leading to city. It was a plan whereby all posts were in touch with each other through outposts. Now after two days the men would move out as it would give the men in the country time to move in. If there was anything in the shape of a 33 [?] force left it was to be caught between the two forces. I may be a bit out in the positions as I did not think it out well at the time, but it is a rough sketch as given to me by Mallin.

Imprisoned at Frongoch.[927]

Robert O'Shea; imprisoned at Frongoch.

James O'Sullivan; he was wounded on the Green.

Councillor Capt. William (Bill) Partridge; he led the rosary each night in his sonorous voice. He was wounded in the head. Sentenced to fifteen years' penal servitude, he was released in 1917 because he had Bright's disease. He died in 1918. The handling of the vacancy caused by his early death caused a split in the Dublin Labour Party and eventually in Irish Labour as a whole.

Aubrey George Pepper; he was sent to Jacob's. (Counted in the St Stephen's Green garrison.)

Capt. Christopher (Christy, Kit) Poole; a member of the committee of the ICA from its inception. There is disagreement in the pension applications as to whether Richard McCormick or Poole was the senior ICA officer serving under Mallin. Born in Dublin into a strong nationalist family, Poole had served in the British Army during the Boer War. He held the distinction of having the only Lee-Enfield .303 rifle belonging to the ICA. He had been a full-time labourer for Dublin Port and Docks until he joined the strike in 1913 and did not get his job back. He prowled the Green, making sure the barricades were reinforced and the fields of fire were well laid out, crossing at all the gates to the Green.

Patrick Poole; he was in the College of Surgeons and was interned until December.

Thomas Pugh; he came from Jacob's. (Counted in the Jacob's garrison.)

James Quigley; he was in the College of Surgeons and evaded capture.

Patrick Redmond; he came from Jacob's. (Counted in the Jacob's garrison.)

Augustus Percival Reynolds; he was editor and manager of the Fianna newspaper. He was in the Turkish Baths and was imprisoned at Frongoch.

John Arnold de Vere Reynolds; he came from Jacob's. (Counted in the Jacob's garrison.)

Sgt Frank Robbins; he was from North William Street in Dublin's North Strand. His twenty men were to operate in Hatch Street, and later he led a group of only three men and three women (including Countess Markievicz) that seized the College of Surgeons. He had sought greater cooperation between the ICA and the Volunteers.[928] He was imprisoned at Frongoch. In 1948 he unsuccessfully ran for the Dáil as a National Labour Party candidate from the north Dublin district.

Seán Rogan; he was in Yeates's Post Office in Merrion Row. Imprisoned at Frongoch.

John J. Rooney; he was sent to the garrison at Fumbally Lane and then returned to St Stephen's Green.

Albert Rutherford; he came from Jacob's. (Counted in the Jacob's garrison.)

★★Frederick (Freddie) Ryan (17);[929] a member of the Fianna, he was a Volunteer before joining the ICA. He was killed in Harcourt Street during the attempt to set fire to the Russell Hotel. Margaret Skinnider was wounded in the same incident.[930]

James Ryan; an explosives expert for the Volunteers, he was in the College of Surgeons.

William John Scott; he was in Granby's Music Shop and was wounded.

Tom Scully; he was a seaman and lived at 7 Pitt Street. He is listed on the Roll of Honour.

John (Patrick?) Seery; he was in the College of Surgeons and was interned until August.

Martin Joseph Shannon; he was in Harcourt Street Railway Station.

Denis Shelly; he came from Jacob's. (Counted in the Jacob's garrison.)

Tom Shiels (Shields); he was in Leeson Street and the College of Surgeons. Imprisoned at Frongoch.

Terence Simpson; he came from Jacob's and was in the Turkish Baths. (Counted in the Jacob's garrison.)

Michael Slater; he came from Jacob's and was in the Turkish Baths. (Counted in the Jacob's garrison.)

James Smith; he lived at 3 Pile's Buildings, Wood Street, and is listed on the Roll of Honour.

Richard (Dick) Stokes; he came from Jacob's. (Counted in the Jacob's garrison.)

Thomas Sutton; he was in Harcourt Street Railway Station.

John Charles Toomey; he came from Jacob's and was in the Turkish Baths. (Counted in the Jacob's garrison.)

George Tully; he came from the GPO. (Counted in the GPO garrison.)

John Turner; he came from Jacob's. (Counted in the Jacob's garrison.)

Joseph Edward Vize; he came from Jacob's and was in the Turkish Baths. (Counted in the Jacob's garrison.)

John Walker; he came from Jacob's. (Counted in the Jacob's garrison.)

Michael Walker; he came from Jacob's. (Counted in the Jacob's garrison.)

Nicholas Ward; he came from Jacob's. (Counted in the Jacob's garrison.)

John Whelan; he was in the College of Surgeons. Imprisoned at Frongoch.

Peter Williams; he came from Jacob's. (Counted in the Jacob's garrison.)

ST STEPHEN'S GREEN/COLLEGE OF SURGEONS: WOMEN

Christina (Chris) Caffrey (Keely); she was captured while taking a message to the GPO, disguised as a war widow. She was strip-searched but ultimately released, and made her way back to the College. While under guard in Trinity College, she chewed up the dispatch and said that it was 'just a sweet' when she was asked what she was chewing.[931]

Annie Carey (O'Hagen); she was a member of the Hibernian Rifles and went back and forth to Jacob's.

Máire Comerford; she was turned away because of her youth but reported to the GPO.[932] (Counted in the GPO garrison.)

Eileen Conroy; she is listed on the Roll of Honour.

Brigid Dempsey (née Dodd); she lived at 7 York Street, just next to the College of Surgeons. She was pregnant at the time of the Rising, but kept smuggling food to the garrison.

Mary Devereux (Allen); she is listed on the Roll of Honour.

Anastasia (Anne) Devlin; she was a dispatch runner to the other garrisons.

Mary Donnelly; she went out of the College of Surgeons several times to forage for food, and crawled back in through holes in the walls. She found the College quite scary: 'The classrooms of the College seemed huge and draughty. Everywhere were huge glass cases with objects for students, pebbles and specimens. In an adjoining room the jars had parts of humans preserved in liquid.'[933]

Sgt Madeleine ffrench-Mullen; an ICA officer, she commanded the medical detachment. She was imprisoned at Richmond Barracks and Kilmainham Gaol.[934] In 1919, with Dr Kathleen Lynn, she opened St Ultan's Children's Hospital with '£70 and 3 cots'.

Nora Foley (Ni Foghludha) (O'Daly); when the garrison relocated to the College of Surgeons, Nora set up a first-aid department and treated all of the wounded there. Following the surrender, like some of the women she initially was sent to Richmond Prison, and then was held at Kilmainham. She recalled: 'The order was given to lodge us in Kilmainham Jail and hither we were finally marched, arriving after dusk and being received by the light of candles, which only served to intensify the gloom. Finally our quarters were allotted, one cell to each four prisoners, and one blanket and one "biscuit" doled out to us. Our cell doors were banged shut and we were left to make the best we could of the means at our disposal.' Madeleine ffrench-Mullen approached the women on Wednesday and told them that they could go to see their families. Nora said yes at first, but when she realised that it was a ruse to let them escape she declined to go.[935]

Helen Ruth (Nellie) Gifford (Donnelly); she was in charge of the commissary.[936] Later she explained the refusal of women to escape: she felt that 'the Republic promised us equality without sex discrimination, so we were all adjudged soldiers, women and men, whether we worked as dispatch carriers or in Red Cross units'.[937] Nellie was a prisoner at Kilmainham Gaol when her sister, Grace, married Joseph Plunkett. Poignantly, Nellie remembered that she heard the shots on the morning of Joe's execution, but did not know that it was he who was executed—nor did she know that her sister had married Joe during the night.

Nora Margaret Mary Gillies (O'Daly); she had been involved since 1914, and was at the Howth gunrunning. At the Green she was a medical officer and treated Margaret Skinnider, among others.[938]

Brigid Goff (Gough?); she was remembered for entertaining the garrison with her jokes as they worked.[939]

Rosana (Rosie) Hackett; an employee at Jacob's Biscuit Factory, she was one of the most militant in the 1911 strike, was locked out in 1913 and was unable to obtain employment thereafter. One of the founders of the Irish Women's Workers' Union, she went to work full-time as the clerk of the ITGWU. She helped with the printing of the *Proclamation*. At St Stephen's Green she was in charge of a Red Cross station in the College of Surgeons and was imprisoned. Rosie devoted the rest of her life to labour causes and died in 1976. In 2014 a bridge across the Liffey was named in her honour.[940]

Mary (May, Molly) Hyland (Kelly); a noted actress and singer, she commandeered food and brought it in to the garrison. Later she brought a dead Volunteer to Dublin from the Wicklow mountains—to avoid arrest, she had to prop him up in the motorcar seat so that he would look alive.[941]

Margaret (Maggie) Joyce; she had joined the ICA in 1914.

Mary Kavanagh; she was a member of the Hibernian Rifles.

Annie Kelly; she and Rosie Hackett were great friends.

Kate (Katie, Kitty) Kelly; she worked in the commissariat with Nell Gifford and Molly Hyland.

Mary Kelly; prior to the Rising she was involved in gathering information on the British.

Elizabeth Ann 'Lilly' (Lily?) Kempson (McAlerney); a nineteen-year-old worker at Jacob's Factory, she was a member of the Irish Women's Workers' Union and served fourteen days in Mountjoy Jail for her involvement in the Jacob's strike in 1911. She was a member of Cumann na mBan and the Irish Citizen Army. At the Green, she and some of the other women helped to evacuate citizens and defend the gates. She took the bread from a baker in the Green at the point of a pistol to try to replenish the dwindling supplies of the rebels. When a man fighting in the Green said that he wanted to go home, Lilly stopped him, saying: 'You can't. We're all away from home now.' After the Rising she hid in a confessional in Whitefriar Street Church, as the British Army was looking for her and searched her home for guns and ammunition. She escaped to Liverpool, where she boarded the SS *Philadelphia* and went to America with just the clothes on her back. 'Tell Mom I'm off to Amerikay.' Lilly never returned to Ireland and passed away on 22 January 1996 in Seattle, Washington, USA, the last female survivor of the Rising.[942]

Elizabeth (Lily) King (MacCarthy); prior to the Rising she was involved in intelligence-gathering as a waitress in the Vegetarian Restaurant on St Stephen's Green.

Alice — (MacThomais) (15); on Monday, Philip Clarke sent her on his bicycle to his wife in Cork Street. [943] 'If necessary, say goodbye from me to your mother and to all the children and tell her to be of good heart for there are good times coming.' When Alice returned later with some cigarettes from his wife, he was already dead, leaving his widow with eight children.[944] He was killed on Tuesday morning.[945] Alice was very small and had been to St Stephen's Green on Monday, but she was sent home because she began to cry when she saw an ICA man threatening to shoot a man who was trying to pull down a barricade on Kildare Street. As she was leaving, another man came up to her and said, 'Don't cry, little girl, we won't shoot him. Go on down to help the men in Jacob's', so Alice spent the rest of the day going on messages for the men in Jacob's. When she reached the Green on Monday, she asked whether she could help, and Clarke asked her to take a message to his wife and to take his bike home. His wife told her that she was a very brave girl, but Alice said, 'I don't know about that, they sent me home yesterday for crying'.[946]

Áine Malone (Fitzgerald); she was wounded on Easter Monday at St Stephen's Green while carrying a dispatch to Jacob's Biscuit Factory and was brought to Mercer's Hospital.

Major Countess Constance (Gore-Booth) Markievicz (48); Vice-Commandant.[947] Originally she was to liaise between the GPO and St Stephen's Green, but Mallin told her that he needed her as second in command.[948] Early on Monday afternoon she was delivering supplies to City Hall with Dr Lynn. Lynn was called back to the City Hall after Seán Connolly was wounded, and Markievicz only arrived at the Green some time later on Monday afternoon.[949]

Upon her arrival at the Green, some reports have her being detailed by Cmdt Mallin to inspect the defences, and she came to the Harcourt Street corner, where a group of Volunteers were arguing with a DMP member who refused to leave his post. Allegedly, the DMP constable was trying to climb over the closed gate, but was pushed back by the men guarding it and warned that he would be shot if he persisted. It is said that she raised her Mauser handgun and other Volunteers also raised their guns. Two (some say three) shots rang out and Constable Michael Lahiff (29) was killed.[950] She was supposed to have shouted, 'I shot him! I shot him!',[951] but no BMH Witness Statement definitively places her at the Harcourt Street corner at that time.

Nevertheless, an eyewitness account recalls her in the Green with a cigarette in her mouth and a pistol in her hand: '… a lady in a green uniform … breeches, slouch hat with green feathers, the feathers were the only feminine appearance, holding a revolver in one hand and a cigarette in the other, was standing on the footpath giving orders to the men …' Geraldine Fitzgerald was a nurse at the St Patrick's Jubilee Nurses' Home, 101 St Stephen's Green South. She wrote that the nurses had just begun lunch when they saw the woman and 'recognised her as the Countess de Markievicz—such a specimen of womanhood … We had only been looking a few minutes when we saw a policeman walking down the path … he had only gone a short way when we heard a shot and he fell on his face. The Countess ran triumphantly into the Green shouting "I got him" … We rushed for bandages … but we could not stop his life blood ebbing away.'[952]

Markievicz did take part in the firing later that day when a party of Royal Irish Rifles came along Camden Street, and also took part in the sniping from the roof of the College of Surgeons. At the surrender, she kissed her 'Peter the Painter' Mauser before handing it over.[953]

Mary (May) Moore (Wisely, Wisley?); she joined the women in the first-aid station in the duck-keeper's house.[954] She was first in the Turkish baths and then went to the College of Surgeons.

Brigid Murtagh (O'Daly); she was a member of the first-aid team of Cumann na mBan.[955]

Christina Máire Ni Dhubhgaill (Doyle); on Monday she delivered first-aid equipment to the Green, and then remained until the surrender.

Mrs — Norgrove; she is listed in Dr Kathleen Lynn's diary.

Margaret Ryan (Dunne); she was involved in intelligence-gathering before the Rising.

Kathleen Seary (Seery) (Redmond); she set up a field kitchen in the summer-house and was imprisoned in Richmond Prison and Kilmainham.

Margaret Skinnider (23); a mathematics teacher from Glasgow, she operated as an ICA member when in Ireland.[956] After she joined Cumann na mBan, she was involved in smuggling weapons and explosives to Ireland.[957] She would carry the detonators in her hat and wrap the wires around her body. At Christmas 1915 she brought detonators to Ireland on the boat from Glasgow. She took holidays from her teaching position in Scotland in order to take part in the Rising.

Skinnider was sent away from the College many times carrying dispatches; when she left her post she changed into civilian clothes, rode on her bicycle, and changed back into her uniform on her return.

She proposed to Mallin that the Shelbourne Hotel be bombed, but he was very dubious about the plan. Finally, she convinced him that a bomb could be placed at the Russell Hotel, and on Wednesday she was one of the party sent to set fire to the hotel.[958] Wounded three times (in the right arm, right side and back), she was carried back to the College by Bill Partridge. She wrote *Doing my bit for Ireland*, in which she described her role as a sniper on the roof of the College of Surgeons: 'It was dark there, full of smoke, a din of firing, but it was good to be in the action; more than once I saw a man I aimed at fall'. She applied for a pension for her service, but was rejected at first because she was a woman. After repeated submissions, her application was finally approved in 1938.

Appendix 1. Women who also served in County Dublin during the Rising

Most were involved in carrying dispatches into and out of the city. It should be noted that women carried many of the dispatches during the Rising, as they did many of the important communications throughout the period. Women were chosen for these missions because they could move about the country more easily than the men, providing that they dressed conventionally in long skirts or dresses. Even Margaret Skinnider, who often dressed as a boy, wore women's clothes when doing dispatch work and when running weapons.[959] British soldiers generally refused to strip-search women unless a lady searcher was available. Since women were less conspicuous and less likely to be searched, they also ran other important errands. Marie Perolz obtained extra revolvers from an arms dealer in Dublin.[960] In one case, the Volunteers sent a group of Cumann na mBan women to save a batch of guns shortly before the Rising; they asked Brighid Foley, Effie Taaffe and Kitty O'Doherty to find and protect the guns that had come into the country in boxes marked as 'cutlery'. The women successfully transported these two boxes across town, past a couple of policemen, and hid them under the stairs in O'Doherty's house.[961]

Eilis Allen; she took messages from Liberty Hall to Belfast and Coalisland, Co. Tyrone.

Kate Brown; it is unclear whether she mobilised in Dublin or in Enniscorthy.

Martha Brown; imprisoned.

Ina Connolly (Heron); she took messages from Liberty Hall to Belfast and Coalisland, Co. Tyrone.[962]

Nora Connolly (O'Brien); she took messages from Liberty Hall to Belfast and Coalisland, Co. Tyrone.[963]

Elizabeth Corr; she took messages from Liberty Hall to Coalisland, Co. Tyrone.[964]

Agnes Daly; she took messages to County Kerry.

Kathy Doran.

Kathleen Fleming; imprisoned.

Margaret Fleming (Leonard); she was was sent from Dublin to Athlone, Co. Westmeath, with a dispatch for the Irish Volunteer leadership there on Monday.

Cait Foley (Murphy); sister of Brighid, she carried messages to Coalisland, Co. Tyrone.

Eilis (Betsy) Gray; she was briefly in Dublin, and went with Nora and Ina Connolly to Coalisland, Co. Tyrone.[965]

Kathleen Kearney; sister of Peadar Kearney, she married Jack Furlong, who was in Jacob's, and they had two sons, Seán and Rory. Later she married Stephen Behan, and was the mother of Brendan Behan.

K. Kennedy.

Bridie Kenny; imprisoned.

Catherine Liston; imprisoned.

Mary Liston; imprisoned.

Julia McCauley (McAuley); imprisoned.

Anastasia MacLaughlin (McLaughlin).

Maggie McLaughlin; imprisoned.

Agnes McNamara; imprisoned.

Agnes McNanice; imprisoned.

Kathleen Maher; imprisoned.

Kathleen Mahon.

J. Milner.

Katie O'Connor.

Kitty O'Doherty; in March, Marie Perolz asked Brighid Foley, Effie Taaffe and Kitty O'Doherty to find and protect the guns that had come into the country in boxes marked as 'cutlery'. Informers at Dublin Castle warned that the British had discovered what was really in the boxes and that the house where they were kept was to be raided by Castle officials. The women successfully transported these two boxes across town, past a couple of policemen, and hid them under the stairs in O'Doherty's house.[966] She carried dispatches to County Kerry, and on Thursday of Easter week she carried messages to Kinnegad.

Grace O'Sullivan; imprisoned.

Mary Partridge; imprisoned.

Marie (Mary) Perolz (Flanagan); she was assigned to the St Stephen's Green ICA garrison, but spent the week outside Dublin, carrying dispatches on dangerous missions between garrisons, and down to the south-west.[967] She was mobilised on Easter Sunday at Liberty Hall to be told that the orders had been changed. She was told to remain there and then was sent to look for Seán MacDermott. Following this, she was sent to Cork by Pearse and MacDermott and secured six dispatch couriers. She brought dispatches to Cork City, Mallow, Tralee, Dungarvan and Waterford. Her contact in Cork was Tomás MacCurtain. She got back to Dublin on the Friday, was arrested on 2 May and was interned in Kilmainham, Mountjoy and Lewes Prison until August/September 1916.[968]

Barbara Retz; imprisoned.

Agnes Ryan.

Maureen Ryan (Máirín Bean Ni Riain) (Cregan); she carried dispatches for Seán MacDermott and Gearóid O'Sullivan containing information on the landing of the German arms ship *Aud*. She went to Tralee and delivered the messages to Austin Stack and Patrick Cahill. She also took automatic revolvers and ammunition with her.

Nora Thornton; Seán MacDermott sent her to Tralee with dispatches on Monday. She 'stayed in Castlemaine until the first train to Dublin ran; I can't say when that was. During that week I suffered a lot thinking of my three brothers who were in the fight in Dublin and wondering when I could get back there. I was also worried that my dispatch could not be delivered on the Monday of my arrival. The fact that I was not able to get back to Dublin and take part in the fight prevented me getting full credit for Easter Week service when I was claiming a pension. It was not my fault that I could not get back; there were no trains till the following week.'[969]

Appendix 2. British soldiers, police and civilian casualties

Official estimates have 116 British soldiers killed.

Official estimates have 16 policemen killed.

Official estimates have 254 adult civilians killed and over 2,000 wounded; more reliable estimates have approximately 500 killed.

Official estimates have 38 children aged sixteen years and under killed in Dublin.[970]

Appendix 3. Executions after the Rising

3 May: Thomas Clarke, Patrick Pearse and Thomas MacDonagh.

4 May: Edward (Ned) Daly, Willie Pearse, Joseph Plunkett and Michael O'Hanrahan.

5 May: John MacBride.

8 May: Seán Heuston, Michael Mallin, Con Colbert and Éamonn Ceannt.

9 May: Thomas Kent (Cork).

12 May: Seán MacDermott and James Connolly.

3 August: Roger Casement (Pentonville Prison).

Appendix 4. Sentences imposed on male prisoners

Ninety-seven Volunteers were sentenced to death but had the sentences reduced to some years of penal servitude. (Most of those imprisoned were never court-martialled.[971])

Sentenced to death but commuted to penal servitude for life

Thomas Ashe

Robert Brennan[972]

William T. Cosgrave[973]

Éamon de Valera
Thomas Hunter
Henry O'Hanrahan
John (Jack) Shouldice[974]

Sentenced to death but commuted to twenty years' penal servitude
Richard Hayes[975]

Sentenced to death but commuted to ten years' penal servitude
Thomas Bevan
Peter Clancy
Richard Davys
John Doherty
Peter Doyle
Frank Drennan
Francis (Frank) Fahy[976]
James T. Hughes
George Irvine[977]
Frank Lawless
James Lawless
Fionan Lynch[978]
Jeremiah C. Lynch
Patrick McNestry
James (Séamus) Melinn
Michael Mervyn
Bryan Molloy
Denis O'Callahan
George Plunkett
John (Jack) Plunkett[979]
J.J. Reid
P.E. Sweeney
William (Liam) Tobin[980]
J.J. Walsh
Thomas Walsh[981]
John Williams

Sentenced to death but commuted to penal servitude
Charles Bevan, 3 years
Henry James (Harry) Boland, 5 years
Michael Brady, 3 years

J. Brennan, 3 years

Maurice Brennan, 3 years

Robert Brennan, Enniscorthy, 5 years

F. Brooks, 3 years

James Burke, 3 years

John Joseph Byrne, 3 years

J. Clarke, 3 years

R. Coleman, 3 years

William P. Corrigan,[982] 5 years

Philip Cosgrave, 5 years

Gerald Crofts, 5 years

John F. Cullen, 3 years

Michael de Lacey,[983] Enniscorthy, 5 years

James Dempsey, 3 years

J. Derrington, 3 years

John Downey, 3 years

Gerald Doyle, 3 years

James Doyle, Enniscorthy, 5 years

John R. Etchingham, Enniscorthy, 5 years

John Faulkner, 3 years

Patrick Fogarty, 3 years

Peter Galligan,[984] 5 years

James Joyce,[985] 5 years

P. Kelly, 3 years

R. Kelly, 3 years

Richard F. King, Enniscorthy, 5 years

George Levins, 3 years

John McArdle, 3 years

Seán McGarry,[986] 8 years

Philip MacMahon, 3 years

J. Marks, 3 years

W. Meehan, 3 years

Brian Molloy, Galway, 5 years

James Morrissey, 3 years

J. Norton, 3 years

John O'Brien, 3 years

Fergus O'Connor, 3 years

W. O'Dea, 3 years

C. O'Donovan, 5 years

T. O'Kelly, 3 years

James O'Sullivan, 8 years
T. Peppard,[987] 3 years
Vincent Poole, 5 years
John Quinn, 3 years
James Rafter, Enniscorthy, 5 years
Michael Reynolds, 3 years
Michael Scully, 3 years
J. Wilson, 2 years
P. Wilson, 3 years
W. Wilson, 3 years

Sentenced to penal servitude
Thomas Barrett, 1 year
Piaras Béaslaí, 3 years
Thomas Bennett, 1 year
Timothy Brosnan, 20 years (15 remitted)
Joseph Burke, 3 years
Christopher Carrick, 3 years
John Carrick, 3 years
Eddy Corcoran, 3 years
John Corcoran, 3 years
William Corcoran, 3 years
James Crenigan,[988] 1 year
Gerald Crofts, 10 years (5 remitted)
William Derrington, 2 years (1 remitted)
Michael Donohue, 1 year
Frank Drennan, 20 years (10 remitted)
Edward (Éamon) Duggan, 3 years
Murtagh Fahy, 1 year
Patrick Fahy, 10 years
Thomas Desmond FitzGerald, 10 years
Patrick Flanagan, 3 years
Michael Fleming, 3 years
Michael Fleming Jnr, 1 year
Patrick Fury, 3 years
Thomas Fury, 3 years
Thomas (Fred) Fury, 3 years
John Grady, 1 year
Michael Grady, 1 year
John Greaves, 6 months

J. Grenigan, 2 years (1 remitted)
John Haniffy, 1 year
Martin Hansbury, 1 year
Michael Hehir, 3 years
Michael Higgins, 1 year
Michael Higgins (Oranmore), 3 years
Joseph Howley, 3 years
William Hussey, 3 years
Patrick Kennedy,[989] 1 year
Thomas Kennedy, 1 year
Joseph Ledwick, 6 months
James Loughlin, 3 years
Conor McGinley, 3 years
Joseph McGuinness, 3 years
Eoin MacNeill, life
James Murray, 1 year
Charles O'Neill, 1 year
William Partridge, 15 years (5 remitted)
E. Roach, 1 year
Michael Scully, 10 years (7 remitted)
Michael Toole, 3 years
Patrick Weafer, 6 months
Charles White, 1 year

Appendix 5. Women imprisoned after the Rising

Although 77 women were taken prisoner after the Rising, most were soon released.[990] Women were held in Dublin Castle and Kilmainham Gaol.[991] Brighid Foley and Marie Perolz were released in June, Nell Ryan during the autumn; Winifred Carney and Helena Molony were released on Christmas Eve 1916. Countess Markievicz had received a death sentence, commuted to penal servitude for life, but was released in the general amnesty of 1917.

Bridget Brady (Murphy)
Kate Brown
Martha Brown
Catherine (Katie) Byrne
Eileen Byrne
Mary (May) Byrne (Doyle)

Winifred Carney (McBride)

Máire (May, Meg) Carron

Kathleen Daly Clarke

Kathleen (Katie, Kitty) Connolly (Barrett)

Ann (Áine) Cooney (O'Brien)[992]

Eileen Cooney (Harbourne)

Lily Cooney (Curran)

Marcella Cosgrave

Bridget Davis (O'Duffy)

Ellen (Nellie) Ennis (Costigan)

Madeleine ffrench-Mullen

Kathleen Fleming

Brighid Foley (Brid Ni Foghludha, Breeid Martin)

Nora Foley (Ni Fogludha) (O'Daly)[993]

Mary (May) Gahan (O'Carroll)

Nellie Gifford (Donnelly)[994]

Bridget Goff (Gough?)

Julia Grenan

Rosana (Rosie) Hackett[995]

Bridget Hegarty (Harmon)

Annie (O?) Higgins

Ellen Humphries

Margaret (Maggie) Joyce

Kate (Kitty, Katie) Kelly

Martha Kelly (Murphy)

Margaret Kennedy (Hennessey)[996]

Bridie Kenny

Catherine Liston

Mary Liston

Bessie Lynch (Kelly)

Dr Kathleen Lynn[997]

Bridget Lyons (Thornton)[998]

Julia McCauley (McAley)

Josie McGowan (McGavan?)

Maggie McLoughlin

Rose McNamara (Murphy)[999]

Agnes MacNamee

Kathleen Maher

Pauline Markham (Keating)[1000]

Countess Constance Markievicz

Brid S. Martin
Kathleen (Kate) Martin
Florence Mead (Griffin)
Caroline (Carrie) Mitchell (McLoughlin)
Helena Molony[1001]
Lizzie Mulhall
Rosanna (Rose) Mullally (Farrelly)
Kathleen (Kate) Murphy
Bridget Murtagh (O'Daly)
Annie Norgrove (Grange)
Emily Norgrove (Hanratty)
Lily O'Brennan[1002]
Margaret O'Flaherty (Timmons)
Sheila (Sighle) O'Hanlon (Lynch)
Emily O'Keefe (Hendley)
Josephine O'Keefe
Mary (May) O'Moore
Louise (Dolly) O'Sullivan (Pollard)
Mary Partridge
Mary (Marie) Perolz (Flanagan)[1003]
Countess Josephine Plunkett
Maria Quigley (Clince)
Priscilla Quigley (Kavanagh)
Barbara Retz
Ellen (Nellie) Ryan[1004]
Mary Kate Ryan (O'Kelly)[1005]
Kathleen Seary (Seery) (Redmond)
Josephine Spencer (Spicer?)
Mary (Mollie) O'Sullivan (Sullivan?) (O'Carroll)
Catherine (Cathleen?) Treston

Appendix 6. British troops in Ireland during the Rising

Army Service Corps
Connaught Rangers
Duke of Lancaster's Own Yeomen
Grenadier Guards
2nd King Edward's Horse Regiment
Kingstown Volunteer Corps

North Staffordshire Regiment
6th Reserve Cavalry Regiment
Royal Army Medical Corps
4th Battalion Royal Dublin Fusiliers
10th Battalion Royal Dublin Fusiliers
Royal Engineers
Royal Field Artillery
Royal 8th Hussars
Royal Iniskilling Fusiliers
Royal Irish Fusiliers
3rd Battalion Royal Irish Rifles
3rd Battalion Royal Irish Regiment
18th Royal Irish Rifle Regiment
5th and 12th Royal Lancers
Royal Leicestershire Regiment
Royal Leinster Regiment, relieved the OTC at Trinity
Royal Navy, HMY *Helga*
Royal Scots
Sherwood Foresters (Nottingham and Derbyshire) Regiment
South Staffordshire Regiment
Volunteer Officer Training Corps (Trinity)

Notes

1   Matthews 2014; Burke 1926.

2   Carthy 2007, 51–66.

3   According to Éamon de Valera, the plan outlined to the Dublin commandants was for Pearse to be in command of all the Volunteers throughout the country, and Connolly to be in command of the five Dublin battalions (Ó Neill and Ó Fiannachta 1968–70, I, 41). Those ranks were how they were listed in the *Irish War News* printed during Easter Week.

4   'When the time for armed rebellion finally arrived, there was a traditional division of labour between the sexes within the ICA, and a discernible reluctance by many Volunteers about having women involved at all. In most cases, the extent of women's participation depended entirely upon the tenacity of the individual.' Ward 1983, 106, 109.

5   Dalton 1929, 19.

6   Liam Tobin, who served in C Company of the 1st Battalion, stated: 'I was struck by the small numbers who showed up … I had often seen our Company … muster a bigger number than the whole battalion did that morning' (Tobin, Liam: Witness Statement 1753).

7   Fox (2014 [1944], 227) lists the names of 218 ICA men and women in his authoritative book (191 men and 27 women). John Hanratty, one of the founding members of the ICA, claimed that James Connolly told him about six weeks before the Rising that the total strength of the ICA was about '300 armed men' (Hanratty, John: Witness Statement 96). Hayes-McCoy writes that 'less than 1,000 mustered on Monday and about 800 more joined them during the next day or so'; G.A. Hayes-McCoy, 'A military history of the Rising', in Nowlan 1969, 266.

8   Joye and Malone 2006.

9   Matthews 2007a.

10 Gavan-Duffy, Louise: Witness Statement 216.

11 Coffey 1969, 295.

12 Hayes-McCoy, 'A military history of the Rising', in Nowlan 1969, 295.

13 For example, it is estimated that 57 men of the 1st Battalion went to the GPO when their positions in the north of Dublin were overrun; Heuston 1966, 6.

14 http://www.census.nationalarchives.ie/pages/1911/Dublin/South_Dock/Eblana_Villas/92709/.

15 Gillis 2014.

16 Five priests and one brother are listed in the garrisons, as well as two physicians who were also non-combatants.

17 Thomas Kent was executed by firing squad on 9 May at Cork Detention Barracks. His body was buried in the Cork prison yard (it has since been exhumed and reinterred in the family plot in Castlelyons, following a state funeral) (Kent, William: Witness Statement 75; Bateson 2010, 235). Sir Roger Casement was hung in Pentonville Prison on 3 August (Bateson 2010, 243).

18 Volunteers were sent to Cahirsiveen to commandeer a wireless system and transmitter. Denis Daly, Dan (Donal) Sheehan, Charles Monahan, Colm Ó Lochlainn and Con Keating made up the raiding party. They went by train to Limerick, where they met Tommy McInerney, who owned one of the two cars that were to be used in the venture. Keating, Sheehan and Monahan travelled on with McInerney. When Daly and Ó Lochlainn got to Cahirsiveen, the other car never showed up and they decided to return to Dublin. On the train back, they heard that McInerney had driven off the Ballykissane Pier in County Kerry and that Sheehan, Monahan and Keating had drowned. Quilty, John J.: Witness Statement 516 (he was the owner of the car that drove off the pier). Richard Kent was killed in County Cork.

19 Official lists indicate 64 'rebels' killed. The Irish National Aid and Volunteers' Dependants' Fund (INAVDF) issued a list of 'men who were killed whilst fighting for Ireland during Easter Week, 1916'. There were 64 names on that list. When a man who was killed was not on that list, it will

be so indicated in the garrison list that follows. Peter Darcy, D. Murphy and Patrick Sheehy are on the INAVDF list but there is no available information other than that.

20 O'Higgins 1925, 31.

21 Ferguson 2014.

22 Matthews 2010a, 33; Turner 1926a.

23 Hally 1966–7, Part 1, 325.

24 Ward 1983, 115.

25 Dillon, Geraldine Plunkett: Witness Statements 29, 358, 424. The sister of Joseph Plunkett, Mrs Dillon spent much time at Larkfield and her statements give great insight into the activities of the Plunkett family, as well as the goings-on of the garrison prior to the Rising. She married Thomas Dillon on Easter Sunday and they spent their wedding night in the Imperial Hotel. They watched the taking of the GPO from across the street, and when it was secured Joseph Plunkett sent Rory O'Connor over to tell them both to return to Larkfield to get one of the stills running in case the men could use that for ammunition and munitions. Turner 1926a; see also Dillon 2007.

26 Matthews 2010a, 7.

27 Nunan 1967.

28 Agnew, Arthur: Witness Statement 152.

29 Bateson 2010, 173.

30 Fr Columbus, OFM Cap., recorded his experiences in a diary. The manuscript was discovered in the Capuchin Archives in Church Street. See Benedict Cullen, 'Echoes of the Rising's final shots', *Irish Times* (http://www.aohdiv7.org/hist_easter_aftermath.htm).

31 Denis McCullough, who went on to become president of the IRB, bluntly stated: 'I cleared out most of the older men, including my father, most of whom I considered of no further use to us'. McCullough, Denis: Witness Statements 111, 914, 915, 916.

32 Kevin B. Nowlan, 'Tom Clarke, MacDermott, and the I.R.B.', in Martin 1967, 109ff.

33 Seán T. O'Kelly in *An Phoblacht*, 30 April 1926.

34 Caulfield 1995, 183.

35 Clarke 1997, 93.

36 Clarke 1970, 62.

37 Clarke 1997, 94.

38 Bateson 2010, 180; O'Keefe 1932; Burke 1926.

39 N. O'Brien 1932.

40 Aloysius, Revd, OFM Cap.: Witness Statement 200; Fr Aloysius 1942.

41 *Ibid.*

42 Hyland (1997, 54) notes that Connolly 'was not strapped to a chair, but placed seated on a rough wooden box … and then executed'.

43 Warwick-Haller and Warwick-Haller 1995, 13ff.

44 Kendall 2013.

45 Bateson 2010, 187; Travers 1966b; Dore 1968.

46 Mulcahy, Mary Josephine: Witness Statement 399.

47 Letter from MacDermott to his brothers and sisters, written in Kilmainham Gaol, 11 May 1916, in the possession of the MacDermott family. MacLochlainn 1971, 168.

48 Augustine, Revd, OFM Cap.: Witness Statement 920.

49 'Seán MacDermott's last letter', *The Capuchin Annual* (1942).

50 Browne, Rt Revd Msgr Patrick: Witness Statement 719; Browne 1917.

51 Bateson 2010, 177.

52 Aloysius, Revd, OFM Cap.: Witness Statement 200; Fr Aloysius 1942; Dennis 1942; D. MacDonagh 1945a; N. O'Brien 1977; O'Hegarty 1919b; Mac An Tsoir 1962.

53 Bateson 2010, 189.

54 Augustine, Revd, OFM Cap.: Witness Statement 920.

55 Enright 2014.

56   LeRoux 1932.

57   D. Ryan 1917.

58   Bateson 2010, 185; Plunkett 1958.

59   Plunkett 1942.

60   Plunkett, Grace: Witness Statement 257; Donnelly, Nellie: Witness Statement 256; D. MacDonagh 1945b. See the *Weekly Irish Times, Sinn Féin Rebellion Handbook* (1916), 67 (p. 66 in the 1998 Mourne River Press edition).

61   Turner 1926a.

62   Agnew, Arthur: Witness Statement 152.

63   Turner 1926a.

64   Cabra Bridge, in the north of Dublin, was assigned to eight Volunteers. When their position became untenable, they were to try to link up with the 5th Battalion in Fingal, north County Dublin, but most came to the GPO.

65   Henderson, Frank: Witness Statements 249, 851.

66   MacEntee 1944.

67   O'Donovan, Kathleen: Witness Statement 586; Maher 1998; Brasier and Kelly 2000; Fitzpatrick 2003.

68   Caulfield 1995, 184.

69   Turner 1926a.

70   *Ibid.*

71   Caulfield 1995, 100.

72   Turner 1926a.

73   Bracken, Peadar: Witness Statements 12, 361.

74   Turner 1926b.

75   Turner 1926a.

76   *Ibid.*

77   *Ibid.*

78   Brennan-Whitmore 1926a.

79   Brennan-Whitmore 1926b; 1953.

80   Brennan-Whitmore 1996, 20ff; 1953.

81   Brennan-Whitmore 1996, 116ff.

82   See the *Weekly Irish Times, Sinn Féin Rebellion Handbook* (1916), 75 (p. 74 in the 1998 Mourne River Press edition).

83   Brennan-Whitmore 1926c.

84   Those indicated with # reported to the 5th Battalion at Ashbourne but were sent to the GPO on Tuesday 25 April. Many were seconded on to other garrisons. They are counted in the Ashbourne garrison. Lawless, Joseph: Witness Statement 1043.

85   Colgan 1926.

86   See Hanratty, John: Witness Statement 96.

87   Bulfin, Éamonn: Witness Statement 497. (See Walpole, R.H. and FitzGerald, Theobold: Joint Witness Statement 218, below.)

88   Enright 2014.

89   Burke, Fergus (Frank): Witness Statement 694.

90   Byrne, Christopher: Witness Statements 167, 642.

91   Fox 2014, 227.

92   Colgan 1926.

93   Byrne, Thomas: Witness Statement 564.

94   Turner 1926a.

95   Caldwell, Patrick: Witness Statement 638.

96   McGallogly, John: Witness Statement 244.

97   Carpenter, Walter: Witness Statement 583. See Hanratty, John: Witness Statement 96.

98 Fox 2014, 227.

99 Bateson 2010, 223.

100 Carrigan, James: Witness Statement 613.

101 Turner 1926a.

102 Fox 2014, 227.

103 Cremin, Michael: Witness Statement 563.

104 Clarke, Josephine: Witness Statement 699.

105 Turner 1926a.

106 *Ibid.*

107 Colgan 1926.

108 Colley, Harry: Witness Statement 1687.

109 Matthews 2010a, 22.

110 Good, Joe: Witness Statement 388.

111 Turner 1926b.

112 Fox 2014, 227.

113 Bateson 2010, 251.

114 *Irish Worker* No. 43 (3 May 1924).

115 Devine and O'Riordan 2006, 20 (footnote).

116 Cowley, Michael: Witness Statement 553.

117 Bateson 2010, 220.

118 Henderson, Frank: Witness Statement 249.

119 Leahy, Thomas: Witness Statement 660.

120 Turner 1926a.

121 Cremin, Michael: Witness Statements 563, 903.

122 Crenigan, James: Witness Statements 148, 1395.

123 Ó Ruairc 2011, 55.

124 Brennan–Whitmore 1926b.

125 Brennan–Whitmore 1996, 94.

126 Turner 1926a.

127 Daly, Denis: Witness Statements 110, 786.

128 Fitzgerald, Maurice: Witness Statement 326. Fitzgerald was the principal of the Wireless College.

129 Ó Lochalinn, Colm: Witness Statement 751.

130 Quilty, John J.: Witness Statement 516. (He was the owner of the car that drove off the pier.)

131 Ó Mahony 1987 [1995], 127.

132 O'Daly, Patrick: Witness Statements 220, 387.

133 Saurin 1926.

134 Daly, Séamus: Witness Statement 360.

135 Turner 1926a.

136 Daly, Liam: Witness Statement 425.

137 Devine, Thomas: Witness Statement 428.

138 Donnelly, Charles: Witness Statement 824.

139 Dore, Éamonn: Witness Statements 153, 392, 515.

140 Turner 1926b.

141 Doyle, John: Witness Statement 748.

142 Turner 1926a.

143 Brennan–Whitmore 1926b.

144 Turner 1926a.

145 McGallogly, John: Witness Statement 244.

146 Turner 1926a.

147 Fitzgerald 1966.

148 Fitzgerald 1968.

[149] King, Martin: Witness Statement 543; Byrne, Seán: Witness Statement 579.

[150] Turner 1926b.

[151] Turner 1926a.

[152] Flanagan 1918.

[153] Barry, Mrs Tom: Witness Statement 1754.

[154] Turner 1926a.

[155] *Ibid.*

[156] *Ibid.*

[157] Caulfield 1995, 260.

[158] Brennan–Whitmore 1926b.

[159] Turner 1926a.

[160] Gleeson, Joseph: Witness Statement 367.

[161] Turner 1926a.

[162] Fox 2014, 227.

[163] Good, Joe: Witness Statement 388.

[164] Good 1996.

[165] Colgan 1926.

[166] Turner 1926a.

[167] Colgan 1926.

[168] Harris, Tom: Witness Statement 320.

[169] Dick Healy in *The Banba Review*, January 1963.

[170] Turner 1926a.

[171] Ó Ruairc 2011, 55.

[172] Henderson, Frank: Witness Statements 249, 821; Hopkinson 1998.

[173] Turner 1926a.

[174] Humphreys 1966.

[175] Kavanagh, Séamus: Witness Statements 208, 1053.

[176] Bateson 2010, 191.

[177] Bulfin, Éamon: Witness Statement 497; Connelly, Charles (Keely's brother-in-law): Witness Statement 824.

[178] Kelly, Edward: Witness Statement 1094.

[179] Turner 1926a.

[180] *Ibid.*

[181] Kennedy, Luke: Witness Statement 165.

[182] Bateson 2010, 195.

[183] J.J. Reynolds 1926.

[184] *The Catholic Bulletin*, November 1916.

[185] Turner 1926a.

[186] *Ibid.*

[187] Joseph Sweeney; he made a statement describing his experiences in the GPO: 'Personal narratives of the Rising of 1916' (NLI MS 10915).

[188] Turner 1926a.

[189] Ó Mahony 1987 [1995], 123, 129, 138.

[190] Colgan 1926.

[191] Knightly, Michael: Witness Statements 833, 834, 835.

[192] Turner 1926a.

[193] Turner 1926b.

[194] Leahy, Thomas: Witness Statement 660.

[195] Colgan 1926.

[196] Lemass 1966, 7.

[197] MacEntee 1944.

[198] Lynch, Diarmuid: Witness Statements 4, 120, 121, 364, 651; BMH Contemporary Document 16.
[199] Turner 1926a.
[200] *Ibid*.
[201] Saurin 1926.
[202] McCrea, Patrick: Witness Statement 413.
[203] Turner 1926a.
[204] McDonagh, Joseph: Witness Statement 1082.
[205] MacEntee, Seán: Witness Statement 1052; McInerney 1974; Gregory 1917.
[206] Turner 1926a.
[207] McGallogley, John: Witness Statement 244.
[208] Turner 1926a.
[209] McGarry, Milo: Witness Statement 356.
[210] Perolz, Marie: Witness Statement 246.
[211] McGarry, Seán: Witness Statement 368.
[212] Turner 1926a.
[213] *Ibid*.
[214] McGowan, Séamus: Witness Statement 542.
[215] Turner 1926a.
[216] McLoughlin, Seán: Witness Statement 290; McLoughlin 1948.
[217] McGuire 2006.
[218] Caulfield 1995, 277.
[219] Fox 2014, 227.
[220] Turner 1926a.
[221] *Ibid*.
[222] Turner 1926b.
[223] Bateson 2010, 225.
[224] De Burca, Frank: Witness Statement 694.
[225] Colgan 1926.
[226] *Ibid*.
[227] Turner 1926a.
[228] Caulfield 1995, 99.
[229] *The Irish Times, 1916 Rebellion Handbook* (Mourne River Press edn, 1998), 73.
[230] Turner 1926a.
[231] Colgan 1926.
[232] Brennan–Whitmore 1926b.
[233] Turner 1926a.
[234] Ann Devlin Branch, Glasgow, 1916–1922 (UCDA, Coyle papers, p. 61/4[67], p. 1).
[235] Bateson 2010, 226.
[236] Turner 1926a.
[237] Henderson, Frank: Witness Statement 249.
[238] Murphy, Fintan: Witness Statement 370.
[239] Murphy, Séamus: Witness Statement 1756; BMH Contemprorary Document 128.
[240] See Hanratty, John: Witness Statement 96.
[241] Turner 1926a.
[242] See http://mspcsearch.militaryarchives.ie/detail.aspx?parentpriref= .
[243] Saurin, Charles: Witness Statement 288.
[244] Bateson 2010, 228.
[245] Fallon 2014.
[246] Saurin 1926.
[247] Good 1996, 58–9.
[248] Caulfield 1995, 260.

[249] Fox 2014, 227.

[250] Nunan 1966; 1967.

[251] Turner 1926a.

[252] Ó Mahony 1987 [1995], 106, 125, 129, 130.

[253] Nunan, Seán: Witness Statement 1744.

[254] Turner 1926a.

[255] Duffy 2013.

[256] Good, Joe: Witness Statement 388.

[257] Turner 1926a.

[258] McGallogley, John: Witness Statement 244.

[259] Tannam, Liam: Witness Statement 242.

[260] John O'Connor, personal memoir, BMH Contemporaneous Document 152.

[261] Bateson 2010, 208.

[262] *The Catholic Bulletin*, March 1919.

[263] Turner 1926a.

[264] Ó Mahony 1987 [1995], 158.

[265] Turner 1926a.

[266] *Ibid.*

[267] O'Higgins 1925, 17–18; 1935.

[268] Brennan-Whitmore 1926b.

[269] Turner 1926b.

[270] Turner 1926a.

[271] Caulfield 1995, 100.

[272] O'Kelly, Fergus: Witness Statement 351.

[273] Foy and Barton 1999, 131–2; Townshend 2005, 137.

[274] Colgan 1926.

[275] Turner 1926a.

[276] *Ibid.*

[277] Fox 2014, 227.

[278] *Ibid.*

[279] Bateson 2010, 209.

[280] Forty—Hayes-McCoy, 'A military history of the Rising', in Nowlan 1916, 295. Eleven—Caulfield 1995, 257; O'Higgins 1925, 35. Twenty-five—MacEntee 1966, 160. Two groups of twenty each, to move up both sides of Moore Street—Daly, Denis: Witness Statement 110. Thirty-five—Tannam, Frank: Witness Statement 242. Jack Plunkett's unpublished memoir indicated that there were a dozen men in the party.

[281] Staines, Michael: Witness Statement 284.

[282] Devine, Thomas: Witness Statement 428.

[283] Mitchell made the following statement: 'While driving through Moore St. to Jervis St. Hospital one afternoon towards the end of the week the sergeant drew my attention to the body of a man lying in the gutter in Moore Lane. He was dressed in a green uniform. I took the sergeant and two men with a stretcher and approached the body which appeared to be still alive. We were about to lift it up when a young English officer stepped out of a doorway and refused to allow us to touch it. I told him of my instructions from H.Q. but all to no avail. When back in the lorry I asked the sergeant what was the idea? His answer was—"he must be someone of importance and the bastards are leaving him there to die of his wounds. It's the easiest way to get rid of him". We came back again about 9 o'clock that night. The body was still there and an officer guarding it, but this time I fancied I knew the officer—he was not the one I met before. I asked why I was not allowed to take the body and who was it? He replied that his life and job depended on it being left there. He would not say who it was. I never saw the body again but I was told by different people that it was The Ó Rahilly.' Mitchell began his recollections by reminding the questioner that it was more than

30 years after the event. Mitchell, Albert: Witness Statement 196.

284 McLoughlin 1948.

285 D. Ryan 1949 [1957], 253–4.

286 Colgan 1926.

287 Turner 1926a.

288 O'Reilly, M.W.: Witness Statement 886.

289 McCrea, Patrick: Witness Statement 413.

290 Bateson 2010, 206.

291 O'Mara, Peadar: Witness Statement 377.

292 Thomas O'Reilly, letter to the National Graves Association, 23 October 1935.

293 Turner 1926a.

294 Ó Ruairc 2011, 55. Bevan, Séamus: Witness Statement 1058. 'In those days I had a keen interest in the Flags of Nations and their significance. And hence, when on the Wednesday of Easter Week I arrived within sight of the G.P.O. with a dispatch from Commandant Daly of the Four Courts area, I was immediately struck by the appearance of the flag which flew from the Henry St. corner of the G.P.O. I have a vivid recollection of that flag. It was very large, much larger than any flag I had ever seen. It blew in a stiff breeze almost halfway across Henry St. and the bottom edge of this flag almost touched the top of the balustrade.' See notes regarding Éamon Bulfin, above, and R.M. Walpole, below.

295 Gearóid O'Sullivan, BMH Contemporaneous Document 90.

296 Turner 1926a.

297 Peppard, Thomas: Witness Statement 1399.

298 Turner 1926a.

299 Agnew, Arthur: Witness Statement 152.

300 Plunkett, John: Witness Statements 488, 864. BMH Contemporaneous Documents 320, 179.

301 Caulfield 1995, 236.

302 Price, Seán: Witness Statement 769.

303 McGallogly, John: Witness Statement 244; Reader, Séamus: Witness Statements 627, 933, 1767; BMH Contemporaneous Document 205.

304 Clarke 1997, 130.

305 Saurin 1926.

306 Turner 1926a.

307 Turner 1926b.

308 Robinson, Séamus: Witness Statement 156.

309 Turner 1926a.

310 Turner 1926b.

311 MacThomais 1965, 22.

312 Henderson, Frank: Witness Statements 249, 821.

313 Ryan, Desmond: Witness Statement 724.

314 J. Ryan 1942.

315 Ryan, James: Witness Statement 70; McInerney 1967.

316 Turner 1926a.

317 Colgan 1926.

318 Saurin 1926.

319 Saurin, Charles: Witness Statement 288.

320 Colgan 1926.

321 Scollan, John J.: Witness Statements 318, 341.

322 Turner 1926a.

323 McGallogley, John: Witness Statement 244.

324 Turner 1926a.

325 *Ibid.*

326 Ward 1997, 155.

327 *Ibid.*

328 Bateson 2010, 221.

329 Turner 1926a.

330 Desmond Lynch, National Library of Ireland MS 31420.

331 Devine, Thomas: Witness Statement 428.

332 Bulfin, Éamonn: Witness Statement 497.

333 Good, Joe: Witness Statement 388.

334 Peadar Slattery, BMH Contemporaneous Document 176.

335 Staines, Michael: Witness Statements 284, 943, 944.

336 Joseph Stanley, BMH Contemporaneous Documents 4, 39. See Reilly 2005.

337 Steinmeyer 1926.

338 Stephenson 2006.

339 Turner 1926a.

340 Brennan-Whitmore 1926b.

341 See Griffith and O'Grady 2002 [1982].

342 Saurin 1926.

343 Tannam, Liam: Witness Statement 242; BMH Contemporaneous Document 289.

344 Thornton, Frank: Witness Statements 510, 615; BMH Contemporaneous Documents 188, 200.

345 Caulfield 1995, 250.

346 Turner 1926a.

347 *Ibid.*

348 Caulfield 1995, 216.

349 Traynor, Oscar: Witness Statement 340; BMH Contemporaneous Documents 120, 214.

350 See Hanratty, John: Witness Statement 96.

351 Turner 1926a.

352 McGallogley, John: Witness Statement 244.

353 McGarry, Milo: Witness Statement 356.

354 Turner 1926b.

355 Twamley, John: Witness Statement 629; Byrne, Seán: Witness Statement 579; King, Martin: Witness Statement 543.

356 Colgan 1926.

357 Turner 1926a.

358 Walker, Charles: Witness Statements 241, 266. See Reilly 2005.

359 Walpole, R.H.: Witness Statement 218.

360 Ó Ruairc 2011, 55. Ó Ruairc has Hegarty helping Gearóid O'Sullivan.

361 Two flags were raised over the GPO, the *Irish Republic* flag on the Prince's Street corner and the Tricolour on the Henry Street corner. Walpole, R.H. and FitzGerald, Theobold: Joint Witness Statement 218. Their statement, which deals solely with raising the flag, seems to have been in response to the obituary of Gearóid O'Sullivan in 1948, in which O'Sullivan was given credit for raising this flag. It is claimed that Gearóid O'Sullivan and Seán Hegarty raised the *Irish Republic* flag over the Prince's Street corner. It is also claimed that Gearóid O'Sullivan or Michael Staines raised the Tricolour on the Henry Street corner. It is claimed that Éamonn Bulfin, Paddy Moran or Robert Walpole raised the *Irish Republic* flag on the Prince's Street corner. (See notes on Éamonn Bulfin, Paddy Moran, Gearóid O'Sullivan and Michael Staines, above.) See http://www.generalmichaelcollins.com/life-times/1916-to-1919/map/flags-gpo/.

362 Bateson 2010, 32.

363 Turner 1926a.

364 *Ibid.*

365 Colgan 1926.

366 Bateson 2010, 200. O'Farrell (1997, 100) gives the name as 'Patrick' Weafer.

[367] Caulfield 1995, 98.

[368] Daly, William: Witness Statement 291. De Burca, Aoife: Witness Statement 359.

[369] O'Kelly, Fergus: Witness Statement 351; O'Higgins 1925, 27.

[370] Bateson 2010, 231.

[371] *Irish Worker* No. 43 (3 May 1924).

[372] Turner 1926a.

[373] White 1930 [2005]; Doyle 2007.

[374] Matthews 2007a.

[375] Weston, Charles: Witness Statement 149.

[376] Taillon 1996, 81–2.

[377] Rooney, Catherine: Witness Statement 648.

[378] Woggan 2000a; 2000b; McCoole 2003, 145.

[379] Leslie De Barra, interview in Ó Dulaing 1984, 97–8.

[380] O'Connor 1986, 61.

[381] See Griffith, Kenneth and Timothy O'Grady 2002 [1982]; Comerford 1986; Máire Comerford, BMH Contemporaneous Document 59; McCoole 2003, 149.

[382] Taillon 1996, 46.

[383] Dore, Nora: Witness Statement 154.

[384] Dore, Éamon T.: Witness Statements 53, 515, 392.

[385] De Burca, Aoife: Witness Statement 359.

[386] Taillon 1996, 51.

[387] *Ibid.*, 28.

[388] Coffey 1969, 295.

[389] McCoole 2003, 615.

[390] Gavan-Duffy, Louise: Witness Statement 216. Her statement is more reflective and politically aware than most of the others, and is one of the most astute views of the political tenor of the times.

[391] Tannam, Liam: Witness Statement 242.

[392] O'Doherty, Kitty: Witness Statement 355.

[393] Breeid Martin, Pension Application ref. MSP34REF64289/.

[394] McCoole 2003, 163.

[395] 'Cumann na mBan in Easter Week: tribute from a hostile source', *Wolfe Tone Annual* (n.d.).

[396] O'Farrell 1997, 39; O'Higgins 1925, 88.

[397] MacLochlainn 1971, 183.

[398] Grenan 1916; 1917a.

[399] McCoole 2003, 172.

[400] Perolz, Marie: Witness Statement 246.

[401] Gertrude Gaffney, private letter.

[402] McCoole 2003, 173.

[403] See Hanratty, John: Witness Statement 96.

[404] Fox 2014, 117.

[405] McWhinney, Linda: Witness Statement 404; Kearns 1922; Ó Duigneain 1991; McCoole 2003, 179.

[406] McLoughlin, Mary: Witness Statement 934.

[407] Taillon 1996, 92.

[408] *Ibid.*, 28.

[409] Turner 1926b.

[410] Murphy, Eileen: Witness Statement 480.

[411] Taillon 1996, 43.

[412] Murray 1922; Taillon 1996, 51.

[413] Perolz, Marie: Witness Statement 246.

[414] Ryan 1949 [1957], 253–4.

[415] O'Farrell 1930; McHugh 1966, 206ff; McCoole 2003, 193. Miss O'Farrell's account of her role in

the surrender negotiations with the British is most completely given in *An t-Éireannach*, 12–29 Feabhra 1936, in two chapters of 'Cu Uladh's' *Blaidhain na h-Aiserighe*, a complete history of the Rising in Irish based on the original statements of the participants and translations of documents, and covering all the Volunteer positions throughout Dublin.

[416] McCoole 2003, 203.

[417] Caulfield 1995, 215.

[418] Barry, Mrs Tom: Witness Statement 1754.

[419] M. Reynolds 1926.

[420] Reynolds, Molly: Witness Statement 195; BMH Contemporaneous Document 290.

[421] Ward 1983, 110.

[422] Mulcahy, Mary Josephine: Witness Statement 399.

[423] Ward 1997, 155.

[424] Colbert, Elizabeth M. (Lila): Witness Statement 856.

[425] O'Doherty, Kitty: Witness Statement 355.

[426] Diary of Cesca Chenevix Trench, quoted in Fletcher 2006.

[427] Wyse-Power, Nancy: Witness Statement 541.

[428] Caulfield 1995, 232.

[429] *Ibid.*, 165.

[430] *Ibid.*, 234.

[431] *Ibid.*, 257.

[432] D. O'Neill 2006.

[433] Liam Tobin, who served in C Company of the 1st Battalion, stated: 'I was struck by the small numbers who showed up … I had often seen our Company … muster a bigger number than the whole battalion did that morning' (Tobin, Liam: Witness Statement 1753). 'If it was not for the invaluable work of carrying messages inside Dublin and out to the countryside that was undertaken by the women, the Rising would have been an even more confused venture than it was' (Ward 1983, 108).

[434] P. O'Brien 2012a, 3ff.

[435] Hally 1966.

[436] D. O'Neill 2006.

[437] J.J. Reynolds 1926.

[438] *The War History of the 2/6th South Staffordshire Regiment* (London, 1924).

[439] Holohan, Garry: Witness Statement 328.

[440] Bateson 2010, 87.

[441] Morkan, Phyllis: Witness Statement 210.

[442] P. O'Brien 2012a.

[443] D. O'Neill 2006.

[444] Liam Tobin, who served in C Company of the 1st Battalion, stated: 'I was struck by the small numbers who showed up … I had often seen our Company … muster a bigger number than the whole battalion did that morning' (Tobin, Liam: Witness Statement 1753).

[445] P. O'Brien 2012a, 3ff.

[446] Hally 1966.

[447] D. O'Neill 2006; J.J. Reynolds 1926.

[448] *The War History of the 2/6th South Staffordshire Regiment* (London, 1924).

[449] Golden, Gerry: Witness Statements 177, 521, 522.

[450] Fr Columbus, OFM Cap., recorded his experiences in a diary. The manuscript was discovered in the Capuchin Archives in Church Street. See Benedict Cullen, 'Echoes of the Rising's final shots', *Irish Times* (http://www.aohdiv7.org/hist_easter_aftermath.htm).

[451] Daly, Madge: Witness Statements 209, 855.

[452] Bateson 2010, 110.

[453] Fr Albert 1926; 1942.

WHO'S WHO IN THE DUBLIN RISING, 1916

454 Browne, Rt Revd Msgr Patrick: Witness Statement 729.

455 Fr John Heuston, OP; BMH Contemporaneous Document 309.

456 MacLochlainn 1971, 106ff.

457 Bateson 2010, 94.

458 Smart, Thomas: Witness Statement 255; J.J. Reynolds 1926.

459 McDonough, Joseph: Witness Statement 1082; Kennedy, Seán: Witness Statements 842, 885.

460 Archer, Liam: Witness Statement 819.

461 Balfe, Richard: Witness Statement 251.

462 Thornton, Brighid Lyons: Witness Statement 259.

463 J.J. Reynolds 1926.

464 Bevan, Séamus: Witness Statements 1058, 1059.

465 Bibby, Fr Albert, OFM: Witness Statement 200.

466 Balfe, Richard: Witness Statement 251.

467 J.J. Reynolds 1926.

468 O'Duffy, Seán: Witness Statement 313.

469 Caulfield 1995, 57.

470 Byrne, Seán: Witness Statement 579.

471 Callender, Ignatius: Witness Statement 923.

472 Callender 1939.

473 J.J. Reynolds 1926.

474 Art MacEoin, 'Murder in the Castle', *An Phoblacht*, 22 November 2001; Ó Mahony 2000.

475 Those indicated with # reported to the 5th Battalion at Ashbourne but were sent to the GPO on Tuesday 25 April. Many were seconded on to other garrisons. They are counted in the Ashbourne garrison. Lawless, Joseph: Witness Statement 1043.

476 Cody, Seán: Witness Statement 1035.

477 Coghlan, Francis X.: Witness Statement 1760.

478 Collins, Maurice: Witness Statement 550.

479 O'Donovan, Con: Witness Statement 1750.

480 Conlon, Mrs Martin: Witness Statement 419; Foy and Barton 1999, 131–2; Townshend 2005, 137.

481 Conlon, Martin: Witness Statement 798.

482 Bateson 2010, 90.

483 *Ibid.*, 93.

484 Caulfield 1995, 157.

485 Flanagan, M.: Witness Statement 800.

486 Dowling, Thomas: Witness Statement 533.

487 Bateson 2010, 97.

488 Caulfield 1995, 266.

489 J.J. Reynolds 1926.

490 Caulfield 1995, 340.

491 Fahy, Frank: Witness Statement 442; Fahy, Anna: Witness Statement 202.

492 Bateson 2010, 98.

493 O'Flanagan, Michael: Witness Statement 800; J.J. Reynolds 1926.

494 Keating, Pauline: Witness Statement 432.

495 Turner 1926a.

496 Gaskin, Frank: Witness Statement 386.

497 Golden, Gerry: Witness Statements 177, 521, 522.

498 Griffith and O'Grady 2002 [1982], 56ff.

499 Harling, Seán: Witness Statement 935.

500 J.J. Reynolds 1926.

501 Hayden, Fr Augustine, OFM Cap.: Witness Statement 920.

502 Report of 'A' Company, Allen Library.

503 Caulfield 1995, 266.

504 Holohan, Garry: Witness Statement 328. In fact, 'Gerald' Playfair, who was seventeen at the time, was not killed in the Rising. His older brother George (23) was the Playfair son who was shot and 'died from bullet wounds to the abdomen'. He died in 1 Park Place, beside the Islandbridge Gate to Phoenix Park. See Duffy 2013.

505 Holohan 1942.

506 Holohan, Garry: Witness Statement 328; Augustine, Revd, OFM Cap.: Witness Statement 920; Fr Aloysius 1942.

507 Bateson 2010, 99; Duffy 2013.

508 *An tÓglach*, 12 June 1926.

509 Bateson 2010, 102.

510 J.J. Reynolds 1926.

511 Cullen, Mrs Martin: Witness Statement 419.

512 Kelly, Patrick: Witness Statement 781.

513 Laffan, Nicholas: Witness Statements 201, 703.

514 Leahy, Thomas: Witness Statement 660.

515 Michael Lennon, BMH Contemporaneous Document 56.

516 Lynch, Fionan: Witness Statement 192.

517 Béaslaí 1926, 234.

518 McLoughlin 1948.

519 McLoughlin, Seán: Witness Statement 290.

520 McGuire 2006.

521 Fox 2014, 227.

522 Bateson 2010, 106.

523 Laffan, Nicholas: Witness Statement 201; J.J. Reynolds 1926.

524 Holohan, Garry: Witness Statement 1043.

525 J.J. Reynolds 1926; Martin, Éamon: Witness Statements 591, 592, 593; BMH Contemporaneous Document 238.

526 Murphy, Gregory: Witness Statement 150.

527 Murphy, John (Seán): Witness Statement 204.

528 Caulfield 1995, 266.

529 Murray, Joseph: Witness Statement 254.

530 Report of 'A' Company, Allen Library.

531 Caulfield 1995, 157.

532 J.J. Reynolds 1926.

533 Kelly, Patrick: Witness Statement 78.

534 O'Carroll, Liam: Witness Statements 314, 594.

535 O'Connell, Mortimer: Witness Statement 804.

536 O'Dea, Michael: Witness Statement 115.

537 O'Duffy, Seán: Witness Statements 313, 618, 619; BMH Contemporaneous Document 210.

538 O'Flanagan, George: Witness Statement 131.

539 O'Flanagan, Michael: Witness Statements 800, 908.

540 Bateson 2010, 103.

541 Shouldice, John: Witness Statement 162.

542 Caulfield 1995, 270.

543 Royal Commission of Inquiry, London (18 May 1916).

544 O'Sullivan, Séamus: Witness Statement 393.

545 Reynolds, Joseph: Witness Statement 191.

546 Roche, Liam: Witness Statement 1698; BMH Contemporaneous Documents 23, 26.

547 Caulfield 1995, 266.

548 *Ibid.*, 185.

549 Shouldice, John: Witness Statements 162, 679.
550 Stephenson 1966.
551 Stephenson 2006.
552 Lawless, Joseph: Witness Statement 1043.
553 O'Sullivan, Séamus: Witness Statement 393.
554 Tobin, Liam: Witness Statement 1753.
555 Aloysius, Revd, OFM Cap.: Witness Statement 200; Fr Aloysius 1942.
556 Bateson 2010, 107.
557 Laffan, Nicholas: Witness Statements 201, 703.
558 Whelan, William: Witness Statement 369.
559 Caulfield 1995, 266.
560 Bateson 2010, 112.
561 Brennan 1966; Crenigan, James: Witness Statement 148.
562 Conlon, Mrs Martin: Witness Statement 419.
563 Taillon 1996, 66.
564 Ibid., 66, 91.
565 Ibid., 28; Fahy, Anna: Witness Statement 202.
566 Bateson 2010, 155.
567 McHugh 1966, 320.
568 Heron, Áine: Witness Statement 239.
569 See Stephenson 2006.
570 See Griffith and O'Grady 2002 [1982].
571 See Cowell 2005; Thornton 1975; McCoole 2003, 182.
572 McCoole 2003, 216.
573 McQuaile, Charles S.: Witness Statement 276.
574 Keating, Pauline: Witness Statement 432.
575 Morkan, Phyllis: Witness Statement 210.
576 Ui Chonaill 1966, 184.
577 Bermingham, DMP Constable Patrick J.: Witness Statement 697.
578 Ó Maitiu 2001.
579 Hally 1966–7, Part 1, 321.
580 'Jacob's and Stephen's Green area', The Catholic Bulletin, September 1918.
581 Bateson 2010, 146; McCracken 2000.
582 Peadar Kearney, 'Reminiscences of Easter Week', Trinity College Dublin MS 3560.
583 Augustine, Revd, OFM Cap.: Witness Statement 920.
584 Enright 2014.
585 Bateson 2010, 144.
586 Kenna 2014.
587 Aloysius, Revd, OFM Cap.: Witness Statement 200; Fr Aloysius 1942.
588 Fr Columbus, OFM Cap., recorded his experiences in a diary. The manuscript was discovered in the Capuchin Archives in Church Street. See Benedict Cullen, 'Echoes of the Rising's final shots', Irish Times (http://www.aohdiv7.org/hist_easter_aftermath.htm).
589 MacDonagh, Sr Francesca: Witness Statement 717.
590 Bateson 2010, 148. See O'Hanrahan 1917.
591 O'Reilly, Eily O'Hanrahan: Witness Statements 270, 415.
592 McInerney 1968.
593 Bateson 2010, 157.
594 The Catholic Bulletin, October 1916.
595 O'Farrell 2014.
596 De Brun, Seosamh: Witness Statement 312.
597 Byrne, Vincent: Witness Statement 423.

[598] Hayes, Michael: Witness Statement 215.

[599] Bateson 2010, 155; Duffy 2013.

[600] McHugh 1966, 320.

[601] P. Ó Ceallaigh 1966.

[602] Lawless, Michael: Witness Statement 727.

[603] Leonard, Joe: Witness Statement 547.

[604] MacDonagh, John: Witness Statements 219, 532.

[605] O'Donnell, Michael: Witness Statement 225.

[606] Art MacEoin, 'Murder in the Castle', *An Phoblacht*, 22 November 2001.

[607] Molloy 1966.

[608] Molloy, Michael: Witness Statement 716.

[609] See Moran 2010.

[610] Murphy, John J. (Seán): Witness Statement 204; BMH Contemporaneous Document 111.

[611] Bateson 2010, 157.

[612] D. Ryan 1949 [1957], 168.

[613] Bateson 2010, 150.

[614] P. Ó Ceallaigh 1966; Stapleton, William: Witness Statement 822.

[615] O'Reilly, Eily O'Hanrahan: Witness Statements 270, 415.

[616] O'Kelly, Patrick: Witness Statement 376; P. Ó Ceallaigh 1966.

[617] Lawless, Michael: Witness Statement 727.

[618] Pounch, Séamus: Witness Statements 267, 294.

[619] Price, Major–Gen. Éamon (Bob): Witness Statement 995.

[620] Pugh, Thomas: Witness Statement 397.

[621] Bateson 2010, 157.

[622] Slator, Thomas: Witness Statement 263.

[623] Slattery, James: Witness Statement 445.

[624] Stapleton, William James: Witness Statement 822.

[625] Slator, Thomas: Witness Statement 263.

[626] See Griffith and O'Grady 2002 [1982].

[627] Turner 1926a.

[628] Taillon 1996, 97.

[629] *Ibid.*, 63.

[630] *Ibid.*, 97.

[631] O'Reilly, Eily O'Hanrahan: Witness Statements 270, 415.

[632] Nic Shiubhlaigh 1955, 165. See Reilly 2005.

[633] Nic Shiubhlaigh 1955, 174–6.

[634] Lyons 1926.

[635] Ó Ruairc 2011, 73: 'De Valera's leadership of the Boland's Mills garrison during the Rising had been less than spectacular'. See Pinkman 1998, 201: 'Suffering from battle hysteria, Cmdt de Valera had to be forcibly restrained by some of his men of the Boland's Mill garrison before the end of the Easter Week's fighting and removed to Sir Patrick Dun's Hospital. It was in a room of the hospital that de Valera made his formal surrender to Captain Hitzen of the 5th Lincolnshire Regiment at about 1 pm on Sunday, 30 April 1916.'

[636] Caulfield 1995, 197–8, 216–17.

[637] Ó hUid 1966.

[638] Fitzpatrick 2002.

[639] Helferty 2006.

[640] *Dáil Éireann, Official Report*, Vols 67–8 (13 May 1937), 462.

[641] Lyons 1926. Hanna Sheehy-Skeffington later swore that de Valera sheepishly admitted to her that he wished he had not acted in this high-handed way—but only because it had meant that some of his best men had to spend time cooking: *An Phoblacht*, 16 July 1932; also see *Prison Bars*, July 1937.

642 Foley, Mrs Michael: Witness Statement 539.

643 Murphy, Mrs Eileen: Witness Statement 480.

644 Byrne, Seán: Witness Statement 422.

645 Banks, Henry T.: Witness Statement 1637.

646 Bateson 2010, 134.

647 O'Connor, Joseph: Witness Statement 157.

648 Caulfield 1995, 153.

649 Byrne, Seán: Witness Statement 422.

650 Christian, William: Witness Statement 646; Doyle, Very Revd James: Witness Statement 311; BMH Contemporaneous Document 149.

651 Bateson 2010, 133.

652 Coogan 2001, 118.

653 Grace, James: Witness Statement 310.

654 *Ibid.*

655 Lyons 1926.

656 *Ibid.*

657 Caulfield 1995, 220.

658 Donnelly, Simon: Witness Statements 113, 433, 481; BMH Contemporaneous Documents 62, 63, 65, 93, 106, 132. Donnelly 1922; Simon Donnelly, 'Thou shalt not pass—Ireland's challenge to the British forces at Mount Street Bridge, Easter 1916', IMA CD 62/3/7 (pamphlet).

659 Doyle, James: Witness Statements 127, 309.

660 Caulfield 1995, 203.

661 Doyle, Séamus: Witness Statement 166.

662 Bateson 2010, 126.

663 Caulfield 1995, 202.

664 O'Keefe, Seán: Witness Statement 188; Walsh, Thomas and James jointly: Witness Statement 309.

665 Bateson 2010, 141.

666 Ward, Patrick: Witness Statement 1140.

667 Thomas Fitzgerald, BMH Contemporaneous Document 91.

668 Caulfield 1995, 56.

669 Grace, James: Witness Statement 310.

670 Caulfield 1995, 62.

671 Lyons 1926.

672 *Ibid.*

673 Kavanagh, Séamus: Witness Statements 208, 1053.

674 Peter Kavanagh, BMH Contemporaneous Document 86.

675 Lyons, George: Witness Statements 11, 104; BMH Contemporaneous Documents 54, 300.

676 Lyons 1926.

677 Caulfield 1995, 250.

678 McDonnell, Andrew: Witness Statement 1768.

679 Bateson 2010, 136.

680 Lyons 1926.

681 MacThomais 1965, 30.

682 Lyons 1926.

683 Kavanagh, Séamus: Witness Statement 208.

684 Lyons 1926.

685 Bateson 2010, 118.

686 *The Catholic Bulletin*, June 1917.

687 Caulfield 1995, 159.

688 Grace, James: Witness Statement 310.

689 Lyons 1926.

690 Bateson 2010, 127.

691 Walsh, Thomas and James, jointly: Witness Statement 309.

692 Murray, Séamus: Witness Statement 308.

693 Lyons 1926.

694 *Ibid.*

695 O'Connor, Joseph: Witness Statements 157, 487, 544; Joseph O'Connor, NLI MS 13735; O'Connor 1966. See Hanratty, John: Witness Statement 96.

696 O'Connor, Joseph: Witness Statement 157.

697 Caulfield 1995, 174.

698 *Ibid.*, 147.

699 Doyle, James: Witness Statements 127, 309.

700 Lyons 1926.

701 Caulfield 1995, 134.

702 See http://mspcsearch.militaryarchives.ie/detail.aspx.

703 Lyons 1926.

704 Caulfield 1995, 60.

705 Bateson 2010, 128.

706 MacThomais 1965, 28.

707 Walsh, Thomas and James, jointly: Witness Statement 309.

708 Foy and Barton 1999, 81.

709 *Ibid.*, 81ff.

710 Caulfield 1995, 173.

711 T. Walsh 1966.

712 Ward, Patrick: Witness Statement 1140.

713 Bateson 2010, 130.

714 O'Shea, Seán: Witness Statement 129.

715 Collins 1997, 9.

716 Burke, James J.: Witness Statement 1758.

717 Mannion, Annie: Witness Statement 297. Miss Mannion was a Matron in the Union during the Rising.

718 Hally 1966.

719 B. O'Neill 1939, 59.

720 'Easter Week, 1916, General Maxwell's Report', *An tOglach*, 19 June 1926.

721 Bateson 2010, 43.

722 Gallagher 2014.

723 Ceannt, Áine B.E.: Witness Statement 264; BMH Contemporaneous Documents 94, 295.

724 Augustine, Revd, OFM Cap.: Witness Statement 920; MacDonagh 1946.

725 Ceannt, Áine B.E.: Witness Statement 264; BMH Contemporaneous Documents 94, 295.

726 Bateson 2010, 45.

727 Augustine, Revd, OFM Cap.: Witness Statement 920.

728 Colbert, Elizabeth (Lila): Witness Statement 856.

729 Fr Augustine, OFM Cap., *Dublin Evening Herald*, 1 June 1916.

730 Joyce 1926.

731 Burgess, Alfred: Witness Statement 1634.

732 Burke, J.: Witness Statement 1758.

733 Bateson 2010, 266.

734 Joyce 1926.

735 Coughlan, James: Witness Statement 304.

736 Collins 1997, 10.

737 Coughlan, James: Witness Statement 304.

738 Byrne, Joseph: Witness Statement 461.

739 Corrigan, William P.: Witness Statement 250.

740 Cosgrave, William T.: Witness Statements 268, 449; BMH Contemporaneous Documents 18, 125.

741 Collins 1997, 10.

742 Coughlan, James: Witness Statement 304.

743 Bateson 2010, 50; Duffy 2013.

744 *The Catholic Bulletin*, April 1918.

745 Doolan, Joseph: Witness Statement 199; Joseph Doolan, NLI MS 10915; Doolan 1918.

746 Downey, Kieran: Witness Statement 753.

747 Doyle, Peadar: Witness Statement 155.

748 Doyle, Thomas: Witness Statement 186.

749 Egan, Patrick: Witness Statement 327.

750 Joyce 1926.

751 O'Flaherty, Liam: Witness Statement 248; McCarthy, Dan: Witness Statement 722; BMH Contemporaneous Document 211. See McCarthy, Thomas: Witness Statement 307.

752 Coughlan, James: Witness Statement 304.

753 Foran, James: Witness Statement 243.

754 Gay, Col. Thomas B.: Witness Statement 780.

755 Holland, Robert: Witness Statement 280.

756 Holland, Robert: Witness Statements 280, 371; BMH Contemporaneous Document 147.

757 Irvine, George: Witness Statement 265.

758 Gaskin, Frank: Witness Statement 386.

759 Joyce, John V.: Witness Statement 1762; Joyce 1926.

760 Ceannt, Áine B.E.: Witness Statement 264.

761 Kenny, James: Witness Statement 174.

762 Holland, Robert: Witness Statement 280.

763 McCarthy, Dan: Witness Statement 722; BMH Contemporaneous Document 211.

764 O'Flaherty, Liam: Witness Statement 248.

765 McCarthy, Thomas: Witness Statement 307.

766 Bateson 2010, 58.

767 Coughlan, James: Witness Statement 304.

768 Irvine, George: Witness Statement 265.

769 Joyce 1926; Murphy, Séamus: Witness Statement 1756; BMH Contemporaneous Document 128.

770 Murphy, Seán: Witness Statement 1598; McCarthy, Dan: Witness Statement 722; BMH Contemporaneous Document 211. See McCarthy, Thomas: Witness Statement 307.

771 Murphy, William: Witness Statement 352.

772 Nevin, Fr Eugene, CP: Witness Statement 1605.

773 Nolan, George: Witness Statement 596.

774 O'Brien, Annie (née Cooney): Witness Statement 805.

775 O'Brien, Laurence: Witness Statement 252.

776 See McCarthy, Thomas: Witness Statement 307.

777 O'Brien, Liam: Witness Statement 323.

778 Joyce 1926.

779 O'Carroll, Joseph: Witness Statement 728.

780 Young 1926.

781 O'Neill, Edward: Witness Statement 203.

782 Caulfield 1995, 80.

783 *The Catholic Bulletin*, September 1916.

784 Bateson 2010, 53.

785 *The Catholic Bulletin*, April 1918.

786 Egan, Patrick: Witness Statement 327.

787 Bateson 2010, 47.

[788] Doolan, Joseph: Witness Statement 199.

[789] Bateson 2010, 52.

[790] *The Catholic Bulletin*, September 1916.

[791] Bateson 2010, 54; Duffy 2013.

[792] Caulfield 1995, 79.

[793] Irvine, George: Witness Statement 265.

[794] Burke, James J.: Witness Statement 1758.

[795] Ward, Patrick: Witness Statement 1140.

[796] Young 1926.

[797] Taillon 1996, 61.

[798] Cooney 1930; McCoole 2003, 153.

[799] O'Brien, Annie (née Cooney): Witness Statement 805 (made jointly with her sisters, Eileen (Cooney) Harbourne and Lily (Cooney) Curran).

[800] McCoole 2003, 155.

[801] Kennedy, Margaret: Witness Statement 185.

[802] Ward 1983, 115.

[803] McNamara, Rose: Witness Statement 482.

[804] McCoole 2003, 189.

[805] Taillon 1996, 38, 43.

[806] Ceannt, Áine B.E.: Witness Statement 264; O'Brennan 1936; 1947.

[807] Coogan 2013; O'Brien 2012b.

[808] Crenigan, James: Witness Statements 148, 1395.

[809] Ryan 1949 [1957], 229.

[810] Lawless, Joseph: Witness Statement 1043—this runs to 418 pages and provides a remarkably complete and detailed account of the Fingal Volunteers in the Ashbourne engagement and the north Dublin area from 1913 through the entire revolutionary period. Lawless 1926; 1941–2.

[811] Austin, John: Witness Statement 904; Bratton, Eugene: Witness Statement 467; 'Graphic story of Ashbourne', *Gaelic American*, 23 September 1916.

[812] Lawless 1926.

[813] Lawless 1946; Ó Luing 1968.

[814] Ashe, Nora: Witness Statement 645.

[815] Those indicated by # reported to the 5th Battalion but were sent to the GPO on Tuesday 25 April. They are listed in both garrisons but are counted only in the Ashbourne garrison. Lawless, Joseph: Witness Statement 1043.

[816] Crenigan, James: Witness Statements 148, 1395.

[817] Bateson 2010, 163.

[818] Austin, John: Witness Statement 904.

[819] Lawless, Joseph: Witness Statement 1043.

[820] Daly, Francis: Witness Statement 278.

[821] Golden, Gerry: Witness Statements 177, 521, 522; Gerry Golden, 'Description of the Battle of Ashbourne', Allen Library.

[822] Hayes, Dr Richard: Witness Statements 97, 876; BMH Contemporaneous Documents 46, 50, 51, 299.

[823] Lawless 1926.

[824] Lawless, Joseph: Witness Statement 1043. This runs to 418 pages and provides a remarkably complete and detailed account of the Fingal Volunteers in the Ashbourne engagement and the north Dublin area from 1913 through the entire revolutionary period. BMH Contemporaneous Documents 17, 251.

[825] Lawless 1926; 1941–2; 1966.

[826] McAllister, Bernard: Witness Statement 147.

[827] McAllister, Michael: Witness Statement 1494.

828 Gen. Richard Mulcahy, BMH Contemporaneous Document 139.

829 O'Connor, James: Witness Statement 142.

830 Peppard, Thomas: Witness Statement 1399.

831 Bateson 2010, 166.

832 Gerry Golden, 'Description of the Battle of Ashbourne', Allen Library; Lawless, Joseph: Witness Statement 1043.

833 Ó Luing 1970, 241.

834 Weston, Charles: Witness Statement 149.

835 Lawless, Sister Eithne: Witness Statement 414.

836 See 'Dublin Castle from the inside', *An tOglach*, 3 February 1926.

837 *The Irish Times*, 25 April 1916.

838 Foy and Barton 1999, 54–5; Townshend 2005, 110, 162–4.

839 D. Ryan 1949 [1957], 116–18; Fox 2014, 149. 'There was never any question of taking the Castle. The forces were too small for the Castle to be taken and held. It was hoped, however, that by holding the Guardroom and commanding the entrance from adjacent posts, the effectiveness of the Castle as an attacking base would be destroyed. Here, again, the plan was crippled by the small number taking part. But the success achieved by the audacious attack created panic on the other side.'

840 Béaslaí 1926, 97; Peadar Kearney, quoted in De Burca 1958, 116.

841 LeRoux 1932, 384.

842 See Lynch 1957, 77ff and 105ff, where he alleges that the original plan was to take the City Hall first and then to take the Castle guardroom.

843 Bateson 2010, 25.

844 See 'Dublin Castle from the inside', *An tOglach*, 3 February 1926.

845 Lynn, Dr Kathleen: Witness Statement 357.

846 See Hanratty, John: Witness Statement 96.

847 Bateson 2010, 38.

848 See Hanratty, John: Witness Statement 96.

849 Connolly, Matthew: Witness Statement 1746; M. Connolly 1966.

850 Bateson 2010, 30; Duffy 2013.

851 Fox 2014, 134.

852 James Donnelly, BMH Contemporaneous Document 98.

853 Bateson 2010, 39.

854 MacThomais 1965, 15.

855 *The Catholic Bulletin*, December 1916.

856 Robbins, Frank: Witness Statement 585; Robbins 1977, 118.

857 King, Martin: Witness Statement 543; Byrne, Seán: Witness Statement 579.

858 See Hanratty, John: Witness Statement 96.

859 Oman, William: Witness Statement 421.

860 Bateson 2010, 29.

861 See Hanratty, John: Witness Statement 96.

862 Bateson 2010, 32.

863 Scallon, John Joseph: Witness Statement 318; Byrne, Thomas: Witness Statement 364.

864 Hanratty, John: Witness Statement 96.

865 Taillon 1996, 23.

866 *Ibid.*, 105.

867 Lynn, Dr Kathleen: Witness Statement 357; McCoole 2003, 181.

868 Diary of Kathleen Lynn, 24 April 1916.

869 There are various spellings of her surname in the sources. 'Molony' is the one she used. Her birth certificate (15 January 1883) has 'Moloney' but her death certificate (29 January 1967) has 'Molony'.

[870] P. Kelly 1966.

[871] McCoole 2003, 188.

[872] Molony, Helena: Witness Statement 391; Helena Molony, 'Women of the Rising', RTÉ Archive, 16 April 1963.

[873] Caulfield 1995, 92.

[874] 'Remembering the past: Helena Molony', *An Phoblacht*, 30 January 1997.

[875] *Unfurling the flag*, The Irish Republican Digest, Book 1 (pamphlet; Cork, 1956), 31–2.

[876] *Workers' Republic*, 22 April 1916.

[877] Letter from Clare Cowley, Molly O'Reilly's granddaughter; *Workers' Republic*, 22 April 1916.

[878] Fox 1938, 153.

[879] Taillon 1996, 55.

[880] *Unfurling the flag*, The Irish Republican Digest, Book 1 (pamphlet; Cork, 1956), 31–2.

[881] McGowan, Séamus: Witness Statement 542. See Hanratty, John: Witness Statement 96.

[882] Oman, William: Witness Statement 421.

[883] Hally 1966–7, Part 1, 321.

[884] There is a graphic account of events at St Stephen's Green in the memoirs of Breda Grace and Dr D.A. Courtney, De Valera Papers, Killiney MSS 94/385. See also the Easter Week diary of Douglas Hyde, who lived on Earlsfort Terrace: TCD MS 10343/7.

[885] Bateson 2010, 67.

[886] Mallin, Thomas: Witness Statement 382.

[887] Browne, Rt Revd Msgr Patrick: Witness Statement 729.

[888] Bibby, Fr Albert, OFM Cap.: Witness Statement 200.

[889] MacLochlainn 1971, 121ff. The original of this letter is in the possession of the Mallin family.

[890] See http://www.cathinfo.com/index.php/Fr-Joseph-Mallin-SJ.

[891] Bateson 2010, 70.

[892] *The Catholic Bulletin*, November 1918.

[893] Nicholas Alexander, BMH Contemporaneous Document 148.

[894] Bateson 2010, 71.

[895] *The Catholic Bulletin*, December 1916.

[896] Caulfield 1995, 166.

[897] MacThomais 1965, 17–18. Alice was his mother.

[898] Bateson 2010, 76.

[899] Crothers's Witness Statement uses that spelling of his name, and he is so listed in the 1911 census (http://www.census.nationalarchives.ie/pages/1911/Dublin/South_Dock/Eblana_Villas/92709/).

[900] Fox (2014, 227) lists him as 'Carruthers'.

[901] Crothers, Christopher: Witness Statement 1759.

[902] See Hanratty, John: Witness Statement 96.

[903] Townshend 1978–9.

[904] Bateson 2010, 73; Duffy 2013.

[905] Robbins, Frank: Witness Statement 585.

[906] Fox 2014, 227.

[907] Caulfield 1995, 152.

[908] Private statement of Ned Keogh.

[909] See Hanratty, John: Witness Statement 96.

[910] Byrne, Seán: Witness Statement 579.

[911] King, Martin: Witness Statement 543.

[912] Lawless, Michael: Witness Statement 727.

[913] Bateson 2010, 82.

[914] Ó Briain 1966.

[915] Fox 2014, 227.

[916] Molloy 1966.

917 Molloy, Michael: Witness Statement 716.

918 Bateson 2010, 78.

919 Hackett, Rosana: Witness Statement 546.

920 Nicholls, Harry: Witness Statement 296.

921 Ó Briain 1966.

922 Ó Briain 1923.

923 Ó Briain, Liam: Witness Statements 3, 6, 7.

924 Oman, William: Witness Statement 421.

925 Lawless, Michael: Witness Statement 727.

926 See Hanratty, John: Witness Statement 96.

927 O'Shea, James: Witness Statement 733.

928 Robbins, Frank: Witness Statement 585; Robbins 1928; 1977, 118.

929 Bateson 2010, 80; Duffy 2013.

930 Fox 2014, 164.

931 Robbins 1977, 118.

932 See Griffith and O'Grady 2002 [1982]; Máire Comerford, BMH Contemporaneous Document 59.

933 Caulfield 1995, 130.

934 McCoole 2003, 161.

935 Taillon 1996, 71; O'Daly 1926.

936 Donnelly, Mrs Nellie: Witness Statement 256; Donnelly 1930; McCoole 2003, 167.

937 Taillon 1996, 98.

938 O'Daly 1926; McCoole 2003, 192.

939 Taillon 1996, 57.

940 Hackett, Rose: Witness Statement 546. 'Local woman helps name bridge after trade unionist', *Irish Independent*, 11 September 2013. 'Political Left teamed up to secure naming of bridge', *Irish Independent*, 22 September 2013.

941 Robbins 1977, 94–5.

942 Laura Friel, '"Tell Mom I'm off to America." The story of Lily Kempson and her fight for freedom', *An Phoblacht*, 16 April 1998.

943 Bateson 2010, 71.

944 *The Catholic Bulletin*, December 1916.

945 Caulfield 1995, 166.

946 MacThomais 1965, 17–18. Alice was his mother.

947 McCoole 2003, 185.

948 See Matthews 2010b, 126–30, for a contrasting view of the countess's role at St Stephen's Green.

949 Philip Rooney, 'The Green Jacket: the story of the Countess', *The Sunday Press*, 15, 18 and 25 September and 2 October 1960.

950 P. O'Brien 2013, 18.

951 Caulfield 1995, 66.

952 Extract from the diary of Geraldine Fitzgerald, dated 24 April 1916. War Office Papers, WO 35/207/127.

953 This type of 7.63mm Mauser pistol converted into a rifle with a removable stock. It was nicknamed a 'Peter the Painter' after Peter Piaktow, a Latvian anarchist in London, a painter, who was sought but never caught following the 1911 London riots on Sidney Street.

954 Taillon 1996, 57.

955 See 'A Dublin woman's story of the Rebellion', *Gaelic American*, 18 November 1916.

956 Skinnider 1966.

957 Skinnider 1917, 9–10.

958 Ward 1983, 113.

959 Skinnider 1917, 50–1, 76–8.

960 Perolz, Marie: Witness Statement 246.

961 O'Doherty, Kitty: Witness Statement 355.

962 Heron, Ina: Witness Statement 919.

963 O'Brien, Nora: Witness Statement 286; McCoole 2003, 151; N. O'Brien 1932.

964 Corr, Elizabeth and Nell, jointly: Witness Statement 179.

965 Gray 1948.

966 O'Doherty, Kitty: Witness Statement 355.

967 McCoole 2003, 198.

968 Perolz, Marie: Witness Statement 246.

969 Thornton, Nora: Witness Statement 655.

970 Duffy 2013.

971 Enright 2014.

972 Brennan, Robert: Witness Statements 125, 779, 790.

973 Cosgrave, William T.: Witness Statements 268, 449.

974 Shouldice, John F.: Witness Statements 162, 679.

975 Hayes, Dr Richard: Witness Statements 97, 896.

976 Fahy, Frank: Witness Statement 442.

977 Irvine, George: Witness Statement 265.

978 Lynch, Fionan: Witness Statement 192.

979 Plunkett, John (Jack): Witness Statements 488, 865.

980 Tobin, Major-Gen. Liam: Witness Statement 1753.

981 Walsh, Thomas: Witness Statement 196.

982 Corrigan, William: Witness Statement 250.

983 DeLacey, Michael: Witness Statement 319.

984 Galligan, Peter: Witness Statement 170.

985 Joyce, Col. J.V.: Witness Statement 1762.

986 McGarry, Seán: Witness Statement 368.

987 Peppard, Thomas: Witness Statement 1399.

988 Crenigan, James: Witness Statements 148, 1395.

989 Kennedy, Patrick: Witness Statement 499.

990 Matthews 2007b; see the *Weekly Irish Times, Sinn Féin Rebellion Handbook* (1916), 92 (p. 91 in the 1998 Mourne River Press edition); McCoole 2003, 216–17.

991 For the treatment of women prisoners in Dublin Castle following the Rising see 'Dublin Castle from the inside', *An tOglach*, 3 February 1926.

992 O'Brien, Annie (née Cooney): Witness Statement 805 (made jointly with her sisters, Eileen (Cooney) Harbourne and Lily (Cooney) Curran).

993 O'Daly 1926.

994 Donnelly, Nellie Gifford: Witness Statement 256.

995 Hackett, Rose: Witness Statement 546.

996 Kennedy, Margaret: Witness Statement 185.

997 Lynn, Dr Kathleen: Witness Statement 357.

998 Thornton, Dr Brigid Lyons: Witness Statement 259.

999 McNamara, Rose: Witness Statement 482.

1000 Markan, Pauline: Witness Statement 432.

1001 Molony, Helena: Witness Statement 391.

1002 McCoole 2003, 189.

1003 Perolz, Marie: Witness Statement 246.

1004 McCoole 2003, 206.

1005 *Ibid.*

Bibliography

MANUSCRIPT, NEWSPAPERS AND PRINTED PRIMARY SOURCES

1916 Papers, Box 5608, No. 5688, National Archives, Dublin.

An Claidheamh Soluis.

An tÓglach.

An Phoblacht.

Bean na hÉireann.

Piaras Béaslaí Papers, National Library of Ireland.

Augustine Birrell Papers, Trinity College Dublin.

British Parliamentary Archive Papers, 'The Irish Uprising, 1914–1921'.

Cathal Brugha Papers, University College Library.

Máire Ni Shuibhne Brugha Papers, University College Library.

The Capuchin Annual.

The Catholic Bulletin.

Daniel Cohalan Papers, National Library of Ireland.

Éamon de Valera Papers, University College Dublin.

John Devoy Papers, National Library of Ireland MS 18157.

Documents relative to the Sinn Féin movement (London, 1921, Cmd. 1108).

The Easter Commemoration Digest, 1964.

Forward.

The Freeman's Journal.

The Gaelic American.

Gerry Golden, 'The story of the fight at Rath Cross Roads or the Battle of Ashbourne', Allen Library.

The Harp.

Mary Hayden diaries, National Library of Ireland.

Mrs Augustine Henry diary, National Library of Ireland.

Bulmer Hobson Papers, National Library of Ireland.

Paddy Houlihan, 'The Battle of Ashbourne', National Library of Ireland MS 18098.

The Irish Catholic.

The Irish Citizen.

Irish Freedom.

The Irish Independent/Sunday Independent.

The Irish Independent, Golden Jubilee Supplement (1966)/*Sunday Independent*, Easter Rising Commemorative Supplement (1966).

Irish Republican Brotherhood Papers, University College Library.

The Irish Times.

The Irish Volunteer.

Irish Volunteers Papers, University College Library.

The Irish Worker.

Pte J. Jameson, 2635/Sherwood Foresters, 'My experiences whilst in Ireland',
Document Reference No. 999/519, National Archives, Dublin.

Patrick Little Papers, University College Library.

Diarmuid Lynch, 'Recollections and comments on the IRB', National Library of
Ireland MS 11128.

Denis McCullough Papers, University College Library.

Joseph McGarrity Papers, National Library of Ireland.

Eoin MacNeill Papers, National Library of Ireland.

Mary Martin diary, Trinity College Library, http://dh.tcd.ie/martindiary/.

Military Archives of Ireland, Cathal Brugha Barracks, Dublin:

Introduction to the Bureau of Military History 1913–1921 (Defence Forces Printing
Press, 2003).

Bureau of Military History Witness Statements:

Aghlas (Ashe), Nora: Statement 645. Agnew, Arthur: Statement 152. Aloysius,
Revd, OFM Cap.: Statements 200, 207. Archer, Liam: Statement 819. Augustine,
Revd, OFM Cap.: Statement 920. Austin, John: Statement 904. Balfe, Richard:
Statement 251. Béaslaí, Piaras: Statements 261, 675. Beaumont, Mrs Seán
(Maureen McGavock): Statement 385. Bermingham, Patrick J.: Statement 697.
Bevan, Séamus: Statements 1058, 1059. Bloxam, Elizabeth: Statement 632. Boylan,
Peter: Statement 269. Boylan, Seán: Statements 212, 1715. Bracken, Peadar:
Statements 12, 361. Brady, Christopher J.: Statement 705. Bratton, RIC Constable
Eugene: Statement 467. Brennan, Frank J.: Statement 49. Browne, Revd Michael:
Statement 538. Browne, Msgr Patrick: Statement 729. Buckley, Tim: Statement 43.
Bucknill, Sir Alfred: Statement 1019. Bulfin, Éamon: Statement 497. Burgess,
Alfred: Statement 1634. Burke, Fergus (Frank): Statement 694. Byrne,
Christopher: Statements 167, 642. Byrne, Gerald: Statement 143. Byrne, Joseph:
Statement 461. Byrne, Seán (F Co., 1st Btn, 1916): Statement 422. Byrne, Seán (C
Co., 3rd Btn, 1916): Statement 579. Byrne, Tom: Statement 564. Caldwell, Patrick:
Statement 638. Callender, Ignatius: Statement 923. Carpenter, Walter: Statement
583. Carrigan, James: Statement 613. Cavanaugh, Maeve: Statement 258. Ceannt,
Áine Bean Éamon: Statement 264. Christian, William: Statement 646. Clarke,
Josephine (née Stallard): Statement 699. Cody, Seán: Statement 1035. Coffey,
Diarmuid: Statement 1248. Coghlan, Francis X.: Statement 1760. Colbert,
Elizabeth: Statement 856. Colley, Harry: Statement 1687. Collins, Con (Conor,
Cornelius): Statement 90. Collins, Maurice: Statement 550. Conlon, Martin:
Statement 798. Conlon, Mrs Martin: Statement 419. Connolly, Joseph: Statement
124. Connolly, Matthew: Statement 1746. Corkery, Dan: Statements 93, 1719.
Corrigan, William: Statement 250. Cosgrave, William T.: Statements 266, 449.
Coughlan, James: Statement 304. Cregan, Máirín: Statement 416. Cremin, Mary
A. (née Sheehan): Statement 924. Crenegan, James: Statements 148, 1395.
Crothers, Christopher: Statement 1759. Curran, Lily (née Cooney): Statement

Thomas Weafer, GPO. Capt. Thomas Joseph (Tom) Weafer was killed in the Hibernian Bank on Lower Abbey Street on Wednesday. The strategic importance of the building is clear. The building was completely destroyed and his body was totally consumed in the fire. Some reports, however, note that he was killed on Monday in the Reis's Jewellers building, where he was sent to erect a wire. (*Come here to me! Dublin life and culture* blog)

Oscar Traynor, GPO. After Fairview Strand fell, Lt Oscar Traynor led the Fairview Volunteers and ICA members to the GPO. He was then sent to the Metropole Hotel, and after its fall he returned to the GPO. He led his men to bore through the walls of the hotel to the corner of Messrs Manfield's premises on the corner of Abbey Street Middle. (Courtesy of the Trustees of the National Library of Ireland)

GPO Garrison. This photograph of survivors of the GPO garrison was taken in Croke Park on the 20th anniversary of the Easter Rising (1936) and was published in the *Irish Press*. Two hundred and eighty-eight men and women are seen, and the number of women in the photograph confirms the large number of women in the garrison. (Courtesy of Clare Cowley)

Richard Mulcahy, 5th Battalion. On Sunday evening he was sent by James Connolly to Howth to cut the undersea telephone wires between Dublin and London. It was impossible to return to Dublin, so he went to Ashbourne and Ashe appointed him Vice-Commandant for the Rising. He succeeded Michael Collins as Commander in Chief of the Free State Army. (Courtesy of the Trustees of the National Library of Ireland)

Michael Walker, 2nd Battalion. Michael was in the 2nd Battalion with his brother John. Both brothers were Olympic bicyclists. In the 1912 Olympic Games, Michael cycled for Ireland, but under the banner of Great Britain. He finished 67th in the individual road race. He is shown here in the uniform of the Old IRA, c. 1910–20. (Courtesy of the Trustees of the National Library of Ireland)

Piaras Béaslaí, 1st Battalion. Piaras Béaslaí was the Battalion Vice-Commandant, and became editor of *An tÓglach* (*The Soldier*). Born and educated in Liverpool, he moved to Dublin at the age of 23. He was TD for Kerry East in the first three Dáils and published one of the first biographies of Michael Collins. (Courtesy of the Trustees of the National Library of Ireland)

Michael Mallin, St Stephen's Green. Cmdt Michael Mallin assembled the Citizen Army detachment at Liberty Hall and marched about 100 Citizen Army men and women to St Stephen's Green. His command was placed to block British troop movements into Dublin from the south, generally, and to counter attempts by British troops coming from Portobello Barracks to support Dublin Castle. (Courtesy of the Trustees of the National Library of Ireland)

Winifred Carney (McBride), GPO.
She was James Connolly's secretary in
Belfast, and came to Dublin to take part
in the Rising. In Moore Street she knelt
at Connolly's side and asked of the
surrender, 'Was there no other way?'
Connolly replied that he would not see
his brave boys burned to death and
there was no other way.

Jack White, GPO. Capt. John J. (Jack)
White DSO was an original member of
the Irish Citizen Army, and was the first
chair of the Army council. He left the
ICA in 1914 and became a member of
the Volunteers. During the Rising he
was in the GPO.

Lucy Agnes Smyth (Byrne). She was sent to 27 Hardwicke Street to get some rifles, then reported to the GPO and was sent to the Hibernian Bank, where she remained until going to Jervis Street Hospital with the other women. Prior to the Rising, she was romantically involved with Con Colbert. (Maeve O'Leary)

Máire Comerford, GPO. Máire Comerford pictured on her wedding day. Originally from Wexford, she reported to St Stephen's Green, but was turned away because she was deemed too young and spent the week carrying dispatches from the GPO. During the Civil War she was imprisoned and endured a hunger strike as well as being wounded in Mountjoy Prison. (Comerford.com)

Boland's Garrison. Surviving members of the garrisons often met in the decades following the Rising. This photo is of surviving members of the 3rd Battalion of Volunteers who served in Boland's Mills. The photo was taken at UCD on the 50th Anniversary of the Rising. (Courtesy of the Trustees of the National Library of Ireland)

805. Cusack, Brian: Statement 736. Czira, Sidney Gifford: Statement 909. Daly, Denis: Statement 110. Daly, Francis: Statement 278. Daly, Madge: Statements 209, 855. Daly, Séamus: Statement 360. Daly, Una: Statement 610. De Barra, Leslie Price Bean: Statement 1754. De Brun, Seosamh: Statement 312. De Burca, Aoife: Statement 359. De Burca, F.: Statement 105. De Roiste (Roche), Liam: Statement 1698. Dillon, Geraldine Plunkett: Statements 29, 358, 424. Dolan, Edward: Statement 1078. Donnelly, Charles: Statement 824. Donnelly, Nellie (née Gifford): Statement 256. Donnelly, Simon: Statements 113, 433, 481. Doolan, Joseph: Statement 199. Dore, Éamon: Statement 392. Dore, Nora (née Daly): Statement 154. Doyle, Revd James: Statement 311. Doyle, James: Statements 127, 309. Doyle, James (Gresham Hotel): Statement 771. Doyle, Séamus: Statement 166. Doyle, Thomas: Statement 186. Egan, Patrick: Statement 327. Fahy, Anna: Statement 202. Fahy, Frank: Statement 442. Fay, Bridget (née Diskin): Statement 484. Fitzgerald, Maurice: Statement 326. Fitzgibbon, Seán: Statement 130. Flanagan, M.: Statement 800. Fogarty, Revd Dr Michael: Statement 271. Foley, Mrs Michael: Statement 539. Foran, James: Statement 243. Fox, Thomas: Statement 365. Fulham, James: Statement 630. Gaskin, Frank: Statement 386. Gavan-Duffy, George: Statement 381. Gavan-Duffy, Louise: Statement 216. Gerrard, Capt. E.: Statement 348. Gleeson, Joseph: Statement 367. Gogan, Liam: Statement 799. Golden, Gerry: Statements 177, 206, 521, 522. Good, Joe: Statement 388. Grace, Seumus: Statement 310. Griffith, Maud: Statement 205. Hackett, Rose: Statement 546. Hales, Tom: Statement 20. Handley, Sgt Edward: Statement 625. Hayes, Michael: Statement 215. Hayes, Dr Richard: Statements 97, 876. Healy, Seán: Statements 686, 1479, 1643. Hehir, Hugh: Statement 683. Henderson, Frank: Statements 249, 821. Heron, Áine: Statement 293. Heron, Ina (née Connolly): Statement 919. Hobson, Bulmer: Statements 30, 31, 50, 51, 52, 53, 81, 82, 83, 84, 85, 86, 87, 652, 1089, 1365. Hobson, Claire (née Gregan): Statement 685. Holland, Robert: Statements 280, 371. Holohan, Garry: Statements 328, 336. Hughes, Julia: Statement 880. Hynes, James: Statement 867. Hynes, Thomas: Statement 714. Irvine, George: Statement 265. Jackson, Valentine: Statement 409. Joyce, Col. J.V.: Statement 1762. Kavanagh, Séamus: Statements 208, 998. Keating, Pauline: Statement 432. Keegan, John: Statement 217. Kelly, Edward: Statement 1094. Kelly, Patrick: Statement 78. Kennedy, Senator Margaret: Statement 185. Kennedy, Patrick (Paddy): Statement 499. Kennedy, Seán: Statements 842, 885. Kenny, Lt James (Howth, Kilcoole): Statement 174. Kenny, James (E Co., 4th Btn, 1916): Statement 141. Kent, William: Statement 75. Keogh, Margaret: Statement 273. King, RIC Constable Frank: Statement 635. King, Martin: Statement 543. Laffan, Nicholas: Statements 201, 703. Lalor, Mary (née Hyland): Statement 295. Larkin, James: Statement 906. Lavin, Revd Thomas: Statement 1407. Lawless, Sr Eithne (Evelyn, Eibhlin): Statement 414. Lawless, Col. Joseph V.: Statement 1043. Leahy, Thomas: Statement 660. Lonergan, Michael: Statement 140. Lynch, Diarmuid: Statements 4, 120, 121, 364, 651. Lynch, Fionan: Statement 192. Lynn, Dr Kathleen: Statement 357. Lynskey, William: Statement 1749. McAllister, Michael: Statement 1494. Macardle, Dorothy: Statement 457. McBride, Maud Gonne: Statement 317. McCartan, Patrick: Statements 99, 100, 766. McCarthy,

Cathleen: Statement 937. McCarthy, Dan: Statement 722. McCarthy, Thomas: Statement 307. MacCarvill, Eileen: Statement 1752. McCrea, Patrick: Statement 413. McCullough, Denis: Statements 111, 636, 914, 915, 916. MacDonagh, Sr Francesca: Statement 717. MacDonagh, John: Statements 219, 532. McDonnell, Andrew: Statement 1768. McDonnell, Michael (Mick): Statement 225. McDowell, Maeve (née Cavanagh): Statement 258. McElligott, Patrick: Statement 1013. McEllistrom, Thomas: Statement 275. MacEntee, Margaret (née Browne): Statement 322. MacEntee, Seán: Statement 1052. McEoin, Capt. James: Statement 436. McGaley, Jack: Statement 126. MacGarry, Maeve: Statement 826. MacGarry, Milo: Statement 356. McGarry, Seán: Statement 368. McGowan, Séamus: Statement 542. McGuinness, Joseph: Statement 607. McKenna, Kathleen (née Napoli): Statement 643. McLoughlin, John (Seán): Statement 290. McLoughlin, Mary: Statement 934. McNamara, Rose: Statement 482. MacNeill, Agnes: Statement 213. MacNeill, Niall: Statement 69. McWhinney, Linda (née Kearns): Statement 404. Mallin, Thomas: Statement 382. Malone, Bridget (née Walsh): Statement 617. Martin, Brigid (née Foley): Statement 398. Martin, Éamon: Statements 591, 592, 593. Mernin, Lily: Statement 441. Mitchell, Albert: Statement 196. Molloy, Michael: Statement 716. Molony, Helena: Statement 391. Moriarty, Maurice: Statement 117. Morkan, Phyllis: Statement 210. Mulcahy, Mary Josephine (née Ryan): Statement 399. Mullen, Patrick: Statement 621. Murphy, Eileen (née Walsh): Statement 480. Murphy, Fintan: Statement 370. Murphy, Gregory: Statement 150. Murphy, John J. (Seán): Statement 204. Murphy, Séamus: Statement 1756. Murphy, Stephen: Statement 545. Murphy, William: Statement 352. Murray, Joseph: Statement 254. Murray, Séamus: Statement 308. Nevin, Revd Eugene: Statement 1605. Ni Bhriain, Máire: Statement 363. Nicholls, Harry: Statement 296. Nolan, George: Statement 596. Nugent, Laurence: Statement 907. Nunan, Seán: Statement 1744. Ó Briain, Liam: Statements 3, 6, 7, 565, 784. O'Brien, Annie (née Cooney): Statement 805 (jointly with her sisters: Eileen (Cooney) Harbourne and Lily (Cooney) Curran). O'Brien, Laurence: Statement 252. O'Brien, Liam: Statement 323. O'Brien, Nora (née Connolly): Statement 286. O'Brien, William: Statement 1766. Ó Brolchain, Máire: Statements 302, 321. Ó Buachalla, Domhnall: Statement 194. O'Byrne, Máire (née Kennedy): Statement 1029. O'Carroll, Joseph: Statement 728. O'Carroll, Liam: Statements 314, 594. Ó Ceallaigh, Padraig: Statement 376. O'Connor, Éamon: Statement 114. O'Connor, James: Statement 142. O'Connor, Joseph: Statements 157, 487, 544. O'Connor, Patrick J. ('Ninepence'): Statement 608. O'Daly, Patrick: Statements 220, 387. O'Doherty, Kitty: Statement 355. O'Donnell, Mrs Bernard (née Eithne Coyle): Statement 750. O'Donoghue, Very Revd Thomas: Statement 1666. O'Donovan, Con: Statement 1750. O'Duffy, Seán M. Statements 313, 618, 619. O'Flaherty, Liam: Statement 248. O'Flanagan, George: Statement 131. O'Flanagan, Michael: Statements 800, 908. O'Grady, Charles: Statement 282. O'Hegarty, P.S.: Statements 26, 27, 28, 259, 839, 840, 841, 897. O'Hegarty, Seán: Statement 54. O'Keefe, Seán: Statement 188. O'Kelly, Fergus: Statement 351. O'Kelly, J.J. (Sceilg): Statements 384, 427. O'Kelly, Kathleen (née Murphy): Statement 180. O'Kelly, Séamus: Statement 471. O'Kelly, Seán T.: Statements 611,

1765. O'Leary, Mortimer: Statement 107. Ó Lochlainn, Colm: Statement 751. Oman, William: Statement 421. Ó Monachain, Ailbhe: Statement 298. O'Mullane, Brigid (Bridie): Statements 450, 485. O'Neill, Edward: Statement 203. Ó Rahilly, Áine: Statement 333. O'Reilly, Eily (née O'Hanrahan): Statements 270, 415. O'Reilly, Michael W.: Statement 886. Ó Riain, Padraig: Statement 98. O'Rourke, Joseph: Statement 1244. O'Shea, James: Statement 733. O'Sullivan, Dermot: Statement 508. O'Sullivan, Séamus: Statement 393. Perolz, Marie (née Flanagan): Statement 246. Plunkett, Grace Gifford: Statement 257. Plunkett, John (Jack): Statements 488, 865. Pounch, Séamus: Statements 267, 294. Prendergast, Seán: Statements 755, 820. Price, Gen. Éamon: Statement 995. Price, Seán: Statement 769. Pugh, Thomas: Statement 397. Quilty, John J.: Statement 516. Reilly, RIC Constable Bernard: Statement 349. Reynolds, Molly: Statement 195. Reynolds, Peter: Statement 350. Rigney, Mary: Statement 752. Robbins, Frank: Statement 585. Robinson, Séamus: Statements 156, 1721, 1722. Rooney, Catherine (née Byrne): Statement 648. Rosney, Joseph: Statement 112. Ryan, Desmond: Statements 724, 725. Ryan, Dr James: Statement 70. Ryan, Máirín (née Cregan): Statement 416. Saurin, Charles: Statement 288. Saurin, Frank: Statement 715. Scollan, John J.: Statements 318, 341. Scully, Thomas: Statement 491. Shelly, Charles: Statement 870. Shouldice, Jack (John F.): Statement 162. Slater, Thomas (Tom): Statement 263. Slattery, James (Jim): Statement 445. Smart, Thomas: Statement 255. Smith, Eugene: Statement 334. Smyth, Patrick: Statement 305. Soughley, Michael T.: Statement 189. Stack, Una: Statements 214, 418. Stafford, Jack: Statement 818. Staines, Michael: Statements 284, 943, 944. Stapleton, William James (Bill): Statement 822. Styles, John J.: Statement 175. Tannam, Liam: Statement 242. Thornton, Dr Brigid (née Lyons): Statement 259. Thornton, Frank: Statements 510, 615. Thornton, Nora: Statement 655. Traynor, Oscar: Statement 340. Twamley, John: Statement 629. Ui Chonnaill, Eilis Bean (née Ryan): Statement 568. Walker, Charles: Statements 241, 266. Walker, Michael: Statement 139. Walpole, R.H. (Harry): Statement 218. Walsh, James and Thomas: Statement 198. Ward, Patrick: Statement 1140. Weston, Charles: Statement 149. Whelan, William: Statement 369. Woods, Mary (née Flannery): Statement 624. Wylie, W.E.: Statement 864. Wyse-Power, Charles: Statement 420. Wyse-Power, Nancy: Statements 541, 587, 732. Young, Thomas: Statement 531.

General Maxwell Report to Field Marshal, Commanding-in-Chief, Home Forces, 25 May 1916.

General Richard Mulcahy Papers, University College Dublin.

New Ireland.

Diarmuid Ó Donnabhain Rossa, 1831–1915: Souvenir of Public Funeral.

Florence O'Donoghue Papers, National Library of Ireland.

Agnes O'Farrelly Papers, University College Library.

The Ó Rahilly (Michael Joseph) Papers, University College Library.

James Pearse Papers, National Library of Ireland.

Patrick Pearse Papers, National Library of Ireland.

Count George Noble Plunkett Papers, National Library of Ireland.

Royal Commission on the Landing of Arms at Howth on 26th July 1914, Report (1914), Cd. 7631.

Royal Commission on the Rebellion in Ireland, Report (1916), Cd. 8279, Minutes of Evidence, Cd. 8311.

Royal Commission on the Arrest and Subsequent Treatment of Mr Francis Sheehy Skeffington, Mr Thomas Dickson and Mr Patrick James McIntyre, Report (29 September 1916), Cd. 8376.

Desmond Ryan Papers, University College Library.

Dr James Ryan Papers, University College Library.

St Enda's School Papers, University College Library.

Sinn Féin.

The Spark.

Austin Stack Papers, National Library of Ireland.

Thom's Irish Almanac and Official Directory.

Trinity College Library, Manuscript Department:

Henry Hanna, a member of the GRs, eyewitness account, MS 10066/192.l.

Elise Mahaffy, 'Ireland in 1916: an account of the Rising in Dublin', MS 2074.

A.A. Luce Papers, MS 4874.

Peadar Ó Cearnaigh, 'Reminiscences of the Irish Republican Brotherhood and Easter Week 1916', MS 3560/1.

Peadar Ó Cearnaigh, 'Founding of the Irish Republican Brotherhood', MS 2560/2.

The Voice of Labour.

The Worker.

The Workers' Republic.

SECONDARY SOURCES

Aan de Wiel, J. 2000 Archbishop Walsh and Mgr Curran's opposition to the British war effort in Dublin, 1914–1918. *Irish Sword* **22** (88).

Aan de Wiel, J. 2003 *The Catholic Church in Ireland 1914–1918*. Dublin.

Aan de Wiel, J. 2004–5 Easter Rising 1916: Count Plunkett's letter to Pope Benedict XV. *Irish Sword* **24**.

Adams, G. 2001 *Who fears to speak? The story of Belfast and the 1916 Rising*. Belfast.

Albert, Fr, OFM Cap. 1926 Seán Heuston's last moments. *Fianna* (May 1926).

Albert, Fr, OFM Cap. 1942 Seán Heuston: how Seán Heuston died. *Capuchin Annual* (1942).

Alberti, J. 1998 *Beyond suffrage: feminists in war and peace, 1914–1928*. Basingstoke.

Alderman, C.L. 1972 *The wearing of the green: the Irish Rebellion, 1916–1921*. New York.

Allen, K. 1990 *The politics of James Connolly*. London.

Aloysius, Fr, OFM Cap. 1942 Easter Week: personal recollections. *Capuchin Annual* (1942).

Andrews, C.S. 1979 *Dublin made me*. Cork.

Anon. 1917 *Arthur Griffith: a study of the founder of Sinn Féin*. Dublin.

Anon. 1926a Easter Week, 1916, special pictorial edition. *An tÓglach*, 26 June 1926.

Anon. 1926b Pictures of Easter Week. *An tÓglach*, 3 July 1926.

Anon. 1926c Éamonn Ceannt's letter. *An tÓglach*, 10 July 1926.

Anderson, W. 1994 *James Connolly and the Irish Left*. Dublin.

'An Rathach' 1948 London Volunteers. *Irish Democrat* (April 1948).

Arthur, Sir G. 1932 *General Sir John Maxwell*. London.

Asquith, Lady C. 1968 *Diaries, 1915–1918*. London.

Bartlett, T. and Jeffrey, K. (eds) 1996 *A military history of Ireland*. Cambridge.

Barton, B. 2002 *From behind a closed door: secret court martial documents of the 1916 Rising*. Belfast.

Bateson, R. 2010 *They died by Pearse's side*. Dublin.

Béaslaí, P. 1926 *Michael Collins and the making of a new Ireland* (2 vols). Dublin.

Béaslaí, P. 1952a The Connolly 'kidnapping'. *Irish Independent*, 24 April 1952.

Béaslaí, P. 1952b The fixing of the date of the 1916 Rising. *Irish Independent*, 24 April 1952.

Béaslaí, P. 1953 The National Army is founded. *Irish Independent*, 5 January 1953.

Béaslaí, P. 1961–5 Moods and memories. *Irish Independent*, October 1961–June 1965.

Beckett, J.C. 1963 *The making of modern Ireland, 1603–1923*. New York.

Bergin, J.J. 1910 *History of the Ancient Order of Hibernians*. Dublin.

Bew, P. 1994 The real importance of Roger Casement. *History Ireland* **2** (2).

Bew, P. 1996 *John Redmond*. Dublin.

Bew, P. 2007 *Ireland: the politics of enmity, 1789–2006*. Oxford.

Birmingham, G.A. 1919 *An Irishman looks at his world*. London.

Birrell, A. 1937 *Things past redress*. London.

Boland, K. 1977 *Up Dev*. Dublin.

Bolger, D. (ed.) 1989 *16 on 16*. Dublin.

Bouch, J.J. 1933 Republican Proclamation of 1916. *Bibliographical Society of Ireland* **5** (3).

Bouchier-Hayes, F. 2008a An Irishman's Diary: Darrell Figgis. *Irish Times*, 21 April 2008.

Bouchier-Hayes, F. 2008b An Irishman's Diary: The Irish Republican Brotherhood. *Irish Times*, 4 August 2008.

Bouchier-Hayes, F. 2008c An Irishman's Diary: Cathal Brugha. *Irish Times*, 18 August 2008.

Bouchier-Hayes, F. 2009 An Irishman's Diary: Bulmer Hobson. *Irish Times*, 11 August 2009.

Bourke, M. 1967 *The Ó Rahilly*. Tralee.

Bourke, M. 1968 Thomas MacDonagh's role in the plans for the 1916 Rising. *Irish Sword* (1968).

Bowen, E. 1951 *The Shelbourne: a centre in Dublin life for more than a century*. London.

Bowman, T. 2002 The Ulster Volunteers 1913–1914: force or farce? *History Ireland* **10** (1).

Boyce, D.G. and Hazelhurst, C. 1977 The unknown chief secretary. *Irish Historical Studies* **20** (79).

Boyle, A. 1977 *The riddle of Erskine Childers*. London.

Boyle, J.F. 1916 *The Irish rebellion of 1916*. London.

Boyle, J.W. 1967 Irish Labour and the Rising. *Éire-Ireland* **2**.

Boyle, J.W. 1986 *Leaders and workers*. Cork.

Bradbridge, Lt Col. E.U. 1928 *Fifty-ninth Division, 1915–1918, a compilation*. Chesterfield.

Brasier, A. and Kelly, J. 2000 *Harry Boland: a man divided*. Dublin.

Brennan, J. 1958 The Castle Document. *Irish Times*, 28 March 1958.

Brennan, J. 1966 Mendicity Institution area. *Capuchin Annual* (1966).

Brennan, L.M. 1926 We surrender. *An tÓglach*, 12 June 1926.

Brennan-Whitmore, W.J. 1917 *With the Irish in Frongoch*. Dublin.

Brennan-Whitmore, W.J. 1926a How the Irish troops took the GPO. *An tÓglach*, 16 January 1926.

Brennan-Whitmore, W.J. 1926b The occupation of the North Earl Street area. *An tÓglach*, 30 January and 6 February 1926.

Brennan-Whitmore, W.J. 1926c In captivity with the Irish in Frongoch. *An tÓglach*, 28 August–25 December 1926.

Brennan-Whitmore, W.J. 1953 My part in the Easter Rising. *Irish Weekly Independent*,

6 August–3 September 1953.

Brennan-Whitmore, W.J. 1966 How long could they hold out? *Irish Independent*, 11 April 1966.

Brennan-Whitmore, W.J. 1996 *Dublin burning: the Easter Rising from behind the barricades.* Dublin.

Brewer, J.D. 1990 *The Royal Irish Constabulary: an oral history.* Belfast.

Briollay, S. [writing as Roger Chauvire] 1922 *Ireland in rebellion.* Dublin.

Browne, Revd P. (ed.) 1917 *Aftermath of Easter Week.*

Brugha, M. MacSwiney 2005 *History's daughter.* Dublin.

Burke, J.J. 1926 The Citizen Army in 1916. *An tÓglach,* 20 February 1926.

Burke, T. 2005 The other women of 1916. *20th Century Social Perspectives, 20th Century Contemporary History* 5.

Butler, R.M. 1916 The reconstruction of O'Connell Street. *Studies: The Irish Jesuit Quarterly Review* 5.

Callan, P. 1987 Recruiting for the British Army in Ireland during the First World War. *Irish Sword* 17 (66), 42–56.

Callender, I. 1939 A diary of Easter Week. *Dublin Brigade Review* (1939).

Campbell, Cmdt L. 2006a A military analysis of the Rising. *An Cosantóir* (April/May 2006).

Campbell, Cmdt L. 2006b A tale of two soldiers. *An Cosantóir* (April/May 2006).

Canavan, T. 2006 Pearse Museum. *History Ireland* 14 (2).

Cardozo, N. 1979 *Maud Gonne.* London.

Carroll, F.M. 1978 *American opinion and the Irish question, 1910–1923.* Dublin.

Carty, J. 1951 *Ireland—from the Great Famine to the Treaty of 1921.* Dublin.

Carty, X. 1978 *In bloody protest: the tragedy of Patrick Pearse.* Dublin.

Casement, Sir R. 1914 *Ireland, Germany and the freedom of the seas.* New York.

Casement, Sir R. 1958 *The crime against Europe* (ed. H.O. Mackey). Dublin.

Caulfield, M. 1995 *The Easter Rebellion, Dublin 1916.* Dublin.

Ceannt, Á. 1946 Looking back to Easter Week. *The Leader*, 20 April 1946.

Ceannt, É. 1914 The founding of the Irish Volunteers. *Irish Volunteer*, 20 June 1914.

Chatterton, E.K. 1934 *Danger zone: the story of the Queenstown command.* London.

Clare, A. 2011 *Unlikely rebels: the Gifford girls and the fight for Irish freedom.* Cork.

Clarke, K. 1997 *Revolutionary woman. My fight for Ireland's freedom* (ed. H. Litton). Dublin.

Clarke, T. 1970 *Glimpses of an Irish felon's prison life* (with foreword by P.S. O'Hegarty). Cork.

Clery, A.E. 1917 Pearse, MacDonagh and Plunkett: an appreciation. *Studies: The Irish Jesuit Quarterly Review* 6.

Clery, A.E. 1919 The Gaelic League, 1893–1919. *Studies: The Irish Jesuit Quarterly Review* 8.

Clery, A.E. 1922 A review of Pearse's political writings and speeches. *Studies: The Irish Jesuit Quarterly Review* 11.

Clifford, B. 1997 *War, insurrection and election in Ireland, 1914–21*. Belfast.

Clifford, B. 2002 *Casement as traitor patriot*. London.

Coady, S. 1966 Remembering St John's Convent. *Capuchin Annual* (1966).

Coakley, J. 1983 Patrick Pearse and the 'noble lie' of Irish nationalism. *Studies in Conflict and Violence* 62.

Coates, T. (ed.) 2000 *The Irish uprising, 1914–1921: papers from the British Parliamentary Archive*. London.

Coffey, T.M. 1969 *Agony at Easter*. London.

'Coilin' 1917 *Patrick H. Pearse: a sketch of his life*. Dublin.

Colgan, P. 1926 The Maynooth Volunteers in 1916. *An tÓglach*, 8 May 1926.

Collins, L. 2012 *16 Lives: James Connolly*. Dublin.

Collins, L., Kostick, C. and MacThomais, S. 2004 Tragedy in the Connolly family. *History Ireland* 12 (3).

Collins, S. 1997 *The Cosgrave legacy*. Dublin.

Colum, P. 1931 The career of Roger Casement. *Dublin Magazine* (October–December 1931).

Colum, P. 1959 *Arthur Griffith*. Dublin.

Comerford, A. 1969 *The Easter Rising, Dublin 1916*. New York.

Comerford, M. 1986 Women in struggle. In P. McGlynn (ed.), *Eiri amach na casca*. Dublin.

Conlon, L. 1969 *Cumann na mBan and the women of Ireland, 1913–1972*. Kilkenny.

Connell, J.E.A. Jnr 2006 *Where's where in Dublin: a directory of historic locations 1913–1923*. Dublin.

Connell, J.E.A. Jnr 2009 *Dublin in rebellion*. Dublin.

Connell, J.E.A. Jnr 2011a The Proclamation of the Irish Republic. *History Ireland* 19 (1).

Connell, J.E.A. Jnr 2011b Role of the GAA in formation of nationalism. *History Ireland* 19 (2).

Connell, J.E.A. Jnr 2011c St Enda's School/St Ita's School. *History Ireland* 19 (3).

Connell, J.E.A. Jnr 2011d The Irish Republican Brotherhood. *History Ireland* 19 (6).

Connell, J.E.A. Jnr 2012a Tom Clarke's return to Ireland. *History Ireland* 20 (1).

Connell, J.E.A. Jnr 2012b Home Rule rally on O'Connell Street, March 1912. *History Ireland* 20 (2).

Connell, J.E.A. Jnr 2012c Liberty Hall. *History Ireland* 20 (3).

Connell, J.E.A. Jnr 2012d Reaction to Home Rule in Ulster and the Ulster Covenant. *History Ireland* 20 (5).

Connell, J.E.A. Jnr 2012e Fianna na hÉireann. *History Ireland* 20 (6).

Connell, J.E.A. Jnr 2013a Irish Women's Franchise League/Irish Women's Workers'

Union. *History Ireland* **21** (1).

Connell, J.E.A. Jnr 2013b 'A Soldier's Song'/*Amhrán na bhFiann*. *History Ireland* **21** (2).

Connell, J.E.A. Jnr 2013c Founding of Cumann na mBan. *History Ireland* **21** (3).

Connell, J.E.A. Jnr 2013d Founding of the Irish Citizen Army. *History Ireland* **21** (5).

Connell, J.E.A. Jnr 2013e Founding of the Irish Volunteers. *History Ireland* **21** (6).

Connell, J.E.A. Jnr 2014a Larne landing of weapons. *History Ireland* **22** (2).

Connell, J.E.A. Jnr 2014b Howth/Kilcoole landing of weapons. *History Ireland* **22** (3).

Connolly, J. 1898 *The workers' republic*. Dublin.

Connolly, J. [writing as 'Setanta'] 1899 The Mendicity and its guests. *Workers' Republic*, 27 August 1899.

Connolly, J. 1913 Arms and the man. *Irish Worker*, 13 December 1913.

Connolly, J. 1915 *The re-conquest of Ireland*. Dublin.

Connolly, J. 1916a The programme of Labour. *Workers' Republic*, 19 January 1916.

Connolly, J. 1916b Cannon fodder for British imperialism. *Workers' Republic*, 12 February 1916.

Connolly, J. 1916c We will rise again. *Workers' Republic*, 25 March 1916.

Connolly, J. 1916d The call to arms. *Workers' Republic*, 1 April 1916.

Connolly, J. 1916e The Irish flag. *Workers' Republic*, 8 April 1916.

Connolly, J. 1916f Labour and Ireland. *Workers' Republic*, 22 April 1916.

Connolly, J. and De Leon, D. (n.d.) *Connolly/De Leon Controversy on Wages, Marriage and the Church* (undated pamphlet).

Connolly, J. and Walker, W. (n.d.) *The Connolly/Walker Controversy on Socialist Unity in Ireland* (undated pamphlet). Cork.

Connolly, J. 1949 *Labour and Easter Week: a selection from the writings of James Connolly* (ed. D. Ryan). Dublin.

Connolly, L. 2002 [2003] *The Irish women's movement*. New York [Dublin].

Connolly, M. 1952 James Connolly: socialist and patriot. *Studies: The Irish Jesuit Quarterly Review* **41**.

Connolly, M. 1966 City Hall area. *Capuchin Annual* (1966).

Connolly, N. 1918 *The Irish rebellion of 1916, or, The unbroken tradition*. New York.

Connolly, N. (O'Brien) 1975 *Portrait of a rebel father*. Dublin and London.

Connolly, N. (O'Brien) 1981 *We shall rise again*. London.

Connolly-Heron, I. 1966a James Connolly, the search for roots. *Liberty* (May 1966).

Connolly-Heron, I. 1966b James Connolly—a biography. *Liberty* (August 1966).

Conroy, J. 2005 The Plough and Stars: sixteen characters in search of analysis. *Red Banner* **21**.

Coogan, O. 2013 *Politics and war in Meath—1913–1923*. Meath County Council.

Coogan, T.P. 1966 *Ireland since the Rising*. London.

Coogan, T.P. 1990 *Michael Collins*. London.

Coogan, T.P. 1993 *De Valera: Long Fellow, long shadow.* London.

Coogan, T.P. 2001 *1916: the Easter Rising.* London.

Cooke, P. 1986 *Scéal Scoil Éanna.* Dublin.

Cooney, A. 1930 The Marrowbone Lane Post. *An Phoblacht,* 26 May 1930.

Corkery, D. (n.d.) *What's this about the G.A.A.?* (undated pamphlet).

Cornish, V. 1916 The strategic geography of the British Empire. *Royal Colonial Institute Journal* (February 1916).

Costello, F. 2003 *The Irish Revolution and its aftermath, 1916–1923.* Dublin.

Cottrell, P. 2006 *The Anglo-Irish War: the Troubles of 1913–1922.* Oxford.

Coulter, C. 1993 *The hidden tradition: feminism, women, and nationalism in Ireland.* Cork.

Courtney, D.A. 1916 [1980] *Reminiscences of the Easter Rising.* Nenagh.

Cowell, J. 1997 *Dublin's famous people and where they lived.* Dublin.

Cowell, J. 2005 *A noontide blazing. Brigid Lyons Thornton: rebel, soldier, doctor.* Dublin.

Coxhead, E. 1965 *Daughters of Erin.* London.

Coyle, E. 1933 The History of Cumann na mBan. *An Phoblacht,* 8 April 1933.

Crawford, F. 1947 *Guns for Ulster.* Belfast.

Creel, G. 1919 *Ireland's fight for freedom.* New York.

Cronin, S. 1966 *Our own red blood: the story of the 1916 Rising.* Dublin.

Cronin, S. 1972 *The McGarrity Papers.* Tralee.

Cronin, S. 1978 *Young Connolly.* Dublin.

Cuffe, T.S. 1942 They lit a torch. *Capuchin Annual* (1942).

Cullen, C. (ed.) 2013 *The world upturning: Elsie Henry's Irish wartime diaries, 1913–1919.* Dublin.

Cullen, M. and Luddy, M. (eds) 1995 *Women, power and consciousness.* Dublin.

Cullen, M. and Luddy, M. 2001 *Female activists: Irish women and the change, 1900–1960.* Dublin.

Curran, C.P. 1966 Griffith, MacNeill and Pearse. *Studies: The Irish Jesuit Quarterly Review* (Spring 1966).

Curran, J. 1975 The decline and fall of the I.R.B. *Éire-Ireland* **10** (1).

Curry, C.E. 1922 *Sir Roger Casement's diaries.* Munich.

Czira, S.G. 1974 *The years flew by.* Dublin.

Dalton, C. 1929 *With the Dublin Brigade.* London.

Daly, D. 1974 *The young Douglas Hyde.* Dublin.

Daly, M.E. (ed.) 2006 *Roger Casement in Irish and world history.* Dublin.

Daly, M.E. and O'Callaghan, M. (eds) 2007 *1916 in 1966: commemorating the Easter Rising.* Dublin.

D'Arcy, W. 1947 *The Fenian Movement in the United States.* Washington, DC.

Dargan, P. 2005–6 The Fianna Eireann and the War of Independence—a personal experience. *Irish Sword* **25**.

Davison, J. 2005 Feature: Remembering James Connolly. *An Phoblacht,* 9 May 2005.

Deasy, J. 1963 [2004] *The fiery cross: the story of Jim Larkin*. Dublin.

De Barra, É. 1969 A valiant woman: Margaret Mary Pearse. *Capuchin Annual* (1969).

De Blacam, A. 1918 *Towards the Republic*. Dublin.

De Blaghd, E. 1962 Ireland in 1915. *An tÓglach* **1** (5).

DeBurca, M. 1980 *The G.A.A.: a history of the Gaelic Athletic Association*. Dublin.

De Burca, S. 1958 *The Soldier's Song: the story of Peadar Kearney*. Dublin.

Deeney, A.T. 2001 What effects did Eoin MacNeill's Countermanding Order have on the Easter Rising in 1916? Unpublished MA thesis, University of Ulster.

Dempsey, J. 1993 Jennie Wyse Power, 1858–1941. Unpublished MA thesis, St Patrick's College, Maynooth.

Denieffe, J. 1906 [1969] *A personal narrative of the Fenian Brotherhood (Irish Republican Brotherhood)*. New York [Dublin].

Denman, T. 1994 'The Red Livery of Shame': the campaign against army recruitment in Ireland, 1899–1914. *Irish Historical Studies* **29** (114).

Dennis, A. 1942 A memory of P.H. Pearse. *The Capuchin Annual* (1942).

De Paor, L. 1997 *On the Easter Proclamation and other declarations*. Dublin.

Depuis, N. 2009 *Mna na hÉireann: the women who shaped Ireland*. Cork.

Derwin, D. 2000 The taming of Jim Larkin. *Red Banner* **2**.

Desmond, S. 1923 *The drama of Sinn Féin*. London.

Devine, F. (ed.) 2013 *A capital in conflict: Dublin City and the 1913 Lockout*. Dublin.

Devine, F. and O'Riordan, M. 2006 *James Connolly, Liberty Hall, and 1916*. Dublin.

Devoy, J. 1929 *Recollections of an Irish rebel*. New York.

Dillon, G.P. 1936a Casement and Easter Week. *Irish Press*, 3 January 1936.

Dillon, G.P. 1936b How much did the Castle know? *Irish Press*, 14 January 1936.

Dillon, G.P. 1958 Joseph Plunkett: origin and background. *University Review* (1958).

Dillon, G.P. 1960 The Irish Republican Brotherhood. *University Review* **2** (9).

Dillon, G.P. 1968 Joseph Plunkett's diary of his journey to Germany. *University Review* (1968).

Dillon, G.P. 2007 *All in the blood: a memoir of the Plunkett family, the 1916 Rising, and the War of Independence* (ed. H. O'Brolchain). Dublin.

Doerries, R. 2000 *Prelude to the Easter Rising: Sir Roger Casement in Imperial Germany*. London.

Doherty, G. and Keogh, D. 2003 *De Valera's Ireland*. Cork.

Doherty, G. and Keogh, D. (eds) 2007 *1916. The long revolution*. Cork.

Doherty, S. 1995 Elizabeth O'Farrell and the women of 1916. Unpublished MA thesis, National University of Ireland.

Doherty, S. 1998 Will the real James Connolly please stand up? *International Socialism* **80**.

Donnelly, N. 1930 With the Citizen's Army in Stephen's Green. *An Phoblacht*, 19 April 1930.

Donnelly, S. 1917 Mount Street Bridge. *Catholic Bulletin* (October 1917).

Donnelly, S. 1922 With the 3rd Battalion. *Poblacht na hÉireann*, 20 April 1922.

Doolan, J. 1918 The South Dublin Union [a four-part account]. *Catholic Bulletin* (March, April, May and June 1918).

Dooley, P. 1944 *Under the banner of Connolly*. London.

Dore, É. 1968 Seán MacDermott as I knew him. *Leitrim Guardian*, Christmas 1968.

[Douglas, Harry] 2005–6 The 1916 diary of 2nd Lieutenant Harry Douglas, Sherwood Foresters. *Irish Sword* **25**.

Doyle, J., Clarke, F., Connaughton, E. and Somerville, O. 2002 *An introduction to the Bureau of Military History, 1913–1921*. Dublin.

Doyle, K. 2007 A revolutionary misfit: Jack White. *Red Banner* **24**.

Doyle, S. 1932 With Pearse in Arbour Hill. *Irish Press*, 3 May 1932.

Duff, C. 1966 *Six days to shake an empire*. London.

Duff, D. 1934 *Sword for hire*. London.

Duff, D. 1940 *The rough with the smooth*. London.

Duffy, J. 2013 Children of the Revolution. *History Ireland* **21** (3).

Duggan, J.P. 1966 Asserting it in arms. *An Cosantóir* **26**.

Duggan, J.P. 1970 German arms and the 1916 Rising. *An Cosantóir* **30**.

Duggan, J.P. 1995 Poltergeist pistol. *History Ireland* **3**.

Dunleavy, M. 2002 *Dublin barracks*. Dublin.

Dunsany, Lord 1939 Recollections of 1916. *Irish Digest* (April 1939).

Durney, J. 2004 *The Volunteer: uniforms, weapons, and history of the Irish Republican Army, 1913–1917*. Naas.

Dwane, D.T. 1922 *The early life of Éamon de Valera*. Dublin.

Dwyer, T.R. 1980 *Éamon de Valera*. Dublin.

Dwyer, T.R. 2014 *Thomas MacDonagh*. Dublin.

Ebenezer, L. 2006 *Fron-Goch and the birth of the IRA*. Llanrwst.

Edmunds, Capt. G.J. 1960 *The 2/6th Battalion: the Sherwood Foresters, 1914–1918*. Chesterfield.

Edwards, O.D. 1987 *Éamon de Valera*. Cardiff.

Edwards, O.D. and Pyle, F. (eds) 1968 *1916: the Easter Rising*. London.

Edwards, O.D. and Ransom, B. (eds) 1973 *James Connolly: selected political writings*. London.

Edwards, R.D. 1977 *Patrick Pearse: the triumph of failure*. London.

Edwards, R.D. 1981 *James Connolly*. Dublin.

Ellis, P.B. (ed.) 1973 *James Connolly: selected writings*. Harmondsworth.

Enright, S. 2014 *Easter Rising, 1916—the trials*. Dublin.

Ervine, St J. 1917 The story of the Irish rebellion. *Century Magazine* (1917).

Fallon, D. 2014 *The Pillar: the life and afterlife of the Nelson Pillar*. Dublin.

Fallon, L. 2013 *Dublin Fire Brigade and the Irish Revolution*. Dublin.

Fanning, R. 2013 *Fatal path: British government and Irish revolution 1910–1922*. London.

Feeney, B. 2014 *Seán MacDiarmada*. Dublin.

Feeney, T. 2008 *Seán MacEntee: a political life*. Dublin.

Ferguson, S. 2014 *The GPO: 200 years of history*. Cork.

Figgis, D. 1917 *A chronicle of jails*. Dublin.

Figgis, D. 1924 *Recollections of the Irish war*. London.

Fingall, Elizabeth, Countess of 1937 [1991] *Seventy years young*. London [Dublin].

Finnan, J.P. 2004 *John Redmond and Irish unity, 1912–1918*. Syracuse, NY.

Fitzgerald, D. 1939 *Prelude to statescraft*. London.

Fitzgerald, D. 1966 Inside the GPO. *Irish Times Supplement*, 7 April 1966.

Fitzgerald, D. 1968 *Desmond's Rising*. Dublin.

Fitzgerald, G. 1966 The significance of 1916. *Studies: The Irish Jesuit Quarterly Review* (Spring 1966).

Fitzgerald, W.D. (ed.) (n.d.) The historic Rising of Easter Week, 1916. *The Voice of Ireland* (undated).

Fitzgibbon, C. 2004a Easter 1916, Part I. *An Phoblacht*, 5 April 2004.

Fitzgibbon, C. 2004b Easter 1916, Part II. *An Phoblacht*, 7 April 2004.

Fitzgibbon, S. 1949 The Easter Rising from the inside. *Irish Times*, 18–21 April 1949.

Fitzhenry, E.C. 1935 *Nineteen sixteen—an anthology*. Dublin.

Fitzpatrick, D. 1986 *Ireland and the First World War*. Dublin.

Fitzpatrick, D. 2002 'Decidedly a personality': de Valera's performance as a convict, 1916–1917. *History Ireland* **10** (2).

Fitzpatrick, D. 2003 *Harry Boland's Irish revolution*. Cork.

Flanagan, Fr J. 1918 The General Post Office area. *Catholic Bulletin* (August 1918).

Fletcher, A. 2006 A young nationalist in the Easter Rising. *History Today* **56** (4).

Fox, R.M. 1935 *Rebel Irishwomen*. Dublin and Cork.

Fox, R.M. 1938 *Green banners: the story of the Irish struggle*. London.

Fox, R.M. 1946 *James Connolly, the forerunner*. Tralee.

Fox, R.M. 1947 How the women helped. In The Kerryman, *Dublin's fighting story 1916–1921, told by the men who made it*. Tralee.

Fox, R.M. 2014 [1944] *History of the Irish Citizen Army*. Dublin.

Foy, M.T. and Barton, B. 1999 *The Easter Rising*. Stroud.

French, G. 1931 *The life of Field Marshal Sir John French*. London.

Gallagher, F. [writing as David Hogan] 1953 *The four glorious years*. Dublin.

Gallagher, M. 2014 *Éamonn Ceannt*. Dublin.

Garnham, N. 2004 Accounting for the early success of the Gaelic Athletic Association. *Irish Historical Studies* **34** (133).

Garvin, T. 1986 The anatomy of a nationalist revolution: Ireland, 1858–1928. *Contemporary Studies in Society and History* (July 1986).

Gaughan, J.A. 1977 *Austin Stack: portrait of a separatist*. Dublin.

Gerson, G. 1995 Cultural subversion and the background of the Irish 'Easter Poets'. *Journal of Contemporary History* **30** (2).

Gibbon, M. 1966 Murder in Portobello Barracks. *Dublin Magazine* **5**.

Gibney, J. 2013 *Seán Heuston*. Dublin.

Gilley, S. 1986 Pearse's sacrifice: Christ and Cuchulainn crucified and risen in the Easter Rising, 1916. In Y. Alexander and A. O'Day (eds), *Ireland's terrorist dilemma*. Dartrecht.

Gillis, E. 2013 *Revolution in Dublin: a photographic history 1913–1923*. Cork.

Gillis, L. 2014 *Women of the Irish revolution: a photographic history*. Cork.

Gilmore, G. (n.d.) *The relevance of James Connolly in Ireland today*. Dublin.

Ginnell, L. 1918 *D.O.R.A. at Westminster*. Dublin.

Githens-Mazer, J. 2006 *Myths and memories of the Easter Rising: cultural and political nationalism in Ireland*. Dublin.

Goldring, D. [writing as 'An Englishman'] 1917 *Dublin explorations and reflections*. Dublin.

Golway, T. 1998 *Irish rebel: John Devoy and America's fight for Irish freedom*. New York.

Good, J. 1996 *Enchanted by dreams: the journal of a revolutionary* (ed. M. Good). Tralee.

Gray, B. [E.] 1948 A memory of Easter Week. *Capuchin Annual* (1948).

Greaves, C.D. 1961 *The life and times of James Connolly*. London.

Greaves, C.D. 1968 James Connolly, Marxist. *Marxism Today* (June 1968).

Greaves, C.D. 1982 *The Irish Transport and General Workers' Union: the formative years: 1909–1923*. Dublin.

Greaves, C.D. 1991 *1916 as history: the myth of the blood sacrifice*. Dublin.

Green, A.S. 1922 Arthur Griffith. *Studies: The Irish Jesuit Quarterly Review* **11**.

Gregory, P. 1917 Poets of the insurrection: John F. MacEntee. *Studies: The Irish Jesuit Quarterly Review* **6**.

Grenan, J. 1916 After the surrender. *Wolfe Tone Annual*, Special 1916 Edition.

Grenan, J. 1917a Events of Easter Week. *Catholic Bulletin* (June 1917).

Grenan, J. 1917b Story of the surrender. *Catholic Bulletin* (June 1917).

Griffith, A. 1904 *The resurrection of Hungary: a parallel for Ireland*. Dublin.

Griffith, K. and O'Grady, T. (eds) 2002 *Ireland's unfinished revolution: an oral history*. Boulder, CO. [First published as *Curious journey: an oral history of Ireland's unfinished revolution* (London, 1982).]

Grob-Fitzgibbon, B. 2008 *Turning points of the Irish Revolution: the British government, intelligence and the cost of indifference, 1912–1921*. Dublin.

Gunther, J. 1936 Inside de Valera. *Harper's Magazine* (August 1936).

Gwynn, D. 1923 Patrick Pearse. *Dublin Review* (January–March 1923).

Gwynn, D. 1931 *The life and death of Roger Casement*. London.

Gwynn, D. 1932 *The life of John Redmond*. London.

Gwynn, D. 1933 *De Valera*. London.

Gwynn, D. 1948 *Young Ireland*. Cork.

Gwynn, D. 1950 *The history of Partition, 1912–1925*. Dublin.

Hadden, P. 1986 *Divide and rule*. London and Dublin.

Hall, W.G. 1920 *The Green Triangle: being the history of the 2/5th Battalion The Sherwood Foresters (Notts & Derby Regiment) in the Great European War, 1914–1918*. Garden City.

Hally, Col. P.J. 1966 The Easter Rising in Dublin: a military evaluation of Easter Week. *An Cosantóir* **7** (29).

Hally, Gen. P.J. 1966–7 The Easter Rising in Dublin, the military aspects (Parts 1 and 2). *Irish Sword* **7** (29) (1966) and **8** (30) (1967).

Hartnett, S. 1971 Comradeship Kilmainham. *Irish Press*, 30 December 1971.

Haswell, J. 1973 *Citizen armies*. London.

Haverty, A. 1988 *Countess Markievicz: an independent life*. London.

Hay, M. 2005 Bulmer Hobson: the rise and fall of an Irish nationalist, 1900–16. Unpublished Ph.D thesis, University College Dublin.

Hay, M. 2009 *Bulmer Hobson and the nationalist movement in twentieth-century Ireland*. Manchester.

Haydon, A. 1976 *Sir Matthew Nathan*. Queensland.

Hayes, A. (ed.) 2000 *The years flew by: recollections of Madame Sydney Gifford Czira*. Galway.

Hayes, A. and Urquhart, D. 2001 *The Irish women's history reader*. London.

Hayes, J. 1919 *Patrick H. Pearse: storyteller*. Dublin.

Hayes-McCoy, G.A. (ed.) 1964 *The Irish at war*. Cork.

Headlam, M. 1947 *Irish reminiscences*. London.

Hearn, D. 1992 The *Irish Citizen*, 1914–1916: nationalism, feminism, militarism. *Canadian Journal of Irish Studies* **18** (1).

Hegarty, P. 2010 *The Easter Rising: a momentous week in Irish history seen through the eyes of a young boy*. Dublin.

Hegarty, S. and O'Toole, F. 2006 *The* Irish Times *Book of the 1916 Rising*. Dublin.

Helferty, S. 2006 1916 in the de Valera Papers. *History Ireland* **14** (2).

Henry, R.M. 1922 Arthur Griffith. *Studies: The Irish Jesuit Quarterly Review* **11**.

Henry, W. 2005 *Supreme sacrifice: the story of Éamonn Ceannt, 1881–1916*. Cork.

Henry, W. 2014 *John MacBride*. Dublin.

Hepburn, A.C. 1998 *Ireland, 1905–1925. Volume II*. Newtownards.

Herlihy, J. 1997 *The Royal Irish Constabulary*. Dublin.

Herlihy, J. 2001 *The Dublin Metropolitan Police: a complete alphabetical list of officers and men, 1836–1925*. Dublin.

Heuston, J.M. 1966 *Headquarters Battalion, Army of the Irish Republic, Easter Week 1916*. Carlow.

Higgins, R. 2013 *Transforming 1916: meaning, memory and lore of the fiftieth anniversary of the Easter rising.* Cork.

Higgins, R. and Ui Chollatain, R. (eds) 2009 *The life and after-life of P.H. Pearse.* Dublin.

Higgins, R., Holohan, C. and O'Donnell, C. 2006 1966 and all that. *History Ireland* **14** (2).

Hill, M. 2003 *Women in Ireland.* Belfast.

Hobson, B. 1918 *A short history of the Irish Volunteers, 1913–1916.* Dublin.

Hobson, B. 1931 The origin of Óglaigh na hÉireann. *An tÓglach* (June 1931).

Hobson, B. 1968 *Ireland, yesterday and tomorrow.* Tralee.

Hoff, J. and Coulter, M. (eds) 1995 Irish women's voices: past and present. *Journal of Women's History* **6** (4) and **7** (1).

Hoff, M. 2006 The foundations of the Fenian uprising. Senior thesis, United States Military Academy.

Hoff, M. 2007 A successful failure: the catalyst of the 1916 Easter Rising. MA thesis, United States Military Academy.

Holohan, P. 1942 Four Courts area. *Capuchin Annual* (1942).

Holt, E. 1960 *Protest in arms: the Irish Troubles, 1916–1923.* London.

Hopkinson, M. (ed.) 1998 *Frank Henderson's Easter Rising: recollections of a Dublin Volunteer.* Cork.

Horgan, J.J. 1948 *Parnell to Pearse.* Dublin.

Horgan, J.J. 1997 *Lemass.* Dublin.

Hourihane, A.M. 2014 Children of the Revolution. *Irish Times*, 21 March 2014.

Hoy, H.C. 1932 *40 O.B. or How the war was won.* London.

Hughes, B. 2012 *Michael Mallin.* Dublin.

Humphreys, R. 1966 A rebel's diary. *The Belvederian* (Belvedere College Annual) **25** (2).

Hunt, G. 2009 *Blood upon the rose. Easter 1916: the rebellion that set Ireland free.* Dublin.

Hyland, J.L. 1997 *Life and times of James Connolly.* Dundalk.

Igoe, V. 2001 *Dublin burial grounds and graveyards.* Dublin.

Ireland, J. de Courcy 1966 *The sea and the 1916 Rising.* Dublin.

Irish Life 1916 The record of the Irish rebellion of 1916 [pamphlet].

Irish Republican Digest 1965 *Irish Republican Digest, featuring the Rising of 1916, Book 1.* National Publications Committee, Cork.

Irish Times 1917 [1998] *1916 Rebellion handbook.* Dublin.

Jackson, A. 1993 Larne gunrunning, 1914. *History Ireland* **1** (1).

Jackson, A. 2004 *Home Rule, an Irish history 1800–2000.* Oxford.

James, L. 1994 *The rise and fall of the British Empire.* London.

James, W. 1956 *The code breakers of Room 40: the story of Admiral Sir William Hall, genius of British counter-intelligence.* New York.

Jamie, Lt Col. J.P.W. 1931 *The 177th Brigade, 1914–1918*. Leicester.

Jeffery, K. 1994 Irish culture and the Great War. *Bullan* (1994).

Jeffery, K. (ed.) 1999 *The Sinn Féin Rising as they saw it* [incorporating *The Sinn Féin Rising as I saw it* by M. Norway and *Experiences in war* by A. Hamilton Norway]. Dublin.

Jeffrey, K. 2000 *Ireland and the Great War*. Cambridge.

Jenkins, R. 1964 *Asquith*. London.

Johnson, T. 1918 *A handbook for rebels: a guide to successful defiance of the British government*. Dublin.

Johnston, A., Larragy, J. and McWilliams, E. 1990 *Connolly: a Marxist analysis*. Dublin.

Jones, F.P. 1917 *History of the Sinn Féin movement and the Irish rebellion of 1916*. New York.

Jones, M. 1988 *These obstreperous lassies: a history of the Irish Women Workers' Union*. Dublin.

Jordan, A. 1991 *Major John MacBride: MacDonagh and MacBride, Connolly and Pearse*. Westport.

Joy, M. (ed.) 1916 [2007] *The Irish rebellion of 1916 and its martyrs: Erin's tragic Easter*. New York.

Joyce, J. 2009 June 30th, 1915: O'Donovan Rossa's death famous for oratory at grave. *Irish Times*, 29 June 2009.

Joyce, J.V. 1926 Easter Week, 1916: the defence of the South Dublin Union. *An tÓglach,* 12 June 1926.

Joyce, M. 1966 The story of Limerick and Kerry in 1916. *Capuchin Annual* (1966).

Joye, T. 1996 The American Civil War and Irish nationalism. *History Ireland* **4** (2).

Joye, L. 2010 TSS *Helga*. *History Ireland* **18** (2).

Joye, L. and Malone, B. 2006 The Roll of Honour of 1916. *History Ireland* **14** (2).

Kain, R. 1980 A diary of Easter Week: one Dubliner's experience. *Irish University Review* **10**.

Kavanaugh, Sub-Lt P. 1966 John Mitchel's place in Irish military thinking. *An Cosantóir* **26**.

Kautt, W.H. 1999 *The Anglo-Irish War, 1916–1921*. Westport, CT, and London.

Kearns, L. 1922 *In times of peril*. Dublin.

Kee, R. 1972 *The green flag* [combining three separate volumes entitled *The most distressful country*, *The bold Fenian men* and *Ourselves alone*]. London.

Keith, J. 2006 *The GPO and the Easter Rising*. Dublin.

Kelly, M. 2006 *The Fenian ideal and Irish nationalism, 1882–1916*. Dublin.

Kelly, M. 2008 Nationalism's pilot light? *History Ireland* **16** (6).

Kelly, P. 1966 The women of Easter Week: Helena Molony. *Evening Herald*, 31 March 1966.

Kelly, S. [published anonymously] 1916 *Pictorial review of 1916*. Dublin.

Kelly, T. 1942 I remember. *Capuchin Annual* (1942).

Kendall, T. 2013 Lost memoir tells how James Connolly returned to his faith before execution. *Irish Independent*, 25 May 2013.

Kenna, S. 2014 *16 Lives: Thomas MacDonagh*. Dublin.

Kennedy, C.M. 2003 Genesis of the rising, 1912–1916: a transformation of nationalist opinion? Unpublished Ph.D thesis, University College Cork.

Kennerk, B. 2012 *Moore Street—the story of Dublin's market district*. Cork.

Kennerk, B. 2013 Compensating for the Rising. *History Ireland* **21** (2).

Kenny, M. 1993 *The road to freedom: photographs and memorabilia from the 1916 Rising and afterwards*. Dublin.

Keny, C. 2012 Face of hope for all that might have been. *Sunday Independent*, 8 January 2012.

Keogh, D. 1978 William Martin Murphy and the origins of the 1913 Lockout. *Saothar* **4**.

Keohane, L. 2015 *Captain Jack White: imperialism, anarchism and the Irish Citizen Army*. Dublin.

Kerryman, The 1947 *Dublin's fighting story, 1916–1921: told by the men who made it*. Tralee.

Kilcullen, J. 1967 Appreciation: Headmaster of St Enda's. *Éire-Ireland* (Summer 1967).

Killeen, R. 1995 *The Easter Rising*. Hove.

Kostick, C. 2013 James Connolly in the Bureau of Military History. *Irish Marxist Review* **1** (5).

Kostick, C. 2014 *Michael O'Hanrahan*. Dublin.

Kostick, C. and Collins, L. 2000 *The Easter Rising: a guide to Dublin in 1916*. Dublin.

Laing, Cmdt V., Donovan, Sgt C. and Manning, Pte A. 2006 The Ashbourne engagement. *An Cosantóir* (April/May 2006).

Larkin, E. 1965 *James Larkin: Irish Labour, 1876–1947*. London.

Larkin, F.M. 2006 A great daily organ: *The Freeman's Journal*, 1763–1924. *History Ireland* **14** (3).

Larkin, J. Jnr (n.d.) *In the footsteps of Big Jim: a family biography*. Dublin.

Lawless, Cmdt F. 2006 Personal recollections: Ashbourne. *An Cosantóir* (April/May 2006).

Lawless, Col. J.V. 1926 Ashbourne. *An tÓglach* **5** (4) (31 July 1926).

Lawless, Col. J.V. 1941–2 Ashbourne. *An Cosantóir* **1** (24 and 25) (1941) and **2** (11) (1942).

Lawless, Col. J.V. 1946 Thomas Ashe. *An Cosantóir* (November 1946).

Lawless, Col. J.V. 1966 The fight at Ashbourne. *Capuchin Annual* (1966).

Lawless, Col. J.V. 2006 From the archives: a contemporary view. *An Cosantóir* (April/May 2006).

Lawlor, B. 1991 *The ultimate Dublin guide*. Dublin.

Lawlor, D. 2009 *Na Fianna Éireann and the Irish Revolution—1909 to 1923*. Dublin.

Lee, J.J. 2006 1916 as virtual history. *History Ireland* **14** (2).

Leiberson, G. (ed.) 1966 *The Irish uprising, 1916–1922*. New York.

Lemass, S. 1966 I remember 1916. *Studies: The Irish Jesuit Quarterly Review* (Spring 1966).

Lennon, M.J. 1922 A retrospect. *Banba* (April 1922).

Lennon, M.J. 1948 Easter Week diary. *Irish Times*, 29 March–3 April 1948.

Lennon, M.J. 1949 'The Easter Rising from the inside': the account of Seán Fitzgibbon. *Irish Times*, 18–22 April 1949.

LeRoux, L.N. 1932 *Patrick H. Pearse* (trans. D. Ryan). Dublin.

LeRoux, L.N. 1936 *Tom Clarke and the Irish freedom movement*. Dublin.

Leslie, S. (ed.) 1924 *Memoirs of Brigadier-General Gordon Shephard*. Privately printed.

Leslie, S. (n.d.) *The Irish tangle for English readers*. London.

Levenson, L. 1983 *With wooden sword: a portrait of Francis Sheehy Skeffington*. Boston, MA.

Levenson, L. and Natterstad, J. 1986 *Hanna Sheehy Skeffington: Irish feminist*. Syracuse, NY.

Levenson, S. 1973 *James Connolly: a biography*. London.

Levenson, S. 1977 *Maud Gonne*. London.

Limond, D. 2006 A work for other hands. *History Ireland* **14** (2).

Little, P.J. 1942 A 1916 document. *Capuchin Annual* (1942).

Litton, H. 2013 *Edward Daly*. Dublin.

Litton, H. 2014 *Thomas James Clarke*. Dublin.

Longford, Lord and O'Neill, T.P. 1966 De Valera in the Easter Rising. *Sunday Telegraph*, 27 March 1966.

Luddy, M. 1995 *Hanna Sheehy Skeffington*. Dundalk.

Luddy, M. 1999 *Women in Ireland 1800–1918: a documentary history*. Cork.

Luddy, M. 2012 Ireland Rising. *History Today* **62** (9).

Luddy, M. and Murphy, C. 1990 *Women surviving: studies in Irish women's history in the 19th and 20th centuries*. Dublin.

Lynch, B. 2006 Through the eyes of 1916. *History Ireland* **14** (2).

Lynch, D. 1957 *The I.R.B. and the 1916 insurrection* (ed. F. O'Donoghue). Cork.

Lynch, D. 1966 The countermanding orders of Holy Week, 1916. *An Cosantóir* **26**.

Lynd, R. 1917 *If the Germans conquered England, and other essays*. Dublin.

Lynd, R. 1919 *Who began it?* (Pamphlet issued by the Peace in Ireland Council.)

Lyons, F.S.L. 1971 *Ireland since the Famine*. London.

Lyons, F.S.L. 1981 De Valera revisited. *Magill* (March 1981).

Lyons, G. 1926 Occupation of the Ringsend area. *An tÓglach*, 10, 17 and 24 April 1926.

Lysaght, D.R. O'Connor 2003 The rhetoric of Redmondism, 1914–16. *History*

Ireland **11** (1).

MacAnBheatha, P. 1981 *James Connolly and the workers' republic.* Dublin.

Mac An Tsoir 1962 Padraig MacPiaras. *Comhair* **21**.

MacAonghusa, P. (ed.) 1979 *Quotations from P.H. Pearse.* Cork.

MacAonghusa, P. (ed.) 1983 *Quotations from Éamon de Valera.* Dublin.

MacAonghusa, P. (ed.) 1995 *What Connolly said.* Dublin.

Macardle, D. 1937 [1965] *The Irish Republic.* New York.

MacAtasney, G. 2005 *Seán MacDiarmada, the mind of the revolution.* Dublin.

MacAtasney, G. 2013 *Tom Clarke: life, liberty, revolution.* Dublin.

MacBride, M.G. 1950 *Servant of the queen.* Dublin.

McCallum, C. 2005 *And they'll march with their brothers to freedom—Cumann na mBan, nationalism, and women's rights in Ireland, 1900–1923.* Dublin.

McCann, B.P. 1996–7 The diary of 2nd Lieutenant A.V.G. Killingley, Easter Week, 1916. *Irish Sword* **20**.

McCann, J. 1946 *War by the Irish.* Tralee.

McCarthy, C. 2007 *Cumann na mBan and the Irish Revolution.* Cork.

McCarthy, M. 2013 *Ireland's 1916 Rising: explorations of history-making, commemorations and history in modern times.* Ashgate.

McCay, H. 1966 *Padraic Pearse: a new biography.* Cork.

McCoole, S. 1997 *Guns and chiffon.* Dublin.

McCoole, S. 2003 *No ordinary women: Irish female activists in the revolutionary years.* Dublin.

McCormack, W.J. 2012 *Dublin 1916 and the French connection.* Dublin.

McCracken, D.P. 2000 MacBride's Brigade in the Anglo-Boer War. *History Ireland* **7** (1) (Spring 2000).

McCullough, D. 1966 The events in Belfast. *Capuchin Annual* (1966).

MacCurtain, F. 2006 *Remember, it's for Ireland.* Cork.

MacCurtain, M. and O'Corrain, D. (eds) 1978 *Women, the vote and revolution. Women in Irish society: the historical dimension.* Dublin.

McDermott, N. 2005 Jim Larkin: a man on a mission. *Red Banner* **20**.

McDermott, P. 2006 Brothers in arms. *Irish Echo*, 19–25 April 2006.

McDermott, P. 2006b One family's Rising. *Irish Echo*, 3–9 May 2006.

MacDonagh, D. 1945a Patrick Pearse. *An Cosantóir* (August 1945).

MacDonagh, D. 1945b Joseph Plunkett. *An Cosantóir* (November 1945).

MacDonagh, D. 1946 Éamonn Ceannt. *An Cosantóir* (October 1946).

MacDonagh, M. 1916 *The Irish at the Front.* London.

McDonagh, M. 2009 Call for memorial to be put up to citizens of Dublin killed in Rising. *Irish Times*, 22 June 2009.

MacDonnacha, M. 2002 Deserting the Starry Plough. *An Phoblacht*, 19 December 2002.

MacDonnell, J.M. (n.d.) *The story of Irish Labour*. Cork.

McDonnell, K.K. 1972 *There is a bridge at Bandon*. Cork.

McDowell, R.B. 1967 *Alice Stopford Green: a passionate historian*. Dublin.

McEneany, K.T. (ed.) 1982 *Pearse and Rossa*. New York.

MacEntee, S. 1944 Easter Week in the GPO. *The Irish Digest* (May 1944).

MacEntee, S. 1966 *Episode at Easter*. Dublin.

MacEoin, U. (ed.) 1980 *Survivors*. Dublin.

McGahern, J. 1991 *Amongst women*. New York.

McGarry, F. 2006 Keeping an eye on the usual suspects: Dublin Castle's 'Personality Files', 1899–1921. *History Ireland* **14** (6).

McGarry, F. 2010 *The Rising: Easter 1916*. Oxford.

McGarry, F. 2011 *Rebels: voices from the Easter Rising*. Dublin.

MacGarry, M. 1942 Memories of Scoil Eanna. *Capuchin Annual* (1942).

McGee, O. 2005 *The I.R.B.: the Irish Republican Brotherhood from the Land League to Sinn Féin*. Dublin.

McGill, P.J. 1966 Padraic Pearse in Donegal. *Donegal Annual* (1966).

MacGiolla, C.B. (ed.) 1966 *Intelligence notes 1913–1916, preserved in the State Paper Office*. Baile Átha Cliath.

McGough, E. 2013 *Diarmuid Lynch: a forgotten Irish patriot*. Cork.

McGowan, J. 2005 *Countess Markievicz: the people's countess*. Sligo.

McGuigan, J. 2005–6 A duty to execute: the 1916 pocket book of Captain Annan Dickson of the Sherwood Foresters. *Irish Sword* **25**.

McGuire, C. 2006 Seán McLoughlin: the boy commandant of 1916. *History Ireland* **14** (2).

McGuire, C. 2011 *Seán McLoughlin: Ireland's forgotten revolutionary*. Dublin.

McHugh, R. (ed.) 1966 *Dublin, 1916*. London.

McInerney, M. 1967 James Ryan. *Irish Times*, 15–17 March 1967.

McInerney, M. 1968 Gerald Boland's story. *Irish Times*, 8–19 October 1968.

McInerney, M. 1971 *The riddle of Erskine Childers*. Dublin.

McInerney, M. 1974 Seán MacEntee. *Irish Times*, 22–25 July 1974.

McIntosh, G. and Urquhart, D. 2010 *Irish women at war: the twentieth century*. Dublin.

McKay, F. 1966 Clann na nGaedheal Girl Scouts. *Irish Press*, 3 May 1966.

McKenna, L. 1920 [1991] *The social teachings of James Connolly*. Dublin.

MacKenna, S. [writing as Martin Daly] 1917 *Memories of the dead*. Dublin.

McKenzie, F.A. 1916 *The Irish Rebellion: what happened and why*. London.

McKeown, E. 1966 A family in the Rising. *Electricity Supply Board Journal* (1966).

McKillen, B. 1982 Irish feminism and national separatism. *Éire-Ireland* **17**.

McKittrick, D. 1991 Rebels of 1916 leave mixed legacy. *Irish Independent*, 12 March 1991.

McLaughlin, T. 2006 The aftermath. *An Cosantóir* (April/May 2006).

MacLochlainn, P. 1971 *Last words, letters and statements of the leaders executed after the Rising at Easter, 1916.* Dublin.

McLoughlin, S. 1948 Memories of the Easter Rising. *Camillian Post* (Spring 1948).

MacManus, M.J. 1944 *Éamon de Valera.* Dublin.

McManus, R. 2002 *Dublin 1910–1940: shaping the city and suburbs.* Dublin.

MacManus, S. 1921 [1978] *The story of the Irish race.* Dublin [Old Greenwich, CT].

McNally, F. 2009 An Irishman's Diary: Dublin in rebellion. *Irish Times,* 12 June 2009.

MacNeill, E. 1913 The North began. *An Claidheamh Soluis,* 1 November 1913.

MacNeill, E. 1915 Ireland for the Irish nation. *Irish Volunteer,* 20 February 1915.

MacNeill, E. 1919 Recollections of Pearse. *New Ireland,* 14 June 1919.

MacNeill, E. 1937 *Phases of Irish history.* Dublin.

MacSwiney, T. 1921 [1936] *Principles of freedom.* Dublin.

MacThomais, É. 1965 *Down Dublin streets, 1916.* Dublin.

MacThomais, S. 2005 The historical significance of 16 Moore Street. *An Phoblacht,* 1 September 2005.

MacThomais, S. 2012 *Dead interesting: stories from the graveyards.* Dublin.

McVeigh, J. 1998 Constance Markievicz: aiming for the stars. *An Phoblacht,* 17 September 1998.

Maher, J. 1998 *Harry Boland: a biography.* Cork.

Malins, E. 1965 *Yeats and the Easter Rising.* Dublin.

Mandle, W. 1977 The IRB and the beginning of the Gaelic Athletic Association. *Irish Historical Studies* **20** (80).

Mandle, W. 1979 Sport as politics: the Gaelic Athletic Association 1884–1924. In R. Cashman and M. McKernan (eds), *Sport in history.* Queensland.

Mandle, W. 1987 *The Gaelic Athletic Association and Irish nationalist politics, 1884–1924.* Dublin.

Mansergh, N. 1966 *The Irish Question, 1840–1921.* Toronto.

Mansergh, N. 1991 *The unresolved question: the Anglo-Irish Settlement and its undoing, 1912–1972.* London.

Mansergh, N. 1997 *Nationalism and independence: selected Irish papers.* Cork.

Manzor, P.J. 2002 The impact of the American Civil War on the emergence of Irish-American nationalism. Unpublished MA thesis, NUI Galway.

Marcus, L. 1964 The G.A.A. and the Castle. *Irish Independent,* 9–10 July 1964.

Markievicz, Countess C. 1909 *Women, ideals and the nation* [pamphlet, reissued 1918]. Dublin.

Markievicz, Countess C. 1918 *A call to the women of Ireland.* Dublin.

Markievicz, Countess C. 1923 *What Irish republicans stand for.* Glasgow.

Markievicz, Countess C. 1926 Cumann na mBan. *Cumann na mBan* **11** (10).

Markievicz, Countess C. 1987 *Prison letters of Countess Markievicz.* London.

Marreco, A. 1967 *The rebel countess: the life and times of Constance Markievicz.* London.

Martin, A.E. 1966 To make a right rose tree. *Studies: The Irish Jesuit Quarterly Review* **55**.

Martin, F.X. 1961 Eoin MacNeill on the 1916 Rising. *Irish Historical Studies* **12**.

Martin, F.X. (ed.) 1963 *The Irish Volunteers, 1913–1915*. Dublin.

Martin, F.X. 1964 *The Howth gunrunning and the Kilcoole gunrunning*. Dublin.

Martin, F.X. 1966a 1916—myth, fact and mystery. *Studia Hibernica* **7**.

Martin, F.X. (ed.) 1966b The McCartan Documents, 1916. *Clogher Record* (1966).

Martin, F.X. (ed.) 1966c *The Easter Rising, 1916, and University College, Dublin*. Dublin.

Martin, F.X. (ed.) 1967 *Leaders and men of the Easter Rising*. London.

Martin, F.X. 1968 The 1916 Rising—a *coup d'état* or a 'bloody protest'? *Studia Hibernica* **8**.

Martin, F.X. and Byrne, J.F. (eds) 1973 *The scholar revolutionary: Eoin MacNeill*. Shannon.

Martin, H. 1921 *Ireland in insurrection*. London.

Matthews, A. 2007a Citizen Army women in the GPO in 1916. *Red Banner* **28**.

Matthews, A. 2007b Rebel women in prison in 1916. *Red Banner* **29**.

Matthews, A. 2008 Vanguard of the Revolution. In R. O'Donnell (ed.), *The impact of the 1916 Rising among the nations*. Dublin.

Matthews, A. 2010a *The Kimmage garrison, 1916: making billy-can bombs at Larkfield*. Dublin.

Matthews, A. 2010b *Renegades: Irish republican women 1900–1922*. Dublin.

Matthews, A. 2010c Cumann na mBan and the Red Cross. In J. Kelly and R.V. Comerford (eds), *Associated culture in Ireland and abroad*. Dublin.

Matthews, A. 2014 *The Irish Citizen Army*. Cork.

Matthews, M.E. 2002 Women activists in Irish republican politics, 1900–1941. Unpublished Ph.D thesis, NUI Maynooth.

Maume, P. 1994 Lilly Connolly's conversion. *History Ireland* **2** (3).

Maume, P. 1995a *D.P. Moran*. Dundalk.

Maume, P. 1995b Parnell and the I.R.B. oath. *Irish Historical Studies* **29** (115).

Maume, P. 1999 *The long gestation: Irish nationalist life, 1892–1921*. Dublin.

Maume, P. 2001 From deference to citizenship: Irish republicanism, 1870–1923. *The Republic* **2**.

Maume, P. 2006 The man with thirty lives? *History Ireland* **14** (2).

Maye, B. 1997 *Arthur Griffith*. Dublin.

Mayhew, G. 1963 A corrected typescript of Yeats' 'Easter 1916'. *Huntington Library Quarterly* **27**.

Meakin, Lt W. 1920 *The 5th North Staffords and the North Midland Territorials, 1914–1919*. Longton.

Meleady, D. 2014 *John Redmond: the national leader*. Dublin.

Mellows, L. 1946 An account of the Irish rebellion [partial reprint]. *Wolfe Tone Annual* (1946).

Mitchell, A. 1997 Casement's Black Diaries: closed books reopened. *History Ireland* 5 (3).

Mitchell, A. 2001 The Casement 'Black Diaries' debate: the story so far. *History Ireland* 9 (2).

Mitchell, A. 2003 Robert Emmet and 1916. *History Ireland* 11 (3).

Mitchell, A. 2014 *Roger Casement*. Dublin.

Mitchell, A. and Ó Snodaigh, P. 1985 *Irish political documents, 1916–1949*. Dublin.

Mitchell, D. 1990 *A 'peculiar' place: the Adelaide Hospital, Dublin, 1839–1989*. Dublin.

Molloy, M.J. 1966 He helped to print the proclamation. *Evening Herald*, 4 April 1966.

Molyneux, D. and Kelly, D. 2015 *When the clock struck in 1916*. Cork.

Monteith, R. 1953 *Casement's last adventure*. Dublin.

Mooney, J.E. 1991 Varieties of Irish republican womanhood: San Francisco lectures during their United States tours: 1916–1925. Unpublished MA thesis, San José State University, California.

Moore, Col. M. 1938 The rise of the Irish Volunteers [serial]. *Irish Press*, 4 January–2 March 1938. [Apparently written in 1917. See National Library of Ireland ILB 94109.]

Moran, B. 1978 Jim Larkin and the British Labour Movement. *Saothar* 4.

Moran, M. 2010 *Executed for Ireland*. Dublin.

Moran, S.F. 1989a Patrick Pearse and the European revolt against reason. *Journal of the History of Ideas* 50 (4).

Moran, S.F. 1989b Patrick Pearse, the Easter Rising and Irish history. *Graduate Review* (Summer 1989).

Moran, S.F. 1994 *Patrick Pearse and the politics of redemption*. Washington, DC.

Morgan, A. 1988 *James Connolly: a political biography*. Manchester.

Mulcahy, Gen. R. 1980 The development of the Irish Volunteers, 1916–1922. *An Cosantóir* 40.

Mulcahy, R. 1999 *Richard Mulcahy (1886–1971): a family memoir*. Dublin.

Mulcahy, R. 2003 The Mulcahy Tapes and Papers. *History Ireland* 8 (1).

Mulcahy, R. 2009 *My father, the general, and the military history of the revolution*. Dublin.

Mulholland, M. 2002 *The politics and relationships of Kathleen Lynn*. Dublin.

Mulqueen, J. and Wren, J. 1989 *De Valera: an illustrated life*. Dublin.

Munck, R. 1985 *Ireland: nation, state and class struggle*. Boulder, CO.

Murphy, B.P. 1991 *Patrick Pearse and the lost republican ideal*. Dublin.

Murphy, C. 1989 *The women's suffrage movement and Irish society in the early twentieth century*. London.

Murphy, Major H.L. 1996 Countess Markievicz. *An Cosantóir* (June 1946).

Murray, J. 1996 *Erskine Childers*. London.

Murray, M. 1922 A girl's experience in the GPO. *Poblacht na hÉireann*, 20 April 1922.

Murray, R.H. 1916 The Sinn Féin rebellion. *The Nineteenth Century and After* (June 1916).

Murtagh, P. 2014 Equally audacious: the Kilcoole gun-running. *Irish Times*, 17 July 2014.

Myers, K. 1991 The glory that was hijacked. *Guardian*, 30 March 1991.

Neeson, E. 2007 *Myths from Easter 1916*. Aubane.

Nelson, C. 2014 Murderous renegade or agent of the crown? The riddle of Erskine Childers. *History Ireland* **22** (3).

Nevin, D. (ed.) 1964 *1913: Jim Larkin and the 1913 Lockout*. Dublin.

Nevin, D. 1968 *Connolly bibliography*. Dublin.

Nevin, D. (ed.) 1978 [1998] *James Larkin: lion in the fold*. Dublin.

Nevin, D. 2005 *James Connolly: a full life*. Dublin.

Nevin, D. (ed.) 2008 *Between friends: James Connolly letters and correspondence, 1889–1916*. Dublin.

Newsinger, J. 1979 Revolution and Catholicism in Ireland, 1848–1923. *European Studies Review* **9**.

Newsinger, J. 1986 James Connolly, the German Empire, and the Great War. *Irish Sword* **16** (65).

Newsinger, J. 1993 The Devil it was who sent Larkin to Ireland: the Liberator, Larkinism, and the Dublin Lockout of 1913. *Saothar* **18**.

Newsinger, J. 2002 Irish Labour in a time of revolution. *Socialist History* **22**.

Ní Chorra, E. 1936 A rebel remembers. *Capuchin Annual* (1936).

Ní Chumnaill, E. 1933 The history of Cumann na mBan. *An Phoblacht*, 8 April 1933.

Ní Dhonnchadha, M. and Durgan, T. (eds) 1991 *Revising the Rising*. Derry.

Ní Dhuibhne, E. 2002 Family values: the Sheehy Skeffington Papers in the National Library of Ireland. *History Ireland* **10** (1).

Ní Ghairbhí, R. 2015 *Willie Pearse*. Dublin.

Níc Shiubhlaigh, M. 1955 *The splendid years* (as told to E. Kenny). Dublin.

Nixon, W. and Healy, E. 2000 *Asgard*. Dublin.

Nolan, L. and Nolan, J.E. 2009 *Ireland and the war at sea, 1914–1918*. Cork.

Norman, D. 1988 *Terrible beauty: a life of Constance Markievicz*. London.

Norman, E.R. 1965 *The Catholic Church and Ireland in the age of rebellion*. Ithaca, NY.

Norstedt, J.A. 1980 *Thomas MacDonagh: a critical biography*. Charlottesville, VA.

Norway, M. 1916 *The Sinn Féin rebellion as I saw it*. London.

Novak, R. 2008 Keepers of important secrets: the Ladies Committee of the IRB. *History Ireland* **16** (6).

Nowlan, K. (ed.) 1969 *The making of 1916: studies in the history of the Rising*. Dublin.

Nunan, E. 1966 The Irish Volunteers in London. *An tÓglach* (Autumn 1966).

Nunan, E. 1967 The Kimmage Garrison. *An tÓglach* (Winter 1967).

Oates, Lt Col. W.C. 1920 *The Sherwood Foresters in the Great War, 1914–1919.* Nottingham.

Ó Braonain, C. 1916 Poets of the insurrection II—Patrick H. Pearse. *Studies: The Irish Jesuit Quarterly Review* **5**.

O'Brennan, L. 1922 Letter to the Editor: An appreciation of Erskine Childers. *Irish Independent*, 21 November 1922.

O'Brennan, L.M. 1936 The dawning of the day. *Capuchin Annual* (1936).

O'Brennan, L.M. 1947 We surrender. *An Cosantóir* (June 1947). [Reprinted in *An Cosantóir* (April/May 2006).]

Ó Briain, L. 1923 *The historic Rising of Easter Week, 1916.* Dublin.

Ó Briain, L. 1966 Saint Stephen's Green area. *Capuchin Annual* (1966).

O'Brien, N. Connolly 1932 Women in Ireland, their part in the revolutionary struggle. *An Phoblacht*, 25 June 1932.

O'Brien, N. Connolly 1977 The Pearse I knew. *Hibernia* **10** (15 April 1977).

O'Brien, P. 2007 *Blood on the streets: 1916 and the battle of Mount Street Bridge.* Cork.

O'Brien, P. 2010 *Uncommon valour: 1916 and the battle for the South Dublin Union.* Cork.

O'Brien, P. 2012a *Crossfire—the battle of the Four Courts.* Dublin.

O'Brien, P. 2012b *Field of fire—the battle of Ashbourne.* Dublin.

O'Brien, P. 2013 *Shootout: the battle for St Stephen's Green, 1916.* Dublin.

O'Brien, W. 1916 An Irish soldier and the rebellion. *Irish Times*, 9 May 1916.

O'Brien, W. 1936 Was the date changed? *Irish Press*, 25 January 1936.

O'Brien, W. 1959 *Fifty years of Liberty Hall.* Dublin.

O'Brien, W. 1969 *Forth the banners go* (ed. E. MacLysaght). Dublin.

O'Brien, W. and Ryan, D. 1953 *Devoy's postbag, 1871–1928.* Dublin.

Ó Brochláin, H. 2012 *Joseph Plunkett.* Dublin.

Ó Broin, L. 1966 *Dublin Castle and the 1916 Rising.* London.

Ó Broin, L. 1969 *The chief secretary: Augustine Birrell in Ireland.* London.

Ó Broin, L. 1976 *Revolutionary underground: the story of the I.R.B., 1858–1924.* Dublin.

Ó Broin, L. 1989 *W.E. Wylie and the Irish Revolution, 1916–1921.* Dublin.

Ó Buachalla, S. (ed.) 1980a *The letters of P.H. Pearse.* London.

Ó Buachalla, S. (ed.) 1980b *A significant educationalist: the educational writings of P.H. Pearse.* Dublin.

O'Callaghan, J. 2015 *Con Colbert.* Dublin.

O'Callaghan, S. 1956 *The Easter lily.* London.

O'Callaghan, S. 1974 *Execution.* London.

O'Carroll, J.P. and Murphy, J.A. (eds) 1983 *De Valera and his times.* Cork.

O'Casey, S. [writing as P. Ó Cathasaigh] 1919 [1980] *The story of the Irish Citizen Army.* Dublin and London [London].

Ó Cathasaigh, A. (ed.) 1997 *James Connolly, the lost writings.* Harmondsworth.

Ó Ceallaigh, P. 1966 Jacob's Factory area. *Capuchin Annual* (1966).

Ó Ceallaigh, S.T. 1936 The founding of the Irish Volunteers. *An Phoblacht*, 30 April 1936.

Ó Ceallaigh, S.T. 1961 Memoirs. *Irish Press*, 3 July–9 August 1961.

Ó Ceallaigh, S.T. 1963 The founding of the Irish Volunteers. *Capuchin Annual* (1963).

Ó Ceallaigh, S.T. (n.d.) *A trinity of martyrs.* Dublin.

O'Ceirin, K. and O'Ceirin, C. 1996 *Women of Ireland.* Galway.

Ó Clerigh, G. 2008 John Redmond and 1916 [letter]. *Irish Times*, 7 April 2008.

Ó Conluain, P. (ed.) 1963 *Seán T.* Dublin.

O'Connor, E. 1988 *Syndicalism in Ireland, 1917–1923.* Cork.

O'Connor, E. 1992 *A labour history of Ireland, 1824–1960.* Dublin.

O'Connor, J. 1966 Boland's Mill area. *Capuchin Annual* (1966).

O'Connor, J. 1986 *The 1916 Proclamation.* Dublin.

O'Connor, U. 1975 *A terrible beauty is born: the Irish Troubles, 1912–1922.* London.

O'Connor Lysaght, D.R. 2006 The Irish Citizen Army, 1913–16. *History Ireland* **14** (2).

O'Daly, N. 1926 The women of Easter Week: Cumann na mBan in Stephen's Green and the College of Surgeons. *An tÓglach*, 3 April 1926.

O'Day, A. 1998 *Irish Home Rule, 1867–1921.* Manchester.

O'Doherty, L. 1970 Dublin, 1920. *Capuchin Annual* (1970).

O'Donnell, J. 1990–1 Recollections based on the diary of an Irish Volunteer. *Cathair na Mart* **10** (1) (1990) and **11** (1991).

O'Donnell, P.D. 1972 Dublin military barracks. *Dublin Historical Record* **25** (4).

O'Donnell, R. (ed.) 2008 *The impact of the 1916 Rising among the nations.* Dublin.

O'Donnell, R. 2014 *Patrick Pearse.* Dublin.

O'Donoghue, F. 1949 A review of the 1916 Rising. *Irish Historical Studies* (September 1949).

O'Donoghue, F. 1955 A review of *Casement's last adventure. Irish Historical Studies* (March 1955).

O'Donoghue, F. 1963 Plans for the 1916 Rising. *University Review* **3**.

O'Donoghue, F. 1966 The failure of the German arms landing at Easter 1916. *Journal of the Cork Historical and Archaeological Society* **71**.

O'Donovan Rossa, D. 1898 [1972] *Rossa's recollections, 1838–1898* (introduction by S. Ó Luing). New York [Shannon].

O'Donovan Rossa, J. 1872 [1991] *Irish rebels in English prisons.* New York [Dingle].

Ó Dubghaill, M. 1966 *Insurrection fires at Eastertide.* Cork.

Ó Duigneain, P. 1991 Linda Kearns—the Sligo nurse in the 1916 Rising. *Sligo Champion*, 5 April 1991.

Ó Duigneain, P. 2002 *Linda Kearns.* Manorhamilton.

Ó Dulaing, D. 1984 *Voices of Ireland*. Dublin.

O'Dwyer, R. 2010 *The Bastille of Ireland: Kilmainham Gaol, from ruin to restoration*. Dublin.

Ó Faolain, S. 1933 *The life of de Valera*. Dublin.

Ó Faolain, S. 1934 *Constance Markievicz*. London.

Ó Faolain, S. 1939 *De Valera*. London.

O'Farrell, E. 1917 Events of Easter Week. *Catholic Bulletin* (May 1917).

O'Farrell, E. 1930 Recollections. *An Phoblacht*, 26 April and 10 May 1930.

O'Farrell, M. 1999 *A walk through rebel Dublin, 1916*. Cork.

O'Farrell, M. 2014 *The 1916 diaries of an Irish rebel and a British soldier*. Cork.

O'Farrell, P. 1997 *Who's who in the Irish War of Independence and Civil War*. Dublin.

O'Hanrahan, M. 1917 *Irish heroines*. Cumann na mBan pamphlet.

O'Hegarty, P.S. 1918 *An indestructible nation*. Dublin.

O'Hegarty, P.S. 1919a *Sinn Féin: an illumination*. Dublin and London.

O'Hegarty, P.S. 1919b P.H. Pearse. *Irish Commonwealth* (St Patrick's Day issue).

O'Hegarty, P.S. 1924 [1998] *The victory of Sinn Féin*. Dublin.

O'Hegarty, P.S. 1931 Patrick Pearse. *Dublin Magazine* (July–September 1931).

O'Hegarty, P.S. 1952 *A history of Ireland under the Act of Union*. London.

O'Higgins, B. 1925 *The soldier's story of Easter Week*. Dublin.

O'Higgins, B. 1935 The soldier's story of Easter Week. *Wolfe Tone Annual* (1935).

O'Keefe, J. 1932 Easter Week and Connolly. *Workers' Voice*, 14 May 1932.

O'Kelly, S. 1996 *The glorious seven*. Dublin.

O'Leary, J. 1896 *Recollections of Fenians and Fenianism*. London.

Ó Luing, S. 1953 *Art Ó Griofa*. Dublin.

Ó Luing, S. 1961 Talking to Bulmer Hobson. *Irish Times*, 6 May 1961.

Ó Luing, S. 1968 Thomas Ashe. *Capuchin Annual* (1968).

Ó Luing, S. 1970 *I die in a good cause: a study of Thomas Ashe, idealist and revolutionary*. Tralee.

O'Mahony, S. 1987 [1995] *Frongoch, university of revolution*. Killiney.

Ó Mahony, S. 2000 *Three murders in Dublin Castle* [pamphlet]. Dublin.

Ó Maitiu, S. 2001 *W & R Jacob: celebrating 150 years of Irish biscuit-making*. Dublin.

O'Neill, B. 1939 *Easter Week*. New York.

O'Neill, Cmdt D. 2006 The Four Courts: Easter 1916. *An Cosantóir* (April/May 2006).

O'Neill, Col. E. 1966 The Battle of Dublin, 1916. *An Cosantóir* 26.

O'Neill, É. 1935 Patrick Pearse, some other memories. *Capuchin Annual* (1935).

O'Neill, M. 1991 *From Parnell to de Valera: a biography of Jennie Wyse-Power, 1858–1941*. Dublin.

O'Neill, M. 2000 *Grace Gifford Plunkett and Irish freedom: tragic bride of 1916*. Dublin.

Ó Neill, T. and Ó Fiannachta, P. 1968–70 *De Valera* (2 vols). Dublin.

Ó hÓgartaigh, M. 2005 *Kathleen Lynn, patriot doctor.* Dublin.

Ó Rahilly, A. 1991 *Winding the clock: The Ó Rahilly and the 1916 Rising.* Dublin.

Ó Rahilly, M.J. (The) 1915a *The secret history of the Irish Volunteers.* Dublin.

Ó Rahilly, The 1915b The history of the Irish Volunteers. *Gaelic American,* 2 January 1915.

Ó Rahilly, The 1915c The Volunteer colours: flags for the regiments. *Irish Volunteer,* 23 May 1915.

Oram, H. 1983 *The newspaper book.* Dublin.

O'Riordan, M. 1979 *The Connolly Column.* Dublin.

Ó Ruairc, P. Óg 2011 *Revolution.* Cork.

O'Shannon, C. (ed.) 1959 *Fifty years of Liberty Hall, 1909–1959.* Dublin.

O'Shea, Cmdt B. and White, CQMS G. 2006 The Volunteer uniform. *An Cosantóir* (April/May 2006).

Ó Siochain, S. 2007 *Roger Casement: imperialist, rebel, revolutionary.* Dublin.

Ó Snodaigh, A. 1997 Arming the Volunteers. *An Phoblacht,* 20 June 1997.

Ó Snodaigh, A. 1998 The Irish Volunteers founded. *An Phoblacht,* 26 November 1998.

Ó Snodaigh, A. 1999 The first 1916 Rising casualty. *An Phoblacht,* 1 April 1999.

Ó Snodaigh, A. 2000 Remembering the past: the Battle of Mount Street Bridge. *An Phoblacht,* 20 April 2000.

O'Sullivan, M. 1994 *Seán Lemass.* Dublin.

O'Sullivan, M. and O'Neill, B. 1999 *The Shelbourne and its people.* Dublin.

O'Sullivan, N. 2007 *Every dark hour: a history of Kilmainham Jail.* Dublin.

O'Sullivan, N. 2009 *Written in stone: the graffiti in Kilmainham Jail.* Dublin.

O'Sullivan, T.F. 1916 *The story of the G.A.A.* Dublin.

O'Toole, F. 1999 *The* Irish Times *book of the century.* Dublin.

Ó Tuile, P. (n.d.) *Life and times of Brian O'Higgins.* Navan.

Ó hUid, Ceannaire T.C. 1966 The Mount Street action, April 26, 1916. *An Cosantóir* 26.

Owens, R.C. 1984a *Did your granny have a hammer?* Dublin.

Owens, R.C. 1984b *Smashing times: a history of the Irish women's suffrage movement, 1889–1922.* Dublin.

Parks, E.W. and Parks, A.W. 1967 *Thomas MacDonagh: the man, the patriot, the writer.* Athens, GA.

Paseta, S. 1999 *Before the revolution: nationalism, social change and Ireland's Catholic elite, 1879–1922.* Cork.

Paseta, S. 2014 *Irish nationalist women, 1900–1918.* Cambridge.

Pearse, J. 1886 *England's duty to Ireland as plain to a loyal Irish Roman Catholic.* Dublin.

Pearse, M.B. (ed.) 1934 *The home life of Padraig Pearse.* Dublin.

Pearse, M.M. 1942 St Enda's. *Capuchin Annual* (1942).

Pearse, M.M. 1943 Patrick and Willie Pearse. *Capuchin Annual* (1943).

Pearse, P. 1913 The coming revolution. *An Claidheamh Soluis*, 8 November 1913.

Pearse, P.H. 1914 At last—an Irish army! *Irish Volunteer*, 4 July 1914.

Pearse, P.H. 1915 Why we want recruits. *Irish Volunteer*, 22 May 1915.

Pearse, P.H. 1915 The Irish flag. *Irish Volunteer*, 20 March 1915.

Pearse, P.H. 1916 *The murder machine*. Dublin.

Pearse, P.H. 1918 *The Singer and other plays*. Dublin.

Pearse, P.H. 1922 *Collected works of Padraic H. Pearse. Political writings and speeches*. Dublin.

Pearson, P. 2000 *The heart of Dublin*. Dublin.

Phillips, W.A. 1923 *The revolution in Ireland, 1906–1923*. London.

Pinkman, J.A. 1998 *In the legion of the vanguard* (ed. F.E. Maguire). Dublin.

Plunkett, G. 1958 Joseph Plunkett: origin and background. *University Review* (1958).

Plunkett, G. 1968 Joseph Plunkett's diary of his journey to Germany. *University Review* (1968).

Plunkett, G. Gifford 1922 The white flag of 1916. *Poblacht na h-Éireann* **1** (12).

Plunkett, J.M. 1942 Joseph Plunkett's last message. *The Capuchin Annual* (1942).

Poets of the insurrection 1918 [Essays originally published in *Studies: The Irish Jesuit Quarterly Review*.] Dublin and London.

Pollard, H.B.C. 1922 *The secret societies of Ireland: their rise and progress*. London.

Porter, R. 1973 *P.H. Pearse*. New York.

Prunty, J. 1998 *Dublin slums, 1800–1925*. Dublin.

Reddin, K. 1943 A man called Pearse. *Studies: The Irish Jesuit Quarterly Review* (June 1943).

Redmond, J. 1916 *The Rising*. London.

Redmond-Howard, L.G. 1916 *Six days of the Irish Republic*. Dublin.

Rees, R. 1998 *Ireland, 1905–1925*, Vol. 1. Newtownards.

Reeve, C. and Barton, A. 1978 *James Connolly and the United States: the road to the 1916 Irish rebellion*. Atlantic Highlands, NJ.

Reid, B.L. 1976 *The lives of Roger Casement*. New Haven, CT.

Reilly, J. 2006 Mater nuns supported Rising, R.I.C. files claim. *Irish Independent*, 2 April 2006.

Reilly, T. 2005 *Joe Stanley, printer to the Rising*. Dingle.

Reynolds, J.J. 1919 *A fragment of 1916 history*. Dublin.

Reynolds, J.J. 1926 The Four Courts and North King Street in 1916. *An tÓglach*, 15, 22 and 29 May 1926.

Reynolds, M. 1926 Cumann na mBan in the GPO. *An tÓglach*, 27 March 1926.

Ring, J. 1996 *Erskine Childers*. London.

Robbins, F. 1928 The Citizen Army and Easter Week. *Irishman*, 19 May 1928.

Robbins, F. 1977 *Under the Starry Plough: recollections of the Irish Citizen Army*. Dublin.

Robertson, N. 1960 *Crowned harp: memories of the last years of the crown in Ireland*.

Dublin.

Roche, A.J. (ed.) 2000 *A family in revolution*. Dublin.

Roper, E. (ed.) 1934 *Prison letters of Countess Markievicz*. London.

Rowbotham, S. 1997 *A century of women*. New York and London.

Ruane, M. 1991 *Ten Dublin women*. Dublin.

Ryan, A. 2005 *Witnesses: inside the Easter Rising*. Dublin.

Ryan, A. 2007 *Comrades: inside the War of Independence*. Dublin.

Ryan, D. (ed.) 1917 *The story of a success by P.H. Pearse, being a record of St Enda's College, September 1908 to Easter 1916*. Dublin.

Ryan, D. 1919 *The man called Pearse*. Dublin.

Ryan, D. 1924 *James Connolly and his life*. Dublin.

Ryan, D. 1934 *Remembering Sion: a chronicle of storm and quiet*. London.

Ryan, D. 1936 *Unique dictator: a study of Éamon de Valera*. London.

Ryan, D. 1937 *The phoenix flame*. London.

Ryan, D. 1942 Margaret Pearse. *Capuchin Annual* (1942).

Ryan, D. 1948 *Socialism and nationalism: a collection of the writings of James Connolly*. Dublin.

Ryan, D. 1949 [1957] *The Rising: the complete story of Easter Week*. Dublin.

Ryan, D. 1957 Pearse, St Enda's, and the Hound of Ulster. *Threshold* (1957).

Ryan, D. 1958 St Enda's—fifty years after. *University Review* (1958).

Ryan, D. 1961 The Easter Rising. *Irish Press*, 24–29 April 1961.

Ryan, D. (ed.) 1963 [1995] *The 1916 poets*. Dublin.

Ryan, D. (ed.) (n.d.) *Collected works of Padraic H. Pearse: St Enda's and its founder*. Dublin.

Ryan, J.T. 1931 The origin of the *Aud* expedition. *An Phoblacht*, 25 April 1931.

Ryan, Dr J. 1942 The General Post Office area. *Capuchin Annual* (1966).

Ryan, L. 1992 The *Irish Citizen*, 1912–1920. *Saothar* 17.

Ryan, L. 1994 Women without votes: the political strategies of the Irish suffrage movement. *Irish Political Studies* 9.

Ryan, L. 1996 *Irish feminism and the vote: an anthology of the* Irish Citizen *newspaper, 1912–1920*. Dublin.

Ryan, L. and Ward, M. (eds) 2004 *Irish women and nationalism: soldiers, new women and wicked hags*. Dublin.

Ryan, M. 2014 *Thomas Kent*. Dublin.

Ryan, M., Browne, S. and Gilmour, K. (eds) 1995 *No shoes in summer: days to remember*. Dublin.

Salmon, L.M. 1923 *The newspaper and the historian*. New York.

Saurin, C. 1926 Hotel Metropole Garrison. *An tÓglach*, 13 and 20 March 1926.

Sawyer, R. 1993 *'We are but women': women in Ireland's history*. London.

Sceilg [J.J. O'Kelly] (n.d.) *Stepping stones* (undated pamphlet). Irish Book Bureau,

Dublin.

Sceilg (J.J. O'Kelly) (n.d.) *A trinity of martyrs* (undated pamphlet). Irish Book Bureau, Dublin.

Schuller, G. 1986 *James Connolly and Irish freedom: a Marxist analysis.* Cork.

Schmuhl, R. 2013 Ambiguous reprieve: Dev and America. *History Ireland* **21** (3).

Severn, B. 1971 *Irish statesman and rebel: the two lives of Éamon de Valera.* Folkstone.

Sexton, S. 1994 *Ireland: photographs, 1840–1930.* London.

Shaw, Revd F. 1972 The canon of Irish history: a challenge. *Studies: The Irish Jesuit Quarterly Review* (Summer 1972).

Sheehy, J. 1980 *The rediscovery of Ireland's past: the Celtic Revival, 1830–1930.* London.

Sheehy-Skeffington, A.D. 1982 The Hatter and the Crank. *Irish Times*, 5 February 1982.

Sheehy-Skeffington, A. and Owens, R. (eds) 1975 *Votes for women: Irish women's struggle for the vote.* Dublin.

Sheehy-Skeffington, F. 1914 *War and feminism.* Dublin.

Sheehy-Skeffington, H. 1902 Women and the university question. *New Ireland Review* **17**.

Sheehy-Skeffington, H. 1912 The women's movement—Ireland. *Irish Review* (July 1912).

Sheehy-Skeffington, H. 1917 *British militarism as I have known it.* New York.

Sheehy-Skeffington, H. 1919 *Impressions of Sinn Féin in America.* Dublin.

Sheehy-Skeffington, H. 1928 Constance Markievicz in 1916. *An Phoblacht*, 14 April 1928.

Sheehy-Skeffington, H. 1943 Women in politics. *The Bell* **7** (2).

SIPTU 1997 *Tribute to Lames Larkin, orator, agitator, revolutionary, trade union leader.* Services, Industrial, Professional and Technical Union publication. Dublin.

Sissen, E. 2004 *Pearse's patriots.* Cork.

Skinnider, M. 1917 *Doing my bit for Ireland.* New York.

Skinnider, M. 1966 In Stephen's Green. *Irish Press* Supplement, 9 April 1966.

Small, S. 1998 *An Irish century, 1845–1945.* Dublin.

Smith, N.C. 2008 *A 'manly study'? Irish women historians, 1868–1949.* Dublin.

Smith, W.G. 1916 *Report of work done by St John's Ambulance Brigade during the Sinn Féin rebellion, April–May 1916.* Dublin.

Smyth, H.P. 1997 Kathleen Lynn, MD, FRCSI (1874–1955). *Dublin Historical Record* **30**.

Spindler, K. 1931 *The mystery of the Casement ship.* Berlin.

Staines, M. and O'Reilly, M. 1926 The defence of the GPO. *An tÓglach*, 23 January 1926.

Stanley, D. 1999 *Images of Ireland: central Dublin.* Dublin.

Steele, K. 2007 *Women, press and politics during the Irish Revival.* Syracuse, NY.

Steinmeyer, C. 1926 The evacuation of the GPO. *An tÓglach*, 27 February 1926.

Stephens, J. 1916 [1978] *The insurrection in Dublin*. Gerrard's Cross.

Stephens, J. 1922a *Arthur Griffith, journalist and statesman*. Dublin.

Stephens, J. 1922b Arthur Griffith. *Studies: The Irish Jesuit Quarterly Review* **11**.

Stephenson, J. 2006 *Patrick Joseph Stephenson: 'Paddy Joe'*. Sheffield.

Stephenson, P.J. 1966 *Heuston's fort: a participant's account of the fight by the Mendicity Institute Garrison in Dublin, Easter Week 1916*. Whitegate.

Taillon, R. 1996 *When history was made: the women of 1916*. Belfast.

Talbot, H. 1923 *Michael Collins' own story*. London.

Tansill, C.C. 1957 *America and the fight for Irish freedom, 1866–1922*. New York.

Tarpey, Sr M.V. 1970 The role of Joseph McGarrity in the struggle for Irish independence. Unpublished MA thesis, University of Michigan.

Thompson, W.I. 1967 *The imagination of an insurrection. Dublin, Easter 1916: a study of an ideological movement*. London.

Thornly, D. 1966 Patrick Pearse. *Studies: The Irish Jesuit Quarterly Review* (Spring 1966).

Thornly, D. 1971 Patrick Pearse and the Pearse family. *Studies: The Irish Jesuit Quarterly Review* (Autumn/Winter 1971).

Thornton, Cmdt B.L. 1975 Women and the Army. *An Cosantóir* (November 1975).

Throne, J. 1976 Easter Rising—1916: 60 years after, what are the lessons? *Militant Irish Monthly* **43**.

Tierney, M. 1964a *Bibliographical memoir of Eoin MacNeill*. Dublin.

Tierney, M. 1964b Eoin MacNeill: a biographical study. *Saint Patrick* (1964).

Tierney, M. 1980 *Eoin MacNeill, scholar and man of action, 1867–1945*. Oxford.

Tobin, F. 2013 *The Irish Revolution, 1912–1925: an illustrated history*. Dublin.

Toby, T. 1997 *Exemplary violence used in British colonial policy: one explanation for General John Maxwell's violent reaction to the Easter Rising of 1916*. Boston, MA.

Toibin, C. 1966 Playboys of the GPO. *London Review of Books*, 18 April 1966.

Townshend, C. 1978–9 The Irish railway strike of 1920—industrial action and civil resistance in the struggle for independence. *Irish Historical Studies* **21**.

Townshend, C. 1979 Martial law: legal and administrative problems of civil emergency in Britain and the Empire, 1800–1940. *Historical Journal* **25**.

Townshend, C. 1983 *Political violence in Ireland: government and resistance since 1848*. Oxford.

Townshend, C. 1989 Military force and civil authority in the United Kingdom, 1914–1921. *Journal of British Studies* **28**.

Townshend, C. 1993 Militarism and modern society *Wilson Quarterly* (Winter 1993).

Townshend, C. 1994 The suppression of the Easter Rising. *Bullan* **1** (1).

Townshend, C. 2005 *Easter 1916: the Irish rebellion*. London.

Townshend, C. 2006 Making sense of Easter 1916. *History Ireland* **14** (2).

Travers, C. 1966a *Seán MacDiarmada (1883–1916)*. Dublin.

Travers, C. 1966b Seán MacDiarmada, 1883–1916. *Breifne* (1966).

Travers, P. 1994 *Éamon de Valera*. Dublin.

Trimble, D. 1992 *The Easter Rebellion of 1916*. Belfast.

Turner, C. 1926a The Kimmage Garrison in 1916. *An tÓglach,* 1 May 1926.

Turner, C. 1926b The defence of Messrs Hopkins and Hopkins, O'Connell St., Dublin, in Easter Week, 1916. *An tÓglach,* 5 June 1926.

Ui Chonaill, E. Bean 1966 A Cumann na mBan recalls Easter Week. *Capuchin Annual* (1966).

Ui Dhonnachadha, S. Bean 1986 Memories of Easter Week. *An Phoblacht*, 27 March 1986.

Valiulis, M.G. 1992 *Portrait of a revolutionary: General Richard Mulcahy and the founding of the Irish Free State*. Blackrock.

Valiulis, M.G. 2008 *Gender and power in Irish history*. Dublin.

Van Voris, J. 1967 *Constance de Markievicz: in the cause of Ireland*. Amherst, MA.

Vane, Sir F. 1929 *Agin the government*. London.

'Volunteer, A' 1966 South Dublin Union area. *Capuchin Annual* (1966).

Walker, J. Crampton 1916 Red Cross work and stretcher bearing during the Irish Republic. *Irish Life*, 26 May 1916.

Walsh, B. 2013 *Boy republic: Patrick Pearse and radical education*. Dublin.

Walsh, L.J. 1921 *On my keeping and in theirs*. Dublin and London.

Walsh, L.J. 1934 *Old friends: being memories of men and places*. Dundalk.

Walsh, M. 2008 *The news from Ireland: foreign correspondents and the Irish Revolution*. Dublin.

Walsh, O. 2002 *Ireland's independence, 1880–1923*. London.

Walsh, P. 1928 *William J. Walsh, archbishop of Dublin*. London.

Walsh, P. and Malcomson, A.P.W. 2010 *The Connolly archive*. Dublin.

Walsh, S.P. 1979 *Free and Gaelic: Pearse's idea of a national culture*. Dublin.

Walsh, T. 1966 The epic of Mount Street Bridge. *Irish Press* Supplement, April 1966.

Ward, A.J. 1980 *The Easter Rising: revolution and Irish nationalism*. Arlington Heights, IL.

Ward, M. 1983 *Unmanageable revolutionaries: women and Irish nationalism*. Dingle.

Ward, M. 1994 The missing sex: putting women into Irish history. In A. Smythe (ed.), *A dozen lips*. Dublin.

Ward, M. (ed.) 1995 [2001] *In their own voice*. Dublin.

Ward, M. 1997 *Hanna Sheehy Skeffington: a life*. Cork.

Warwick-Haller, A. and Warwick-Haller, S. (eds) 1995 *Letters from Dublin, Easter 1916: Alfred Fannin's diary of the Rising*. Dublin.

Wells, W.B. 1917 *An Irish apologia. Some thoughts on Anglo-Irish relations and the war*. Dublin.

Wells, W.B. 1919 *John Redmond: a biography.* London.

Wells, W.B. and Marlowe, N. 1916 *A history of the Irish rebellion of 1916.* Dublin.

West, N. 1981 *MI-5: British Secret Service operations, 1900–1945.* London.

Whearity, P.F. 2013 *The Easter Rising of 1916 in north County Dublin: a Skerries perspective.* Dublin.

Whelan, G. 1996 *The guns of Easter.* Dublin.

White, G. and O'Shea, B. 2003 *Irish Volunteer soldier, 1913–1923.* Northants.

White, J. 1919 *The significance of Sinn Féin.* Dublin.

White, J. 1930 [2005] *Misfit: a revolutionary life.* Dublin.

White, V. (ed.) 2009 *Cullenswood House: old ghosts and new dreams.* Dublin.

Wilkinson, B. 1974 *The zeal of the convert: the life of Erskine Childers.* Washington, DC.

Williams, D.T. (ed.) 1966 *The Irish struggle, 1916–1921.* London.

Williams, D.T. (ed.) 1973 *Secret societies in Ireland.* Dublin.

Wills, C. 2009 *Dublin 1916: the siege of the GPO.* London.

Woggan, H. 2000a *Silent radical: Winifred Carney 1887–1943. A reconstruction of her biography.* Dublin.

Woggon, H. 2000b The silent radical: Winifred Carney, 1887–1943. *Studies in Irish Labour* 6.

Wohl, R. 1979 *The generation of 1914.* Cambridge, MA.

Wrench, J.E. 1935 *Struggle, 1914–1920.* London.

Wright, A. 1914 *Disturbed Dublin: the story of the great strike of 1913–1914.* London.

Yeates, P. 2000 *Lockout: Dublin 1913.* Dublin.

Yeates, P. 2001 The Dublin Lockout, 1913. *History Ireland* 9 (2).

Yeates, P. 2011 *A city in wartime.* Dublin.

Yeates, P. 2014 How a Volunteer's role in Howth gun-running created an irreparable family breach. *Irish Times*, 17 July 2014.

Young, Capt. T. 1926 Fighting in South Dublin: with the garrison in Marrowbone Lane during Easter Week, 1916. *An tÓglach*, 6 March 1926.

Dublin participants

Men

A

John Adams, 4th Battalion
John Francis Adams, St Stephen's Green
Arthur P. Agnew, GPO
Nicholas Alexander, St Stephen's Green
Thomas Allen, 1st Battalion
Joseph Allwell, 3rd Battalion
Liam Aloysius Archer, 1st Battalion
James Arnold, 4th Battalion
Thomas Ashe, 5th Battalion
William Francis Ashton, 1st Battalion
Thomas R. Atkins, 3rd Battalion
Richard (Dick) Aungier, 5th Battalion

B

Patrick J. Bailey, 4th Battalion
Richard (Dick) Balfe, 1st Battalion
Henry Banks, 3rd Battalion
Seán Banks, 3rd Battalion
John Bannon, St Stephen's Green
Tom Bannon, 1st Battalion
Benedict Barrett, 1st Battalion
James Barrett, 2nd Battalion
William Barrett, 2nd Battalion
John Barry, St Stephen's Green
Piaras Béaslaí, 1st Battalion
Robert Beggs, 1st Battalion
Daniel Joseph Begley, 1st Battalion
David Timothy Begley, GPO
Joseph Patrick Begley, 2nd Battalion, St
    Stephen's Green
P. Begley, 3rd Battalion
James Behan, GPO
Michael Behan, GPO
John Bent, 1st Battalion
Andrew J. Bermingham, GPO
John Bermingham, 2nd Battalion
John Bermingham, 3rd Battalion
John Joseph Bermingham, GPO
Peter Bermingham, St Stephen's Green
William Berry, 2nd Battalion
Charles Stewart Bevan, 1st Battalion
James (Séamus) Bevan, 1st Battalion
Joseph Bevan, 1st Battalion
Thomas J. Bevan, 1st Battalion

Fr Albert Bibby, 1st Battalion
Joseph Billings, GPO
James Bird, 1st Battalion
Patrick Bird, GPO
Patrick Birney, 5th Battalion
Peter (Peadar) Blanchfield, 1st Battalion, 5th
    Battalion
Thomas (Tom) Blanchfield, GPO, 5th Battalion
William J. Blake, 2nd Battalion
Edmund (Ned) Boland, GPO
Gerald Boland, 2nd Battalion
Harry Boland, GPO
Michael Boland, GPO
Patrick (Paddy) Boland, 1st Battalion
James Bolger, GPO
John Bolger, GPO
David J. Bourke (Dáithí de Burca), GPO
William Patrick Bowles, 4th Battalion
Joseph Bowman, 4th Battalion
William Bowman, 4th Battalion
John Boylan, GPO
Stephen Boylan, 3rd Battalion
Thomas J. Boylan, 4th Battalion
John Boyne, 2nd Battalion
Joseph Brabazon, 1st Battalion
John Bracken, 3rd Battalion
John Bracken Jnr, 3rd Battalion
Joseph Bracken, GPO
Peadar Bracken, GPO
Luke Bradley, 2nd Battalion, St Stephen's Green
Patrick Bradley, St Stephen's Green
Christopher (Christy) Brady, City Hall
Francis Brady, 2nd Battalion
James Joseph Brady, 2nd Battalion
Michael Brady, GPO
Michael Brady, 4th Battalion
Patrick Brady, 2nd Battalion, St Stephen's
    Green
——(1) Breaslin, GPO
——(2) Breaslin, GPO
John (Seán) Breen, 3rd Battalion
Liam Breen, GPO
Edward Brennan (Éamonn Ó Braoináin), 1st
    Battalion
James Brennan, 2nd Battalion, St Stephen's
    Green
James Joseph (Séamus) Brennan, 1st Battalion

James Michael (Séamus) Brennan, GPO
Laurence Brennan, 2nd Battalion
Maurice Brennan, GPO
Patrick Brennan, 3rd Battalion
Patrick Brennan, 3rd Battalion
W.J. Brennan-Whitmore, GPO
James Breslin, 1st Battalion
Patrick Breslin, 2nd Battalion
Peadar Breslin, 1st Battalion
Thomas Breslin, 1st Battalion
Tobias (Toby) Breslin, 3rd Battalion
Edward Bridgeman, 1st Battalion
John Brien, 2nd Battalion
Joseph A. Briggs, GPO
Patrick (Paddy) Brogan, 5th Battalion
Frederick John Brooks, 1st Battalion
Daniel (Dan) Brophy, GPO, 5th Battalion
Thomas Brophy, GPO
James Brougham, 2nd Battalion, St Stephen's
    Green
Joseph Brown (Browne), 2nd Battalion
James Browne, 3rd Battalion
William Browne, 3rd Battalion
William Bruen, 3rd Battalion
Cathal Brugha, 4th Battalion
Thomas Bryan, St Stephen's Green
Donal Buckley (Domhnall Ó Buachalla), GPO
William Joseph Buckley, 2nd Battalion
Edward (Éamon) Bulfin, GPO
Bartholomew (Bart) Burke, GPO
Edward Burke, St Stephen's Green
Fergus (Frank) Burke, GPO
James Joseph Burke, 4th Battalion
Matt Burke, St Stephen's Green
Matthew Burke, 4th Battalion
Nicholas Burke, GPO
Thomas Burke, 2nd Battalion, St Stephen's
    Green
William Francis (Frank) (Goban) Burke, 4th
    Battalion
James Burns, 1st Battalion
Frederick Burton, 3rd Battalion
Christopher Butler, 4th Battalion
Con Butler, 4th Battalion
George Butler, 1st Battalion
James Butler, 4th Battalion
Patrick (Paddy) Buttner, St Stephen's Green
Alphonsus (Alfie) Byrne, 4th Battalion
Ambrose Byrne, 1st Battalion
Andrew Joseph Byrne, 3rd Battalion
Bernard Christopher Byrne, 1st Battalion

Charles Byrne, 4th Battalion
Charles Bernard Byrne, 1st Battalion
Christopher Byrne, 3rd Battalion
Christopher Byrne, 4th Battalion
Christopher Byrne (O'Byrne), St Stephen's
    Green
Christopher Columba Byrne, GPO
Daniel Byrne, 3rd Battalion
Denis Byrne, 2nd Battalion, St Stephen's Green
Denis Byrne, 3rd Battalion
Denis Byrne, 4th Battalion
Dermot Byrne, 3rd Battalion
Edward Byrne, GPO
Frank Byrne, 4th Battalion
George Byrne, 4th Battalion
Henry Byrne, 3rd Battalion
James Byrne, GPO
James Byrne, 1st Battalion
James Byrne, 2nd Battalion
James Byrne, 3rd Battalion
James Byrne (Séamus Ó Broin), 4th Battalion
James Byrne, St Stephen's Green
Joe Byrne, GPO
John Byrne, City Hall
John (Seán) Byrne, City Hall
John (Seán) Byrne, 3rd Battalion
John Joseph Byrne, 1st Battalion
John Joseph Byrne, 4th Battalion
Joseph Byrne, St Stephen's Green
Joseph John Byrne, 2nd Battalion
Joseph P. Byrne, 4th Battalion
Laurence Byrne, 1st Battalion
Liam Byrne, 4th Battalion
Louis Byrne, GPO
Louis Byrne, GPO, City Hall
Michael Byrne, 3rd Battalion
Michael Byrne, 3rd Battalion
Michael Byrne, 3rd Battalion
Michael Byrne, 4th Battalion
Michael Byrne, 4th Battalion
Patrick Byrne, 1st Battalion
Patrick Byrne (Pádraig Ó Broin), 2nd Battalion
Patrick Byrne, 3rd Battalion
Patrick (Paddy) Byrne, 3rd Battalion
Patrick Byrne, 4th Battalion
Patrick Byrne, 4th Battalion
Patrick Byrne, City Hall
Patrick Joseph Byrne, GPO
Peter Byrne, 3rd Battalion
Peter Sylvester Byrne, GPO
Seán Byrne, 1st Battalion

Séamus Byrne, 1st Battalion
Thomas Byrne, 3rd Battalion
Thomas Francis (Tom) Byrne, GPO, City Hall
Vincent (Vinnie) Byrne, 2nd Battalion
William Byrne, 1st Battalion
William Byrne, 2nd Battalion
William Byrne, 3rd Battalion

C
Patrick Caddell, GPO, 5th Battalion
John Caffrey, GPO
Mathew Caffrey, GPO
Patrick Cahalan, 2nd Battalion
Arthur John Cahill (Ó Cahill), 2nd Battalion
James Cahill, 1st Battalion
Patrick Caldwell, GPO
Joseph Callen, GPO
Ignatius Callender, 1st Battalion
George Campbell, St Stephen's Green
Michael John Campbell, 1st Battalion
Daniel Canny, GPO
Joseph Canny, GPO
Christopher Carberry (Carbury), 3rd Battalion
James Carberry (Carbury), 2nd Battalion
Alex Carmichael, GPO
Bernard Carmichael, GPO
Francis Joseph Carney, 2nd Battalion, St
    Stephen's Green
Peter Carpenter, GPO
Walter Patrick Carpenter, GPO
Charles E. Carrigan (Caragan, Kerrigan), GPO
James Carrigan, GPO
Bartholomew Leo Carroll, 4th Battalion
Dudley Carroll, 3rd Battalion
James Carroll, 4th Battalion
John Carroll, GPO
Michael Carroll, St Stephen's Green
Patrick Carroll, GPO
Peter Carroll (Peadar Ó Cearbhail), GPO
Peter Carroll, 1st Battalion
Eugene (Owen) Carton, St Stephen's Green
Thomas Carty, 4th Battalion
Hugh Casey, 1st Battalion
James Joseph Casey, 2nd Battalion
Leo Casey, 3rd Battalion
James Cassels, GPO, 2nd Battalion
Henry Cassidy, St Stephen's Green
James Philip Cassidy, GPO
Thomas Cassidy, 1st Battalion
Thomas Cassidy, 3rd Battalion
John Patrick Catlin, 1st Battalion

Éamonn Ceannt, 4th Battalion
Daniel Francis Chambers, 2nd Battalion, St
    Stephen's Green
Patrick Chaney, St Stephen's Green
William Chaney, St Stephen's Green
Michael Charlton (Charleton), St Stephen's
    Green
William Christian, 3rd Battalion
Peter Christie, 2nd Battalion, St Stephen's
    Green
Peadar (Peter) Clancy, 1st Battalion
James Clarke, 1st Battalion
Joe Clarke, 3rd Battalion
John Clarke, GPO, 1st Battalion, 5th Battalion
Joseph Clarke, 4th Battalion
Liam Clarke, GPO
Philip Clarke, St Stephen's Green
Robert John Clarke, 2nd Battalion
Thomas (Tom) Clarke (Tomás Ó Clerigh),
    GPO
Peter Clifford, GPO
Thomas (Tom) Clifford, St Stephen's Green
Patrick J. Clinch, GPO
William Coady, 4th Battalion
John (Seán) Coate, GPO
Peter Coates, 3rd Battalion
Peter Coates, St Stephen's Green
John (Seán) Cody, 1st Battalion
Joseph Coffey, 1st Battalion
Francis Xavier Coghlan, 1st Battalion
Joseph Coghlan, GPO
Cornelius (Con) Colbert, 4th Battalion
Seán Colbert, 2nd Battalion
Patrick Cole, 1st Battalion
Seán Cole, GPO
Thomas Cole, 1st Battalion
Richard (Dick) Coleman, GPO, 1st Battalion,
    5th Battalion
Daniel Colgan, 3rd Battalion
Michael John (Mick) Colgan, 2nd Battalion
Patrick Colgan (Padraic Colgain), GPO
Henry Edward (Harry) Colley, GPO
Charles Tottenham Collins, 2nd Battalion
Maurice John Collins, 1st Battalion
Michael Collins, GPO
Éamon Comber, 1st Battalion
Andrew Comerford, 2nd Battalion
Luke Condron, 1st Battalion
William (Liam) Condron, 4th Battalion
Martin Conlon, 1st Battalion
Patrick (Paddy) Connaughton, GPO

Éamonn (Eddie) Connolly, City Hall
George Connolly, City Hall
James Connolly, GPO
Joseph Connolly, GPO
Joseph Connolly, St Stephen's Green
Matt (Mattie) Connolly, City Hall
Rory (Rauri, Roderick, Roddy) Connolly, GPO
Seán Connolly, City Hall
James (Jimmy) Connor, 5th Battalion
Herbert 'Andy' Conroy, GPO
James Conroy Snr, 1st Battalion
James Patrick Conroy, GPO
Jimmy Conroy Jnr, 2nd Battalion
John (Seán) Conroy, St Stephen's Green
William Conroy, 3rd Battalion
Seán Joseph Conway, GPO
Patrick Vincent Coogan, 1st Battalion
Joseph Cooling, 1st Battalion
James Cooney, 2nd Battalion
John Dutton Cooper, GPO
Robert Cooper, 3rd Battalion
Laurence Corbally, GPO
Richard Corbally, GPO
Thomas Corbally, GPO
James Corcoran, St Stephen's Green
Brother Joseph Louis Corcoran, 4th Battalion
Patrick John Christopher Corless, GPO
James Corrigan, 4th Battalion
William Patrick (Willie) Corrigan, 4th Battalion
Edward Cosgrave, GPO
John Cosgrave, 3rd Battalion
Michael Cosgrave, 1st Battalion
Philip Cosgrave, 4th Battalion
William T. Cosgrave, 4th Battalion
Edward J. Costello, 1st Battalion
John (Seán) Costello, 3rd Battalion
Joseph Alphonsus Francis Cotter, 2nd Battalion, St Stephen's Green
Richard (Dick) Cotter, 2nd Battalion
James John Coughlan, 4th Battalion
Bernard Courtney (Courtnay?), St Stephen's Green
Daniel Courtney, GPO
Michael Patrick Cowley (Mícheál Padraig Mac Amhalghaidh), GPO
Redmond Cox, 1st Battalion
Henry (Harry) Coyle, GPO
John Thomas Coyle, City Hall
William Coyle, 1st Battalion

Thomas Coyne, 3rd Battalion
Barney Craven, St Stephen's Green
Thomas Craven, GPO
Michael Cremin, GPO
James Crenigan, GPO, 1st Battalion, 5th Battalion
John (Jack) Crenigan, 5th Battalion
Joseph Cripps, GPO
Gerald Crofts, GPO
Michael Croke, GPO
Thomas Croke, GPO
John Cromien, 1st Battalion
Christopher Crothers (Carruthers), St Stephen's Green
John Cullen, 4th Battalion
John Christopher (Seán) Cullen, 3rd Battalion
John Francis (Frank) Cullen, 1st Battalion
Joseph Cullen, 1st Battalion
Michael Cullen, 3rd Battalion
Patrick Cullen, St Stephen's Green
Peter Cullen, 2nd Battalion
Thomas Cullen, 1st Battalion
Thomas Cullen, 4th Battalion
William F. (Liam) Cullen, GPO
Mark Joseph Cummins, GPO
Tom Cummins, GPO
James Cunningham, 2nd Battalion
Michael Cunningham, 4th Battalion
Joseph Michael Curran, 3rd Battalion
William Curran, 4th Battalion
Michael Curtain (Curtin), 2nd Battalion
John Cusack, GPO

D

Patrick Dalton, GPO
Denis (Dinny) Daly, GPO
Edward (Ned) Daly, 1st Battalion
Francis (Frank) Daly, 1st Battalion, 5th Battalion
James Daly, 3rd Battalion
Patrick Daly, 1st Battalion
Patrick (Paddy) Daly (O'Daly) (Pádraig Ua Dalaigh), 1st Battalion
Patrick (Paddy) J. Daly (O'Daly), GPO
Séamus Daly, GPO
Thomas (Tom) Daly, City Hall
William Daniel (Liam) Daly, GPO
William Joseph Daly, 2nd Battalion
Henry (Harry) Daniels, St Stephen's Green
Charles Darcy (D'Arcy, Darcey), City Hall
James Darcy, 2nd Battalion
John Francis Darcy, 4th Battalion

Patrick Leo Darcy, 2nd Battalion
William Darcy, GPO
Michael Darker, 1st Battalion
William Darker, GPO
Luke Darling, 1st Battalion
Daniel Davitt, GPO
Richard Patrick Davys, 2nd Battalion, St
    Stephen's Green
Robert (Bob) DeCoeur, St Stephen's Green
Seán Deegan, 2nd Battalion
Henry Delaney, 1st Battalion
Michael Delaney, City Hall
Edward Delemere, 1st Battalion
James Dempsey, GPO
James Dempsey, 1st Battalion
William Dempsey, 4th Battalion
Patrick Dennany (Dennahy), GPO
Joseph Derham, GPO
Michael Derham, 1st Battalion
John (Seán) Derrington, 1st Battalion
William Patrick (Liam) Derrington, 1st
    Battalion
Paul Dervin, 1st Battalion
Éamon de Valera, 3rd Battalion
Patrick Devereux, GPO
Francis Devine, GPO, City Hall
Frederick Victor Devine, 2nd Battalion
John (Johnny) Devine, 5th Battalion
Thomas William Devine, GPO
James Joseph (Séamus) (Peter, Peadar?) Devoy,
    GPO
William Dickinson, GPO
Christopher Doggett, 1st Battalion
John Joseph (Jack) Doherty (O'Doherty), 4th
    Battalion
Michael (Mick) Doherty, St Stephen's Green
Peter Dolan, 2nd Battalion, St Stephen's Green
John (Seán) Domican, 1st Battalion
Brendan Donelan (Donnellan, Donolan), 4th
    Battalion
Charles Donnelly, GPO
James Donnelly, City Hall
James Donnelly, St Stephen's Green
John Donnelly, 2nd Battalion
Michael Donnelly, St Stephen's Green
Patrick (Paddy) Donnelly, GPO
Simon Donnelly, 3rd Battalion
Robert Donohoe, 1st Battalion
Sylvester Donohoe, 1st Battalion
Michael Donovan, 3rd Battalion
John Doogan, 2nd Battalion

Joseph (Joe) Doolan, 4th Battalion
Éamonn T. Dore, GPO
Andrew Dowling, 1st Battalion
James Thomas Dowling, 1st Battalion
John Dowling, 1st Battalion
John (Seán) Dowling, 4th Battalion
Michael Dowling, GPO
Thomas Dowling, 1st Battalion
John (Seán) Downey, 4th Battalion
Joseph Downey, 4th Battalion
Christopher Doyle, 4th Battalion
Denis (Dennis) Doyle, St Stephen's Green
David Doyle, 3rd Battalion
Edward Doyle, GPO
Gerald Doyle, 4th Battalion
James H. Doyle, 3rd Battalion
James Joseph (Séamus) Doyle, 3rd Battalion
John Doyle, GPO
John Doyle, GPO
John Doyle, 1st Battalion
John Joseph (J.J.) Doyle, GPO
John William Doyle, 3rd Battalion
Joseph Doyle, St Stephen's Green
Joseph Doyle (Daly?), St Stephen's Green
Joseph Francis Doyle, 4th Battalion
Michael Doyle, 3rd Battalion
Patrick Doyle, 2nd Battalion
Patrick Doyle, 3rd Battalion
Patrick Doyle, 3rd Battalion
Patrick J. Doyle, 3rd Battalion
Patrick (Paddy) Doyle, 5th Battalion
Peadar Seán Doyle, 4th Battalion
Peter Doyle, GPO, City Hall
Seán (John J.) Doyle, GPO
Sylvester Joseph Doyle, St Stephen's Green
Thomas Doyle, GPO
Thomas Doyle, 2nd Battalion, St Stephen's
    Green
Thomas J. Doyle, 4th Battalion
William Doyle, GPO, 5th Battalion
James Drannon (?), 2nd Battalion
Frank Drennan, GPO
William Drennan, 1st Battalion
Thomas Drumm, 2nd Battalion, St Stephen's
    Green
Patrick Joseph Drury, GPO
Christopher Duffy, 1st Battalion
Edward Duffy, GPO
Joseph Duffy, GPO
Joseph Duffy, St Stephen's Green
Patrick Duffy (O'Duffy), St Stephen's Green

Éamonn J. Duggan, 1st Battalion
Francis Duggan, 2nd Battalion
Richard Duke, 5th Battalion
Thomas Patrick Duke, 5th Battalion
Andrew (Andy) Dunne, St Stephen's Green
Denis K. Dunne, 4th Battalion
Francis (Frank) Dunne, GPO
John Dunne, GPO
John Dunne, 3rd Battalion
John Dunne, 3rd Battalion
Joseph Dunne, GPO
Patrick Dunne, GPO
Patrick Joseph Dunne, 4th Battalion
Peter (Peadar) Dunne, 4th Battalion
Thomas Dunne, GPO
Thomas Dunne, 1st Battalion
Thomas Dunne, 3rd Battalion
Thomas John Dunne, 1st Battalion
John Dwan, 1st Battalion
James Dwyer, St Stephen's Green
Michael Dwyer, GPO, St Stephen's Green
Michael Dwyer, 4th Battalion
Albert Dyas, GPO
Christopher Dynan, St Stephen's Green

E
John Early, GPO
Patrick Joseph Early, 5th Battalion
John Edwards, 4th Battalion
Michael Edwards, 1st Battalion
Joseph Egan, GPO
Patrick Egan, 4th Battalion
William Egan, St Stephen's Green
John (Seán) Ellis, 1st Battalion
Samuel Ellis, 2nd Battalion
Elliot (Ellett) Elmes (Ellems), City Hall
Patrick English, GPO
Patrick Francis (Frank) English (Frainnc Inglis),
    GPO
Christopher Ennis, 2nd Battalion
Edward Ennis, 3rd Battalion
Michael Ennis, 2nd Battalion
Thomas James (Tom) Ennis, GPO
Robert Eustace, GPO
Robert J. Evans, 4th Battalion

F
Brian Fagan, 4th Battalion
James Fagan, 3rd Battalion
John Fagan, 1st Battalion
Michael Fagan, 1st Battalion

Patrick Fagan, 1st Battalion
William Fagan, 4th Battalion
Frank Fahy, 1st Battalion
James Fairhill (Séamus Ó Maoilfinn), 2nd
    Battalion
Denis Farrell, GPO, City Hall
James Farrell, 2nd Battalion
James Farrell, St Stephen's Green
John Farrell, 1st Battalion
John Farrell, 1st Battalion
Michael Farrell, 4th Battalion
Patrick Farrell, 1st Battalion
Thomas Farrell, 1st Battalion
Christopher Farrelly, 1st Battalion
Christopher Farrelly, 2nd Battalion
Seán Farrelly, 1st Battalion
Walter Farrelly, 5th Battalion
Stephen Farren, 1st Battalion
John Faulkiner, GPO
Peter Fearon, 1st Battalion
James Feehan, 4th Battalion
Christopher Feekery, GPO
Gerald Feeny, 1st Battalion
Douglas ffrench-Mullen, 4th Battalion
Michael Finegan, GPO
John Finlay (Finley, Findlay), City Hall
Timothy Finn, 3rd Battalion
John Fisher, 1st Battalion
Desmond FitzGerald, GPO
James FitzGerald, 3rd Battalion
Leo FitzGerald, 3rd Battalion
Theobold Wolfe Tone Fitzgerald, 3rd Battalion
Thomas FitzGerald, 3rd Battalion
William (Willie) FitzGerald, 3rd Battalion
John J. Fitzharris, GPO, St Stephen's Green
Gerald Fitzmaurice, 2nd Battalion
Andrew Joseph (Andy) Fitzpatrick, GPO
Denis Fitzpatrick, 1st Battalion
Francis (Frank) Fitzpatrick, City Hall
James Fitzpatrick, 4th Battalion
Michael Fitzpatrick, 2nd Battalion
Maurice Fitzsimons, 1st Battalion
James Flaherty (O'Flaherty, Ó Florbheartaigh),
    4th Battalion
William (Liam) Flaherty (O'Flaherty, Ó
    Florbheartaigh), 4th Battalion
Francis Flanagan, GPO
James Michael Flanagan, GPO
Fr John (O') Flanagan, GPO
Matthew Flanagan, GPO
Matthew Flanagan, 2nd Battalion

Maurice Daniel Flanagan, GPO
Michael (Mick) Flanagan, GPO
Michael Flanagan, 1st Battalion
Patrick (Paddy) Flanagan, 3rd Battalion
James Fleming, GPO
Michael Fleming, 2nd Battalion
Michael Fleming, 3rd Battalion
Michael (Mick) Fleming, 5th Battalion
Seán Flood, 1st Battalion
Ignatius George Flynn, GPO
John A. Flynn, 3rd Battalion
Patrick Flynn, GPO
James Fogarty, 4th Battalion
John Fogarty, 1st Battalion
Joseph Fogarty, 2nd Battalion
Patrick Fogarty, 1st Battalion
Thomas Fogarty, GPO
Michael Patrick Foley, 1st Battalion
William Foley, 4th Battalion
James Foran, 4th Battalion
Seán Forde, 1st Battalion
James (Séamus) Fox, St Stephen's Green
James Joseph (Jimmy) Fox, St Stephen's Green
Michael Fox, GPO
Frederick Foy, 1st Battalion
Martin Foy (Fay?), St Stephen's Green
Denis Frawley, 1st Battalion
Bernard Friel (Frick?), GPO
Thomas Fulham (Fullam?), 3rd Battalion
George Fullerton, St Stephen's Green
Andrew Furlong, GPO
John (Jack) Furlong, 2nd Battalion
Joseph Furlong, 2nd Battalion
Matthew Furlong, GPO
Matthew Furlong, 2nd Battalion

G

Joseph Gahan, GPO
Matthew Gahan, 1st Battalion
Tadhg Gahan, 2nd Battalion, St Stephen's Green
Patrick Gallagher, GPO
Peter Paul Galligan, GPO
Peter Ganley, 5th Battalion
Henry Gannon, GPO
Laurence Gannon, 4th Battalion
Patrick Garland, GPO
Patrick Gartlan, 1st Battalion
Francis Gaskin, 4th Battalion
Frank Gaskin, 1st Battalion
Henry Gaskin, 4th Battalion

Thomas Gaskin, 4th Battalion
John James Gavan, GPO
Thomas Ernan (Tomás Ernán) Gay, 4th Battalion
Arthur Gaynor, 1st Battalion
George Geoghegan, City Hall
John Joseph Geoghegan, GPO
Christopher (Christy) Geraghty, 1st Battalion
Eugene Geraghty, St Stephen's Green
John (Seán) Geraghty, 1st Battalion
Edward (Edmund) Gibson, 4th Battalion
Michael Gibson, 4th Battalion
Richard Gibson, GPO
Michael Giffney, GPO
James T. Gill, 3rd Battalion
Robert (Bob) Gilligan, 1st Battalion
Patrick Gilsenan, 1st Battalion
Daniel Patrick (Dr P.) Gleeson, 2nd Battalion
Joseph Gleeson, GPO
Martin Gleeson, GPO
Thomas Gleeson, GPO, St Stephen's Green
William Gleeson, GPO, St Stephen's Green
James Glynn, 4th Battalion
John Gerard Gogan, 4th Battalion
Richard P. (Dick) Gogan, GPO
Vincent Joseph Gogan, 1st Battalion
David Thomas Golden, GPO
Gerry Golden, 5th Battalion
Alfred Joseph (Joe) Good, GPO
Edward Gordon, 3rd Battalion
James Gough, 5th Battalion
James (Jim) Gough, St Stephen's Green
Charles Goulding, 2nd Battalion
James Goulding, 2nd Battalion
Seán Goulding, 3rd Battalion
Jack Gowan, 5th Battalion
James J. Grace, 3rd Battalion
James Graham, 1st Battalion
Thomas Graham, 4th Battalion
Patrick (Paddy) Grant, 5th Battalion
Richard Grattan, 2nd Battalion
John (Jack) Graves, GPO
Patrick Green, 1st Battalion
Owen Greene, 3rd Battalion
William Greene, 1st Battalion
John Gregory, 2nd Battalion, St Stephen's Green
James Grehan, 4th Battalion
Martin Griffin, 3rd Battalion
Gerald Griffin, 1st Battalion
William Griffith, 1st Battalion

Michael Grimley, 1st Battalion
John (Seán) Guilfoyle, 3rd Battalion
Joseph Guilfoyle, 3rd Battalion

H
John Halpin, GPO
John Halpin, 1st Battalion
Patrick Halpin, GPO
Peter (Peadar) Halpin, 1st Battalion
William Halpin, GPO, City Hall
William Halpin, 3rd Battalion
William Halpin, St Stephen's Green
William Thomas Halpin, City Hall
Thomas Hamill, 1st Battalion
James Hampton, St Stephen's Green
Matthew Hand, St Stephen's Green
Stephen Hanlon, 1st Battalion
Thomas Hannigan, 1st Battalion
Arthur Hannon, GPO
James Joseph Hannon, 2nd Battalion
D. Haran, 4th Battalion
Patrick Harbourne, 4th Battalion
Seán Harbourne, 4th Battalion
Frank Harding, 1st Battalion
John Harling, GPO
Seán Harling, 1st Battalion
James Harmon, 1st Battalion
Patrick Joseph Harmon, 4th Battalion
Alfred (Alf) Harnett, 1st Battalion
John Harpur, 1st Battalion
Seán Harrington, 1st Battalion
Thomas (Tom) Harris, GPO
Christopher Haughton, 1st Battalion
Augustine Hayes, 3rd Battalion
James Hayes (Séamus Ó hAodha), 2nd Battalion
James Joseph (J.J., Séamus) Hayes, GPO
Michael Hayes (Ó hAodha), 2nd Battalion
Dr Richard Hayes, 5th Battalion
Seán Hayes, GPO
Diarmuid Healy, 1st Battalion
Peadar Healy, 1st Battalion
Richard (Dick) Healy, GPO
Seán Healy, 2nd Battalion
Thomas Healy, City Hall
James Michael Heery, GPO
Michael Heffernan, GPO
John Hegarty, 1st Battalion
Seán Hegarty, GPO
Michael Hemming, 3rd Battalion
Frank Henderson, GPO
Leo James Henderson, GPO

Thomas Henderson, 1st Battalion
Edward Hendrick, 1st Battalion
James Joseph Hendrick, 1st Battalion
John Joseph Hendrick, St Stephen's Green
Francis Henry, St Stephen's Green
Frederick (Fred) Henry, St Stephen's Green
James Henry, 3rd Battalion
James Heron, St Stephen's Green
George Heuston, 2nd Battalion
John (Seán) Heuston, 1st Battalion
Michael Hickey, 3rd Battalion
Richard Hickey, GPO
Frederick Paul Higgins, GPO
James Higgins, 1st Battalion
Peter Higgins, GPO
Patrick Joseph Hogan, 1st Battalion
William Conor Hogan, 1st Battalion
James Patrick Holden, St Stephen's Green
Daniel (Dan) Holland, 4th Battalion
Francis Michael (Frank) Holland, 4th Battalion
Robert Holland, 4th Battalion
Walter (Watty) Holland, 4th Battalion
Denis Holmes, 1st Battalion
Gerard (Garry) Holohan, 1st Battalion, 5th Battalion
Hugh Aloysius Holohan, GPO
Paddy Holohan, 1st Battalion, 5th Battalion
Patrick Hugh (Paddy) Holohan (Holahan, Houlihan), 1st Battalion
Daniel Horan, 4th Battalion
John Joseph Horan, GPO
Martin Hore, GPO
Con Howard, 1st Battalion
George Howard, 4th Battalion
Seán Bernard Howard, 1st Battalion
Michael Howlett, 1st Battalion
James J. Hughes, 2nd Battalion
Patrick Hughes, GPO
Thomas Hughes, GPO
Richard (Dick) Humphreys, GPO
Robert Humphreys, 2nd Battalion, St Stephen's Green
James Hunter, GPO
Thomas (Tom) Hunter, 2nd Battalion
John (Jack, Seán) Hurley, 1st Battalion
Joseph Hutchison, GPO
Christopher Hyland, 1st Battalion
James Hyland, St Stephen's Green
Thomas Hyland, 1st Battalion
John Francis (Jack) Hynes, GPO, 5th Battalion
Seán Hynes, 1st Battalion

I

George Irvine, 4th Battalion
Samuel Patrick Irwin, 3rd Battalion

J

Nicholas Jackman, 1st Battalion
Francis Jackson, 3rd Battalion
Joseph Jackson, 3rd Battalion
Peter Jackson, GPO
Peter Jackson, St Stephen's Green
Thomas Michael Jennings, 2nd Battalion, St Stephen's Green
Thomas Jones, GPO
Brian Joyce (Seoighe), GPO
Edward Joyce, St Stephen's Green
James Joyce, St Stephen's Green
John Joyce, 2nd Battalion
John Vincent Joyce, 4th Battalion
Joseph James Joyce, 2nd Battalion, St Stephen's Green
John Patrick Judge, 4th Battalion

K

Thomas (Tom) Kain (Kane?), City Hall
Thomas Kane, 1st Battalion
Daniel Kavanagh, 2nd Battalion
Denis Kavanagh, 1st Battalion
James (Séamus) Kavanagh, 3rd Battalion
James Joseph (Séamus) Kavanagh, 1st Battalion
James Joseph Kavanagh, 4th Battalion
John Kavanagh, 2nd Battalion, St Stephen's Green
Martin Kavanagh, 4th Battalion
Michael Kavanagh, 3rd Battalion
Patrick Kavanagh, 2nd Battalion
Patrick Kavanagh, 3rd Battalion
Peter (Peadar) Kavanagh, 3rd Battalion
Séamus Kavanagh, GPO
Séamus Kavanagh, 2nd Battalion, St Stephen's Green
Thomas (Tom) Kavanagh, 4th Battalion
William (Liam) Kavanagh, 3rd Battalion
Liam Keane, 4th Battalion
Michael Kearney, 3rd Battalion
Peadar Kearney, 2nd Battalion
Thomas Kearney, GPO
Thomas Kearney, 4th Battalion
Frank Kearns, 2nd Battalion
Hubert (Hugh) Kearns, GPO, 2nd Battalion
John Kearns, 2nd Battalion
Joseph John Kearns, 2nd Battalion

Patrick Kearns, 1st Battalion
Thomas Kearns, 2nd Battalion
Cornelius (Con) Keating, GPO
Edward Laurence (Éamonn) Keegan, 4th Battalion
Christopher Keeling, GPO
Joseph Keeley, St Stephen's Green
John Keely (Kealy, Kiely), GPO
Thomas Patrick (Tommy) Keenan, St Stephen's Green
Thomas Kehoe, 2nd Battalion
Edward (Éamonn) J. Kelly, GPO, City Hall
Fergus Kelly, GPO
Francis Kelly, 2nd Battalion, St Stephen's Green
Francis Matthew (Matt) Kelly, GPO
Frank Kelly, GPO
Hugh Kelly, 2nd Battalion, St Stephen's Green
James (Jimmy) Kelly, 5th Battalion
James Kelly, St Stephen's Green
John Kelly, St Stephen's Green
John Emmanuel Kelly, 2nd Battalion
John J. (Jack) Kelly, GPO, 5th Battalion
Joseph Kelly, GPO
Joseph Kelly, 1st Battalion
Joseph Kelly, St Stephen's Green
Joseph Francis Kelly, 4th Battalion
Joseph Patrick Kelly, 5th Battalion
Martin Kelly, City Hall
Matthew Kelly, 5th Battalion
Michael (Mick) Kelly, St Stephen's Green
Michael J. Kelly, 1st Battalion
Patrick Kelly, GPO, 1st Battalion, 5th Battalion
Patrick Kelly, 1st Battalion
Patrick Kelly, 2nd Battalion
Patrick Kelly, 3rd Battalion
Peter Kelly (Peadar Ó Cellaigh), 5th Battalion
Richard (Dick) Kelly, GPO, 1st Battalion, 5th Battalion
Richard Kelly, 3rd Battalion
Seán Kelly, 4th Battalion
Thomas Joseph Kelly, 3rd Battalion
Tom Kelly, 1st Battalion
William (Bill) Kelly, 4th Battalion
William Kelly, St Stephen's Green
Austin (Gilbert?) Kennan, GPO
James J. Kennedy, 1st Battalion
John Kennedy, 1st Battalion
Joseph Kennedy, 1st Battalion
Joseph P. Kennedy, 4th Battalion
Luke Kennedy, GPO
Seán Kennedy, 1st Battalion

Charles Kenny, 3rd Battalion
Henry Vincent Kenny, GPO
James Kenny, GPO
James Kenny, 4th Battalion
James Kenny, 4th Battalion
James Joseph Kenny, 2nd Battalion, St Stephen's
  Green
Joe Kenny, GPO
John Kenny, GPO
John Kenny, 1st Battalion
Kieran Kenny, 4th Battalion
Michael Kenny, GPO
Bernard Patrick Keogh, GPO
Cyril Aloysius Keogh, St Stephen's Green
Edward Patrick (Ned) Keogh, St Stephen's
  Green
Gerald Anthony Keogh, GPO
James Keogh, St Stephen's Green
John Keogh, 4th Battalion
Joseph James Keogh, GPO
Martin Keogh, 4th Battalion
Michael Keogh, GPO
Patrick Keogh, 4th Battalion
John Patrick (Seán) Kerr, GPO
Michael Kerr, 4th Battalion
Thomas Kerr, GPO
Owen Kerrigan, 4th Battalion
John Keys, 4th Battalion
Thomas Kilcoyne, GPO
John A. Kilgallon, GPO
Thomas (Tom) Kilgallon, GPO
Robert Killeen, GPO
Patrick Killion, 1st Battalion
Patrick (Paddy) Kilmartin, GPO
Arthur King, City Hall
Daniel King, 2nd Battalion
George King, GPO
John King, GPO
Martin King, St Stephen's Green
Mick King, City Hall
Patrick King, GPO
Sam King, GPO
Samuel King, City Hall
Seán Joseph Francis King, 2nd Battalion, St
  Stephen's Green
John Kinsella, 3rd Battalion
Edward Kirwan, 3rd Battalion
Patrick Kirwan, GPO, City Hall
Michael Knightly, GPO

L

Philip Lacey, St Stephen's Green
Nicholas Laffan, 1st Battalion
John Lafferty, GPO
John Watson Lake, 2nd Battalion
Edward (Éamonn) Lalor, 3rd Battalion
Patrick Joseph Lalor (Lawlor), St Stephen's
  Green
Patrick Lamb, 4th Battalion
J. Lambert, St Stephen's Green
James Lambert, City Hall
Thomas Lambert, GPO, City Hall
Séamus Landy (Lundy), GPO
Edward (Ned) Lane, 2nd Battalion
Patrick Lanigan, 2nd Battalion
Michael Largan, GPO
John Larkin, 1st Battalion
Patrick Lawler, GPO
Colm Lawless, 5th Battalion
Edward Lawless, GPO, 5th Battalion
Frank Lawless Snr, 5th Battalion
James Joseph Lawless, 2nd Battalion
James Vincent (Jim) Lawless, 5th Battalion
Joseph Vincent Lawless, 5th Battalion
Michael J. Lawless, 2nd Battalion, St Stephen's
  Green
Francis J. (Frank) Lawlor, 1st Battalion
John (Seán) Lawlor, 1st Battalion
Laurence James (Larry) Lawlor, 1st Battalion
Thomas Leahy, 1st Battalion, GPO
Thomas Leaver (Seaver?), 5th Battalion
Peter Leddy, St Stephen's Green
Joseph Ledwith (Ledwidge?), GPO
Peter Ledwith, 1st Battalion
Hugh Lee, GPO
Joseph Lee, GPO
Robert Leggett, 1st Battalion
James Leigh, 4th Battalion
Noel Lemass, GPO
Seán Francis Lemass, GPO
Michael Lennon, 3rd Battalion
Michael John Lennon, 1st Battalion
Nicholas Lennon, 1st Battalion
Edward Leonard, 3rd Battalion
Joseph (Joe) Leonard, 2nd Battalion
Patrick Leonard, 3rd Battalion
George Levins, 1st Battalion
Leo Lifforoi (Laffoy?), 3rd Battalion
Michael (Mick) Liston, 4th Battalion
James (Jem) Little, St Stephen's Green
Patrick Long, 2nd Battalion

Thomas Losty, 2nd Battalion
Michael Love, 2nd Battalion
Arnold Lowe, 1st Battalion
Edward Luke (Juke, Tuke?), St Stephen's Green
Charles Lynch, 1st Battalion
Dermot (Dairmuid) Lynch, GPO
Fionan Lynch (Fionán Ó Lóingsigh), 1st
    Battalion
Gilbert Lynch, GPO
Gilbert Lynch, 1st Battalion
John Lynch, GPO
Martin Lynch, GPO
Michael Lynch, 1st Battalion
Michael Joseph Lynch, 5th Battalion
Patrick Leo Lynch, GPO
Seán Lynch, 2nd Battalion, St Stephen's Green
William Lynch, 2nd Battalion
Charles (Charlie) Lyons, 1st Battalion
Edward Lyons, 1st Battalion
Edward Lyons, 2nd Battalion
George A. Lyons (Seoirse A. Ó Liathain), 3rd
    Battalion
John E. Lyons, 1st Battalion
Joseph Lyons, 1st Battalion

M
Bernard (Bennie) McAllister, 5th Battalion
John McAllister, 5th Battalion
Michael (Mick) McAllister, 5th Battalion
M. McAntee, 1st Battalion
James McArdle, 5th Battalion
John McArdle, GPO
Patrick McArdle, 1st Battalion
Patrick McArdle, 5th Battalion
Peter (Owen) McArdle, 3rd Battalion
Thomas McArdle, 5th Battalion
Daniel McArt, St Stephen's Green
Garrett (Gearóid) McAuliffe (MacAuliffe),
    GPO
John MacBride, 2nd Battalion
Patrick McBride, 3rd Battalion
Edward McCabe, 4th Battalion
Frank McCabe, 1st Battalion
Jack McCabe, GPO
John McCabe, 4th Battalion
Kevin Joseph McCabe, GPO
Michael McCabe, 1st Battalion
Michael B. McCabe, 4th Battalion
Patrick McCabe, 3rd Battalion
Peter McCabe, 4th Battalion
William McCabe, 4th Battalion

William A. (Liam) McCabe, 3rd Battalion
John McCann, 5th Battalion
Thomas Joseph McCann, 1st Battalion
Bernard McCarthy, 3rd Battalion
Daniel McCarthy, 1st Battalion
Daniel (Dan) McCarthy, 4th Battalion
Michael McCarthy, 3rd Battalion
Patrick McCarthy, 4th Battalion
Thomas (Tommy) McCarthy, 4th Battalion
William McCleane, GPO
Bernard McCormack, GPO
Christopher J. McCormack, 1st Battalion
James McCormack, St Stephen's Green
John McCormack, 1st Battalion
Patrick MacCormack, 3rd Battalion
Thomas McCormack, St Stephen's Green
Richard McCormick (McCormack), St
    Stephen's Green
Miceal MacCraich, GPO
Patrick (Pat) McCrea, GPO
Joseph McCurran, 3rd Battalion
Richard McDavitt, 2nd Battalion
Louis Bernard McDermott, 4th Battalion
Owen McDermott, 2nd Battalion, St Stephen's
    Green
Patrick McDermott, GPO
Rory MacDermott (Ruaidhri MacDiarmada),
    GPO
Seán MacDermott, GPO
Seán McDermott, 3rd Battalion
John MacDonagh, 2nd Battalion
Joseph McDonagh, GPO
Joseph MacDonagh, 1st Battalion
Thomas MacDonagh, 2nd Battalion
Andy MacDonald, 1st Battalion
John McDonald, GPO
John Bernard McDonald, 2nd Battalion, St
    Stephen's Green
Andrew McDonnell, 3rd Battalion
James McDonnell, City Hall
John Quinlan MacDonnell (McDonald?), GPO
Matthew McDonnell, 2nd Battalion
Michael (Mick) McDonnell, 2nd Battalion, St
    Stephen's Green
Patrick McDonnell, 2nd Battalion, St Stephen's
    Green
Thomas McDonnell, 1st Battalion
William McDonnell, 2nd Battalion, St
    Stephen's Green
Cathal MacDowell, 3rd Battalion
Patrick McDowell, 3rd Battalion

William McDowell (MacDowell), 4th Battalion
Seán McEffroy, 3rd Battalion
James John McElligott, GPO
John McEntagart, GPO
Seán MacEntee, GPO
Louis McEvatt, 1st Battalion
Christopher McEvoy, 1st Battalion
Christopher McEvoy, 4th Battalion
Christopher James McEvoy, 4th Battalion
Dominick McEvoy, GPO
James McEvoy, GPO
Patrick McEvoy, 2nd Battalion
Thomas Richard McEvoy, GPO
James (Séamus) McGallogly, GPO
John (Seán) McGallogly, GPO
Milo McGarry, GPO
Seán McGarry, GPO
Michael McGarvey, GPO
Joseph McGill, 1st Battalion
Patrick McGill, 3rd Battalion
C. McGinley, GPO
Edward (Eunan) MacGinley, 1st Battalion
Patrick McGinley, GPO
William (Liam) McGinley, GPO
Michael McGinn, St Stephen's Green
Michael Conway McGinn, GPO
Tom McGinn, GPO
John McGlure, 2nd Battalion
John (Seán) McGlynn, 4th Battalion
Charles McGowan, 3rd Battalion
Claude McGowan, 2nd Battalion
Jack McGowan, 5th Battalion
Séamus McGowan, GPO
Christopher McGrane, GPO
Thomas McGrane, 2nd Battalion, St Stephen's Green
Daniel McGrath, 2nd Battalion
James (P.B.?) McGrath, 3rd Battalion
Joseph (Joe) McGrath, 4th Battalion
Michael McGrath (Miceál MacGraith), GPO
Patrick McGrath, 4th Battalion
Patrick McGrath, 4th Battalion
Patrick Joseph McGrath Jnr, GPO
Patrick Joseph McGrath Snr, GPO
Peter Paul MacGrath, St Stephen's Green
Seán McGrath, 3rd Battalion
Seán McGrath, 4th Battalion
Thomas (Tom) McGrath, GPO
Frank McGuinness, 1st Battalion
Jim McGuinness, 5th Battalion
Joseph McGuinness, 1st Battalion

Michael McHugh, 1st Battalion
Richard (Dick) McKee, 2nd Battalion
Bernard McKenna, 4th Battalion
John (Seán) McKenna, 4th Battalion
William McKeon, 1st Battalion
Owen McKeown, 1st Battalion
Leo MacKey, GPO
Michael MacKey, GPO
Dan McLaughlin, GPO
Dr Daniel Aloysius MacLaughlin, GPO
Peter McLaughlin, 1st Battalion
John (Seán) McLoughlin (MacLoughlin), GPO, 1st Battalion
Bernard J. MacMahon, 2nd Battalion
Charles Eugene MacMahon, GPO
Daniel Joseph McMahon, 4th Battalion
Donal (Dan?) McMahon, GPO
John (Seán) MacMahon, 3rd Battalion
John (Seán) McMahon, 3rd Battalion
John MacMahon, St Stephen's Green
Patrick MacMahon, GPO
Patrick McMahon, GPO
Peter McMahon, 1st Battalion
Peter (Peadar) MacMahon (Peadar MacMathghamhna), 2nd Battalion, St Stephen's Green
Seán McMahon, GPO
Patrick McManus, GPO
Maighnas MacMearigh (McMerry), 1st Battalion
Francis Joseph McMenamy, 1st Battalion
Manus McMenamy, 1st Battalion
Joseph McMenarigh, 1st Battalion
Bernard McMullan, GPO
Henry Russell MacNab, St Stephen's Green
Francis (Frank) McNally, 1st Battalion
John McNally, GPO, 5th Battalion
Peter McNally, 1st Battalion
James McNamara (MacNamara), 1st Battalion
Patrick J. McNamara (MacNamara), 1st Battalion
James Kevin McNamee, 4th Battalion
Dermot John (Diarmuid) MacNeill, 4th Battalion
William (Liam) MacNeive (Liam MacNiamh), GPO
Patrick McNestry, 1st Battalion
Michael McNulty, 1st Battalion
Peadar Joseph McNulty, 1st Battalion
James McParland, 2nd Battalion
Frank McPartland, GPO

Peter Celestine McPartlin, GPO
Thomas McQuaid, 1st Battalion
Seán MacTialaghoigh (?), 3rd Battalion
James McVeigh, 4th Battalion
Francis (Frank) Macken, GPO
Patrick Macken, 1st Battalion
Peadar Macken, 3rd Battalion
Laurence Mackey, GPO
Michael Mackey, GPO
John (Seán) Madden, GPO
Michael Magee, 1st Battalion
James Maguire, 3rd Battalion
James Maguire, 4th Battalion
James Maguire (McGuire), St Stephen's Green
John (Jack) Maguire, GPO
Matthew Maguire, GPO
Patrick J. Maguire, GPO
Thomas (Tomás) Maguire, 1st Battalion
Daniel Maher, 3rd Battalion
William Joseph Maher, 2nd Battalion
John Mahon (Maher?), St Stephen's Green
Patrick Mahon, GPO
Patrick (Paddy) Joseph Mahon Jnr, GPO
Thomas Christopher Mahon, GPO
Antle (Tony) Makapaltis, GPO
Michael Mallin, St Stephen's Green
James Mallon, 3rd Battalion
Jerome Joseph Malone, GPO
Michael Malone, 3rd Battalion
Robert Malone, 3rd Battalion
Thomas Mangan, GPO
Edward Mannering, St Stephen's Green
Henry Manning, GPO
Patrick Manning, 2nd Battalion
Peter (Peadar) Paul Manning, 1st Battalion
Louis Marie, GPO, 1st Battalion
Thomas Markham, GPO
James Marks, GPO, 1st Battalion, 5th Battalion
Edward Marrinan, 4th Battalion
Christopher Martin, 1st Battalion
Éamon Martin, 1st Battalion
Joseph Patrick (Joe) Martin, 3rd Battalion
Peter Martin, 2nd Battalion
D.H. Mason, 4th Battalion
Frank Mason, 1st Battalion
George Mason, 1st Battalion
Patrick Mason, 4th Battalion
Thomas Mason, GPO
James Masterson, 5th Battalion
Thomas (Tom) Maxwell, 5th Battalion
Daniel Meade, 4th Battalion

Henry Meade, 1st Battalion
Michael Meade, 2nd Battalion
Owen Meade, 2nd Battalion
Walter Meade, 1st Battalion
William Christopher Meade, 1st Battalion
John William Meagher, St Stephen's Green
Michael Meagher, 3rd Battalion
Patrick Meagher, GPO
Patrick Meagher, 3rd Battalion
William Meehan, GPO, 1st Battalion, 5th
      Battalion
John Meldon, 2nd Battalion
Thomas J. Meldon, 2nd Battalion
Herbert Charles (Barney) Mellows, 1st
      Battalion
James (Séamus) Melvinn, 2nd Battalion
Seán Merlahan, 3rd Battalion
Michael Merrigan, 1st Battalion
Thomas Merrigan, 1st Battalion
Edward Merriman, 4th Battalion
Michael Merriman, 3rd Battalion
Michael Mervyn, 1st Battalion
Seán Milroy, GPO, City Hall
James Minihan, GPO
Patrick Mitchell, St Stephen's Green
Joseph Molloy, 3rd Battalion
Michael J. Molloy, 2nd Battalion, St Stephen's
      Green
Richard Molloy, 2nd Battalion
John Joseph Moloney, 4th Battalion
Patrick Moloney, 4th Battalion
Philip Monaghan, 1st Battalion
Andrew Monks, 2nd Battalion, St Stephen's
      Green
Thomas Joseph Monroe, 1st Battalion
James Mooney, GPO
John Francis Mooney, GPO, 1st Battalion
Patrick Mooney, GPO
Patrick Mooney, 1st Battalion
Edward John Moore, GPO
John Moore, GPO
John W. Moore, 1st Battalion
Laurence Moore, 3rd Battalion
Patrick Thomas Moore, GPO
Christopher Moran, 5th Battalion
James Moran, 2nd Battalion
Patrick (Paddy) Moran, 2nd Battalion
Peter Moran, 5th Battalion
Éamonn (Ned) Morcan, 1st Battalion
John Morgan, 1st Battalion
John Morgan, 4th Battalion

Seán Morgan, 2nd Battalion
Patrick J. (Paddy) Morrin (Moran?), GPO
James Morrissey, 4th Battalion
Patrick Stephen (Paddy) Morrissey, 4th
    Battalion
Henry Moughan, GPO
Patrick Mulcahy, 4th Battalion
Richard Mulcahy, 5th Battalion
Andrew J. Mulhall, GPO, 1st Battalion
James Joseph Mulkearns, 1st Battalion
Michael Mullally (Mullalley), City Hall
Frank Mullen, 3rd Battalion
Martin Mullen, 2nd Battalion, 3rd Battalion
Martin Mullen, 4th Battalion
Michael Mullen, 1st Battalion
Patrick Mullen, 3rd Battalion
Patrick Mullen, 4th Battalion
Peter Mullen, 1st Battalion
Andrew Mulligan, GPO
Dominick Mulvey, GPO
Stephen Mulvey, GPO
William Robert Mulvey, GPO
Michael Mulvihill (Moynihan?), GPO
William (Liam) Murnane, 1st Battalion
Bernard (Barney) Murphy, 1st Battalion
Charles Murphy (Colm Ó Murchadha), GPO
Charles Murphy, 3rd Battalion
Christopher Murphy, 1st Battalion
Christopher J. Murphy, 3rd Battalion
Colm Murphy, 1st Battalion
Éamonn Murphy, 5th Battalion
Edward Murphy, 1st Battalion
Fintan Patrick Murphy, GPO
Francis (Frank) Murphy, 4th Battalion
Francis Ciaran Murphy, 5th Battalion
Frederick Murphy, 2nd Battalion, St Stephen's
    Green
Frederick (Fred) Murphy, City Hall
Frederick Charles Murphy, 1st Battalion
Gregory Murphy, 1st Battalion
Hubert Joseph Murphy, 1st Battalion
James Murphy, 4th Battalion
John (Seán) Murphy, 1st Battalion
John Christopher (Seán) Murphy, 4th Battalion
John J. (Seán) Murphy, 2nd Battalion
John J. (Seán) Murphy, 3rd Battalion
Martin Murphy, GPO
Martin Murphy, 1st Battalion
Michael Murphy, GPO
Michael Murphy, 1st Battalion
Michael Murphy, 1st Battalion

Michael Murphy, 4th Battalion
Patrick Murphy, St Stephen's Green
Peter Murphy (Peadar Ó Murchadha), GPO
Richard (Dick) Murphy, 3rd Battalion
Robert Joseph Murphy, GPO
Séamus Murphy, GPO
Stephen Murphy, GPO
Thomas Murphy, GPO
Thomas Murphy, 4th Battalion
William Murphy, GPO
William Murphy, 1st Battalion
William Murphy, 4th Battalion
William P. (Liam) Murphy, 3rd Battalion
James Joseph Murran, 2nd Battalion, St
    Stephen's Green
Daniel Murray, St Stephen's Green
Edward Joseph Murray, 4th Battalion
Frank Murray, 3rd Battalion
Gabriel B. Murray, 4th Battalion
Henry S. (Harry) Murray, 4th Battalion
James (Séamus) Murray, 3rd Battalion
Joseph Murray, GPO
Joseph Michael Murray, 1st Battalion
Michael Murray, 3rd Battalion
Patrick Joseph (Paddy) Murray, GPO
Thomas Murray, GPO
Bernard Murtagh, 2nd Battalion, St Stephen's
    Green
Francis Dominic (Frank) Murtagh, GPO
Joseph Murtagh, GPO
Laurence Joseph Murtagh, 1st Battalion
Patrick Murtagh, 1st Battalion
Denis Joseph Musgrave, 1st Battalion

N
John Neale (Neal, Neill), GPO
Denis Neary, 1st Battalion
Joseph Neary, 1st Battalion
Joseph Neary, 2nd Battalion
Arthur James Neilan, 1st Battalion
James Nelson, St Stephen's Green
Thomas Nelson, City Hall
Fr Eugene Nevin, 4th Battalion
Patrick Nevin, 1st Battalion
John Patrick Newman, GPO
Henry (Harry) Nicholls, St Stephen's Green
Arthur Nolan, 3rd Battalion
George Leo Nolan, 4th Battalion
Patrick Nolan, 2nd Battalion, St Stephen's
    Green
Patrick Nolan, 3rd Battalion

Peter Nolan, 3rd Battalion
Shaun (John Michael) Nolan, GPO, City Hall
Thomas Nolan, 4th Battalion
Thomas Francis Nolan, 1st Battalion
Christopher Noonan, 1st Battalion
Alfred George Norgrove, GPO, City Hall
Frederick Norgrove, GPO
James Norton, GPO
Joe Norton, GPO, 1st Battalion, 5th Battalion
William (Bill) Norton, 5th Battalion
Christopher (Christy) Nugent, 5th Battalion
John Nugent, 3rd Battalion
John Nugent, 4th Battalion
Joseph Nugent, 3rd Battalion
Michael Nugent, GPO
Patrick Nugent, GPO
Ernest Nunan, GPO
Seán Nunan, GPO

O
Liam Ó Briain, St Stephen's Green
Tomas Ó Briain, GPO
John O'Brian, 1st Battalion
Denis O'Brien, 4th Battalion
Denis O'Brien, 4th Battalion
Eugene (Eoghan) O'Brien (Ó Briain), GPO
Francis (Frank) O'Brien (Proinsías Ó Broin), St
    Stephen's Green
John O'Brien, GPO
John O'Brien, 1st Battalion
John O'Brien (Seán Ó Briain), 1st Battalion
Joseph O'Brien, 1st Battalion
Laurence (Larry, Lorcan) O'Brien, 4th Battalion
Liam O'Brien, 4th Battalion
Matthew O'Brien, GPO
Michael O'Brien, GPO
Michael O'Brien, 1st Battalion
Patrick O'Brien, 4th Battalion
Patrick O'Brien (Padraig Ó Broin), 4th
    Battalion
Patrick J. O'Brien, 1st Battalion
Peter (Peadar) O'Brien, 4th Battalion
Stephen L. O'Brien, 4th Battalion
Thomas O'Brien, 1st Battalion
Thomas O'Brien, 1st Battalion
Thomas O'Brien, 1st Battalion
William (Liam) Ó Brien (Ó Broin), 3rd
    Battalion
William O'Brien, 4th Battalion
William Joseph O'Brien, GPO
Séamus Ó Broin, 4th Battalion

Charles (Cathal) O'Byrne, 1st Battalion
Hugh O'Byrne, 4th Battalion
James O'Byrne, GPO
James O'Byrne, GPO
John (Seán) O'Byrne, 4th Battalion
Joseph Michael O'Byrne, 3rd Battalion
Patrick O'Byrne, 2nd Battalion
Seán O'Byrne, 3rd Battalion
Thomas Joseph O'Byrne, 3rd Battalion
William O'Byrne, 1st Battalion
William O'Byrne, 3rd Battalion
William (Liam) O'Byrne, 4th Battalion
Denis (Duncan?) O'Callahan (Donnchadh Ó
    Ceallacháin), 1st Battalion
Dominick O'Callahan, St Stephen's Green
John O'Callahan, GPO
John O'Callahan (Seán Ó Ceallachain), 2nd
    Battalion
John O'Callahan, St Stephen's Green
Michael (Mick) O'Callahan, 4th Battalion
Padraig Ó Caoimh, GPO
Miceal Ó Caoinhanadh, 3rd Battalion
James (Jim) O'Carroll, 2nd Battalion
James Joseph O'Carroll, 2nd Battalion, St
    Stephen's Green
John Stephen O'Carroll, 1st Battalion
Joseph O'Carroll, 4th Battalion
Kevin O'Carroll, GPO
Michael O'Carroll, 1st Battalion
Peter (Peadar) James O'Carroll, 1st Battalion
Richard O'Carroll, 2nd Battalion
Robert J. O'Carroll, 1st Battalion
Seán O'Carroll, 1st Battalion
William (Liam) O'Carroll, 1st Battalion
M. Ó Conallan, 1st Battalion
James O'Connell, 4th Battalion
Mortimer O'Connell, 1st Battalion
Patrick O'Connell, 2nd Battalion
Patrick John (Seán) O'Connell, 1st Battalion
Richard Joseph O'Connell, GPO
Bernard O'Connor, 4th Battalion
Fergus O'Connor, 1st Battalion
James O'Connor, GPO
James O'Connor, 5th Battalion
James S. O'Connor, 1st Battalion
John O'Connor, St Stephen's Green
John Stephen O'Connor, 1st Battalion
John Thomas O'Connor, GPO
Johnny ('Blimey') O'Connor, GPO
Joseph O'Connor, 3rd Battalion
Patrick O'Connor, GPO

Patrick O'Connor, GPO
Patrick J. O'Connor, 1st Battalion
Peter O'Connor, GPO
Rory O'Connor, GPO
Thomas (Tommy) O'Connor, 1st Battalion
Thomas O'Connor, 3rd Battalion
William O'Connor, 3rd Battalion
Michael O'Dea, 1st Battalion
William O'Dea, 1st Battalion
Fionan O'Doherty, 1st Battalion
Florence J. O'Doherty, 1st Battalion
Liam O'Doherty, 1st Battalion
Michael O'Doherty, St Stephen's Green
Séamus Ó Donnagain, GPO
Christopher O'Donnell, 2nd Battalion
James O'Donnell, 2nd Battalion
William O'Donnell, 2nd Battalion
Denis O'Donoghue, 3rd Battalion
Henry Vincent O'Donoghue, St Stephen's
   Green
Patrick (Paddy) O'Donoghue, GPO
Séamus O'Donoghue, GPO
Thomas O'Donoghue (Tomás Ó
   Donnchadha), St Stephen's Green
William O'Donoghue, GPO
Cornelius (Con) O'Donovan, 1st Battalion
Patrick O'Duffy, St Stephen's Green
Seán Martin O'Duffy, 1st Battalion
James O'Dwyer, City Hall
Martin O'Flaherty, 4th Battalion
Francis (Frank) O'Flanagan, 1st Battalion
George O'Flanagan, 1st Battalion
Maurice O'Flanagan, 1st Battalion
Michael O'Flanagan, 1st Battalion
Patrick Joseph O'Flanagan, 1st Battalion
John J. O'Gorman, 4th Battalion
John Patrick O'Gorman, 4th Battalion
Joseph O'Gorman, 4th Battalion
Liam O'Gorman, GPO
Liam O'Gorman, 1st Battalion
Anthony O'Grady, 3rd Battalion
Charles Joseph O'Grady, 4th Battalion
John O'Grady, 2nd Battalion, St Stephen's
   Green
Séamus Ó Greargain, 3rd Battalion
Hugh O'Hagan, 2nd Battalion
James O'Hagan, 4th Battalion
Cornelius (Con) O'Halloran, 4th Battalion
Bernard O'Hanlon, 1st Battalion
John (Seán) O'Hanlon, 3rd Battalion
Patrick O'Hanlon, 1st Battalion

Edward O'Hanrahan, 2nd Battalion
Henry O'Hanrahan, 2nd Battalion
Joseph John O'Hanrahan, 2nd Battalion, St
   Stephen's Green
Michael O'Hanrahan, 2nd Battalion
Jeremiah O'Healy, 1st Battalion
Diarmuid O'Hegarty, 1st Battalion
Brian O'Higgins, GPO
James O'Higgins, GPO
John (Seán) O'Keefe, 3rd Battalion
John Christopher O'Keefe (O'Keeffe), City
   Hall
Michael O'Keefe, 3rd Battalion
Padraig (Patrick, Paudeen) O'Keefe, GPO
Edward (Éamonn) O'Kelly, GPO, City Hall
Fergus Francis O'Kelly, GPO
Joseph O'Kelly, GPO
Joseph O'Kelly, GPO
Michael O'Kelly, 1st Battalion
Michael O'Kelly, St Stephen's Green
Patrick O'Kelly (Padraig Ó Ceallaigh), 2nd
   Battalion
Patrick Anthony O'Kelly, 3rd Battalion
Seán T. O'Kelly, GPO
Ted O'Kelly, GPO
Thomas O'Kelly, 1st Battalion
—— O'Laughlin, GPO
Patrick O'Loughlin, 4th Battalion
David O'Leary, GPO
David O'Leary, St Stephen's Green
Diarmuid O'Leary, GPO
Patrick Joseph O'Leary, 1st Battalion
Philip (Phil) O'Leary, City Hall
Liam Ó Leroin, 3rd Battalion
Patrick O'Loughlin, 4th Battalion
Matthew J. O'Mahoney, GPO
Seán O'Mahoney, 1st Battalion
Edward Joseph (Éamon) O'Mahony, GPO
Seán O'Mahony, GPO
Christopher Robert O'Malley, 2nd Battalion
George Oman, GPO
Robert (Bob) Oman, 1st Battalion
William Edward Oman, City Hall, St Stephen's
   Green
Peter O'Mara, 3rd Battalion
Donagh O'Moore, GPO
Patrick Michael O'Moore, GPO
Seán O'Moore, 1st Battalion
Andrew O'Neill, 3rd Battalion
Charles O'Neill, 1st Battalion
Edward O'Neill, 4th Battalion

James (Jim) (Séamus) O'Neill, GPO
John O'Neill, GPO
John O'Neill, GPO
John J. O'Neill, St Stephen's Green
Joseph O'Neill, 1st Battalion
Joseph O'Neill, 4th Battalion
Michael O'Neill, 4th Battalion
Michael Edward O'Neill, 1st Battalion
Patrick O'Neill, 1st Battalion
Patrick Francis O'Neill, 1st Battalion
Patrick Joseph O'Neill, GPO
Thomas O'Neill, 4th Battalion
Timothy (Tim, Jim) O'Neill, St Stephen's
    Green
William O'Neill, GPO
William O'Neill, 1st Battalion
Michael Joseph (The) Ó Rahilly, GPO
Michael O'Reardon, 1st Battalion
Liam O'Regan, GPO
Anthony (Arthur?) O'Reilly, 5th Battalion
Christopher O'Reilly, 3rd Battalion
Desmond O'Reilly, GPO
Francis Thomas O'Reilly, 2nd Battalion
John O'Reilly, GPO
John O'Reilly, 4th Battalion
John O'Reilly, City Hall
John K. O'Reilly, GPO
Joseph O'Reilly, GPO
Joseph (Joe) O'Reilly, GPO
Joseph Lewis O'Reilly, St Stephen's Green
Kevin O'Reilly, GPO
Luke O'Reilly, 1st Battalion
Martin O'Reilly, GPO
Michael William O'Reilly, GPO
Patrick O'Reilly, 2nd Battalion
Patrick O'Reilly, 3rd Battalion
Patrick O'Reilly, 4th Battalion
Patrick O'Reilly, St Stephen's Green
Peter O'Reilly, 1st Battalion
Richard O'Reilly, 4th Battalion
Samuel Patrick O'Reilly, 1st Battalion
Seán (John, Jack) O'Reilly, City Hall
Thomas O'Reilly, GPO
Thomas O'Reilly, 1st Battalion
Thomas O'Reilly, 1st Battalion
Thomas O'Reilly, 2nd Battalion
William Joseph O'Reilly, GPO
Danny (Domhnall) O'Riordan, 2nd Battalion
Michael O'Riordan, 4th Battalion
Frederick (Fred) O'Rorke (O'Rourke), 2nd
    Battalion, St Stephen's Green

John O'Rorke (O'Rourke), 2nd Battalion, St
    Stephen's Green
Joseph Francis O'Rorke, GPO
John Joseph O'Rourke, 2nd Battalion, St
    Stephen's Green
Michael O'Rourke, 2nd Battalion
Patrick O'Rourke, 4th Battalion
Thomas O'Rourke, 2nd Battalion
Thomas O'Rourke, 3rd Battalion
John (Seán) O'Shaughnessy, 4th Battalion
Theobald O'Shaughnessy (Ó Seachnasaigh),
    4th Battalion
Albert O'Shea, St Stephen's Green
Dermot O'Shea, 2nd Battalion
James O'Shea, 2nd Battalion, St Stephen's
    Green
John James (Seán) O'Shea, 3rd Battalion
Michael O'Shea, GPO
Robert O'Shea, St Stephen's Green
—— Ó Snodaigh, 1st Battalion
Gearóid O'Sullivan (Gearóid Ó Suilleaváin),
    GPO
James O'Sullivan, St Stephen's Green
James J. O'Sullivan, GPO
John O'Sullivan, 1st Battalion
John O'Toole, 4th Battalion
William O'Toole, GPO
Séamus O'Treacy, 3rd Battalion
John (Seán) Owens, 4th Battalion

P

Seosamh Pairceir (Joseph Parker?), 4th Battalion
Bernard Parker, 1st Battalion
Matthew Parnell, GPO
Liam Parr, GPO
William (Bill) Partridge, St Stephen's Green
Richard Pearle, 3rd Battalion
Patrick Pearse, GPO
William (Willie) Pearse, GPO
Thomas Peate, 3rd Battalion
Liam Pedlar, GPO
Denis Peelo, 3rd Battalion
James Peely, 3rd Battalion
Henry Pender, 4th Battalion
James Pender, 3rd Battalion
Thomas Peppard, GPO, 1st Battalion, 5th
    Battalion
Aubrey George Pepper, St Stephen's Green
Michael Phelan, 2nd Battalion
William Phelan, 4th Battalion
John Phillips, 4th Battalion

Matthew Phillips, 4th Battalion
George Plunkett, GPO
James P. Plunkett, 1st Battalion
John (Jack) Plunkett, GPO
Joseph Mary Plunkett, GPO
Frank Dominic Pollard, 1st Battalion
Stephen Patrick Pollard, 1st Battalion
Christopher Poole, St Stephen's Green
John Poole, GPO, City Hall
Patrick Poole, St Stephen's Green
Vincent Poole, GPO
Eugene (Owen) Porter, 3rd Battalion
James S. (Séamus) Pounch, 2nd Battalion
Arthur Power, 4th Battalion
Joseph Power, 4th Battalion
Patrick Power, 3rd Battalion
William (Liam, Billy) Power, 4th Battalion
Seán Prendergast, 1st Battalion
Éamon (Bob) Price, 2nd Battalion
Seán Price, GPO
Thomas Pugh, 2nd Battalion, St Stephen's
    Green
Charles Purcell, GPO
James (John?) Purfield (Purneld, Purfeld?), 3rd
    Battalion
John Purfield, 2nd Battalion

Q
James Quigley, St Stephen's Green
Charles Quinn, 4th Battalion
George J. Quinn, 4th Battalion
James Quinn, GPO
James Joseph Quinn, 4th Battalion
John (Seán) Quinn, 3rd Battalion
John Quinn, 4th Battalion
Thomas Quinn, 3rd Battalion

R
John (Jack) Rafferty, 5th Battalion
Thomas (Tommy) Rafferty, 5th Battalion
Liam Raftis, 3rd Battalion
Patrick Rankin, GPO
Thomas Rath (Roth?), GPO
Albert Sylvester Rawley, 1st Battalion
Séamus Reader, GPO
Daniel Reardon, 2nd Battalion
Laurence Reardon, 2nd Battalion
James Redican, 3rd Battalion
Thomas Christopher Redican, 3rd Battalion
Andrew (Andy) Redmond, GPO
Denis Joseph Redmond, 3rd Battalion

John Redmond, GPO
Patrick Redmond, 2nd Battalion, St Stephen's
    Green
Timothy John Redmond, 1st Battalion
William J. Redmond, 2nd Battalion
Laurence Regan, 1st Battalion
John Reid, GPO
John James (Seán) Reid, 1st Battalion
John Joseph (Seán) Reid, 3rd Battalion
Patrick Reid, 3rd Battalion
Matthew Reilly, GPO
Sam Reilly, GPO
Thomas Reilly, 5th Battalion
James J. Renny, 2nd Battalion
Augustus Percival Reynolds, St Stephen's Green
George Reynolds, 3rd Battalion
John Arnold deVere Reynolds, 2nd Battalion, St
    Stephen's Green
John Richard Reynolds, GPO
Joseph Francis Reynolds, 1st Battalion
Peter Joseph Reynolds, GPO
John Richmond, 1st Battalion
James Rickard, 5th Battalion
Henry (Harry) Ridgeway, GPO
Patrick Joseph (Paddy) Rigney, 4th Battalion
Christopher Ring, GPO
Joseph Ring, GPO
Liam Ring, GPO
Patrick Ring, GPO
T.W. (Leo) Ring, GPO
Edward Joseph (Eddie) Roach, 1st Battalion
Frank Robbins, St Stephen's Green
James (Séamus) Robinson, GPO
Joseph Roche, 1st Battalion
Liam Roche (de Roiste), 1st Battalion
Michael Joseph Roche, 1st Battalion
Seán Augustine Roche, 2nd Battalion
Thomas J. Roche, GPO
Timothy (Tim) Roche, 1st Battalion
William (Liam) Roche, GPO
William Roche, 4th Battalion
Richard Roe, 2nd Battalion
William Charles Roe, 3rd Battalion
Seán Rogan, St Stephen's Green
Michael Rogers (Mícheál Mac Ruaidhri), GPO
Fenton Christopher Ronan, GPO
William (Willie) Ronan (Rownan?), 3rd
    Battalion
Edward N. (Ned) Rooney, 5th Battalion
James Rooney, 5th Battalion
John J. Rooney, St Stephen's Green

Patrick Rooney, 2nd Battalion
William Ross, GPO
Charles Rossiter, GPO
Patrick Joseph (Paddy) Rowe, 3rd Battalion
James Russell, 4th Battalion
Seán Russell, GPO
Albert Rutherford, 2nd Battalion, St Stephen's
    Green
Cornelius Ryan, 3rd Battalion
Desmond Ryan, GPO
Frederick (Freddie) Ryan, St Stephen's Green
Dr James (Jim) Ryan (Séamus Ó Riain), GPO
James Ryan, St Stephen's Green
Laurence Ryan, GPO
Oliver Ryan, GPO, City Hall
Patrick Joseph Ryan, 5th Battalion
Thomas Ryan, GPO
William Ryan, 1st Battalion
William Ryan (Liam S. Ó Riain), 1st Battalion
John Ryder, 2nd Battalion
William Ryder, 2nd Battalion

S

Frank Saul, 4th Battalion
John (Jack) Saul, 4th Battalion
Michael Saunders, 1st Battalion
Charles Saurin, GPO
Martin Savage, GPO
Frederick Schweppe, 2nd Battalion
John Joseph Scollan, GPO
William John Scott, St Stephen's Green
Francis (Frank) Scullen (Scullion), GPO
Leo Patrick Scullen, 1st Battalion
Patrick Scullen (Scullion), GPO
Michael Scully, 1st Battalion
Thomas Scully (Tomás Ó Scolaige), 3rd
    Battalion
Tom Scully, St Stephen's Green
William Scully, 1st Battalion
David Sears, 4th Battalion
Thomas Seaver (Leaver?), 5th Battalion
Patrick Joseph Seely, GPO
James Seerey (Seery), City Hall
John (Patrick?) Seery, St Stephen's Green
James Seville, GPO
James Sexton, GPO
Michael Sexton, GPO, City Hall
Philip Shanahan, 2nd Battalion
Martin Joseph Shannon, St Stephen's Green
Fr Eugene Sheehy, GPO
Thomas P. Sheerin, 1st Battalion

James Sheils, 2nd Battalion
Charles Shelly, 1st Battalion
Denis Shelly, 2nd Battalion, St Stephen's Green
Thomas Shelly, 2nd Battalion
Michael I. Sheppard, 2nd Battalion
Frank Sheridan, GPO
James Sheridan, GPO
James Sheridan, 1st Battalion
John Sheridan, 1st Battalion
Patrick (Paddy) Sherwin, 5th Battalion
Thomas (Tom) Shiel (Shields), St Stephen's
    Green
Arthur Shields, GPO
Henry (Harry) Shiels, 1st Battalion
Seán Shortall, 1st Battalion
William Shortall, 1st Battalion
Patrick (Paddy) Shortis, GPO
Frank Shouldice, 1st Battalion
John Francis (Jack) Shouldice, 1st Battalion
Terence Simpson, 2nd Battalion, St Stephen's
    Green
Liam Siuptal, 1st Battalion
Michael Slater, 2nd Battalion, St Stephen's
    Green
Thomas Slater, 2nd Battalion
William Slater, 2nd Battalion
James Joseph Slattery, 2nd Battalion
Peadar Slattery, GPO
Lawrence Slevin, 1st Battalion
Thomas Smart, 1st Battalion
Albert Smith, 3rd Battalion
Charles (Charlie) Smith, GPO
James Smith, St Stephen's Green
Michael Smith, 4th Battalion
Michael Smyth, 2nd Battalion
Daniel Charles Somers, 2nd Battalion
Edward (Ned) Stafford, 5th Battalion
John Stafford, GPO
Matthew Stafford, GPO
Henry Vincent Staines, 1st Battalion
James Staines, 1st Battalion
Michael Staines (Michael deStainer, Stainar),
    GPO
William F. (Liam) Staines, 1st Battalion
Joseph Michael (Joe) Stanley, GPO
Liam Stanley, 3rd Battalion
William J. (Bill) Stapleton, 2nd Battalion
Charles Steinmayer, GPO
Patrick J. (Paddy) Stephenson, GPO, 1st
    Battalion
John Joseph Stokes, 3rd Battalion

Richard (Dick) Stokes, 2nd Battalion, St
    Stephen's Green
James (Jim) Strich, GPO
James J. Sullivan, GPO, 1st Battalion
Padraig Supple (Stupple?), GPO
Thomas Sutton, St Stephen's Green
Patrick Joseph (Paddy) Swan, 1st Battalion
Anthony (Tony) Swann, GPO
Paddy Swanzy, GPO
James Sweeney, GPO
James Joseph Sweeney, 1st Battalion
Joseph Aloysius Sweeney (Sweeny), GPO
Michael Sweeney, 4th Battalion
Patrick E. Sweeney, GPO
Patrick Emmet Sweeney, 2nd Battalion

T
Charles Tallon, GPO
Christopher Tallon, GPO
James Tallon, GPO
Joseph (Joe) Tallon, GPO
Michael Aloysius (Miceal) Tannam, 3rd
    Battalion
William (Liam) Tannam, GPO
Joseph (Joe) Taylor, 5th Battalion
Thomas Taylor, 5th Battalion
James Teehan, 4th Battalion
Nicholas Teeling (Teehan?), 5th Battalion
Alexander Thompson, 3rd Battalion
Francis Joseph (Frank) Thornton, GPO
Hugh Thornton, GPO
Joseph (Joe) Thornton, 5th Battalion
Patrick Thornton, GPO
Éamonn Tierney, 1st Battalion
Michael Tierney, 1st Battalion
Liam Tobin, 1st Battalion
Michael Tobin, 1st Battalion
William Toole (O'Toole), GPO
John Charles Toomey, 2nd Battalion, St
    Stephen's Green
Joseph (Joe) Toomey, GPO
Joseph Tormey (Seosamh Ó Torma), 2nd
    Battalion
John (Seán) Tracey, 4th Battalion
Fr Aloysius Travers, OFM, 1st Battalion
Edward Travers, 1st Battalion
John (Seán) Joe Traynor, 4th Battalion
Oscar Traynor, GPO
Thomas Traynor, 3rd Battalion
Joseph George Trimble, GPO
Daniel (Dan) Troy, 4th Battalion

Paddy Troy, 4th Battalion
George Tully, GPO, St Stephen's Green
Dr J.J. Tuohy, GPO
Patrick Coleman Tuohy, GPO
Cormac Turner, GPO
Francis (Frank) Turner, GPO
Henry (Harry) Turner, GPO
John Turner, 2nd Battalion, St Stephen's Green
Joseph Turner, GPO
John Joseph Twamley, GPO
Daniel Tynan, 1st Battalion
Andrew Tyrrell, 2nd Battalion
Timothy Tyrrell, GPO

V
Thomas Venables, 4th Battalion
Patrick Villiams, GPO
Joseph Vize, GPO
Joseph Edward Vize, 2nd Battalion, St Stephen's
    Green

W
Michael Wade, GPO
Charles Walker, GPO
John Walker, 2nd Battalion, St Stephen's Green
John Walker, 3rd Battalion
Michael Walker, 2nd Battalion, St Stephen's
    Green
Leo Walpole, 3rd Battalion
Robert Henry (Harry) Walpole, GPO
Christopher Walsh, GPO, City Hall
Edward (Ned) Walsh, City Hall
James Walsh, 1st Battalion
James Walsh, 3rd Battalion
James Walsh, 4th Battalion
James Walsh (Séamus Breathnach), 4th Battalion
James Joseph (J.J.) Walsh, GPO
John Peter Walsh, 2nd Battalion
Mark William Walsh, GPO
Martin Walsh, GPO
Patrick (Paddy) Walsh, 2nd Battalion
Patrick Joseph Walsh, 4th Battalion
Philip Walsh, 1st Battalion
Thomas (Tom) Walsh, GPO, City Hall
Thomas Walsh, 1st Battalion
Thomas Walsh, 3rd Battalion
Willie Walsh, 5th Battalion
Martin Walton, 2nd Battalion
Bernard Ward, 4th Battalion
George Ward, 1st Battalion
George Ward, 2nd Battalion

Gilbert Ward, GPO
Nicholas Ward, 2nd Battalion, St Stephen's
　　Green
Patrick Ward, 3rd Battalion
Patrick Ward, 4th Battalion
Patrick Joseph Ward, 4th Battalion
Peter Ward, 4th Battalion
Seán Ward, 1st Battalion
James Watters (Waters), 3rd Battalion
Patrick Weafer, GPO
Thomas Joseph (Tom) Weafer (Wafer), GPO
Arthur Abraham Weekes (Weakes, Wicks?),
　　GPO
James Weldon, 1st Battalion
Bartholomew (Bartle) Weston, 5th Battalion
Charles Weston, 5th Battalion
Thomas Weston, 5th Battalion
Thomas Wheatley, GPO
George Whelan, 1st Battalion
John Whelan, St Stephen's Green
Joseph Whelan, GPO
Laurence Whelan, GPO
Michael Whelan, 4th Battalion
Patrick Whelan, 3rd Battalion
Richard Whelan, 4th Battalion
William Whelan, GPO
William Whelan, 1st Battalion
Christopher John Whelehan (Whelan?), GPO,
　　2nd Battalion
John J. (Jack) White, GPO
Michael (Mick) White, GPO, 4th Battalion
Henry Joseph Williams, GPO
John Joseph Williams, 1st Battalion
Patrick Williams, 3rd Battalion
Patrick Joseph Williams, City Hall
Peter Williams, 2nd Battalion, St Stephen's
　　Green
John Williamson, 1st Battalion
Henry Christopher Willis, GPO
James Wilson, GPO, 1st Battalion, 5th Battalion
Mark Wilson, 1st Battalion
Peter Wilson, GPO, 1st Battalion, 5th Battalion
William Wilson, 1st Battalion, 5th Battalion
William (Beck) Wilson, GPO, 5th Battalion
William (Cody, Cooty?) Wilson, GPO, 5th
　　Battalion
Henry Winstanley, City Hall
William Joseph Woodcock, 3rd Battalion
James Wren, GPO

Y

Éamon Christopher Young, 4th Battalion
Patrick John Young, 4th Battalion
Robert Martin Young, 4th Battalion
Thomas Laurence (Tom) Young, 4th Battalion
Thomas Yourell, 1st Battalion

Women

A

Mary (Molly, Mollie) Adrien (Adrian), GPO,
　　5th Battalion

B

Brigid Brady (Murphy), City Hall
Kate Brown, unassigned
Martha Brown, unassigned
Elizabeth (Lillie) Burke (née McGinty), GPO
Ellen Sarah Bushell, GPO, 4th Battalion
Catherine Byrne (Rooney), GPO, 1st Battalion
Catherine (Katie) Byrne, 4th Battalion
Elizabeth (Lillie) Byrne, GPO
Margaret Byrne (Copeland), 1st Battalion
Mary Byrne, 1st Battalion
Mary (May) Byrne (Doyle), 4th Battalion
(Marie) Winifred (Winnie) Byrne (Somerville),
　　4th Battalion
Teresa Byrne, St Stephen's Green

C

Christina (Chris) Caffrey (Keely), St Stephen's
　　Green
Annie Carey (O'Hagen), St Stephen's Green
(Maria) Winifred Carney (McBride), GPO
Máire (May, Meg) Carron, 1st Battalion
Catherine Gertrude (Gertie) Colley (Murphy),
　　GPO
Máire Comerford, GPO
Mrs (Martin) Peig Conlon (Peig Bean Ui
　　Channallan [Callanan]), 1st Battalion
Brigid (Bridie, Brid) Connolly, GPO
Kathleen (Kitty, Katie) Connolly (Barrett), City
　　Hall
Ina Connolly (Heron), unassigned
Nora Connolly (O'Brien), unassigned
Cecilia Conroy (O'Neill), 2nd Battalion
Eileen Conroy, St Stephen's Green
Áine Cooney (O'Brien), 4th Battalion
Eileen Cooney (Harbourne), 4th Battalion
Elizabeth (Lily) Cooney (Curran), 4th Battalion

Elizabeth Corr, unassigned
Nell Corr, unassigned
Marcella Cosgrave, 4th Battalion
Mary (May) Cullen, GPO

D
Agnes Daly, unassigned
Katie Daly (Beatty), 1st Battalion
Laura Daly (O'Sullivan), GPO
Nora Daly (Dore), GPO
Brigid Davis (O'Duffy), City Hall
Evelyn Mary (Aoife) de Burca (Eva Burke), GPO
Máire Deegan, 2nd Battalion
Brigid Dempsey (née Dodd), St Stephen's Green
Eileen Dempsey, GPO
Margaret (Maggie) Derham (Mulligan), 1st Battalion
Mary Devereux (Allen), St Stephen's Green
Anastasia (Anne) Devlin, St Stephen's Green
Brid Dixon, GPO
Mary Donnelly, St Stephen's Green
Kathy Doran, unassigned
Frances Downie, GPO
Margaret (Peggy) Downie (Viant), GPO

E
Eilis Elliott (Ni Briain), 1st Battalion
Emily Elliott (Ledwith), 1st Battalion
Máire English, GPO
Ellen (Nellie) Ennis (Costigan), 1st Battalion

F
Margaret Mary (Madge) Fagan (MacSherry), St Stephen's Green
Anna (Mrs Frank) Fahy, 1st Battalion
Madeleine ffrench-Mullen, St Stephen's Green
Kathleen Fleming, unassigned
Margaret Fleming (Leonard), unassigned
Monica (Dot) Fleming (Lawless), 5th Battalion
Brighid Foley (Brid Ni Foghludha, Breeid Martin), GPO
Cait Foley (Murphy), unassigned
Nora Foley (Ni Fogludha) (O'Daly), St Stephen's Green

G
Mary (May) Gahan (O'Carroll), GPO
Louise Gavan-Duffy, GPO
Lucie Gethings, GPO

Maura (May) Gibney (O'Neill), GPO
Helen Ruth (Nellie) Gifford (Donnelly), St Stephen's Green
Nora Margaret Mary Gillies (O'Daly), St Stephen's Green
Brigid Goff (Gough), St Stephen's Green
Brigid Grace, GPO
Eilis (Betsy) Gray, unassigned
Julia Grenan ('Sheila Grennan'), GPO

H
Rosana (Rosie) Hackett, St Stephen's Green
Mary Hanley (Máire Ni Ainle), GPO
Mary Christina Hayes (O'Gorman), GPO, 1st Battalion
Saoirse Hayes (MacAodha), 2nd Battalion
Cathleen Healy, 1st Battalion
Teresa Healy (Byrne), 1st Battalion
Bridget Hegarty (Harmon), 4th Battalion
Margaret Kennedy (Hennessey), 4th Battalion
Margaret Agnes Kennedy, 1st Battalion
Áine Heron, 1st Battalion
Annie Higgins (O'Higgins?), GPO
Patricia Hoey, GPO
Ellen (Nell) Humphreys, GPO
Mary (May, Molly) Hyland (Kelly), St Stephen's Green

J
Margaret (Maggie) Joyce, St Stephen's Green

K
Maeve (Maud) Kavanagh (Cavanagh) (McDowell), GPO
Mary Kavanagh, St Stephen's Green
Mary (May) Kavanagh (Duggan), 1st Battalion
Sara Kealy, 2nd Battalion
Kathleen Kearney (Furlong, Behan), unassigned
Linda Kearns (McWhinney), GPO
Annie Kelly, St Stephen's Green
Kate (Katie, Kitty) Kelly, St Stephen's Green
Kathleen J. Kelly (Barber), GPO
Josephine Kelly (Greene), 4th Battalion
Martha Kelly (Murphy), GPO
Mary (May) Kelly (Chadwick), GPO
Mary Kelly, St Stephen's Green
Elizabeth Anne (Lilly) Kempson (McAlerney), St Stephen's Green
K. Kennedy, unassigned
Bridie Kenny, unassigned
Kathleen Kenny (Blackburn), 1st Battalion

Mary (Mamie) Kilmartin (Stephenson), 1st Battalion
Elizabeth (Lily) King (MacCarthy), St Stephen's Green

L

Bridget Lambert (Doran), GPO
Ellen (Nellie) Lambert (Stynes), GPO
Kathleen Lane (McCarthy), 2nd Battalion
Eileen Lawless (Sister Eithne), 5th Battalion
Kathleen Lawless (McAllister), 5th Battalion
Mary Lawless, GPO
Catherine Liston, unassigned
Mary Liston, unassigned
Elizabeth (Bessie) Lynch (Kelly), City Hall
Thomasina Lynders (Weston), 5th Battalion
Dr Kathleen Lynn, City Hall
Dr Brigid (Brighid) Lyons (Thornton), 1st Battalion

M

Julia McCauley (McAuley), unassigned
Mabel McConnell (FitzGerald), GPO
Mairead McElroy, GPO
Josie McGowan (Mac Gabhan) (McGavan), 4th Battalion
Catherine (Katy) McGuinness, 1st Battalion
Rose McGuinness, 1st Battalion
Anastasia MacLaughlin (McLaughlin), unassigned
Maggie McLaughlin, unassigned
Mary McLoughlin, GPO
Sarah (Sorcha) MacMahon (Sorcha Bhean Mhic Ruaidhri) (Rogers), GPO
Rose McManners, 1st Battalion
Agnes McNamara, unassigned
Rose McNamara (Murphy), 4th Battalion
Sarah McNamara (MacNamara), 1st Battalion
Agnes MacNamee, 4th Battalion
Agnes McNanice, unassigned
Alice ——— (MacThomais), St Stephen's Green
Teresa Magee (McGee), 2nd Battalion
Kathleen Maher, unassigned
Kathleen Mahon, unassigned
Aine Malone (Fitzgerald), 2nd Battalion, St Stephen's Green
Máire Mapother, GPO
Constance Markievicz (née Gore-Booth), St Stephen's Green
Brid S. Martin, 1st Battalion
Kathleen (Kate) Martin, 1st Battalion

Margaret Martin (Murnane), 1st Battalion
Florence (Flossie) Meade (Griffin), 1st Battalion
J. Milner, unassigned
Caroline (Carrie) Mitchell (McLoughlin), 1st Battalion
May Moloney (McQuaile), 1st Battalion
Helena Molony, City Hall
Mary (May) Moore (Wisley), St Stephen's Green
Mary Pauline Morkan (Keating), 1st Battalion
Philomena Morkan (née Lucas), 1st Battalion
Phyllis Morkan, 1st Battalion
Lizzie Mulhall, 4th Battalion
Rosanna (Rose) Mullally (Farrelly), 4th Battalion
Brigid Murnane (McKeon), 1st Battalion
Elizabeth (Lily) Murnane (Coleton), 1st Battalion
Eileen Murphy (née Walsh), GPO
Eileen (Mrs Séamus) Murphy, 1st Battalion
Kathleen Murphy (Patton), GPO
Kathleen (Kate) Murphy, 4th Battalion
Rose Ann Murphy (née Byrne), GPO
Eileen Murray, GPO
Mary (May) Murray, GPO
Mary Murray (Allen), Four Courts
Brigid Murtagh (O'Daly), St Stephen's Green

N

Josephine Neary (Flood), 1st Battalion
Christina Máire Ni Dhubhgaill (Doyle), St Stephen's Green
Eilis Ni Riain (Bean Ui Chonaill), 1st Battalion
Máire Nic Shiubhlaigh (Molly Walker) (Mrs Éamonn Price), 2nd Battalion
Ellen Noone, GPO
Annie Norgrove (Grange), City Hall
Emily Norgrove (Hanratty), City Hall
Mrs —— Norgrove, St Stephen's Green

O

Lily M. O'Brennan, 4th Battalion
Elizabeth (Eilis) O'Brien, GPO
Mary (Dolly) O'Carroll (Lawlor), 1st Battalion
Mary O'Connell, GPO
Aileen Mary O'Connor (O'Reilly), GPO
Katie O'Connor, unassigned
Kitty O'Doherty, unassigned
Elizabeth More O'Farrell, GPO
Cissie O'Flaherty, 4th Battalion
Margaret O'Flaherty (Timmons), 4th Battalion

Ellen O'Flanagan (Parker), 1st Battalion
Emily O'Keefe (Hendley), 1st Battalion
Annie O'Hagan (McQuade), 2nd Battalion
Mary (Molly, Máire) O'Hanlon, 4th Battalion
Sheila (Sighle) O'Hanlon (Lynch), 4th Battalion
Eileen (Eily) (Lily) O'Hanrahan (O'Reilly),
    2nd Battalion
Mary O'Hanrahan, GPO
Annie O'Keefe (O'Carroll), 1st Battalion
Emily O'Keefe (Hendley), 4th Battalion
Josephine O'Keefe (McNamara), 4th Battalion
Josephine (Josie) O'Keefe, 4th Battalion
Máire O'Neill, GPO
Maura O'Neill (Mackay), 1st Battalion
Cathleen O'Reilly, GPO
Mary Teresa (Molly) O'Reilly (Corcoran),
    GPO, City Hall
Nora O'Reilly (Sister Lourdes), GPO
Grace O'Sullivan, unassigned
Louisa (Louise?) (Dolly) O'Sullivan (Pollard),
    1st Battalion
Mary (Mollie) O'Sullivan (O'Carroll), 1st
    Battalion

P

Mary Partridge, unassigned
Marie (Mary) Perolz (Flanagan), unassigned
Josephine (Josie) Pollard (Daly), 2nd Battalion
Kathleen Pollard (McDonald), 2nd Battalion
Leslie Price (Barry), GPO

Q

Maria (Mary) Quigley (Clince), 4th Battalion
Priscilla (Cilla) Quigley (Kavanagh), 4th
    Battalion
Margaret Quinn, GPO

R

Annie Redmond, GPO
Barbara Retz, unassigned
Mary Catherine (Molly, Mollie) Reynolds,
    GPO
Bridie Richards, GPO
Agnes Ryan, unassigned
Ann Noreen Ryan (Ni Riain), GPO
Margaret Ryan (Dunne), St Stephen's Green
Mary Josephine (Min) Ryan (Mulcahy), GPO

Maureen Ryan (Máirín Bean Ni Riain)
    (Cregan), unassigned
Phyllis (Eilis Ni Rian) Ryan (O'Kelly) (Ui
    Cheallaigh), GPO
Veronica (Bheronica) (Ni Rian) Ryan
    (Gleeson) (Ui Glasam), GPO

S

Kathleen Seary (Seery) (Redmond), St
    Stephen's Green
Jane (Jenny, Jinny) Shanahan, City Hall
Mary Shannon, City Hall
Matilda (Tillie) Simpson, GPO
Hanna Sheehy-Skeffington, GPO, St Stephen's
    Green
Margaret Skinnider, St Stephen's Green
Lucy Agnes Smyth (Byrne), GPO
Josephine Spicer, 4th Battalion
Christina Stafford (Brooks), GPO
Mrs M.J. Stapleton (née Slevin), GPO

T

Aoife (Effie) Taaffe, GPO
Nora Thornton, unassigned
Annie Tobin (Soalfield), GPO
Anastasia (Statia) Toomey (Byrne), GPO
Sesca Chevenix Trench (Sadhbh Trinseach),
    GPO
Cathleen (Catherine?) Treston, GPO

U

Brigid Bean Ui Faoithe (White, Whyte), GPO

W

Bridie Walsh (Slater), GPO
Helena Walsh, GPO
Margaret (Martha) Walsh (Jenkinson), GPO
Mary Josephine (Mary Jo) Walsh (Rafferty),
    GPO
Mary Julia Weston, 5th Battalion
Esther Wisley (Wisely) (O'Moore), GPO
May Wisely, St Stephen's Green
Dr Nancy Wyse-Power (de Poer), GPO